AMERICAN AIRPOWER STRATEGY
IN WORLD WAR II

AMERICAN AIRPOWER STRATEGY IN WORLD WAR II

BOMBS, CITIES, CIVILIANS, AND OIL

CONRAD C. CRANE

 UNIVERSITY PRESS OF KANSAS

Photographs are from the USAF Photographic Collection, National Air and Space Museum, Smithsonian Institution, unless otherwise noted.

The views expressed herein are those of the author and do not purport to reflect the positions of the United States Military Academy, Department of the Army, or Department of Defense.

Published by the University Press of Kansas (Lawrence, Kansas 66045), which was organized by the Kansas Board of Regents and is operated and funded by Emporia State University, Fort Hays State University, Kansas State University, Pittsburg State University, the University of Kansas, and Wichita State University

Library of Congress Cataloging-in-Publication Data

Names: Crane, Conrad C., author.
Title: American airpower strategy in World War II : bombs, cities, civilians, and oil / Conrad C. Crane.
Other titles: Bombs, cities, civilians, and oil
Description: Lawrence, Kansas : University Press of Kansas, [2016]
Series: Modern war studies | Includes bibliographical references and index.
Identifiers: LCCN 2015044252
ISBN 9780700622092 (cloth : alk. paper)
ISBN 9780700629022 (paperback : alk. paper)
ISBN 9780700622108 (ebook)
Subjects: LCSH: World War, 1939–1945–Aerial operations, American. | Bombing, Aerial–United States. | Air power–United States–History–20th century. | World War, 1939–1945–Moral and ethical aspects.
Classification: LCC D790 .C69 2016 | DDC 940.54/4973–dc23
LC record available at http://lccn.loc.gov/2015044252

British Library Cataloguing-in-Publication Data is available.

Printed in the United States of America

10 9 8 7 6 5 4 3 2

The paper used in this publication is recycled and contains 30 percent postconsumer waste. It is acid free and meets the minimum requirements of the American National Standard for Permanence of Paper for Printed Library Materials Z39.48–1992.

For Conrad L. Crane,
World War II veteran, mentor, father, and friend

CONTENTS

List of Illustrations   ix

List of Acronyms   xi

Preface   xiii

1. Introduction   1

2. Developing Doctrine   14

3. From Doctrine to Practice: Executing the Air Offensive
   against Germany   31

4. Attitudes of Leaders and the Public   64

5. Attitudes and Perceptions of American Airmen   85

6. The Lure of Technological Innovation: Bombing Aids   101

7. The Lure of Technological Innovation: Better Bombs   116

8. The Lure of the Deathblow in Europe   133

9. Delivering the Deathblow to Germany   146

10. Torching Japan   161

11. Strategic Airpower in Limited Wars   187

12. Legacies   210

Appendix: Suggested Reply to Letters Questioning
   Humanitarian Aspects of Air Force   217

Notes   219

Bibliography   245

Index   257

ILLUSTRATIONS

Two views of Allied strategic bombing, Munich and Harburg   2–3

Brig. Gen. William "Billy" Mitchell   18

Maj. Gen. H. H. "Hap" Arnold and his staff, 1941   29

Submarine pens at Hamburg   36

Target photo of Leipzig, 20 February 1944   42

Target photo of Amiens, 25 June 1944   45

Crashed B-24 near airfield at Shipdham   50

Damaged railroad viaduct at Bielefeld   53

Burning B-24 over Vienna   57

Arnold traveling with Secretary of War Henry Stimson   72

Maj. Gen. Jimmy Doolittle in his plane, 1943   76

Eighth Air Force B-24 Liberators bombing Dunkirk   79

Gen. Carl Spaatz and his staff brief Eisenhower, 1942   81

B-17 with its nose shot off by flak   87

Squadron Cmdr. Jimmy Stewart   92

B-24s bombing Frankfurt, February 1944   103

Radar operator Sgt. W. C. Yoder searches for targets over Omura   107

Bomb-damage assessment of radar bombing of Maruzen   114

Diagrams of the Azon system   119

Two GB-1 glide bombs slung under a B-17 for testing   124

The American JB-2 buzz bomb   127

Destruction caused by Doolittle's attack on marshaling yards near
    Rome   135

The shadow of a B-24 over the shattered marshaling yard in
    Munich   151

Ruins of Johanne Strasse in Dresden after the raid of
    14–15 February 1945   155

Brig. Gen. Haywood Hansell Jr. and Maj. Gen. Curtis LeMay   164–165

B-29s dispersed at one of their bases at Isley Field, Saipan   172

Area of Tokyo in flames on the night of 26 May 1945   178

Devastation caused by Allied planes and artillery, Mannheim,
    19 April 1945   189

Bombed marshaling yard and dam in North Korea   195

Army Chief of Staff William Westmoreland confers with
    President Lyndon Johnson and Walt W. Rostow   199

Devastation caused by LeMay's fire raids on Tokyo   213

ACRONYMS

AAF	Army Air Forces
ACTS	Air Corps Tactical School
AEAF	Allied Expeditionary Air Force
AEF	American Expeditionary Forces
AFB	Air Force Base
AWPD	Air War Plans Division
BC	Bomber Command
CBO	Combined Bomber Offensive
CCS	Combined Chiefs of Staff
CGSS	Command and General Staff School
CSI	Combat Studies Institute
CWS	Chemical Warfare Service
FEAF	Far Eastern Air Forces
HE	high explosives
JCS	Joint Chiefs of Staff
MAAF	Mediterranean Allied Air Forces
MEWS	Microwave Early Warning Stations
ORSA	operations research & systems analysis
OSRD	Office of Scientific Research & Development
ROTC	Reserve Officer Training Corps

SHAEF   Supreme Headquarters, Allied Expeditionary Forces

USASTAF   US Army Strategic Air Forces

USMA   US Military Academy

USSBS   US Strategic Bombing Survey

USSTAF   US Strategic Air Forces

WPD   War Plans Division

PREFACE

There are two primary reasons that I asked the University Press of Kansas to allow me to revise and update my 1993 book *Bombs, Cities, and Civilians: American Airpower Strategy in World War II*. The first is that there has been much new scholarship in the more than two decades since the original book was published. Revealing work by Tami Biddle, Richard Davis, Rob Ehlers, Gian Gentile, Donald Miller, Richard Overy, Ken Werrell, and many others have unearthed much new information that requires reshaping my original arguments. I also uncovered new sources that needed to be incorporated into the revision during subsequent research for my second book with the University Press of Kansas that dealt with the Korean air war. In addition, my archive at the Army Heritage and Education Center was privileged to acquire the extensive operational records of the 44th Bomb Group of the Eighth Air Force, and a close examination of those files required me to adjust some of my conclusions about the conduct of the European bombing campaign, especially in its later stages.

The second reason goes back to the original title selection in 1993. My initial proposal to the press was for *The Temptations of Total War*, which I thought best reflected the concentration of the book on moral aspects of bombing civilians. However, the editors at Kansas felt differently, and as a new author I was not prepared to be combative over the title. The main title, *Bombs, Cities, and Civilians*, was fine, but the subtitle did not accurately depict what the book was about. I did not really analyze the whole development of US airpower strategy in the way that I did in my Korean air war book. Perhaps those editors were wiser than I, forcing me to realize in hindsight that my focus should have been broader. Clausewitz tells us that the amount of a nation's resistance in war is a product of total means times strength of will. My original work focused primarily on the ways American airmen attacked the civilian will to resist, directly or indirectly. However, their main objective was always to destroy military and economic means or war-making capacity, which was seen as the surest way to end the bloody conflict as quickly as possible. The revised book deals more with the search for the "panacea" target system or systems that would really prove the efficacy of precision doctrine as well as make the biggest possible contribution to winning the war. Establishing that baseline also provides a better foundation to discuss the lures that distracted American airmen from their precision ideals and to demonstrate that such diversions were not unique to World War II.

The original inspiration for this book came from two questions. The first, asked by a professor during a graduate seminar at Stanford, focused on the precedents leading to the decision to drop the atomic bomb on Hiroshima and on why discussions about the new weapon's employment dealt with how to use it, not whether to do so. The second, posed by a West Point cadet trying to understand the ethical restrictions on his actions in war, asked to what extent moral considerations and other limitations on combat can really be effective in a high-stakes, high-intensity conflict in a heavily populated area like Western Europe. In response to the first question, I believe that I have presented in this book many of the lures that drew American leaders and airmen down the path to total war in World War II, as well as away from the letter, if not the spirit, of precision doctrine. At the same time, I have also described how some leaders, for a variety of reasons, did slow the rush to unlimited aerial warfare. I hope that the material in this volume will provide future civilian and military leaders with some motivations and ideas about how to limit the slide toward total war in future conflicts.

As with any project that takes as long as this one, there are many people to acknowledge for their help and support. Three deserve my special thanks for the original book. Without the patience and guidance of Dr. Barton Bernstein at Stanford University, this work would have never been started or completed. Lieutenant Colonel Charles F. Brower IV at the United States Military Academy provided me with leadership and inspiration to do research and continue work. In a demanding assignment at Fort Bliss, Texas, I was guided by Lieutenant Colonel Michael Putnam, who showed me how to manage my time more efficiently and encouraged me to finish the project; he also furnished me with insightful critiques of my work.

Numerous others deserve mention. Colonel Robert Doughty and the soldier-scholars of the History Department at USMA provided a rich supply of ideas during discussions and seminars. Dr. Kenneth Werrell and Dr. Jesse Stiller gave me the benefit of their criticism in analyzing my early work, as did Colonel Paul Miles. Dr. Werrell also contributed significantly to the original book. Dr. Ronald Schaffer deserves special mention; not only did we have some valuable discussions at historical conferences but also he generously provided me with much important source material from his own research. I received help with photographs from Larry Dodd of the Northwest and Whitman College Archival Collections, Alan Aimone from Special Collections Division of the US Military Academy Library, Gary Johnson at the US Army Heritage and Education Center, and Melissa Kaiser, Tim Cronen, and Nick Parrella of the Smithsonian. Michael Briggs, Larisa Martin, and Karen Hellekson at the University Press of Kansas were invaluable in sharpening my prose and ideas. My parents also gave me support and encouragement during this long and arduous effort, and unfortunately my father, who will always remain my image of a World War II veteran, did not live long enough to see this latest version.

I am very grateful to Mike Briggs and his staff at the University Press of Kansas for allowing me to create this revised edition, and Rob Ehlers for prodding me to look more closely at the activities of the much-neglected Fifteenth Air Force. That inclination was reinforced by Dr. John Geis and his staff at the Air Force Research Institute, who kindly allowed me access to their impressive THOR database of American bombing operations, and archivist Maranda Gilmore at the Air Force Historical Research Agency, who doggedly tracked down 455th Bomb Group information for me. Tami Biddle provided some more insights to fine-tune the manuscript. I also must express gratitude to the leadership of US Army War College and US Army Heritage and Education Center for giving me sabbatical time to do the necessary update. My family had to accept all the time I took away from them to complete another writing project. Although my sons now have their own lives to lead, unlike in 1993 when they had to tolerate my writing obsessions in person, my wife has again had to live with a husband literally and figuratively with his mind in the clouds. I hope this result is worth all the time and faith they and others have invested in me, and a worthy account of the hard decisions made by brave American airmen immersed in the boiling cauldron of the most terrible war the world has ever seen.

The views expressed herein are those of the author and do not purport to reflect the positions of the Army War College, Department of the Army, or Department of Defense.

1. INTRODUCTION

There is no doubt in my mind that the RAF want very much to have the US Air Forces tarred with the morale bombing aftermath which we feel will be terrific.

—*General Carl Spaatz*[1]

If you want to overcome your enemy you must match your effort against his power of resistance, which can be expressed as the product of two inseparable factors, viz. the total means at his disposal and the strength of his will.

—*Carl von Clausewitz*[2]

Allied strategic bombing during World War II has generated considerable controversy among historians, regarding both results and motivations. Perhaps the most heated debate has focused on the intentional bombardment of civilians to break their morale, a practice called morale bombing or terror bombing. Basil Liddell Hart, the noted British military historian, called the practice of indiscriminate Allied area bombing of cities "the most uncivilized method of warfare the world has known since the Mongol devastations." An American counterpart, Walter Millis, termed such tactics "unbridled savagery."[3] Many American historians, including me, have perceived a difference between the practices of the Royal Air Force (RAF) and the United States Army Air Forces (AAF), however, especially in the European theater. While the British embraced a policy of indiscriminate night area bombing as their only realistic option, the Americans pursued daylight aerial offensives against well-selected military and industrial targets that were justified by both "strategic judgment and morality."[4] Reflecting the Clausewitz quote above, the RAF targeted will, while the AAF aimed to destroy means.

During World War II, the United States Army Air Forces did enunciate a policy of pinpoint assaults on key industrial or military targets, avoiding

1

Two contrasting views of Allied strategic bombing of Germany in World War II: a section of Munich razed primarily by British night raids (above) and a destroyed oil refinery at Harburg hit by American daylight bombers (opposite). Note the many craters from near misses in the fields around the oil plant. (Northwest and Whitman College Archival Collections, Penrose Memorial Library, Whitman College, Walla Walla, WA)

indiscriminate attacks on population centers. This seems to differentiate US policy from the policies of Germany, Great Britain, and Japan, all of which resorted to intentional terror attacks on enemy cities during the war.[5] Scholars who have cited the official AAF history emphasize the intention of American leaders to resist bombing noncombatants in Europe for both military and ethical reasons.[6] Many of these writers contend that US airmen regarded civilian casualties as an unintentional and regrettable side effect of bombs

dropped on military or industrial objectives; in contrast, the RAF campaign to destroy the cities themselves and kill or dislocate their inhabitants was a deliberate strategy.[7]

A few British writers, such as Max Hastings, have for some time criticized the claimed ethical superiority of AAF strategic bombing as "moral hairsplitting."[8] Beginning in the 1980s, however, the tar of morale bombing that Spaatz feared was applied by American historians such as Ronald Schaffer and Michael Sherry. In a groundbreaking 1980 article, Schaffer analyzed the statements of AAF leaders as well as numerous wartime bombing documents in Europe and concluded that ethical codes "did little to discourage air attacks on German civilians." In fact, "official policy against indiscriminate bombing was so broadly interpreted and so frequently breached as to become almost meaningless." He argued that both the policy against terror bombing and ethical support for that policy among AAF leaders were "myths." In his subsequent book, *Wings of Judgment*, which also discusses strategic bombing in the Pacific, Schaffer examined the issue in more detail. He softened his harsh judgment somewhat, but he still concluded that although "virtually every major figure concerned with American bombing expressed some views about the moral issue . . . moral constraints almost invariably bowed to what people described as military necessity," another disputed concept.[9]

Sherry's award-winning book focused on the development of American airpower, which ultimately led to the use of the atomic bomb. He concentrated on the bombing campaign against Japan and contended that strategists adopted the policy of indiscriminate firebombing of cities after precision bombing against military and industrial targets proved only marginally effective in 1944. Though racism made such tactics easier to adopt against Japan, firebombing was the inadvertent but inevitable product of an anonymous "technological fanaticism" of Allied bombing and airpower. The assumption that using everything available would lead to eventual victory was key in the decisions to firebomb and eventually to use the atomic bomb. The American press and public at the time accepted such measures as retribution for war crimes or as preparation for invasion. Since 1945, concerned Americans have focused on the decision to use the atomic bomb as "the moment of supreme moral choice"; Sherry argued that the whole bombing campaign was the product of "a slow accretion of large fears, thoughtless assumptions, and incremental decisions."[10]

DOCTRINE, COMMAND AND CONTROL, AND OPERATIONS

Certainly AAF leaders had varying motivations and opinions about terror bombing. But a sophisticated understanding of military processes, particularly of doctrinal development, command and control, and operational execution, is needed to evaluate American strategic bombing. Both Schaffer and Sherry judged that the AAF failed to live up to the letter and spirit of precision-bombing doctrine. Sherry was especially critical because doctrine was not inspired and shaped to a greater degree by technology. Because of the limitations of the bombers of the 1930s, when precision bombing was developed, he argued, wartime technology was "more demonstrably than usual . . . the offspring, not the parent, of doctrine," leading to vague and unrealistic assumptions about the potential of pinpoint strategic bombardment and diminishing utility and support of the doctrine as the war went on.[11]

Doctrine, however, is supposed to be developed to meet national goals, perform battlefield missions, or counter a perceived threat, and technology is then designed to implement the doctrine. Technological developments may force modifications in doctrine; ideally they should not drive it. Otherwise, the result is something like the Army's infamous Sergeant York Air Defense Gun, an expensive piece of sophisticated equipment whose capabilities were shaped more by technological possibilities than by an accurate appraisal of the evolving threat of enemy aircraft.[12] The entire family of US armor and antiarmor weapons in World War II illustrates the problem of allowing current technology to define tactical doctrine. Developed by technical experts to be light and mobile, American tanks and tank destroyers were employed to maximize mobility. However, they could not support the army's overall strategy and doctrine of firepower and direct assault, which was required by the conditions of European combat. This flaw affected US ground operations throughout the war.[13]

Allowing current technology to define doctrine can also limit the scope of doctrine without providing guidance or flexibility for later developments. A study of the evolution of military doctrine in the three decades after World War II by the US Army's Combat Studies Institute concludes that "the great value of doctrine is less the final answers it provides than the impetus it creates toward developing innovative and creative solutions" for future problems.[14] The commander of the AAF, General Henry "Hap" Arnold, understood this process. In his final report to the secretary of war in 1945, he emphasized, "National safety would be endangered by an Air Force whose doctrines and techniques are tied solely to the equipment and processes of the moment." The Air Force must keep "its doctrines ahead of its equipment, and its vision far into the future."[15] It is always better to have technology chasing doctrine, not the other way around.

It can be argued that the technology for precision bombing really did not exist until the smart bombs of the Vietnam War. The destruction of the French embassy during the 1986 air strike on Libya; the few televised misses with guided munitions and admitted poor accuracy with unguided weapons during DESERT STORM; the targeting of the Chinese embassy in Belgrade in 1999; and the continuing debates over civilian casualties in Afghanistan and Iraq demonstrate that the ideal of pinpoint accuracy under all combat conditions has still not been reached.[16] Yet the pursuit of accurate bombing remained a primary goal throughout World War II, influencing American tactics and technology during that conflict and setting precedents for later wars, including DESERT STORM, in which the US Air Force first provided an impressive demonstration of advances in precision methods and munitions in military briefings and media clips. When examined in comparison with the bombing results of other air forces in World War II, the intent, if not always the effect, of American air attacks was consistently to achieve the most precise and effective bombardment possible in pursuit of the destruction of the enemy's capacity to resist in order to end the war as quickly as possible. Wartime improvements in bombing accuracy, as well as the eventual impact on the German economy, demonstrate that such a goal was realistic, not a dream always to be abandoned in favor of military expediency. Changing conditions influencing combat capabilities and effectiveness in the European and Pacific theaters did lead to the AAF's acceptance of greater risks for enemy civilians by 1945, but in Europe at least, the operational record shows that the avoidance of noncombatant casualties in accordance with precision doctrine remained a component of American bombing, especially outside Germany, even if one of decreasing influence.

Military doctrine is simply a condensed expression of an accepted approach to campaigns, major operations, and battles. The general purposes of doctrine during and after World War II remained basically the same: "to provide guides for action or to suggest methods that would probably work best" and to facilitate communication between different elements by defining terms and providing concepts.[17] Historically, American field commanders have felt free to interpret doctrinal guidance generally as they pleased. Indeed, the Soviets taught that "one of the serious problems in planning against American doctrine is that the Americans do not read their manuals nor do they feel any obligation to follow their doctrines."[18] This is certainly an exaggeration, but field commanders have rightly assumed that doctrine is basically a set of guidelines that permits much situational leeway. Traditionally, these same field commanders have been given considerable freedom from strict command and control, far in the rear. Even the official AAF history of World War II admits that "air force commanders actually enjoyed great latitude in waging the air war and sometimes paid scant attention" to directives from higher up.[19]

This means that the attitudes of leaders in Washington do not always determine operations in far-flung theaters of war. As Schaffer and Sherry pointed out, the leader in Washington most concerned about moral issues, Secretary of War Henry L. Stimson, was either ineffective or isolated. His position was basically administrative, and unlike the president or the chiefs of staff, he was not deeply involved in making strategy. Whatever their public pronouncements to the contrary, neither Roosevelt nor Arnold had any aversion to terror bombing when it suited their purposes. However, the extent of their control over commanders in the field should not be overstated. At times Arnold's shifts in commanders had considerable influence on bombing policies, such as when he replaced Lieutenant General Ira Eaker with Major General Jimmy Doolittle and Brigadier General Haywood Hansell Jr. with Major General Curtis LeMay. In addition, Arnold's consuming desire to justify an independent air service put pressure on AAF combat leaders to produce decisive bombing results. Yet whether because of distance, heart trouble, or the complexity of the war, Arnold rarely wielded a great deal of direct influence, especially in key operations late in the conflict. Sherry's contention that he consistently exercised particularly strong direction of American strategic-bombing operations and units is not supported by the operational record.[20]

This loose doctrinal and command direction resulted in a bombing policy that was shaped by the operational and tactical commanders who actually dropped the bombs. To understand fully American strategic bombing, we must look at day-to-day planning and operations in the field, not just policy papers in the Pentagon. In his exemplary study of the escalating air war between Germany and Great Britain in 1940, F. M. Sallagar notes that "changes crept in as solutions to operational problems rather than as the consequences of considered policy decisions. In fact, they occurred almost independently of the formal decision making process."[21] In that case, the operational solutions always led toward terror bombing; the same is not true for the AAF. An examination of the actual execution of operations in Europe, such as CLARION, THUNDERCLAP, and the War-Weary Bomber project, reveals that American air commanders there consciously tried to avoid terror bombing even when superiors were encouraging it. Some, like Carl Spaatz, seemed to have genuine moral concerns about such bombing; others, like Ira Eaker, were apparently more concerned with public opinion against such tactics or believed they were ineffective or inefficient. AAF operations in Europe contrast starkly with the American strategic bombing of Japan, where the destruction of cities by firebombing was adopted. Yet this decision also was made by the commander on the scene, Curtis LeMay, without real direction from Washington. Bombing policy in each theater was shaped by the military necessity of combat, but it was also affected by the individual personality of each commander, who defined that necessity. Air campaigns were also influenced by command relationships. In Europe, US Strategic

Air Forces (USSTAF) commander Spaatz worked closely with the theater commander, General Dwight Eisenhower, to synchronize air and ground operations. The Pacific theater had no such unified command or such a unified strategy. However, while strategic air operations against Japan were primarily conducted by the Twentieth Air Force, both the Eighth Air Force and the Fifteenth Air Force were bombing Germany, and they operated differently.

Certainly air operations in the European and Pacific theaters had come to accept more risks for noncombatants by 1945. In both cases, this evolution came about as planners and commanders in the field interpreted doctrine and searched for optimum bombing strategies. In Europe, the change resulted to a large extent from an increasing resort to attacks on transportation targets as higher-priority industrial objectives were destroyed or dispersed. Such operations assisted ground advances by restricting the movement of reinforcements and supplies, by putting extra burdens on a transport system already strained by the destruction of oil targets, and by facilitating widespread attacks that used the increased air assets present in the theater. Large transportation objectives could also be discerned by radar used for nonvisual bombing through overcast, a technique that allowed American bombers to increase their missions significantly during German winter weather but that also contributed to an acceptance of less accurate bombing results. Precision doctrine recognized the validity of transportation targets as a means to weaken the enemy's economy, but attacks on marshaling yards in cities were bound to increase the number of noncombatant casualties from errant bombs. Targets in Germany were also treated differently from those in other countries, with more pressure to deliver bombs there in poor weather conditions. In the Pacific, the evolution toward total war went much further. The strategic air campaign targeted factories and military facilities, but normal precision tactics did not seem to work. In order to destroy these objectives, LeMay resorted to incendiary attacks on urban areas that were bound to kill thousands of civilians. If European air commanders were showing less concern for noncombatant casualties in 1945, then Pacific air leaders were demonstrating none at all. Proponents of precision bombing had long argued that it was both the most efficient and humane way to fight a war. However, once LeMay became convinced that pinpoint tactics were no longer effective, morality alone was not enough to prevent the firebombing of Tokyo.

In both theaters, air operations were also influenced by growing pressure to end a war that seemed to be increasingly bloody at the same time enemies should be close to collapse. The Battle of the Bulge in Europe and the invasions of Iwo Jima and Okinawa in the Pacific were shocking portents of possible future costs. At the same time, prodigious American industrial output created vast fleets of bombers that could not just sit idle, despite poor weather, at the same time enemy air defenses were depleted so as to be almost nonexistent. It must be noted that even in the Pacific, the primary focus of bombing strategy remained eliminating military and economic capacity, not targeting civilian will.

OTHER INFLUENCES ON COMMANDERS

It is usually difficult to identify moral considerations in the decision making of key US commanders in World War II. Their primary objective was to win the war in the shortest time with the most efficient use of resources and the fewest possible American casualties. Mission requirements usually prevented any sense of morality from being "an overriding criterion" on aerial operations, although one planner stated that his group "took some comfort that our proposals would be much less costly in terms of the lives of civilians."[22] The need for Allied cooperation also tended to mute ethical arguments because the British so strongly supported attacks on civilian morale and the Americans did not want to cause a rift or aid German propaganda. Although it is hard to determine moral positions from official records and correspondence, it is probably true that ethical restraints were not the most important limitations on terror bombing by the USSTAF. Such considerations, however, cannot be completely discounted.

At the same time, it must be noted that psychological effects have always been an important part of air warfare. Like the bayonet or the tank, the airplane has a shock effect that is intended to unnerve an enemy and break the will to resist. Unlike those other weapons, however, the long range of the airplane encompasses vast regions of the enemy's rear area, inhabited mainly by civilians. Once factories became acceptable bombing targets as part of the enemy's capacity for making war, factory workers could no longer be seen as noncombatants. Once the trend to recognize some civilians as belligerents began, it was only a matter of time until the justification would be made, as in Japan, that everyone supported the war effort in some way. The temptation to exploit and magnify the psychological effects of bombing civilians would also be hard to resist. American airmen, even those most devoted to precision doctrine or morally opposed to bombing any civilians, expected that the destruction of economic and industrial infrastructure would have a significant effect on enemy civilian morale. Yet at least in the European theater AAF leaders were not willing to achieve the same goal by intentionally killing women and children or burning down their homes. Even LeMay's fire raids listed the destruction of specific industrial targets as the primary objective. However, once a supplementary campaign of psychological warfare was launched to terrorize the rest of Japan with the threat of more conflagrations, differences lessened even more between this American air campaign and RAF Bomber Command's area raids on German cities or the Luftwaffe's Blitz against London.

Other influences on air commanders also affected their decisions. Pressures from various levels of command and perceptions of public opinion helped shape planning and operations. Any military mission includes implied tasks to fight, win, and return with honor intact, but these elements have different weight, depending on where the soldiers are on the battlefield. Although Arnold hoped to achieve an independent air force with "Victory through Airpower," his bomber crewmen were more concerned with doing the best job they could and surviving. Operational and tactical commanders were caught in the middle; they had to be loyal to the goals of their organization and to the welfare of their men.[23] A quick and overwhelming victory served both purposes and was also in keeping with the "Airpower Ethic" by preventing long and bloody land combat. The lure of achieving the Allies' stated aim of winning the war "as decisively and speedily as possible" through technological solutions or by a single operation to produce a deathblow became especially strong after the success of Operation OVERLORD in Europe and as the invasion of Japan approached.[24] With the exception of some officers like LeMay, devotion to precision-bombing doctrine remained strong in the field, especially with those officers who had helped develop it, though its applications changed as the military situation evolved. Contrary to many American doctrines in our military history, this one was uniformly known, understood, and believed by most of the soldiers who were supposed to follow it. Indeed, it often seems that precision bombing was better understood in the field than in Washington. In his memoir, Wartime, Paul Fussell claims that "precision bombing became a comical oxymoron relished by bomber crews with a sense of black humor," although he provides no real evidence to back up this statement about American strategic bombing.[25] In reality, aircrews and their leaders were convinced of the effectiveness and appropriateness of their tactics and missions and were usually quick to express dissatisfaction with any perceived deviations from proven and accepted techniques and procedures, though admittedly such complaints lessened as the end of the war approached.

This continuity in doctrine is not really evident unless one focuses on day-to-day operations. Though archival sources such as the papers of Spaatz or Arnold provide invaluable topical information, letters or documents are grouped by subject more than by time period, and even unit histories can be narrow in focus. The best source for a full understanding of the milieu of European air operations is the daily operational diaries of Frederick L. Anderson, USSTAF deputy commander for operations. Each daily file contains bound packets of correspondence that passed in and out of USSTAF headquarters, including letters from Arnold and Spaatz, press releases, and battle reports from the field. This concentrated operational- and tactical-level documentation describes the course of the air war in great detail and shows the continuity and persistence of precision-bombing doctrine even while temptations to use terror bombing increased.[26] The mission reports and monthly summaries of individual bombardment groups are also very revealing about the way operational directives were actually executed.

Yet in the Pacific theater, a unique combination of military problems and an innovative commander less committed to prescribed doctrine produced a far different response to these temptations. This contrast makes the European record even more remarkable, especially when one considers the need to cooperate with an ally dedicated to terror bombing. Though adverse weather, technological limitations, or enemy countermeasures such as flak or smokescreens often made it difficult to achieve the standards of precision-bombing doctrine, most AAF airmen did live up to the spirit of it. Moreover, in the Pacific theater, Brigadier General Haywood Hansell, LeMay's predecessor, was replaced because he would not swerve from the tenets he had helped develop.

Most critics of precision bombing have been asking the wrong question, because it is impossible to determine accurately the specific ethical motivations for strategic air attacks from the documentation available. On the narrower issue of the application of precision bombing practices in the field, an impartial observer must conclude that in general most American airmen did the best they could to win the war with consistent application of a doctrine that favored military and industrial targeting over terror bombing. Their intent was to spare noncombatants while reducing enemy means to resist, and they succeeded better than many historians are willing to concede.

Perhaps the survivors of strategic-bombing attacks understood this better than the historians. As one German who lived through the American bombing and the RAF-induced firestorms in Hamburg commented, "The Americans were regarded by us as *soldiers*. Their attacks were during the day-time and were nearly always directed on military targets, even if the civilian population sometimes suffered heavy casualties because of them. They flew in good visibility and risked the aimed fire of our Flak. Hence [we had] a certain respect for the 'Amis' as we called them."[27]

Yet it is undeniable that for a number of reasons strategic-bombing principles and precedents from Europe contributed to "the slide to total [air] war" in the bombing of Japan. Military conditions were different in the Pacific theater, as were perceptions of the enemy; command and control was much looser also. According to the official history of the Joint Chiefs of Staff, "The division of the Pacific Theater between two major commands [Nimitz and MacArthur] complicated the problems of war and undoubtedly reduced the efficiency with which the war was fought."[28] As the Army and Navy pursued competing strategies, the AAF also mounted an essentially independent campaign. Perhaps the most important difference from the European theater was that in the Pacific, the air commander who instituted the firebombing campaign had not been involved in the development of strategic-bombing doctrine, had learned "not much" when he attended the Air Corps Tactical School, and "was always more practical than theoretical."[29] Once LeMay decided on the burning of Japanese cities as the solution to his operational problems and the practice became accepted by leaders in Washington and in the field, the next step in the escalation to total war—dropping the atomic bomb on Hiroshima—was indeed, to use Sherry's words, only an "incremental decision."

An ironic legacy of strategic bombing in World War II, evident in more limited conflicts such as the war in Vietnam and the campaigns against Iraq, is that even though international opinion might focus on the image of the mushroom cloud obliterating cities or on B-52s carpet bombing enemy populations, the American military ideal in both doctrine and practice has remained the pursuit of precise destruction of enemy capacity. The military ethics and accuracy espoused in doctrinal literature on air operations today and first demonstrated so convincingly during Operation DESERT STORM evolved directly from the effort and intent of the experience in World War II. And since that 1991 conflict the expectations of the American public and political leaders about the precision and potential of airpower have exceeded the dreams of even the most idealistic airmen who shaped the AAF, creating the potential for a dangerous policy–capability mismatch. Exorbitant expectations for accuracy, bloodlessness, and speedy victory always clash with the grim realities of war. History reveals that any lengthy American strategic-bombing campaign targeting national capacity, successful or not, eventually diverges from those precision ideals, or at least stretches their boundaries.

2. DEVELOPING DOCTRINE

The consensus of world opinion is not only opposed to the employment of air power in direct attacks against civilian personnel, but such attacks cannot be justified on the basis of efficiency.

—*Draft, 1935 Air Corps Tactical School text*[1]

During June 1918 the director of military aeronautics in the United States prepared a study on strategic bombardment for the chief of staff, General P. C. March, proposing the development of a "long distance independent bombing force" intended "to operate on a bombing campaign against German industrial centers."[2] Despite this growing interest in an official doctrine for strategic bombing, aircraft production could not support it. The July 1918 "202 Squadron Program" for the American Expeditionary Forces (AEF) Air Service allocated sixty pursuit squadrons, 101 for observation planes and only forty-one for bombers. This decision, based on industrial capacity rather than doctrine, had significant repercussions. The American air arm had no operational organizations to determine the course of engineering development or doctrine, and AEF end-of-war reports were generally written by ground-oriented staff officers in the field with little understanding of air warfare or its potential. As a result of the limitations on production that plagued the air service's structure and performance, postwar US Army staff schools taught that "strategical bombing is . . . a luxury."[3]

Nevertheless, some studies would influence the development of future doctrine. These were compiled for Major General Mason M. Patrick, chief of Air Service, AEF, and would eventually be deposited at the Air Corps Tactical School (ACTS) at Maxwell Field in Alabama. In December 1918 he directed his assistant chief of staff, Colonel Edgar S. Gorrell, to prepare a history and final report on US air activities in Europe during the war. The

14

choice of Gorrell ensured that strategic bombing would not be ignored; he had been made head of Strategic Aviation for the AEF because of his work as chief of the Air Service Technical Section, a position that had required him to anticipate production and supply the essentials for bombing operations. From his investigations he developed a bombardment plan in November 1917 characterized later as the "earliest, clearest, and least known statement of the American conception of the employment of air power." His work so impressed Brigadier General Benjamin Foulois, chief of Air Service, AEF, that the general recommended the plan to Pershing in December. As Tami Biddle has pointed out, it is ironic that this "American conception" heavily relied on innovative analysis done earlier by Lord Tiverton, of the British Air Staff's Directorate of Flying Operations. He was the first airman to look systematically at a comprehensive plan to eliminate enemy capacity with a bombing campaign focused on key industrial target sets. Gorrell's November proposal included verbatim excerpts from one Tiverton had written in September.[4]

Gorrell collected all available materials, including his own 1917 plan, "a truly striking forerunner of the doctrine which matured years later at the Air Corps Tactical School." Some of that later doctrine even used the same wording and metaphors of Gorrell's document.[5] His plan aimed to "wreck Germany's manufacturing centers" with a round-the-clock campaign of day and night bombing. Targeting chemical plants would cut artillery shell output, and bombing aircraft engine plants would limit airplane production. He stated: "The object of strategical bombing is to drop aerial bombs upon the commercial centers and the lines of communications" in order to "cut off the necessary supplies without which the armies in the field cannot exist." Also cognizant of the psychological effects of air raids, he proposed concentrated attacks by all available aircraft on single cities, expecting to shatter "the morale of the workmen" as well as the factories. Some towns' morale seemed especially vulnerable, and he surmised from press reports that bombing Cologne "would create such trouble that the German Government might be forced to suggest terms." Gorrell also projected that fire protection in undermanned German villages would break down under a lengthy bombardment, "and therefore the results would be out of proportion to the immediate effect of the bombs." The advantage of this new aerial warfare would be to break the stalemate on the ground and thus save lives and material.[6]

Gorrell's collection also included a short paper, "Area vs. Precision Bombing," from the organization responsible for providing bombsights for the Air

Service. French and British bombardiers favored area-bombing techniques using outboard sights that allowed them to stay at their guns, but the Americans developed a formation technique in which a chosen bombardier protected by other planes climbed inside the fuselage, used his better sight, and picked the bombing point for the whole formation. This practice of using a lead bombardier and the perception of superior American bombsights and technique would appear again in World War II.[7]

As Gorrell accumulated material for General Patrick, the colonel realized that he needed a more systematic analysis of the effects of aerial bombing on the enemy. Air Service officers under the supervision of the Air Intelligence Section of General Headquarters, AEF, were sent out to survey bombed towns and to interview inhabitants. Teams were to determine whether day or night bombing was more effective in damaging both material and morale. In general, the information was scanty and incomplete, but the report's summary provided many ideas for future consideration. Though bomb damage as a whole was relatively slight, bombing did affect the morale of fighting forces as well as the civilian population. In addition, government employees could not perform their work because of bombing, transportation of troops and supplies was hindered, and the manufacture of war material was hampered to some degree. The Germans were also forced to spend much time and effort defending their homeland. The effects on civilian morale described dealt mainly with loss of sleep and lowered worker performance; the idea of a Hamburg or a Tokyo firestorm was far in the future.[8]

Yet the bombing survey did provide a disturbing preview of attitudes that would help create those holocausts. It mentioned that the casualty figures of 641 killed and 1,242 wounded in twenty-two German cities "may not be considered very important, inasmuch as most of these were civilians," but it further explained that helping the wounded and the dependents of those killed could entail considerable additional expenses to the government.[9] Many of the Allied raids that produced these casualties were motivated by similar German attacks, especially on England, where attacks by dirigibles and bombers had killed 1,414 people and wounded 3,416. The British were incensed at what they perceived as "willful murder," but a captured Zeppelin commander denied the accusations in terms that could have been echoed by American airmen in World War II. "You must not suppose that we set out to kill women and children," he tried to explain. "We have higher military aims. You would not find one officer in the German Army and Navy who would go to war to kill women and children. Such things happen accidentally in war."[10]

The conclusions and criticisms in the bombing survey could be seen as a portent for the precision-bombing theory to come. Despite the inferences about benefits of attacks on civilians, the British and French were criticized for inaccurate bombing as well as for "the unintelligent choice of targets," in particular "the bombing of a town rather than some definite objective of military value in the town." Arguments against the bombing of cities were based on practical considerations, not ethics. Directly targeting civilian morale "is not a productive means of bombing. The effect is legitimate and just as considerable when attained indirectly through the bombing of a factory." Instead, the three most important objectives for bombing were war industries, railroad lines, and troops in the field. The survey concluded that the industrial bombing attack should be concentrated night and day on the enemy's most important and vulnerable economic sector and that communications lines were best hit immediately preceding and during major operations. Many of these attitudes and practices would be evident in the next American air war.[11]

THE INFLUENCE OF THEORISTS

Gorrell's exhaustive work eventually ended up at the library of the ACTS, where it undoubtedly influenced the officers who developed precision-bombing doctrine between the wars. A progression of theorists also made their mark on American air doctrine during that period. Perhaps most important was a British major general, Hugh Trenchard, commander of the Royal Flying Corps and a power in the highest military and political circles, who believed in an independent air force pursuing a radical strategic-bombing campaign. His belief in an "incessant and relentless" bombing offensive where moral effects greatly outweighed material ones had great impact on the development of the interwar Royal Air Force. He also exerted a powerful influence on American officers serving in France during World War I, including Brigadier General William "Billy" Mitchell, the most outspoken American airpower advocate in the postwar period.[12]

Mitchell was first exposed to airpower theory as the assistant to Major George O. Squier, commandant of the Signal School at Fort Leavenworth during 1905 and 1906. In 1908 Squier wrote a position paper that anticipated many of the future tactical and strategic roles for American aviation. Because dirigibles outperformed airplanes at that time, he envisioned strategic airships bombing enemy factories and capitals. Like many future air the-

Brigadier General William "Billy" Mitchell displaying his decorations from World War 1. This photo was taken in 1924, a year before a court-martial convicted him of "conduct prejudicial to good order and military discipline" for accusing the War and Navy departments of incompetence and negligence in their air policies. He then resigned from the service and continued his airpower crusade as a civilian.

orists, he predicted that strong air forces would make war less likely because enemy leaders would be in personal danger once war began. Squier was an attaché in London when World War I began, and he kept his American colleagues well informed on developing theory and the conduct of the air war.[13]

Service with Squier and exposure to Trenchard were not the only theoretical influences on Americans such as Mitchell. As the Germans bombed London with Zeppelins and Gothas in 1917, Field Marshal Jan Smuts predicted that in the future "aerial operations, with their devastation of enemy lands and destruction of industrial and populous centers on a vast scale, may become the principal operations of war."[14] French and British airmen exposed their allies to a European outlook on airpower that was perhaps most clearly expressed by the Italian Giulio Douhet, sometimes called the "Father of Airpower Doctrine."[15] Mitchell may have met Douhet on a trip to Italy in 1922, though the American never attributed any special influence on his thinking to the Italian.[16]

The outspoken Douhet had been imprisoned by his government for a year during World War I for criticizing staff policies. His court-martial conviction was repudiated and expunged after the war, and he became a general and head of his nation's aviation programs. Douhet's book *Command of the Air* was published in 1921, but he had been voicing his position since 1910. Although the bulk of his volume dealt with the technical problems of establishing and organizing a large independent air force to be used en masse, he also graphically portrayed a total war with "no distinction any longer between soldiers and civilians." He further expanded these views in a number of revisions and articles until his death in 1930.[17]

Douhet foresaw that attacks of high explosives, gas, and incendiaries on cities would produce effects on morale exceeding material damage. Like intense artillery bombardments, air raids would subject the people in the target area to significant shock and stress. German and British airmen during World War I had noticed the decreases in factory production and the increases in public discontent that had resulted from their primitive attempts to strike targets in urban areas. Trenchard estimated that the psychological yield of his air attacks on Rhine towns was twenty times greater than the damage from actual physical destruction.[18] Other recent precedents existed for attacking civilian morale with distant bombardment. In 1871 the Prussians had decided that the quickest and ultimately the most humane way to conquer Paris was to shell the civil population so that they would force the garrison to surrender. Douhet expanded on that idea to predict the collapse of whole nations. People would panic at the mere sight of airplanes and demand an end to the war, "driven by the instinct of self preservation." He argued that such wars could not last long, "since the decisive blows will be directed at civilians, that element of countries at war least able to sustain them." Douhet also espoused the principle that some writers have called the "Airpower Ethic": such future wars would be more humane because "they may in the long run shed less blood." Never strong on hard data to back up his claims, Douhet seems to have based his conclusions on incidents such as the one at Brescia during the war, where mourners at a funeral for bombing victims panicked when a bird was mistaken for an airplane. He was also supposedly impressed by the reported effects of German bombing on the population of London.[19]

Douhet's effect on the development of American bombing doctrine has been hotly debated, with skeptics of its precision focus contending that the Italian's writings had a particularly strong influence on AAF teachings and practices. Billy Mitchell may have incorporated some of Douhet's ideas, but he tailored his concepts to the American situation. By 1930 Mitchell did consider cities as attractive targets, but only for disruption, not destruction. "It will be sufficient," he wrote, "to have the civilian population driven out so they cannot carry on their usual vocations. A few gas bombs will do that."[20] When for publicity he advocated Douhet's views in 1933, Mitchell was no longer a major influence on those individuals developing AAF doctrine. Whether because of his earlier military experience in the ruthless guerrilla war in the Philippines or from his incessant desire for publicity, Mitchell tended as time went on to become more extreme in support of terror bombing and more out of touch with mainstream views. Ironically, although resigning from the service after his court-martial gave him more freedom to advocate airpower publicly, it also lessened his influence and connection with those actually developing American air doctrine.[21]

By 1923 Army Air Corps schools had access to Douhet's writings, but his theories on mass-area bombings of civilians did not gain any wide acceptance. The Italian expanded his theories with publications in 1926, 1928, 1929, and 1930, and the comprehensiveness of his ideas "has made it a too convenient reference for anyone who would ascribe the origins of American ideas on strategic bombing to a single, overriding influence." At best, "Douhet must rank as no more than one of the multiple influences on Mitchell, his colleagues, and their successors, as they slowly evolved a strategic bombardment doctrine that was sensitive to the American political and military tradition."[22]

Douhet did have significant influence on the strategic level, however. Before his writings appeared, the dominant strategic schools of thought were the Continental School, following the land power theories of Clausewitz that focused on destroying enemy armies, and the Maritime School, based on Mahan's sea power teachings with the goal of dominating critical sea lanes and choke points. Douhet is given credit for founding the Aerospace School, emphasizing that airpower alone can be decisive and that by controlling the air and destroying the enemy's war-making potential it can make protracted wars obsolete. Probably a more accurate epithet for Douhet is the "Father of Airpower Strategy." Though it is hard to find the exact sources for the ideas American airmen generated between the wars, the Army Air Corps did pursue an aerospace strategy as it developed its own precision-bombing doctrine.[23]

In the years preceding World War II, Douhet's ideas had a more significant impact on some European air forces. In England, influential writers such as J. F. C. Fuller and Basil Liddell Hart echoed Douhet's opinion that civilians could not withstand aerial bombardment. Assisted by a hopeful governmental policy that the British could avoid becoming engaged with land forces in another Continental war, the independent Royal Air Force pursued plans to win any future conflict through controlling the air. By the end of 1941 the RAF was the only means available for the British to strike back at Germany, but daylight raids were proving too costly and night bombing too inaccurate for pinpoint targets. Faced with the need to take some offensive action to meet public demands for retaliation and to justify the large resources invested in an independent air service, Sir Arthur "Bomber" Harris's Bomber Command adopted a Douhetian strategy for mass night raids on German cities to "dehouse German workers" and break civilian morale.[24] In contrast, the RAF's American allies developed a different aerial strategy based on daylight precision bombing of key economic and military objectives.

THE CREATION OF PRECISION-BOMBING DOCTRINE

Although Mitchell's doctrinal ideas moved closer to Douhet's in the 1930s and the contrasting official Army position remained that airpower was only an auxiliary force to assist ground troops, a small group of officers at the ACTS were creating their own strategic-bombing doctrine—precision attack on critical points of specified industrial target systems to destroy the war-making capacity of enemy states.[25] This development would soon have added impact because these same airmen would plan America's air war in World War II and also figure prominently in executing it.

There are two prerequisites for creating new military doctrine. First, higher authorities must realize the need for change and support new ideas. Second, a small and creative group of thinkers must work together to synthesize a body of thought expressing a new approach to war. Organizational doctrine arises from an evolutionary process influenced by interpretations of military history, environmental factors like geography and technology, and the fundamental beliefs of a society.[26] In the 1920s and 1930s the Air Corps' leaders sought a coherent doctrine that would be acceptable to the American people and to politicians and that at the same time would be offensive in nature, thus necessitating an independent air service. While congressional and War Department boards continued to relegate the air arm to auxiliary status, the faculty at ACTS pursued their new doctrine. The theory of precision bombing had begun to take shape in the early 1930s, when Colonel John F. Curry was commandant of the school; he performed the essential function of shielding his faculty from Washington while providing much freedom of thought and expression.[27] Rising Air Corps leaders such as Carl Spaatz and Frank Andrews supported and contributed to the new ideas being created, as did ACTS instructors (and future generals) Laurence Kuter, George Kenney, Kenneth Walker, and Haywood Hansell. However, the officers most responsible for solidifying precision-bombing doctrine into a coherent form were Harold George, Donald Wilson, and Robert Webster.[28]

George, Wilson, Webster, and other ACTS instructors did not work in a vacuum; they had many lessons from the 1920s to draw on. Everyone acknowledged that the public opposed terror bombing of civilians, and this led to military corollaries. "No nation will use its air forces to bomb cities, just for the purpose of destroying the morale of the people by instilling them with fear," an infantry lieutenant colonel wrote in 1928. "Such action could only bring on the nation the active resentment of the rest of the civilized world, a thing that no nation can afford." Army and Navy officers as well as members of Congress continually attacked the practice of strategic bombardment as a violation of international law.[29] Precision-bombing doctrine, attacking factories instead of women and children, offered a way for the Air Corps to be decisive in war without appearing immoral. Moreover, improvements in technology made the doctrine feasible. Air Corps maneuvers in 1929 impressed observers with the "invincibility of the bomber," and Walker especially became an outspoken advocate that "the bomber will always get through." Accurate daylight bombardment began to receive increased emphasis during the next decade, with the development of the Norden and Sperry bombsights and the B-17 airplane. Precision bombing also called upon a traditional American respect for marksmanship that dated back to frontier days. Moral, legal, cultural, technical, strategic, and tactical reasons combined to shape the theory of precision bombing of industrial targets by the 1930s. Mark Clodfelter has argued that the new doctrine was also shaped by the impetus of Progressive reform so prominent in American politics in the early decades of the twentieth century. Though many Progressives such as Herbert Hoover were engineers who shared a similar practical and scientific worldview with airmen, there is no evidence that Air Corps officers identified with such political impulses or parties. Perhaps Progressive ideas might have attracted sympathetic members of Congress to support interwar budgets for new aircraft, but such a reform rationale did not influence the airmen who would fly them. The best that can be said for Clodfelter's theory is that the idea systems surrounding Progressivism and precision bombing arose from similar roots: a desire to utilize modern organizational and engineering expertise rationally to solve serious contemporary problems, whether political or military.[30]

Perhaps the most important rationale for the new doctrine was the belief that aerial bombardment of specific industrial objectives constituted the most effective and economical way to wage war, a conclusion drawn from the work of George, Wilson, and Webster. Without their efforts, precision-bombing theory might not have been so coherent, and it definitely would not have been such a powerful influence on the AAF in World War II.

One writer has called the precision-bombing concept "one of those rare creative ideas that generate in several minds at about the same time."[31] It seems to have begun with instructor Donald Wilson, chief of the Air Force section, when he observed in 1933 that the operation of a whole railroad system could be stopped by the lack of one lubricating ingredient. He then applied his observation on a larger scale and looked for specific structures in industrial nations that supported their capability to wage war. Because the War Department, in accordance with public opinion, prohibited any study of offensive actions against other nations, ACTS had no strategic air intelligence. Wilson therefore looked at the American industrial and social fabric for vulnerabilities, assuming that they would pertain to other industrialized nations. The study could also be used to shape US defenses and thus be within War Department guidelines.[32]

When Wilson left ACTS in 1934, his inquiry was expanded by two captains in the Department of Air Tactics and Strategy, Harold George and Bob Webster. In a detailed analysis of American transportation networks, power systems, and factories they found that the number of critical targets was relatively small and vulnerable to accurate bombardment. They then turned to cities, "the most politically and morally sensitive target system of all." After studying New York, they estimated that the destruction of only seventeen targets within its transportation, water, and electrical systems would render the city uninhabitable. They also concluded that "with very precise bombing, this could be done without vast destruction or mass casualties."[33]

The changes in Air Corps thinking were reflected in ACTS texts. In 1926 the position that an air force was auxiliary to ground forces was abandoned in favor of a Trenchard-style independent, offensive strategy in the manual *Employment of Combined Air Forces*. The document declared that the enemy's population and vital points were the true objectives in war. Expressing ideas similar to Douhet's, it argued that air attack was "a method of imposing will by terrorizing the whole population" and preferable to costly land combat; but, as Gorrell had argued, it maintained that large-scale killing was not necessarily required to affect morale. Though this document has been used as evidence of Douhet's influence at ACTS, with its concentration on "complete destruction of vital parts of the enemy's sources of supply," the manual is much more in keeping with Gorrell's work.[34]

A 1931 text claimed that "with the exception of operations against an enemy force, a large proportion of the operations of an air force will be against strategical objectives . . . the enemy's system of supply, reinforcement and evacuation." The course material did not neglect cities, but it called them "political objectives," whose population can be attacked directly with gas or explosives or "indirectly" through their water, food, or power supplies. Air forces should not be used against political objectives "except as the result of a careful estimate of the results to be accomplished, when weighed against the suffering of women and children, and the effect of public opinion in neutral countries." The text emphasized that "some foreign authorities will advocate the direct attack of the enemy civil population to bring about a decision in war," but it did not support such a position.[35]

In 1933 for political effect ACTS was distributing translations of a Douhet article, "La guerre de l'air," to the House Committee on Military Affairs even as instructors were moving further away from his theories on bombing civilians. The 1934 text for the Air Force course described in detail attacking the "social sphere" and stated that "large urban populations and high standards of living broaden the possible range of dislocation and add length to the lever that an air force can apply against morale." Cities were vulnerable and hard to defend. Although it was "an undeniable fact that the consensus of world opinion is opposed to such employment of air power," it was also "common knowledge" that "nearly all of the leading powers" were making plans and training civilians in order to minimize the effects of attacks on cities. Despite the "wrath of world opinion" that such attacks would incur, the threat of such action "will certainly exist in modern war" and might actually prove more persuasive than the results from an actual attack. But, the text continued, "fortunately a more desirable and more effective approach is available to an Air Force, . . . [which] entails the careful selection of certain material targets . . . upon which the social life of the nation depends," such as food and power supplies. This text reflected a move toward precision bombing, but it still envisioned attacks against the social sphere.[36]

The influence of Wilson, George, and Webster was more apparent in the next year's text. Stating that "loss of morale in the civil population . . . is decisive," it also recognized that direct attacks on civilian personnel are inefficient as well as opposed by world opinion. Whether a strategic air attack aims "to deny the enemy the means that are essential for the prosecution of the war" or to so dislocate normal life that people are willing to surrender to regain it, "transportation facilities and sources of energy and raw materials are the vital elements in a nation upon which both the welfare of the population and the ability to wage war depend." The authors of this 1935 text recognized that attacks on some target systems would degrade both capacity and will, recognizing the shock effect implicit in any aerial raid on a modern society. By 1939 ACTS lesson plans bluntly stated: "Direct attack of the civil populace . . . is rejected as an air objective due to humanitarian considerations." The text concentrated on precision-target systems, although terror attacks were considered "as a possible means of retaliation."[37]

In his concise analysis of the emerging unescorted high-altitude daylight precision doctrine, Peter Faber identifies nine faulty assumptions, many common to other airpower theories before and after. First, it assumed that war could be scientifically managed—that the mechanistic and prescriptive approach could impose precise controls over complex activities. Second, technology was perceived as a panacea to overcome any problem, including weather. Third, it forgot that the enemy has a vote; they would react to whatever actions were applied against them to recover from attacks and develop countermeasures. Wars would be so much easier if people were not involved. The fourth bad assumption is a spin-off from the previous one, as the over-emphasis on the offensive power of unescorted massed bomber formations without considering that they might actually have to fight through complex and effective defensive systems almost lost the air war. Fifth, while the new theory did not dwell very much on psychological impacts, it did assume that eventually all the physical destruction would contribute to destroying the will to resist as well. Sixth, the emerging doctrine saw modern industrial states as "brittle and closed economic systems," not open and adaptable as they turned out to be. Seventh, states were seen as rational actors basing political decisions on pure cost–benefit analyses, without nagging distracters like emotional or bureaucratic factors. Eighth, the "frailty and manipulability" of popular morale was greatly exaggerated, without consideration that the backlash against bombing might actually increase support of the government and the will to resist. Last, Faber argues that air planners were guilty of the practice of "mirror imaging," which confused enemy vulnerabilities with our own. Although his fifth and eighth items actually applied to the British more than the Americans, his list is worth pondering, and the impact of those erroneous assumptions would be evident throughout the course of the air war.[38]

PRECISION DOCTRINE BECOMES OFFICIAL POLICY

The teachings at ACTS had a strong impact on the Air Corps. Though former ACTS instructors did try to influence higher military educational institutions such as the Command and General Staff School at Fort Leavenworth, airmen coming to ACTS had rarely been exposed to any coherent air doctrine taught by another military school.[39] The primary flying school at Randolph Field and the advanced school at nearby Kelly Field were designed to give practical flying skills to newly commissioned airmen. There was not a true basic-training program for officers, and specialized training of Air Corps officers in the 1930s was largely limited to Army extension courses. It was hoped that West Point, which produced a large proportion of the new aviators, would provide its graduates with some sort of theoretical base.[40]

Air Service and Air Corps officers were continually frustrated by the ground-oriented nature of the instruction at West Point. Even as late as 1939, the observation mission dominated practical instruction conducted at Mitchell Field on Long Island.[41] In classes on military theory, cadets discussed Clausewitz, Saxe, Jomini, Frederick, Marlborough, Gustavus, and Schlieffen but not Douhet or Mitchell.[42] Aerial warfare in the 1930s could not be ignored, however, and the bombing lessons from conflicts in China and Spain received much attention in class.

Generally, such discussions focused on the tactical ground support role of air operations, which was in keeping with official Army policy and probably reflected a lack of Air Corps instructors as well. Lessons from the Sino-Japanese War showed that aircraft were "very effective in pursuit, useful in artillery spotting, helpful but not decisive in driving infantry from defensive positions." The best target was troop concentrations. The bombing of cities was dealt with in great detail, however, and conclusions supported the new doctrine evolving at ACTS. "The mistaken Japanese policy of indiscriminate airplane bombing" aroused people in Shanghai and brought them together against Japan; a handout for students stated that "frightfulness united them as no peacetime propaganda could have." The chief result of the bombing of Canton "was to change indifference of the South China masses to intense hatred of the Japanese." A primary lesson of the war taught that "Japanese air bombing of crowded cities destroyed millions of dollars worth of property and took an enormous toll of civilian lives, but gained little or no military advantage thereby. In most cases the reaction was exactly the opposite of the desired and anticipated effect of breaking the nation's will to fight and undermining support of the Nationalist Government." A similar handout on the Spanish Civil War concluded that though bombing was quite effective in destroying the morale of untrained troops, "far from demoralizing the populace it seemed to stiffen their determination to resist and to bring home to their leaders the necessity for cooperation to repel the attackers."[43]

Studying terror bombing such as that used in China, Spain, and Ethiopia led to similar conclusions from other military strategists, who also noted that such raids often led to reprisals and destruction of the attackers' cities.[44] Writers in publications such as the *Infantry Journal* condemned "aeromaniacs" who ignored the lessons of history and continued to believe that "the determination of a people to carry on war can be broken by mere punishment."[45] Attacks on Shanghai and Madrid evoked the expected public outcry, expressed by newspaper editors who claimed that the "laws of war are becoming scraps of paper." The League of Nations and the US government condemned the attacks as "contrary to principles of law and humanity."[46]

By 1939 higher-level military schools such as the Army War College were teaching America's senior leaders that despite European acceptance of wanton air attacks on defenseless civilians as inevitable, such tactics were considered "butchery in the eyes of a trained soldier" and signs of "a state of moral chaos among nations." Moreover, bombing cities required too many air resources, and even if these were available, results were uncertain. Communications (transportation and signal facilities) and industrial installations were the best targets for strategic airpower. A 1940 staff study at the War College on the "Desirability of Cities, Towns, and Villages as Bombardment Objectives" concluded, "There is no historical evidence that aerial bombardment of cities, towns, and villages has ever been productive." It recommended that such targets should be bombed only "where they contain definite objectives, military or political, the destruction of which will be productive of decisive military results."[47]

After Mitchell's death in 1936, émigré aircraft designer Alexander P. de Seversky became the best-known American air theorist. A keen observer of the lessons of modern warfare in early World War II, he was also a former Russian naval officer who had been strongly influenced by the sea power theories of Mahan. Civilian morale was not a direct objective but would be affected by the results of an aerial blockade of the enemy homeland that precision bombing made possible. He mentioned industrial targets, but he focused more on destroying social structures without the indiscriminate slaughter of civilians, going beyond George's and Webster's work to meld Douhet's theories with precision techniques, expanding on the ideas mentioned in the 1935 ACTS text. "The will to resist can be broken in a people," he argued, "only by destroying the essentials of their lives—the supply of food, shelter, light, water, sanitation, and the rest." He even saw some uses for terror bombing, either to lure an enemy air force into a tactical engagement defending cities or to embarrass an enemy through propaganda if it could not defend its populace from air attack. Seversky did not advocate such tactics, but he did feel that the public should be prepared for them. His ideas circulated widely among air service officers and in numerous journals.[48] Walt Disney even made Seversky's influential book, *Victory through Airpower*, into a movie and thus exposed the American and British public to his views on strategic-bombing doctrine.[49]

However, Seversky's ideas did not accurately reflect the mature precision-bombing doctrine that ACTS was teaching and that would guide the AAF into and through World War II, a philosophy that focused on destroying "carefully selected targets in the industrial and service systems on which the enemy people, their industries, and the armed forces are dependent."[50] The clearest and most important enunciation of that doctrine came in an August 1941 document known as AWPD/1.

Army Regulation 95-5 of June 1941, creating the AAF, gave the new organization limited autonomy, but despite a growing appreciation for airpower in official circles, the actual role of strategic bombing was unclear.[51] The AAF's opportunity to establish its role in winning the war came in July 1941 when President Roosevelt sent a letter to the secretaries of War and the Navy "requesting the preparation of the Over-All Production requirements required to defeat our potential enemies." Because the services could not agree on a joint strategy, they each estimated their own requirements. The Army's report was the responsibility of the War Plans Division (WPD) of the General Staff. Lieutenant Colonel Clayton Bissell, an Air Corps officer in the WPD, persuaded his bosses to ask Lieutenant General H. H. Arnold, commanding general, US Army Air Corps, to detail some Air Corps officers to produce an aviation annex. With the cooperation of Brigadier General Carl Spaatz, Arnold's chief of staff, and the strong support of Lieutenant Colonel Harold George, the mission was given to George's newly established Air War Plans Division (AWPD) of the equally new Air Staff, Army Air Forces.[52]

By 1941 the development of theories for using airpower had shifted somewhat from ACTS with the reassignment of many key instructors to staff positions in Washington. Lieutenant Colonel George assembled a task force of himself, Lieutenant Colonel Kenneth Walker, Major Laurence Kuter, and Major Haywood Hansell Jr., all of whom had contributed to developing pre-

Major General H. H. "Hap" Arnold and his staff, in 1941, many of whom were instrumental in developing precision doctrine and AWPD/1. From left to right, Lieutenant Colonel Edgar Sorenson, Lieutenant Colonel Harold George, Brigadier General Carl Spaatz, Major General Arnold, Major Haywood Hansell Jr., Brigadier General Martin Scanlon, and Lieutenant Colonel Arthur Vanaman.

cision-bombing doctrine at ACTS. George, Walker, and Hansell made up AWPD, while Kuter was detailed from the operations division of the War Department General Staff. They received their assignment about a week before it was due on 11 August. Meanwhile, Arnold had been called away for the Atlantic Conference in Placentia Bay, Newfoundland. Lacking clear guidance or objectives and pressed for time, the group had to lay out a plan that would determine the future of the AAF, but as one of the planners wrote, "If the task was staggering, so too was the opportunity." They selected an overall strategic concept and air objective and prepared an air plan to achieve that goal. The result was "straight American air power doctrine" as developed at ACTS, with the provision to support an invasion in order to make the plan more acceptable to Army planners who had not yet accepted the AAF's independent strategic role. Using their broad latitude to their advantage, the task force went beyond setting out production requirements and devised a plan for an all-out strategic air offensive. It was an amazing effort. As one writer has described it, "A plan that should have been assembled by dozens of experts in a period of months was written by four young men in nine days while their boss was out of town."[53]

The final document, officially titled "Munitions Requirements of the AAF for the Defeat of our Potential Enemies," accepted the "Germany First" policy of overall strategic direction. AWPD/1 planned to apply airpower "for the breakdown of the industrial and economic structure of Germany" by destroying "a system of objectives vital to the German war effort": primarily power, transportation, and oil industries. Though the plan recognized the drawbacks of bombing cities, it did envision that area bombing of civilian concentrations might commence as a final blow when German morale began to crack. AWPD/1 did not define whether such a move would entail a single assault or a series of attacks, but it did state that "the entire bombing effort might be applied toward this purpose when it becomes apparent that the proper psychological conditions exist." This one-time exception to general policy was sanctioned only as a way to end the war quickly, but late in the war this concept of an aerial *Todestoss* (deathblow) would prove a potent lure for American leaders, also helping to sanction the use of the atomic bomb.[54]

After review by Spaatz and Arnold and discussions with General George C. Marshall, Army chief of staff, and Secretary of War Henry L. Stimson, AWPD/1 was accepted as part of the overall reply to the president's assignment. Its ready acceptance may have been due to the pressure of time to meet the commander in chief's request, for the plan did not conform completely to War Department views. "Tacitly, though not legally, the AAF staff had assumed on this occasion a position of equality with those of the older arms." All future air planning would build on the foundation of AWPD/1. Though the Pacific theater was not addressed, a strategic air offensive based on precision-bombing doctrine was written into official policy. Like Gorrell's initial work, this plan had also been developed in response to a need to predict production requirements, not to create strategy. Yet with the impetus of AWPD/1, the air assault on enemy war industries and transportation lines that Gorrell's study had envisioned over two decades earlier would soon become reality.[55]

3. FROM DOCTRINE TO PRACTICE: EXECUTING THE AIR OFFENSIVE AGAINST GERMANY

The US Army Air Force will concentrate its efforts upon the systematic destruction of selected vital elements of the German military and industrial machine through precision bombing in daylight. The RAF will concentrate upon mass air attacks of industrial areas at night, to break down morale. . . .

There is, of course, a tremendous amount of incidental damage to be expected from the hundreds of bombs which drop near the aiming point but do not strike the particular part of the target selected.

–AWPD-42, 9 September 1942[1]

AWPD/1 had been a projection if war came. After the attack on Pearl Harbor, the Air War Plans Division had to begin planning for a war that had arrived. A supplemental AWPD-2 created in September 1941 promised to give the bulk of aircraft production to the British until the United States entered the war, an arrangement soon curtailed by Pearl Harbor. The Air Staff's immediate reaction to that attack was to consider deploying all available aircraft to defend the Western Hemisphere, Hawaii, and the Philippines, but they soon settled down to think more long term. By 15 December, AWPD-4 had been completed, basically a restatement of AWPD/1 with inflated demands for an air force of three million men and 90,000 planes, which required that the top national industrial priority become the production of aircraft. The Navy would never agree to that, and such an approach would not have been able to shift with war's changing fortunes. However, while the new proposal floundered, the direction generated by AWPD/1 and the initial Operation BOLERO planning to get an expeditionary force to the United Kingdom led the AAF to quickly begin coordination with the RAF to station American bombers there. The first B-17 arrived on 1 July 1942, shortly after Major General Carl Spaatz had established Eighth Air Force headquarters at

Bushy Park, Teddington. Major General Ira Eaker's VIII Bomber Command mounted its first heavy bombardment mission against the continent on 17 August, when twelve Fortresses successfully attacked the marshaling yard at Rouen, an easy target along the coast that allowed the new force to display its daylight bombing skills without having to fight through much resistance.[2]

Such early raids were more a demonstration of a concept than part of an established combined war-fighting strategy, but that deficiency was soon remedied. The same month that the Eighth Air Force officially entered the war, President Roosevelt asked for another estimate of aircraft production, this time for 1943, "in order to have complete air ascendancy over the enemy." The original members of the Air War Plans Division had been promoted and reassigned, but Hansell, a new brigadier general, was recalled from England by General Marshall to head the effort to develop an "immediate detailed war plan." He and his team built on the precedent of AWPD/1. Though Japan's vulnerability to aerial bombardment was recognized, the top priority remained defeating Germany. That would be accomplished by first destroying the German air force, which was always recognized as the first requirement for a successful strategic air campaign, through the targeting of aircraft and engine factories. Recognizing the political realities of working with the British, as well as the combined nature of the offensive described in the opening quote above, the next priority was submarine construction. Then German war-making capacity would be undermined with attacks on transportation, power, oil, aluminum, and rubber, in that order of importance. There was no mention of targeting morale, though there was an assumption that reductions in electric power would have some impact on civilian will. There was a similar list for Japan, though the plan recognized that it would be years before those islands would be within range of the AAF. Surprisingly, Japanese transportation and power facilities were not among the suggested targets. Top priorities were aircraft and engine plants, submarine yards, and naval and commercial bases.[3]

There were many assumptions evident in AWPD-42. There was little concern about fighter escorts because bomber formations were expected to be able to fight their way to the target with acceptable losses, which would decline as the German air force was depleted. Even against defenses, bombing accuracy would be only slightly worse than in practice runs, with a circular error of only 1,000 feet from an altitude of 20,000 feet, though as is evident from the quote opening the chapter, there was also an understanding that many bombs would miss, with resulting collateral damage. The report did not foresee the development of nonvisual bombing techniques, instead expecting only five or six missions a month in Europe, ten over Japan. Most important, there was "no doubt that if the targets included in these systems were successfully destroyed, the effect would be decisive and Germany would be unable to continue her war effort." Although that was a stark claim for the independent effectiveness of strategic airpower, AWPD-42 never denied the need for an invasion of Europe, arguing that the depletion of the German air force and economy was also necessary for its success.[4]

Struggling to meet his deadlines, Hansell sent the final product straight to the printing office. He soon found out that the president had approved it before Secretary of War Stimson or General Marshall got a chance to see their copy. Fearing the wrath of the Army chief of staff, Hansell asked General Arnold to get him back to England immediately, and within an hour, the planner was airborne. As it turned out, AWPD-42 was never accepted by the Navy and the Joint Chiefs of Staff, though it did influence production priorities.[5]

Nevertheless, its vision of strategic bombing was furthered by an almost simultaneous directive from the AAF and RAF in the United Kingdom, which announced a combined offensive of American day and British night bombing. The "Joint American/British Directif on Day Bomber Operations Involving Fighter Co-operation" was the result of negotiations with the RAF to arrange fighter support for Eaker's Bomber Command. The document indicated that the British would support the American attempt to execute its daylight precision-bombing doctrine and foreshadowed the agreement that would be reached in January 1943 at the Casablanca Conference. There an adept presentation from Eaker, now commanding Eighth Air Force with Spaatz taking over the Northwest African air forces for Operation TORCH, convinced Winston Churchill and others not to force the Americans to join the RAF's night bombing campaign and instead to exploit the many ways that day and night raids complemented each other. Executing both reduced airspace congestion and put twenty-four-hour pressure on the Luftwaffe; further, fires from daylight attacks could act as markers in the dark. Eaker also explained the difficulties in transforming the Eighth to conduct night operations and argued that because of better visibility and better bombsights, day bombers could hit smaller targets and were five times more accurate than the best night bombing. Therefore, the same installation could be destroyed with a force only one-fifth as large. In response to questions about the performance of his bombers up to now, especially their small numbers and lack of any attacks on Germany, Eaker projected a bright future, where the success of Operation TORCH would require the diversion of fewer air assets, new aircraft would arrive including more long-range fighter escorts, blind-bombing techniques would circumvent bad weather, and crews would continue to get more experienced.[6]

The Combined Chiefs of Staff issued CCS 166/I/D, usually referred to as the Casablanca Directive, on 21 January 1943. It described the aims and operations for the Combined Bomber Offensive (CBO) from the United Kingdom, describing missions for both the night raiders of RAF Bomber Command and the daylight bombers from the AAF. The overall objective recognized the desires of both air campaigns; "the progressive destruction and dislocation of the German military, industrial and economic system, and the undermining of the morale of the German people to a point where the capacity for armed resistance is fatally weakened." Hedging its bets, the CBO would target both means and will. For the former, objectives in priority were German submarine construction yards, the German aircraft industry, transportation, oil plants, and other targets in enemy war industry. This generally reflected AWPD's products, except that the current U-boat threat to the British Isles made that a top priority for the CCS because it threatened the buildup of American resources in the United Kingdom, if not its very survival. Those objectives could be altered as the strategic situation developed. In addition, the directive mentioned other targets with special political or military significance, such as French submarine pens in the Bay of Biscay, Berlin, and targets to assist amphibious operations in the Mediterranean or Northwest Europe. The day bomber force was ordered to "take every opportunity to attack Germany by day, to destroy objectives that are unsuitable for night attack, to sustain continuous pressure on German morale, to impose heavy losses on the German day fighter force and to contain German fighter strength away from the Russian and Mediterranean theatres of war." In a caveat that would cause much friction later, the directive required that anyone attacking objectives in occupied countries had to conform to "such instructions as may be issued from time to time for political reasons by His Majesty's Government through the British Chiefs of Staff," who also would consult with representatives from exiled governments. It was assumed that the need for timely decisions on such matters could not be met if such matters had to be referred to the CCS in Washington. Though there were no clear instructions included about who was in command of the CBO, the CCS decided to let the British have oversight initially, so the chief of the British Air Staff, Sir Charles Portal, acted as the CCS agent in 1943.[7]

Eaker had successfully sold his precision-bombing campaign to Allied leadership, now he had to prove it would work. During the rest of the year he would be foiled by determined enemy defenses and countermeasures, a lack of resources, inadequate intelligence, typical weather patterns, and bad assumptions. Among the latter was the faith that unescorted bombers could get through to heavily defended targets in Germany without unacceptable losses, that bombing accuracy and available munitions would destroy critical targets quickly and permanently, and that intelligence could properly select those vital objectives. It took until 1944 for American intelligence organizations to truly mature. In the meantime, the rush to build up bomber aircraft came at the expense of the maintenance and support structures necessary to repair all the damage from enemy fighters and flak as well as provide routine services. There were replacement aircrew shortages as well. The Eighth's resource plight was exacerbated by the siphoning off of units to support General Dwight Eisenhower's Mediterranean operations. Not only did Spaatz take considerable heavy bomber assets with him initially but also Eisenhower was continually requesting more bomb groups whenever a major operation hit a snag, such as when he got three B-24 groups diverted after the near debacle at Salerno when he invaded Italy. Light and infrequent attacks on coastal cities with U-boat facilities did little damage while allowing the Germans to develop their daylight defensive system. Further problems resulted from CCS decisions at the Trident and Quadrant conferences in May and August 1943. While endorsing the CBO, eventually designated as Operation POINTBLANK, as a necessary preliminary to the invasion of western Europe, scheduling that landing for 1 May 1944 complicated priorities for the buildup of forces. Not only would ground divisions now be competing for resources but also the AAF had to set up an expeditionary tactical air force to support them on the Continent.[8]

Hardened submarine pens proved an especially frustrating target system, but by 1 July other countermeasures were winning the Battle of Atlantic, and the American air campaign shifted its primary focus to the German aircraft industry. Under the right visual bombing conditions, results could be fantastic. A raid on Marienberg on 9 October knocked the aircraft plant completely out of action for four months. Fifty-eight percent of bombs fell within 1,000 feet of the aiming point and 83 percent within 2,000 feet. However, conditions were rarely right, especially in fall and winter weather.[9] A close examination of the iconic attacks on the ball-bearing plants at Schweinfurt reveals much about the Eighth Air Force's shortcomings at that time, and also about the unique Clausewitzian friction of air war in 1943.[10]

As the maturing intelligence apparatus shaping Eaker's operations focused increasingly on attacking the aircraft industry, they realized that antifriction

Submarine pens such as these in Hamburg were generally invulnerable to any bombs except some especially large RAF ordnance. Though land–water contrast made them good targets for radar-directed bombing, American airmen experienced much frustration trying to cause any meaningful damage. (44th Bomb Group Collection, USAMHI, USAHEC)

bearings were a tempting vulnerability for the production of all armaments. The target was first identified by a special Committee of Operation Analysts established by General Arnold in late 1942 to include civilian experts in developing industrial intelligence. Their initial March 1943 report recommended fighter production as the first targeting priority, and ball bearings second. When it was sent to the United Kingdom, it was quickly accepted by both the British and Americans, and endorsed by Portal. Although aircraft factories needed over two million ball bearings a month (one medium bomber engine required over a thousand), tanks, motor vehicles, and weapons all required them as well. This target system seemed particularly susceptible to a "knockout blow" because it was concentrated primarily in six cities, and about half of all production came from a single facility at Schweinfurt.[11]

The first of forty raids on the ball-bearing industry came exactly one year after the first American heavy bomber operation from the United Kingdom. The attacking force of 376 B-17s was the largest ever dispatched by the Eighth Air Force. (The British had already executed a 1,000-bomber raid on Cologne as early as May 1942.) The ball-bearing plants at Schweinfurt and Messerschmitt aircraft complex at Regensburg were the most important targets on the bombing priority list; they also required the deepest penetration into Germany to date. Eaker thought his force had been pushed into the dangerous mission before it was really ready. The plan called for Colonel Curtis LeMay's Third Bombardment Division, with long-range tanks, to attack Regensburg and then fly to North Africa. The First Bombardment Division would hit Schweinfurt, following ten minutes behind. German fighters would have to choose which force to engage, and where. After a couple weeks of delays, weather forecasts on 16 August finally predicted good flying conditions over Germany and North Africa, and the mission was scheduled for the next day. Unfortunately, but not atypically, English bases were socked in by clouds the next morning. LeMay had trained his crews to take off in such conditions; he got his force airborne, but the other air division remained on the ground. The Regensburg force could not delay and headed for the target. Brigadier General Frederick Anderson, commander of VIII Bomber Command, decided to hold the Schweinfurt force for three and a half hours, to allow the weather to clear over their airfields and the escort fighters to regroup. However, that respite also allowed Luftwaffe fighters to rearm and reorganize. Further, the Allied Spitfires and Thunderbolts did not have the range to cover the bombers all the way to their targets. Consequently, both bomber forces had to face well-prepared German fighters over their objectives without the cover of their own "little friends." Still, bombing results, especially at Regensburg, were very good. At Schweinfurt, bombing was less accurate, and the bombs used were too small to destroy important machine tools on factory floors—a common problem with US Strategic Air Forces (USSTAF) operations throughout the war. However, there was enough damage to spur German efforts to find other sources of ball bearings and to better disperse production facilities.[12]

Losses were horrendous. LeMay lost twenty-four of his 146 bombers over Germany, and after scrounging repair parts, fuel, and bombs in North Africa, he got about eighty of the remainder to fly back to the United Kingdom. Typical of the feisty LeMay, he insisted on bombing Bordeaux on the way back with fifty-seven of them. However, at least half of the planes he took to Regensburg never flew again. The Schweinfurt force also took a beating, losing thirty-six planes on the mission. Such casualties were unsustainable, and everyone knew it.[13]

The Eighth Air Force spent most of the next three months bombing easier coastal and French targets before mounting a sustained effort against
industrial targets within Germany and Poland during the second week in
October. From 8 to 10 October, eighty-eight bombers were lost in attacks
on Bremen, Vegesack, Gdynia, Danzig, Marienberg, Anklam, and Munster.
Several hundred more aircraft were damaged. Then Mission 115 was set for
14 October, a return to Schweinfurt. Again the frictions of war were evident.
Longer-range P-38 fighters had arrived, but they were not ready to fly until
the next day. Weather at the air bases was again a problem, and B-24s from
the Second Bombardment Division never could get assembled to carry out
their part of the operation. The weather also interfered with the ability of
escort fighters to link up with returning bombers. The Luftwaffe used new
weapons and tactics, firing rockets into the bomber formations, mauling
them severely. Two hundred twenty-eight of the 291 dispatched B-17s succeeded in bombing their target, achieving the most damage of any of the
sixteen raids on Schweinfurt during the war. However, the cost of damaging 10 percent of the key machinery was sixty bombers lost on the mission
(with ten-man crews), seventeen more damaged beyond repair, and 121 B-17s
with damage that could be fixed. Reich Minister of Armaments and War
Production Albert Speer reported that he was told the raid cost 67 percent
of production. He was able to substitute slide bearings to make up for some
shortages, but he was out of reserves. He was saved by the cessation of the
attacks until February. When they did restart, he claimed that he faced another crisis, but again the Allies furnished a reprieve by abandoning attacks
on ball-bearing facilities in April 1944. He agreed with the Committee of
Operation Analysts opinion about the vulnerability of that target system,
claiming that adequate decentralization never did occur. He thought the
Allies threw away a great opportunity to bring German military industrial
capacity to the brink of collapse.[14]

Allied intelligence initially greatly exaggerated the results of Mission 115.
Anderson and Arnold proclaimed in official and public documents that the
ball-bearing works were out of action. However, that is not the reason no
Allied bombers would return there for four months. On the same day that
German fighters were chewing up VIII Bomber Command, Arnold cabled
Eaker that according to information in Washington, the Luftwaffe appeared
ready to collapse, and that possibility needed investigation. Indeed, a lot of
evidence about the state of the German air force had been gathered in that
second week of October. The resulting verdict was a bitter one for the AAF.
Even the official history acknowledges that the Eighth Air Force had lost air

superiority over Germany. Whether they had ever really had it is worth questioning. They would launch no more deep-penetration missions the rest of the year, initially because of the need to replenish losses and the now-recognized requirement for long-range escort fighters, then in December because of foul weather. The Luftwaffe could now concentrate on defeating RAF Bomber Command, and by the end of the year, "Bomber" Harris was well on his way to losing the equivalent of his entire frontline strength in attempting to unsuccessfully destroy Berlin. An argument could be made that at the beginning of 1944 the Allies had not just lost air superiority over Germany but were also losing the air war, especially in light of the recognized requirements for a successful May invasion.[15]

TURNING THE TIDE

By the time that D-day occurred, the issue in the air war was no longer in doubt. The back of the German air force had been broken not by precision bombing to cripple its supporting industrial structures but rather by a brutal campaign of attrition that destroyed aircraft and killed experienced pilots. This would not have been possible without the advent of the P-51 Mustang, which could fly deep into Germany and then outperform any fighter opposition except jets, as well as operational and tactical adjustments that maximized opportunities for that attrition to occur.

Before the Eighth Air Force made these changes, there was a major command shakeup as the new year opened, orchestrated by General Arnold, who had become increasingly critical of Eaker's performance. At the Second Cairo Conference in early December 1943, Arnold complained bitterly to the CCS about the Eighth's aircraft availability rates and targeting priorities. In a swirl of meetings involving the president and General Eisenhower, the AAF commander hammered out an agreement on a new arrangement to control the American strategic bombing campaign over Europe, after abandoning hopes to get a single Allied strategic air force commander. On 1 January 1944, Lieutenant General Carl Spaatz took over the USSTAF, with a headquarters built on the existing Eighth Air Force structure. Spaatz was concerned his transfer would upset the RAF-AAF balance in the Mediterranean, which reinforced Arnold's decision to move Eaker to be Air Officer Commanding, Mediterranean Allied Air Forces. Major General Jimmy Doolittle, who had been in charge of the Northwest African Strategic Air Forces, would be brought in to command the Eighth, while Major General Nathan

Twining would be sent from the Pacific to take over the newly created Fifteenth Air Force, operating from airfields in Italy.[16]

It is not surprising that Eisenhower wanted to bring his team with him, especially considering that USSTAF would eventually be assigned to him to support the invasion. Though the shift was presented to Eaker as a move up to greater responsibilities, he knew he was really being fired by someone who had been his friend for twenty-five years. He fought angrily to keep command of the Eighth Air Force. He enlisted the help of Lieutenant General Jacob Devers, current commander of the US European theater, who thought that Eaker had done as well as he could considering the conditions he struggled against. Eaker even contacted General Marshall, who sent a stinging telegram to Eisenhower questioning the impending transfers. When Spaatz told his commander that he would not go to London unless Eaker was moved to the Mediterranean, Eisenhower persuaded Marshall to accept the new arrangement. There are no indications that Spaatz's position was based on any consideration other than that he thought American air interests would best be served with strong and experienced leaders in both senior command slots. Though the Fifteenth Air Force really belonged to USSTAF, Spaatz always sent directives to them through Eaker, a man he respected and trusted.[17]

USSTAF did not get off to an auspicious start. Bad weather and requirements to go after the V-1 rocket sites bombarding the United Kingdom limited deep raids. When the Eighth Air Force got a large force into north central Germany to attack aircraft plants at Oschersleben and Halberstadt on 11 January, it lost sixty bombers, just as in the Schweinfurt raids. However, the attacking force was much larger, with a loss rate of 11 percent, as the Eighth now had well over 1,300 heavy bombers and crews on hand to sustain operations. The smaller Fifteenth actually had some better results early in January, pummeling Italian ball-bearing plants and motivating the Bulgarian government to flee Sofia after raids there before diverting its main effort to transportation and communication targets to support landings at Anzio. The Balkan city attacks, perceived by the British as a way to crush the morale of Axis allies and directed by the CCS, would run into much resistance from Spaatz and his subordinates (see chapter 8).[18]

The commander of the Luftwaffe's I Fighter Corps called the 11 January air battle "the last victory of the German Air Force over the American Air Force." The most important action of the month affecting the course of the air war occurred on the ground in England instead of in the skies over Germany. Doolittle considered fighters as offensive machines piloted by aggressive individuals who were best utilized engaging enemy fighters before they reached the bombers. Eighth Air Force policies that kept escorts close to their charges combined with orders from Hermann Göring that his pilots avoid American fighters meant that the long-range Mustangs and Lightnings were getting little chance to engage their foes. The air battles of 1943 might have favored the Germans, but pilot replacements could not keep up with their losses while the American buildup continued. When Doolittle visited the headquarters of Eighth Fighter Command for his initial orientation, he saw a sign on the commander's wall that said, "The First Duty of the Eighth Air Force Fighters is to Bring the Bombers Back Alive." He announced, "That statement is no longer in effect" and directed that a new poster be put up that said, "The First Duty of the Eighth Air Force Fighters is to Destroy German Fighters." Doolittle considered that his most important decision of the war. The fighter pilots loved it. The bomber crews, who would eventually come to see themselves as bait, hated it, and some of their leaders told Doolittle "in polite terms of course" that he was a "murderer." Although the new policy did indeed cause major cracks in bomber crew morale before its positive effects became fully apparent, Adolf Galland, chief of the German fighter forces, considered the day the American fighters were unleashed as the day Germany lost the air war.[19]

Eighth Air Force bomber crew morale was further affected when pressure from Arnold persuaded Doolittle to raise the required number of missions before rotation from twenty-five to thirty. The force was ready for a big push. Maintenance and supply systems were fully staffed and stocked. Over 1,000 bombers were available for daily missions, and another 1,000 were in depots or being serviced. There were enough fighters on hand to unleash whole groups on sweeps to catch the Luftwaffe on the ground. The CCS had narrowed POINTBLANK's priority objectives to fighter and ball-bearing production. The CBO was now purely a counterair campaign. A plan code-named ARGUMENT had been developed by the RAF-AAF Combined Operational Planning Committee in England in 1943 that called for an all-out offensive against German fighter, synthetic rubber, and ball-bearing factories. These attacks were also designed to lure enemy fighters into bloody air battles, all in the hope of creating a situation where German fighter production could not keep up with losses. USSTAF now had the force to execute the plan. All it needed was a period of good weather.[20]

Major General Fred Anderson, now deputy commander for operations, persuaded Spaatz to launch ARGUMENT on 20 February. So-called Big Week actually started on the night of the 19th with an RAF area raid on Leipzig, home of key fighter plants, but the American would do most of the damage.

This target photo of key aircraft plants in Leipzig on 20 February 1944 shows that the Big Week attacks also achieved some excellent bombing results on the ground while luring the Luftwaffe into deadly air battles above. (44th Bomb Group Collection, USAMHI, USAHEC)

A series of daylight attacks featuring over 800 bombers struck designated targets throughout Germany and Austria, supplemented by Bomber Command at night. Losses were heavy: 158 bombers from the Eighth, eighty-nine more from the Fifteenth, and 157 from the British. Forty-two USSTAF fighters went down. About 5,000 airmen were killed or became prisoners of war. The Eighth Air Force lost a fifth of its bomber force during the month of February.[21]

However, results were significant. Some fighter plants were shut down for weeks. Speer was told that his March fighter production would be reduced by 70 percent. In response to the assault he directed increased dispersion of aircraft factories, which saved the industry but lost the efficiencies of mass production and created new vulnerabilities through transportation choke points. By the time production output could be restored, shortages in aviation fuel and chaos in the rail system would keep planes undelivered or grounded. For more immediate impact, during the month of February the Luftwaffe lost more than one third of its single-engine fighters and almost a fifth of its pilots.[22]

Although USSTAF quickly made up its losses in men and matériel, this was not possible for the German air force. Big Week did not destroy it or even make it ineffective, but those operations started a long decline from which the Luftwaffe fighter force never recovered. Pilots especially were irreplaceable. Over the next three months of bloody air attrition, as Spaatz struck targets he knew the Germans had to defend, they lost a total of twenty-eight of their best leaders and aces, responsible for destroying over 2,000 enemy aircraft. Replacements never showed up in enough numbers, and they did not have the fuel or time to train properly. This created a vicious cycle where inexperienced pilots had to be thrown into combat against an American force increasing in numbers and capability every day, and losses then forced the employment of even more hastily trained replacements. Many of them died in accidents. The most dangerous occupation of World War II was being a German fighter pilot. They had no twenty-five-mission rotation policy; they flew until they were killed or maimed. Between January and May 1944, their loss rate in the West was 99 percent. By July, the bulk of available pilots to confront USSTAF had between eight and thirty days' experience. Less than 10 percent of German fighter pilots survived the war.[23]

Although USSTAF still suffered losses after Big Week, including sixty-nine bombers attacking Berlin in March and another sixty-three there on a raid in April, it was soon apparent that the AAF's opportunity to truly prove the efficacy of precision bombing by destroying enemy capacity had arrived. That reality would make the debates over the best way to support the coming invasion with strategic air forces even more acrimonious.

TRANSPORTATION VERSUS OIL

As the German air force declined in capability and withdrew back into the Reich, the Allies asserted solid air superiority over Northwest Europe. Soon they would have total air supremacy over France. The stage was set to hammer out the arrangements for heavy bomber support of Operation OVER-

LORD. Although the Americans were willing to put USSTAF assets under Eisenhower's control, the British continued to argue for more autonomy for Bomber Command. Eventually Eisenhower had to threaten leaving unless Prime Minister Churchill gave Supreme Headquarters Allied Expeditionary Forces command of all air forces during the invasion. Eventually an order that gave the supreme commander "direction of" air operations out of England was issued. Though he began exercising that direction in late March 1944, it did not become official until mid-April.[24]

Now that Eisenhower had the desired control of the heavy bombers, he had to decide how best to use them. He was presented with competing plans. His deputy commander, Air Chief Marshall Sir Arthur Tedder, and the commander of the tactical Allied Expeditionary Air Force, Air Chief Marshall Sir Trafford Leigh-Mallory, both favored an assault on Axis transportation developed by Solly Zuckerman. Trained as a doctor, Zuckerman had written two books on the social and sexual practices of monkeys. As a research fellow and lecturer in the anatomy department at Oxford, he had been drawn into experiments on the physical effects of bomb blasts. He eventually got involved in assessing bombing operations in the Mediterranean and achieved some notoriety for his contribution for air operations against Pantelleria and Sicily. Studying the effects of attacks on the rail systems in Sicily and Italy, which had really not been that successful yet in achieving operational and strategic impact, he wrote a paper for the Allied Expeditionary Air Force in January entitled "Delay and Disorganization of Enemy Movement by Rail." He advocated an attack on the seventy-six most important servicing and repair facilities in Northwest Europe, promising to paralyze movement throughout France. Spaatz had his own proposal, developed during Big Week by the Economic Objectives Unit of the Economic Warfare Division of the US embassy in London. It asserted that attacks on German oil production and stocks were the surest way to hasten German defeat, and they would impede enemy mobility not just in France but in every area of the European theater. Not surprisingly, Bomber Harris wanted to continue just bombing cities.[25]

After dealing with the conflicting plans and personalities, on 25 March Eisenhower decided that the transportation plan had the best chance to achieve the effects he wanted, though he would later have to overcome resistance to it from Churchill, who feared too many French civilian casualties from attacks on marshaling yards. Alfred Mierzejewski gives Tedder the primary credit for getting a plan implemented that would have such a significant impact on the war. Allied intelligence continually overestimated

This target photo of the bombing of marshaling yards in Amiens, France, on 25 June 1944 in support of the continuing operations in Normandy shows the spillage into the city that so worried Churchill and Spaatz about French civilian casualties. (44th Bomb Group Collection, USAMHI, USAHEC)

the capacity and resilience of Germany's railways, and among air leaders, only Tedder seemed to realize their vulnerability. In addition, he had the bureaucratic skills to work effectively within Eisenhower's headquarters to be heard. Spaatz also managed to get permission to launch some oil attacks, first with Fifteenth Air Force raids in April that considerably reduced capacity at the Ploesti refineries, and later with more widespread attacks including the Eighth Air Force in May. As his force grew in size, he could still meet Operation OVERLORD requirements while pursuing the oil campaign, even with diversions to attack V-1 Operation CROSSBOW targets that were threatening

Great Britain. By then the transportation assault had shifted to focus heavily on bridges, which proved to be a key vulnerability of the system in France.[26]

Once control of the bombers returned to air commanders in September, the synergistic assaults on oil and transportation systems continued with devastating impact on the German economy and Axis military capability. Although those target systems had always been included in prewar concepts to bomb the Reich, it was the impetus of the planning to support OVERLORD that really thrust them to the forefront of the strategic air campaign. The Americans had over 7,000 fighters and bombers to throw into battle, while Bomber Command's 1,500 heavy bombers could carry up to ten tons of bombs each. Over 80 percent of the tonnage dropped on Europe was delivered during the last year of the war. Fuel stocks and production plummeted quickly, with a truly calamitous drop in oil produced from 380,000 metric tons in May 1944 to less than 30,000 by September. German tanks in the Battle of the Bulge ran out of diesel, and new pilots could not get aviation fuel for training. By December German freight car traffic was only half of the previous year's, and only half the coal needed by industry could be provided. German military logistics practices also made the Wehrmacht vulnerable to supply disruptions caused by air attacks. Richard Overy has pointed out that the early years of the air campaign also had important effects, putting a ceiling on German production and diverting significant resources into air defenses. This final onslaught carved Germany up "into isolated economic regions." There were plenty of bombers to attack other elements of the economy as well, like steel and munitions. On 30 January 1945 Speer sent Hitler a memorandum declaring, "The war is over in the area of heavy industry and armaments."[27]

Like the invasion, such an expansive air campaign could not have been carried out before the defeat of the Luftwaffe, but once the intensive bombardment began, its effects became inexorable. However, although the results tended to reinforce the tenets of American doctrine, its application during typical German fall and winter weather was far from the envisioned ideal of precision. There were many reasons for this. As Churchill knew, it was difficult to limit collateral damage when bombing marshaling yards in the midst of cities. These were especially attractive targets in periods of poor visibility, when primitive radar aids could pick out city outlines for guidance. Targeting directives were much more lenient about hitting targets in Germany than those in occupied countries. After prodding from General George Marshall, in October 1944 both the Eighth and Fifteenth Air Forces issued guidance that considerably lessened restriction against so-called blind bombing of the

Reich. A new Eighth Air Force directive on "Attack of Secondary and Last Resort Targets" decreed that because any city large enough to be identifiable on a radar scope had viable military targets, it could be classified as an acceptable secondary target if primary objectives were obscured by the same overcast. The Fifteenth issued similar guidance, stressing that "under no circumstances will bombs be returned to bases after being carried over German territory." Restrictions about bombing Axis-occupied areas remained much stricter.[28] Although these policies accepted greater risk for German civilians, they also increased pressure on the Reich's deteriorating transportation network and drew inexperienced German pilots into weather conditions for which they were not prepared. Though Richard Davis considers the target category of marshaling yards to be just a "euphemism for area bombing," he admits that "the bombardment of marshalling yards also broke the back of the German war economy," a position echoed in Mierzejewski's superb analysis of the demise of the Reich.[29] There is no indication that any American leader or airman envisioned such attacks as targeting civilian morale either, which is also a normal feature of typical area bombing such as the RAF practiced. AAF area bombardment still targeted capacity.

The apparent stalemate in fall 1944 after the breakout from Normandy and the surprise German offensive in December also spurred ground commanders to put more pressure on airmen to increase their operations. It should not be forgotten that even while Speer was declaring an end to the industrial war, American soldiers were still struggling to eliminate the remnants of the Bulge. There was no way that air commanders could have avoided bombing in poor visibility while they had so many aircraft and soldiers were dying on the ground. In the end airmen were trying to do everything they could to win the war as soon as possible, and they were willing to risk German civilians to save American soldiers. After a significant diversion of USSTAF assets to tactical targets in December had eased pressure on German oil and industry, Spaatz gained permission from Eisenhower in early January to refocus two-thirds of his force back on oil, with tank and jet production the next priorities. Fears of the new Messerschmitt 262 jet fighters were mounting among the Americans, but the British did not think the war would last long enough for the new weapon to have much effect. Spaatz and Air Marshall Bottomly agreed on a new targeting directive on 12 January that reemphasized oil, transportation, and industrial targets but that also allowed diversions against jet and U-boat facilities—the latter an especially good objective for radar-directed attacks because of the land–water contrasts of coastal targets.[30]

One key aspect of the success of this final air campaign is often overlooked. That is the significant contribution made by the British to sustain the pressure on precision target systems. Many oil facilities were small refineries, often well defended and camouflaged. Not only did British intelligence services provide key information about target characteristics and bombing results but also the RAF's skill at blind bombing, honed during years of night raids over Germany, was essential in keeping oil production suppressed during periods of bad weather. British bombers also dropped larger payloads and could deliver crushing punishment that the Americans could not. It is worth noting that while USSTAF conducted 347 separate missions against oil targets, the RAF added 158 more. While Harris continued to resist diversions of his force to go after "panacea targets," Bomber Command's contributions to both the oil and transportation assaults increased throughout the last six months of the war. Devastating RAF attacks on Ruhr cities showed the meshing of all the air campaigns, as their bombs smashed marshaling yards, obliterated oil targets, and leveled large urban areas.[31]

THE AMERICAN CONDUCT OF THE FINAL AIR CAMPAIGN

A detailed examination of the missions conducted by USSTAF in the last few months of the war reveals how the theory of precision-bombing doctrine matched the realities of 1945. Though there were diversions to pursue morale bombing with operations like THUNDERCLAP and CLARION, which will be described later, the primary focus remained on destroying enemy capacity. However, there was much greater acceptance of the "incidental damage" described in AWPD-42 to achieve that end, especially against Germany. Looking at those later missions also reveals some differences between the practices of USSTAF's subordinate air forces. Although the Eighth Air Force deserves the most credit for the defeat of the Luftwaffe, the smaller Fifteenth had a major impact on Axis oil and transportation targets. Besides the decisive reduction of Ploesti in Romania, a region responsible for over half of the oil produced for Germany and Italy, the Fifteenth also mined the Danube River to bring traffic there to a standstill and created immense logistical chaos for German forces trying to stem the Soviet advance. Eaker's early willingness to embrace blind-bombing techniques meant his airmen also devoted more time and effort to develop them, meaning that the Fifteenth Air Force was the best in the AAF at such missions. They also had an advantage over the Eighth in navigating weather patterns, as aircraft flying from Italy could fly between passing fronts while those coming from England had to fly through them.[32]

Similarities and differences between the two air forces' operations can be illustrated by a detailed analysis of some individual bomb groups. The influence of weather and important reliance on radar-assisted bombing techniques were very evident during the closing months of the air campaign, as Allied flyers exploited their supremacy and smashed the remnants of German capacity. In addition, the friction of war, primarily through mechanical failures and enemy countermeasures, continued to degrade accuracy.

The 44th Bomb Group of the Eighth Air Force, known as the "Flying Eight Balls," consisted of four squadrons of B-24 Liberator bombers, the 66th, 67th, 68th, and 506th. Although it had first made its mark in August 1943 on a temporary deployment to North Africa to participate in the first great Ploesti raid, a legendary one-time early attack on oil, it was back in England by the end of the year and carried its full mission load during Big Week and after. As 1945 opened it was operating out of its usual home airfields at Shipdham in Norfolk.

The first mission of the new year targeted the Koblenz–Lutzel railroad bridge. To show the extent of Eighth Air Force bombing on 1 January, thirty-six different objectives were struck that day. Twenty-seven of the dispatched thirty-one group aircraft attacked, with one squadron dropping its bombs four miles short because the leader launched his load prematurely as a result of battle damage to his bomb racks. Though bombing results were reported to be excellent, thirty-five B-24s were sent back the next day. Thirty-three successfully dropped their bombs through overcast using Gee-H guidance, but their impact on the bridge was unobserved. Bad weather also affected the 3 January mission against a tactical target of road and rail junctions at Landau, as all twenty-three aircraft had to use Gee-H again to bomb through "10/10ths"—that is total overcast—with unobserved results.[33]

Weather continued to play havoc with the following mission schedule. On 5 January twenty-two aircraft were sent to bomb transportation objectives at Oberstein, but as a result of weather and mechanical failures only eleven dropped their loads, and then in a visual attack on the marshaling yard at the secondary target of Neunkirchen. After a weather scrub, the group returned to Landau on 7 January. Of thirty-three B-24s, four turned back from mechanical failures and one lost the formation in bad weather. The remaining twenty-eight again dropped their bombs using Gee-H through 10/10ths overcast with unobserved results. Twenty-two planes sent to hit the railroad junction at Burg Reuland the next day bombed the same way. The same happened for the next mission, when twenty-three aircraft attacked the marshaling yard at Kaiserslautern on 13 January. All missions so far in

Although the danger posed by Luftwaffe fighters was much reduced for USSTAF bombers in 1945, flak, weather, and accidents still took their toll. This B-24 Liberator from the 466th Bomb Group crashed while trying to make an emergency landing at Shipdham on 8 January. All crewmen survived, though some were injured. (44th Bomb Group Collection, USAMHI, USAHEC)

the month had featured meager flak and few enemy fighters, though Shipdham had some extra excitement when a damaged Liberator from the 466th Bomb Group crashed there after returning from the 8 January mission.

Then objectives got more ambitious as the new targeting directive took effect. On 14 January the 44th dispatched thirty-two bombers to lead their combat wing in an assault on the oil refinery at Hemmingstadt. Two squadrons had excellent results in visual conditions, but the third bombed poorly because it was crowded off course during the bomb run by another group. It was much harder to get a large number of bombers over a target in daylight formations than with nighttime bomber streams. The next day's mission against the aircraft component factory at Bounheim was scrubbed, but on the 16th, thirty-three B-24s of the group led the whole Second Bombardment Division in an attack of the synthetic oil plant at Ruhland. There were plenty of jinxing gremlins flying with them that day. Just after crossing the German border, the lead plane had a malfunction of its H2X radar set, so the deputy had to take over to guide the formation to the target. When they arrived, it was obscured by a smoke screen and low clouds, so the aircraft had to shift to the secondary objective of the marshaling yards at Dresden. One squadron bombed over the target because of a rack malfunction of the leader. Another bombed short because the lead bombardier's viewing panel was frosted up. The third missed right because it was again forced off its run by another group. One damaged plane was abandoned in flight (the first combat loss of the month), sixteen landed in France, four more landed at other airdromes, and another ran out of fuel before it could find anywhere to land. Even after such a debacle, the group got eleven bombers in the air the next day to partic-ipate in a successful visual attack on the oil refinery at Harburg.

Recovery time and weather allowed only three more missions that month. On the 21st, eleven Liberators bombed the Pforsheim marshaling yard. The H2X equipment on the lead aircraft failed during the bomb run, but the deputy assumed control and managed to find visual conditions at the tar-get for excellent results. On the 28th, twenty-eight B-24s from the 44th led the Fourteenth Wing, a subsection of the division, against the coking plant at Dortmund. The bombing was disappointing, however, because the lead bombardier was wounded on the bomb run through haze, and aiming had to be done hastily using Gee-H. One Liberator had the misfortune to take a direct flak hit in its bomb bay as it opened those doors. On the 29th, thirty aircraft were dispatched to hit Altenbecken, but clouds forced diver-sion to an H2X attack on the marshaling yard at Hamm. One squadron's lead aircraft had H2X malfunctions, so those planes moved on to bomb the marshaling yard at Munster when the set was operating correctly. No results were observed. A mission on the last day of the month to the steelworks at Hallendorf was recalled before reaching Germany.

February opened with a little excitement, as crews were briefed for pos-sible big raids on Berlin or Dresden, a spin-off of the plans for Operation THUNDERCLAP that will be covered later. When weather cleared on the 3rd, however, and the Eighth Air Force launched almost 1,000 bombers against Berlin, the 44th was instead sent against the Rothensee oil refinery at Mag-deburg. Thirty-three aircraft were launched, and twenty-nine bombed the last-resort target of the marshaling yard there after the lead plane's bomb-sight froze up on the bomb run. Again, results were unobserved through thick overcast. Terrible weather canceled all missions for the next ten days, except for repeat attempts at Magdeburg on the 6th and 9th. In both cases the refinery was obscured and the marshaling yards were hit instead. Despite beautiful weather in England on the 14th, the fourth attempt to pummel Rothensee that month ended up with the same scenario. Not willing to give up yet, a fifth mission was scheduled the next day, with orders to bomb the refinery no matter the conditions. Thirty of thirty-one group B-24s dispatched bombed it with H2X through overcast, though one trailing squadron, which had its lead H2X equipment malfunction, had to drop on the basis of smoke markers from the lead squadron. Results, again, were unobserved.

The mission on the 16th to attack the oil refinery at Salzbergen as the primary target or the Rheine marshaling yard as the secondary target was a debacle. Probably because of distance, the bombers could not pick up the range blip on Gee-H for the primary target and had insufficient time to make an H2X run on the secondary target. All thirty-two planes had to land on the continent but later returned to Shipdham. Once they were reassembled, thirty-four were sent to hit the armament factory at Nuremburg on the 20th, but they were all recalled because of adverse weather.

The rest of the month went better. On the 21st, thirty-two group B-24s led the Second Bombardment Division in a successful H2X attack on the marshaling yard at Nuremburg. In support of Operation CLARION on the 22nd, twenty-nine of thirty-two group aircraft dispatched attacked their secondary target of the Gottingen marshaling yard, after ground haze prevented their picking out the primary objective of the choke point at Hohengandern. The visual bombing, from only 8,000 feet against depleted enemy defenses, was excellent, earning the group a commendation. But clear skies were rare that month. The next day thirty of thirty-one bombers used H2X to hit the rail center at Weimar through 10/10ths overcast, and on the 24th eleven group planes bombed the Misburg oil refinery the same way. In both cases, results were unobserved. In the last case of good weather for February, thirty-four of thirty-five B-24s pummeled the Aschaffenberg marshaling yard with clear visibility on the 25th. The next day feared Berlin was the target, but 10/10ths overcast over the whole route restrained enemy fighters as well as required H2X blind bombing, as twenty-two B-24s hit the Pankow rail yard with a mix of incendiaries and high explosives. Radar set malfunctions reared their head again on the 27th, as problems with the lead aircraft's H2X set spoiled the run on the primary target at the Halle marshaling yard, but the same type of target at Bitterfeld showed up strongly, so twenty-one of twenty-two aircraft bombed it instead, again with unobserved results. On the 28th, twenty-three of twenty-four B-24s bombed the Siegen marshaling yard using Gee-H, with more unobserved results.

As ground forces drove into Germany, and with the end of the war ap-

Narrow transportation targets such as this railroad viaduct at Bielefeld were difficult to hit
with unguided bombs from 20,000 feet, even by large formations. The craters from many
misses are evident. Modern-day precision munitions from single aircraft make quick work of
such objectives. (44th Bomb Group Collection, USAMHI, USAHEC)

pearing to be approaching fast, the pace of USSTAF air operations also
picked up. The 44th Bomb Group would mount twenty-four missions in
March 1945. On average, one or two aircraft assigned to each mission failed
to bomb because of mechanical problems. H2X malfunctions also continued. In the attack on the Ingolstadt marshaling yard on the 1st, both lead
and deputy radar sets failed, requiring the twenty-one group planes to bomb
using smoke markers from earlier formations. Rothensee was again the target on the 2nd and 3rd. Overcast forced another diversion to the Magdeberg
marshaling yard on the first day, but on the second the smokestacks of the
complex peeking up over smoke screens allowed twenty B-24s to bomb visually, causing great damage to docks and storage areas. On the 4th, dense
contrails and thick haze foiled attempts to attack the tank factory at Aschaf-
fenburg, so twenty-two aircraft bombed scattered marshaling yard targets of
opportunity, mostly in visual conditions. An H2X attack the next day by
eleven bombers on the Harburg oil refinery was again affected by overcrowd-

ing on the bomb run by some of the other 120 planes on the raid, which diverted the approach of the 44th Group airmen.

On the 6th and 9th, the group stood down, and it only sent out three planes to bolster other formations on the 7th. The 8th featured another series of confused radar-directed attacks on marshaling yards. Twenty-six aircraft were sent out; thirteen bombed Betzdorf with Gee-H, ten hit what they thought was Frankfurt using H2X but were unsure, and two attacked what they thought was Siegen with H2X but turned out to be Limburg instead. All results were unobserved. Thirty-six group bombers attacked the railroad viaduct at Bielefeld with Gee-H on the 10th, and then thirty-three used H2X to hit the Kiel docks the next day. Though all results were unobserved, the land–water contrast for Kiel provided optimum conditions for radar screen images to guide the bombing there.

The group avoided disaster on the 14th in a good visual attack on the Gutersloh marshaling yard with thirty-six B-24s. One squadron overran the approach for their bomb run and while attempting to turn back into position found themselves on a collision course with another wing. They adeptly pulled into the other formation and bombed with it. The group continued to avoid battle losses; for the fourth straight mission they did not even have damage to any aircraft.

On the 15th thirty-three group aircraft led its wing on a raid against the German military headquarters at Zossen. Though weather was good, ground haze and bomb smoke obscured the target, so most bombs fell short. After a day off, the 44th sent twenty-five aircraft against the Munster marshaling yard. They bombed by Gee-H, and as a result of equipment failure one following squadron had to use smoke markers for guidance. On the 18th, thirty-three B-24s participated in a long mission against the Rheinmetall Borsig Armament Works in Berlin. Over 1,000 Eighth Air Force bombers hit Berlin that day, and poor weather, along with the contrails of preceding groups, made navigation and maintaining formation integrity difficult. Two squadrons hit the primary target visually and the third bombed the city with H2X; all three achieved excellent results. In contrast to the previous week, seventeen aircraft sustained significant battle damage on this raid, mostly from flak.

The group finally lost an aircraft in combat on 19 March. Thirty-three bombers led the Second Bombardment Division to hit the aircraft assembly plant at Neuburg. They ducked 1,500 feet to get under haze at the target but then mounted an excellent visual attack. On the way home one B-24 lost two engines and headed for France, never to be heard from again. On the 20th one squadron sent out eleven planes as part of a Fourteenth Wing mission against the oil refinery at Hemmingstadt. The lead bombardier adjusted improperly for smoke obscuring the target, and all the bombs went past it.

By this time in the war enemy fighters appeared reluctant to engage the large bomber formations surrounded by hungry Mustangs, so on the 21st the group mounted two missions to blast airfield installations to clear the way for strafing runs by USSTAF fighters, who were also hunting for jets. Again gremlins rode along with the 44th Group. Thirty-five bombers hit Achmer airfield in the morning, but only one squadron had excellent results because the others bombed out of sequence. Twelve more aircraft headed out in the afternoon for the airfield at Essen. Late in the bomb run, a flak hit severed the lead aircraft's electrical circuits for the autopilot and bombsight. Before the bombardier could adjust, all bombs were away, landing about 4,000 feet east of the target. The next day an attack by thirty-two bombers on Schwabisch Hall airfield went much better, with superb results, though one aircraft was lost when it crashed on takeoff.

Weather was finally improving, allowing much more visual bombing. Thirty bombers pummeled the Rheine marshaling yard on the 23rd. The next day again featured two missions. Twenty-seven group B-24s led the Fourteenth Wing on a critical supply drop for ground forces that had just crossed the Rhine. Sixty-nine tons of supplies were delivered accurately, but two planes were downed by ground fire and thirteen others received significant damage. In the afternoon twelve Liberators participated in an excellent wing attack on the landing strip at Stormede. On the 25th, two squadrons totaling twenty-two aircraft evaded high clouds to obtain excellent visual results bombing oil storage facilities at Hitzacker.

Then bad weather returned, and only two more missions were launched that month. On the 30th, thirty-three aircraft participated in a large attack on the docks and U-boat facilities at Wilhelmshaven. Two squadrons achieved excellent results bombing visually, but the lead bombardier of the third could not identify his target through the clouds and missed with H2X. On the 31st thirty-three group B-24s led the Fourteenth Wing against the Hoya ammunition depot. A 10/10ths cloud cover forced a diversion to the secondary target of the marshaling yard at Brunswick, where H2X bombing results were unobserved.

Missions for the 44th Bomb Group in the first quarter of 1945 were plagued by crowded skies, bad weather, enemy countermeasures, and many problems with radar equipment. Accuracy suffered accordingly. Still, their B-24s had contributed to the constant pressure that USSTAF strategic bombers were maintaining on the collapsing enemy military forces and economy.

The Fifteenth Air Force was also part of that effort. Its 455th Bombardment Group (Heavy) flew B-24s out of an improvised airdrome at San Giovanni, twenty miles southwest of Foggia, Italy, beginning in February 1944. "The Vulgar Vultures" consisted of the 740th, 741st, 742nd, and 743rd bomb squadrons. During December the unit had not been drawn into the tactical missions to support Allied ground forces fighting in the Bulge and instead had continued to hit oil and transportation targets. It usually flew as part of the 304th Bomb Wing.[34]

January 1945 was an unproductive month for the Vultures. Twenty-seven group B-24s flew their first mission of the new year on 4 January as part of 132 bombers blasting the Porto Nuovo marshaling yard in Verona, with excellent results. Thirteen aircraft were crowded off the bomb run and had to hit the secondary objective, the marshaling yard at Vicenza. Results there were also good. One bomber crash landed from flak damage. Twenty-six bombers took off on the 8th to attack a storage depot at Linz, Austria, but after an eight-hour flight bad weather forced them all to return with their bombs. No missions could be flown for another week, until twenty-nine B-24s launched to attack the Florisdorf marshaling yards at Vienna, a heavily bombed city.[35] Only nineteen planes were able to get through to bomb with H2X through overcast. Bombs were widely scattered. Nine aircraft were turned back by weather, and another could not release its bombs. The mission against the railroad bridge at Broz, Austria, on the 19th did not go much better. Twenty-eight B-24s took off. Five had to turn back because their leader could not open his bomb bays, two had mechanical problems and had to return early, and another crashed from engine failure. The other twenty Liberators bombed through overcast with unobserved results. The next day was worse. Twenty-six aircraft heading for Linz again had to turn back because of impenetrable cloud banks at the head of the Adriatic Sea. On the last day of the month, the group launched thirty-seven aircraft against the oil refinery at Moosbierbaum, Austria. Again they had to bomb with H2X, and again results were unobserved. The good news was that only two bombers had been lost that month, with only one due to enemy action.

The weather did not get much better in February. On the 1st, the Fifteenth Air Force mounted a maximum effort against the Moosebierbaum synthetic oil refinery in Austria that included thirty-eight bombers from the 455th. Because of total overcast few planes could find the target, and all the Vultures returned to base with their bomb loads. Oil remained the group

Vienna was not only heavily bombed but also heavily defended. This doomed B-24 has been ignited by enemy fighters over that target. (44th Bomb Group Collection, USAMHI, USAHEC)

focus for the 5 February raid on the storage facilities at Regensberg, but of the forty-two B-24s dispatched, three returned early, one hit a secondary railroad siding, and the rest bombed by radar through clouds with unobserved results. On the 7th, two waves of twenty bombers each went after Moosebierbaum again. Two aircraft returned early with engine problems. Five did not bomb because the flight leader's bombsight malfunctioned. Nineteen used H2X to bomb through overcast and a smoke screen, but fourteen in the second attack achieved fair results with a visual attack through a hole in the clouds. Almost 500 bombers from the Fifteenth returned to the marshaling yards at Vienna on the 8th, including twenty-eight Vultures, which had to drop their fifty-four tons of bombs with H2X. The next day the Fifteenth launched small "lone-wolf" individual attacks on Moosebierbaum in total overcast. Three Vultures participated, but like everyone else, they missed the target.

The group finally got good weather on the 13th, and results were much better. Again two forces were sent out, designated "red" and "blue," usually about an hour apart. Twenty-one B-24s in the first attack put 41 percent of their bombs within 1,000 feet of the aiming point to help cripple the railroad yards at Vienna. Twenty-four in the second mission had similar results against the marshaling yards at Maribor, Yugoslavia. However, the clouds returned the next day for another dual-force mission by forty bombers headed back to the marshaling yards at Vienna. Both elements had to divert to secondary targets, achieving good visual results and pummeling rail yards at Klagenfurt, Austria, and Maribor. Two waves of Vultures again headed for Vienna on the 15th, with H2X attacks through overcast one hour apart on the Korneuburg oil refinery, but the thirty-eight bombers caused no damage to their target. The Fifteenth went after airfields the next day. Thirty-nine Vultures headed for the Oberstraubling airdrome near Regensburg. Three aircraft had to return early with mechanical difficulties; the rest holed the field and its facilities under good visual conditions.

Although the airfields around Foggia did not have the weather problems of those in England, the Fifteenth Air Force still had to deal with the same winter cloud cover over central Europe as the Eighth did. On the 17th, forty-two Vulture B-24s had to divert from their primary objective again. Two turned back with mechanical problems, another lost the formation, and thirty-eight achieved only fair results against their secondary target of the shipyards at Fiume, Italy. The next day's weather was even worse, as twenty-eight bombers headed for the marshaling yards at Amstaten, Germany, had to turn back with their bomb loads. Headquarters then gave the group a broad range of possible targets to hit in order to get some bombs delivered despite the weather. About half of twenty-eight planes dispatched on the 19th attacked alternate objectives of harbors at Fiume or Pola with poor results, while the rest just brought their loads back. Twenty-eight Vultures had to hit their sixth priority alternate target the next day, the shipyards at Trieste, but 80 percent of the bombs landed within 1,000 feet of the aiming point—a fine demonstration of precision bombing in the right conditions. The Fifteenth mounted another maximum effort against Viennese marshaling yards on the 21st. Twenty-one B-24s from the group contributed to blocking the main rail lines in the central marshaling yards using H2X, but six other bombers had to return early because of various equipment failures.

On the 22nd, the Fifteenth Air Force participated in Operation CLARION, hitting smaller transportation targets throughout Germany, Austria, and occupied Italy. Weather continued to interfere. Two waves of forty-three Vultures were supposed to hit marshaling yards at Straubling, Germany, but instead they had to attack their alternate objective, rail yards at Bischofhofen, Austria, with good results. Twenty-eight bombers dispatched to attack the marshaling yard at Gmund, Germany, the next day returned with their bomb loads when they could not acquire targets through the heavy overcast. Considering the directive about not bringing bombs back from the Reich, it must be assumed the aircraft turned back before reaching their objective in southern Germany, or else they just ignored those instructions. On the 25th, twenty-eight Vultures participated in a successful attack on the marshaling yard at Linz, Austria.

The month ended roughly for the 455th. On the 27th, twenty-eight B-24s headed for the marshaling yards at Augsburg, Germany. Despite H2X problems shared with two other bomb groups on the mission, twenty-one bombers did achieve marginal results there, while six others hit alternate targets. Flak was intense, and effective. The group thought this increasingly dangerous antiaircraft fire was a result of the enemy "circling the wagons" to defend the homeland for the final stages of the war. Three aircraft had to land in Switzerland, while nineteen others returned with noticeable damage, four severe. The next day, thirty-five Vultures attacked the railroad bridge at Isarco–Albes, Italy, in two waves, part of a larger attack force of 226 Fifteenth Air Force B-24s. The first bombed poorly and lost another plane to flak. The second put 60 percent of its bombs within 1,000 feet of the aiming point. The bridge's center span was cut, abutments were damaged, and all approaches were blocked. It is worth noting that modern airmen would have taken out the same target with a few precision-guided munitions dropped from a single aircraft.

March would feature better weather eventually, a primary focus on transportation targets, and the continued absence of the Luftwaffe. Heavy overcast still interfered with missions during the first half of the month. Being able to fly between fronts did not provide much relief. Four of the twenty-six May missions would have to be completely aborted, while many others were partially affected by the poor weather. Sometimes just a half hour could make a difference. To open the month, eighteen B-24s launched against the marshaling yards at Maribor, Yugoslavia. Bad weather prevented getting to that objective, so eleven aircraft bombed the secondary target, rail yards at Jesenice, while the other seven brought their loads back. The sixteen Vultures that took off thirty minutes later in the second wave reached Maribor and bombed visually with good results. The next day only nineteen of twenty-eight aircraft could get through to bomb their primary target of the marshaling yard at Linz, Austria, but they had to use H2X through overcast. On the 4th, seventeen group B-24s bombed the marshaling yards at Wiener-Neustadt with H2X with poor results, while twenty-one heading to Brod, Yugoslavia, had to turn back with their bomb loads.

Frustrated by the continuing bad weather, the whole Fifteenth Air Force stood down for the next three days, hoping for improvement. However, when forty-two Vultures launched on the 8th to attack the marshaling yards at Novezamke, they could not even find a target of opportunity to bomb. Three aircraft ran out of fuel before they could get home, two found a friendly airfield in Yugoslavia, and the third crash-landed behind Soviet lines. Missions on the 9th were a little better. Although the following blue force could find no targets and had to return with full loads, the leading red force at least could identify a secondary target at the Graz marshaling yard with H2X. One aircraft had to abort because of an oil leak, but eighteen others dropped their bombs there, causing moderate damage. The next day the Fifteenth sent 192 bombers after the Parona railroad bridge at Verona. Of twenty-one participating Vultures, two returned early as a result of mechanical difficulties; the other nineteen put 75 percent of their bombs within 1,000 feet of their aiming point with good visibility. Two spans of the bridge were dropped and all approaches blocked.

On the 12th, the Fifteenth went back after its favorite target of Vienna, attacking both oil and transportation targets. The 455th sent forty-two aircraft against the Florisdorf refinery. Thirty-eight used H2X through overcast to drop their bombs, but all missed the target. The next day over 500 Fifteenth Air Force bombers had to drop their loads on the Regensburg marshaling yards with H2X through heavy overcast. Of twenty-eight Vultures on the mission, three had to return early, but the others contributed to fair results that further demonstrated that marshaling yards were much more suitable objectives for blind-bombing methods than smaller refineries. On the 14th, forty-two B-24s had to use H2X to bomb the secondary target of marshaling yards at Wiener-Neustadt, with unobserved results. The 15th of March featured dual missions again. The initial red force included twenty aircraft, thirteen bombed their fourth alternate target, rail yards at Bruck-Leitha, Austria, and the other seven hit Wiener-Neustadt again. The following twenty planes of the blue force were also plagued by the overcast; they attacked a number of different targets of opportunity with little impact. Bad weather forced another diversion the next day, as thirty-seven Vultures achieved fair results against secondary marshaling yards at Amsteten, Austria, when they found a hole in the clouds there.

After poor conditions canceled all heavy bomber operations for two days, the weather finally started to clear on the 19th, when the Fifteenth Air Force delivered its largest daily tonnage of the war, 2,243 against German mar-shaling yards. With better weather came better accuracy and results, and Vulture ground crews managed to get forty-two Liberators into the air for five days in a row. On the first day, one aircraft returned early, but the others pummeled rail yards at Muhldorf, Germany. The next day they put over 80 percent of bombs within 1,000 feet of the aiming point in marshaling yards at Wels, Austria. On the 21st, the Eighth and Fifteenth Air Forces launched a combined raid against the jet airfields around Neuberg, Germany. The Me 262s were the only viable threat the Luftwaffe could mount against the strategic bombing onslaught. One B-24 had to turn back with mechanical problems, but the other forty-one placed 87 percent of their bombs within that 1,000-foot circle around their aiming point. On the 22nd, two aircraft had to abort, seven mistakenly bombed rail yards at Neratovice, Czechoslova-kia, and the rest participated in a successful attack on the nearby oil refinery at Kralupy. On the last day of the streak all forty-two Liberators helped shut down the St. Valentin tank works at Steyr, but two were forced to crash-land with flak damage.

Only thirty-eight aircraft were available on the 24th, and all but one man-aged to unload their bombs on the Riem airdrome in Munich, with fair results. On the next day, thirty-six of thirty-eight Liberators completed the mission against the CKD Leiben tank works at Prague, causing significant damage. Then the bad weather returned. Of twenty-eight planes headed to the marshaling yards at Szombathely, Hungary, on the 26th, six managed to find the target through the cloud cover, seven jettisoned their bombs over the Adriatic, and thirteen brought them back to base. No missions were con-ducted for three days, until four Vultures participated in lone-wolf attacks through cloud cover on the 30th. Two helped damage marshaling yards in Vienna; a third missed the tank factory at Kapfenberg. On the last day of the month, twenty-eight B-24s launched against the locomotive depot at Linz, Austria. Only eighteen were able to reach the primary target to bomb with H2X, and results were unobserved. Four aircraft brought their bombs back to base and three dumped their loads in the Adriatic.

CONCLUSIONS AND OBSERVATIONS

Although this narrative only describes three months' worth of missions by two bomb groups, there are many useful observations that can be made. Weather was the main opposition for the USSTAF during this period. Except for rare appearances by jet fighters, the primary German resistance came from flak and occasional passive measures like smoke screens. With such little opposition, American bombers roamed freely over the Reich and occupied territories, with a broad choice of targets. Though Donald Miller has characterized this period of the air war as "Terror Without End" that did really break German civilian morale,[36] the primary focus for USSTAF remained oil and transportation targets, with occasional diversions after jets or factory complexes.

The use of radar-directed bombing methods was widespread and essential to the conduct of the air campaign during this period. Although useful results were often obtained against marshaling yards, attacking more pinpoint targets, like oil refineries, was extremely problematic. The technology allowed USSTAF to maintain pressure on the collapsed transportation system and contributed to the virtual elimination of oil production by March. Neither of these bomb groups perceived themselves as involved in any sort of attacks on enemy morale, even in the February CLARION attacks. When they did get visual bombing conditions, results were usually superb, helped also by the almost total disappearance of the Luftwaffe.

However, there was much less concern about civilian casualties in Germany compared to other sections of Europe. This situation was exacerbated by the drive to continue to mount maximum air efforts as enemy opposition declined and final German collapse seemed near. Clausewitzian friction was very evident. The Eighth Air Force had much trouble with its H2X equipment, as well as with managing so many bomber formations in crowded skies. The Fifteenth seemed to avoid most of those difficulties. They had more H2X sets assigned to units, allowing bombing by smaller formations, and they appear to have had better maintenance of their radars. The Fifteenth Air Force was not as large as the Eighth, and the 455th often sent out its bombers in two separate waves to avoid overcrowding. Both air forces experienced considerable attrition on missions from mechanical failures. The two bomb groups described above averaged between 5 percent and 10 percent of their launched planes turning back before reaching their objectives. Fifteenth Air Force formations often brought their bombs back to base, something the Eighth Air Force never did. Often at the limits of their range, perhaps Fifteenth Air Force bombers had less fuel to waste looking for secondary targets, as well as fewer secondary targets along their flight routes. In addition there was not the same incentive to expend bombs on northern Italy or the Balkans as there was on Germany, and with the speed of the Russian advance, the front lines were often indistinct. The Mediterranean

Allied Air Forces conducted increasing coordination with their allies during this time to ensure maximum support and a minimum of confrontations.

There is need for a good comparative study of the two major USSTAF air forces. However, their common objective, contributing to winning the war through the destruction of the enemy's economic and military means to resist, remained consistent. Precision bombing, as envisioned in the 1930s and even in AWPD/1 and AWPD-42, however, became much more of a sledgehammer than a rapier—and eventually, in its execution against Japan, a rain of fire. The following chapters will look in more detail how this process happened, and why.

4. ATTITUDES OF LEADERS
AND THE PUBLIC

Last month my son Ted won his wings at Randolph Field. He is now going through a bombardment school, and in a short time expects to go to the front.

Will you tell me—has he become what our enemies call him, "A Hooligan of the Air"? Is he expected to scatter death on men, women, children—to wreck churches and shrines—to be a slaughterer, not a fighting man?

I remember so well when you and Frank Lahm, and Tommy Milling won your wings. We all thought it was a new day in chivalry, bravery, manhood. What do Air Force wings mean today? In winning his wings, has Ted lost his spurs? Please tell me.

—*Katharine A. Hooper to H. H. Arnold, 3 May 1943*[1]

This letter from a concerned mother in Massachusetts to the Army Air Forces commander raised some of the same questions being debated by modern historians. When it was written in May 1943, American daylight bombers had been in action over Europe for nine months; they had already been involved in controversy over civilian casualties in occupied countries and had become the subject of much German propaganda.[2] AAF leaders were especially sensitive to public opinion because the airmen believed they needed all the support they could get to achieve independent status. Between the wars, Army aviators had promoted "air-mindedness" and exploited American dreams that the airplane could revolutionize daily life and transform the world for good, and at the core of precision-bombing doctrine was the belief that the American public would not stand for the indiscriminate aerial bombardment of civilians.[3] AAF leaders interpreted the few letters from concerned correspondents as representative of public opinion, and this viewpoint acted as a restraint on some airmen who might otherwise have been inclined to imitate Air Vice Marshal Arthur "Bomber" Harris, commander of the RAF Bomber Command and architect of the RAF night-bombing campaign against German cities. Stopped one night for speeding by a policeman who warned, "You might have killed someone, sir," Harris allegedly retorted, "Young man, I kill thousands of people every night."[4] American leaders probably could never have been that callous, but actual wartime public opinion was not as intolerant of civilian casualties as the AAF perceived.

Pearl Harbor transformed American public opinion about terror attacks on civilians. A poll on 10 December 1941 revealed that 67 percent of the population favored unqualified and indiscriminate bombing of Japanese cities, and only 10 percent responded with an outright no.[5] The same justification of tit for tat that motivated earlier Luftwaffe and RAF raids on London and Berlin seemed to be evident here.[6] Subsequent surveys produced similar results. A majority of Americans favored urban bombing even if it brought Axis retaliation against US cities, implying either a deep commitment or a resignation to total warfare and reflecting the intense anxiety about a war that appeared to be going so disastrously. For religious reasons, most Americans expressed resistance to bombing Rome, but by early 1944 three-quarters of those polled approved bombing historic religious buildings and shrines if military leaders believed such attacks were necessary.[7]

The only significant flurry of US protest against strategic bombing came in response to a pamphlet, "Massacre by Bombing," written by a British citizen, Vera Brittain, and published in America by the Fellowship of Reconciliation, a small pacifist group. She contended that mass bombing just sped up the slaughter and destruction normally occurring only on fighting fronts, produced a downward spiral of moral values, did not induce revolt or break morale, and caused destruction that would cripple postwar Europe and sow the psychological seeds of a third world war. She also noted that the British in bombed areas were less likely to support RAF attacks on enemy cities than their compatriots who had been spared.[8] Her work did not attract significant attention, however, until March 1944 when the *New York Times* reprinted excerpts along with an introductory petition signed by twenty-eight prominent educators, professionals, and clergy (mostly the last). The article, "Obliteration Raids on German Cities Protested in US," caused intense public reaction, and over 200 articles were written condemning Brittain.[9] The paper received "unusually heavy mail" about the piece and estimated that letters of protest concerning Brittain's views were running "50–1 against."[10] Most responses agreed with author MacKinley Kantor, who deplored the "softheartedness" of those people who worry about "socking the rapacious German nation with every pound of high explosives available." A rabbi declared that "the Germans must reap the fruits of their own wicked deeds." Other clergy echoed his sentiments, citing Nazi precedents as the final justification for American bombing. Editorial comment in general disclaimed moral questions and recognized the raids as a "revolting necessity."[11]

Though relatively few commentaries addressed the ethical issues Brittain had raised, articles discussing the morality of obliteration bombing did appear in *Fellowship*, *Saturday Review of Literature*, *Christian Century*, the *Nation*, *Newsweek*, *Politics*, *Spectator*, *Commonweal*, *America*, the *London Tablet*, and the *Labor Leader*.[12] The issue was even debated on the radio during "America's Town Meeting" on the evening of 30 March. Norman Cousins, editor of the *Saturday Review of Literature*, and military analyst Major George Fielding Eliot were for bombing cities; C. C. Paulding, literary editor of *Commonweal*, and Socialist Party leader Norman Thomas attacked the practice.[13] However, the furor caused by Brittain's article soon abated, with no effect on bombing policy.

Other writers had protested aerial bombing. Oswald Garrison Villard, who had been involved with the Brittain piece, penned critical articles in *Christian Century* beginning in 1943, R. Alfred Hassler wrote "Slaughter of the Innocent" in *Fellowship* in February 1944, and German American Gerhart Segar was condemned for his editorials in *Neue Volkszeitung* and for his commentary on "Town Meeting of the Air," when he stated that American pilots were exhibiting "totalitarian thinking" by "finding satisfaction in blowing up women and children." The national religious press, especially Catholic journals, were also often critical of indiscriminate bombing.[14]

In one of the most penetrating critiques, Father John C. Ford argued that even in industrial cities in wartime, at least two-thirds of the civil population would be immoral targets: "most women, almost all children under 14 years, almost all men over seventy, and a very large number of men who are engaged neither in war manufactures, transport, communications, nor in other doubtful categories." He correctly predicted that the bombing of cities would weaken ethical constraints and take us "a long step in the direction of immoral total war." By using explosives and incendiaries "to a hitherto unheard of degree," the practice left "only one more step to go to the use of poison gas or bacteriological war" (or the atomic bomb).[15] Yet no clear consensus was reached among American church leaders on the immorality of city bombing. In 1944 the theologians of the Federal Council of Churches Commission on the Relation of the Church to the War in the Light of the Christian Faith agreed that "the massacre of civilian populations" was immoral but stated that some of their members "believe that certain other measures, such as rigorous blockades of foodstuffs essential to civilian life, and obliteration bombing of civilian areas, however repugnant to humane feelings, are still justifiable on Christian principles, if they are essential to the successful conduct of a war that is itself justified."[16]

The majority of public opinion on killing enemy civilians was probably accurately represented by the reactions to Brittain's article, ranging between avid support for vengeful urban attacks and resigned acceptance of a regrettably unavoidable practice. The average American might not have been aware of the extent of the destruction that bombing wreaked on cities; posters depicted Allied bombers attacking factories instead of people, and periodicals described B-17s dropping explosives down industrial smokestacks. Even if Americans had known the exact results of bombing, it would not have made much difference. Most families had experienced the deaths of loved ones, friends, or neighbors; if bombing enemy civilians would speed victory and save American lives, it had to be done.

ATTITUDES OF LEADERS IN WASHINGTON

Many Americans were comforted, however, by the belief that the AAF avoided indiscriminate killing of civilians whenever possible. In turn, AAF leaders perceived a public opinion in line with the position of publications like the New Republic, which stated that it did not approve of terror bombing but added that to the best of its knowledge most bombardment was directed at military objectives.[17] A subtle, important interaction was maintained between public perceptions of American strategic bombing and the attitudes of the leaders carrying it out. Air Force planners interpreted public opinion as favoring precision attacks on industrial and military targets without indiscriminate civilian casualties, one of the influences that shaped AAF bombing doctrine. Military reports and news releases designed to demonstrate the accuracy and effectiveness of pinpoint bombardment in turn shaped public opinion. This use of information exemplifies a trend that can be traced to the American Civil War, and "management of, or compliance with, public opinion" has become "an essential element in the conduct of war."[18] In World War II, American leaders worked persistently to dispel any impressions of American terror bombing.

This effort often caused men in high places to present different public and private positions on the bombing of enemy civilians; the commander in chief, Franklin D. Roosevelt, is a good example. When the Germans invaded

Poland on 1 September 1939, he immediately issued a plea to all belligerents to cease "the ruthless bombing from the air of civilians in unfortified centers of population" that "has sickened the hearts of every civilized man and woman, and has profoundly shocked the conscience of humanity." He asked for a public affirmation that all parties would avoid such acts, "upon the understanding that these same rules of warfare will be scrupulously observed by all of their opponents."[19] This plea was largely a political ploy. A week earlier, Ambassador William Bullitt had proposed that such an appeal should be made at the start of hostilities. The assumption was that Britain, Poland, and France would agree but that Germany would not, thus showing the moral superiority of the Allies and swaying world opinion against Germany. After consultation with Cordell Hull, Roosevelt agreed to send the message.[20] The Allies did indeed respond favorably, but so did Germany. The Germans were able to claim by 11 September that the Poles were violating the rules of warfare by resisting in open cities and shelling their own people, thus justifying retaliation from the air.[21]

Roosevelt's true feelings are probably better demonstrated by a statement he made to Henry Morgenthau on 4 August 1941 about defeating Hitler: "Well, the way to lick Hitler is the way I have been telling the English, but they won't listen to me. . . . I have suggested again and again that if they sent a hundred planes over Germany for military objectives that ten of them should bomb some of these smaller towns that haven't been bombed before. There must be some kind of factory in every town. That is the only way to break German morale."[22] Although factories would be the technical targets, Roosevelt's actual objective was to smash civilian will, not the economy. (Operation CLARION, similar in concept, was mounted in 1945 and generated much controversy over its aims.) Roosevelt revealed as early as 1938 that he believed the morale of the German people could be cracked by the terror of aerial bombardment.[23]

The president did emphasize the distinction between obliteration and precision bombing in his message to Congress in 1943, but he revealed no such awareness during the controversy over Brittain's pamphlet. Stephan Early, Roosevelt's secretary, responded to "Massacre by Bombing" with a letter on behalf of the president. Although Roosevelt was "disturbed and horrified" by civilian air-raid casualties, "the bombing is shortening the war, in the opinion of an overwhelming percentage of military authorities." Brittain replied that the president's response was "irrelevant, unjustified, and destructive of the very ideals with which the American people went to war."[24] A bit later, Roosevelt sent a note to Secretary Stimson taking an even harsher stand, stating that "the German people as a whole must have it driven home to them that the whole nation has been engaged in a lawless conspiracy against the decencies of modern civilization."[25]

At least in private, Roosevelt showed a willingness early in the war to attack civilian morale from the air. So did the commander of the AAF, Commanding General Henry "Hap" Arnold, who had what one aide called "an open mind" on terror bombing.[26] In 1941 Arnold wrote that "bombing attacks on civil populace are uneconomical and unwise" because "bombers in far larger numbers than are available today will be required for wiping out people in sufficient numbers to break the will of a whole nation."[27] Arnold kept his options open for future civilian bombardment, and his memoirs and diaries reveal even more flexibility on the subject. He was impressed by the damage and civilian listlessness that a relatively small number of Luftwaffe bombers had caused in London, and he envisioned great results from larger fleets of American planes.[28]

In public Arnold called terror bombing "abhorrent to our humanity, our sense of decency," a policy he himself did not support.[29] In private he told his Air Staff that "this is a brutal war and . . . the way to stop the killing of civilians is to cause so much damage and destruction and death that the civilians will demand that their government cease fighting." He added, however, that "this doesn't mean that we are making civilians or civilian institutions a war objective, but we cannot 'pull our punches' because some of them may get killed." He did confide to reporters once that the AAF could bomb to destroy a city "as well as anybody else" and did sometimes carry out "pattern bombing," which could be used to break morale, though that was really not a preferred AAF objective.[30]

In order to support his desire for a postwar independent air service Arnold wanted to avoid alienating the public with an improper image, but he also needed impressive results to prove the effectiveness of air power. Though he was not really involved in running day-to-day combat operations, his authority to relieve field commanders gave him leverage to influence their actions. Poor health limited his effectiveness late in the war, however, and after he suffered his fourth heart attack in January 1945 his involvement in key decisions was especially limited.[31] However, his pressure for more raids despite bad weather led to increased use of less accurate radar-directed bombardments in Europe, and his demand for increased efficiency in Japan inspired the use of fire raids. His main goal was to make the largest possible contribution to winning the war and to ensure that the AAF received credit for it through proper publicity.

Thus he demanded much from his field commanders in the area of public relations. He wrote to commanders in 1942, "Within the borders of continental United States, two most important fronts exist, namely, aircraft production and public opinion." He thought that the American public was entitled "to see pictures, stories and experiences of our Air Force in combat zones," and he sent out personnel from his staff to gather such information. A year later he complained to his commanders that too much information was being withheld because of secrecy; it was more important that the people be kept informed of the major impact the Air Force was making on the enemy's war effort—an impact that could save millions of lives in ground combat. "For whole-hearted and official support of our Air Forces in their operations, . . . the people [must] understand thoroughly our Air Force precepts, principles, and purposes. . . . In short, we want the people to understand and have faith in *our way of making war*."[32] Field commanders protested when Arnold tried to get them to replace a machine gun from their bombers with a camera to provide combat film footage, but their objections had little effect on his drive for media coverage. Arnold exerted even more pressure for publicity once the Allies invaded Europe and the war seemed to be winding down. He complained that ground and naval commanders such as General George Patton and Admiral William Halsey got the publicity but that the contribution of air power was ignored. He emphasized to the field that he considered "the whole subject of realistic reorientation of the public's concept of the effect of air power upon the outcome of the war so important" that he would "scour the country" to find public relations experts to reinforce press representatives in the theater. Because of his push, by November 1944 fully 40 percent of the total film released by the Army to newsreels came from AAF combat camera units.[33] Even this increased output did not please Arnold, who wanted more front-page stories and sent out to all commanders a list of fifty points applicable to writing proper news releases. Thinking ahead about the future of the AAF, he was determined that "through proper presentation to the press" the American people could get the facts necessary to make "a correct evaluation of the part air power has played in this war" so that "the United States should not make the mistake of allowing through lack of knowledge the tearing down in post-war years of what has cost us so much blood and sweat to build up."[34]

Though Arnold did stress the advantages of precision bombing to his commanders, pushing for increased accuracy and refined tactics to achieve "the maximum attainable with the forces and facilities available," he was also "the prophet and proponent of the most terrifying technologies of war."[35]

He emphasized that his commanders "must be ever on the alert to accept new ideas, must have flexible minds on procedure and technique in our missions."[36] He liked to glean such new ideas from the minds of experts; gadgets and hot ideas fascinated him. In keeping with the impression given in his early writings that he would try almost anything if he had enough aircraft, Arnold commented favorably on plans to bomb volcanoes around Tokyo and schools of fish off the coast of Japan.[37] He was fascinated with pilotless flying bombs like the German V-1s and wanted to retaliate for German booby traps in North Africa by dropping explosive devices in fountain pens and pocketbooks onto German territory. Foreshadowing a tactic eventually adopted by the Japanese, Arnold also had his staff investigate a plan to use "Vinylite" film balloons to drop incendiaries on Japan.[38]

There seemed to be little consideration for ethics in Arnold's decisions, but he did espouse the traditional moral position of air power theory that bombing would cost fewer lives than land warfare and end the war quickly. Like other air leaders, he sincerely believed that the decisive power of modern aerial technology could prevent a repeat of the deadlocked carnage of World War I and achieve swift and relatively bloodless victory. He told his commanders that "when used with the proper degree of understanding, [the bomber] becomes, in effect, the most humane of all weapons." He also realized the political costs of indiscriminate bombardment, writing in 1942 that "careless inaccurate bombing intensifies and spreads those hates which will be stumbling blocks to international amity for years after the war is over."[39] Yet as the war continued and he pushed more and more for decisive results to support his dream of an independent air service, considerations of humanity were never a priority with Arnold.

In contrast, at least one leader in Washington, Secretary of War Henry L. Stimson, did consistently oppose the intentional killing or terrorizing of enemy noncombatants. Repelled by the barbarism of indiscriminate attacks on civilians, he had been instrumental in US government protests against such raids during the 1930s and tried to keep a close watch on American strategic air operations during World War II. Stimson's diary is filled with references to atrocities and war crimes and occasionally with concerns for enemy civilians. He was convinced that the Nazi leaders and the secret police, not the German people, caused the war. The same sentiment motivated those critics of strategic bombing who concluded that workers in Berlin were no more evil than the airmen ordered to bomb them.[40] Stimson complained that only General George Marshall supported him in that view: "It is singular that the man who had charge of the Department which did the killing in the war,

Lieutenant General H. H. Arnold traveling with Secretary of War Henry Stimson. Unlike Arnold, Stimson consistently expressed moral opposition to indiscriminate attacks on enemy civilians.

should be the only one who seemed to have any mercy for the other side."
The secretary of war believed that in general Army officers had a better sense
of justice on the issue of "responsibility of peoples" than civilians.[41]

Though Stimson called the Japanese "barbarians" in speeches, he did
work to restrain "the feeling of war passion and hysteria which seizes hold
of a nation like ours in prosecution of such a bitter war." Reports of the fire
raids against Japan evoked a strong reaction; Stimson felt he had been misled
by Robert Lovett, assistant secretary of war for air, and by AAF leaders who
had promised to restrict operations there to "the precision bombing which
[the AAF] has done so well in Europe." In his diary he wrote, "I am told it
is possible and adequate. The reputation of the United States for fair play
and humanitarianism is the world's biggest asset for peace in the coming
decades."[42] Discussing the topic later with President Truman, Stimson realized the validity of Air Force arguments that the omnipresence of dispersed
Japanese industry made it difficult to prevent area bombing, but he "did
not want to have the United States get the reputation of outdoing Hitler
in atrocities." He often agonized over sanctioning bombing raids and wondered about the lack of public protest. Robert Oppenheimer recalled that
Stimson thought it was "appalling" that no one protested the heavy loss of
life caused by the air raids against Japan. "He didn't say that the air strikes
shouldn't be carried on, but he did think there was something wrong with a
country where no one questioned that."[43]

Ronald Schaffer is especially critical of Stimson for not being more effective, pointing out that his protest of the fire raids came almost two months
after they started and that he could have inquired more into the bombing
of Japan and Dresden. Schaffer speculates that Stimson might have been
too old, ill, and misinformed or that he simply chose not to know what the
AAF was doing.[44] Stimson was suffering from poor health and often could
not work full time, and he was not kept informed on day-to-day operations.
However, in his role as secretary of war he was more concerned with administrative matters than with strategy. As the war went on his diary deals
increasingly with the problems of staffing and supplying his forces as the
sources of recruits and replacements dried up and as public enthusiasm for
the war began to wane. The AAF did respond when Stimson showed strong
interest in a subject, such as the sparing of Kyoto from the atomic bomb
or the Norwegian complaints about stray bombs from raids on heavy-water
plants, but they did not feel obligated to brief him on operations. Stimson
remarked once of Robert Lovett that "his youngsters have run away with the
ball without apparently attracting his attention," but the military treated the

civilians in the War Department in just such a manner.[45] Stimson probably learned more about specific operations from the newspapers than he did from soldiers in his department. The war was planned and directed by the Joint Chiefs of Staff and fought by the operational- and tactical-level commanders in the field.

ATTITUDES OF FIELD COMMANDERS

One field commander effective in restraining indiscriminate bombardment was Lieutenant General Carl Spaatz, commander of the USSTAF and an officer most historians credit with continuing to raise the moral issue in opposition to British attempts to enlist American participation in terror attacks and deviations from precision bombing. Russell Weigley calls him "a pillar of common sense," whom ground commanders could always talk to. Although Spaatz believed that "we have proven the precision bombing principle in this war," he realized that with the limits of technology, "our precision . . . is in a relative not a literal sense," and he continued to strive for "pickle barrel accuracy."[46] He also had a more realistic view of Arnold's publicity campaign, and though he supported his chief, he was wary that "the people back home are getting the idea now [April 1944] that the War is won and apparently we have unintentionally given the impression that more has been accomplished than has actually been accomplished." While Arnold pushed for optimistic reports of the triumphs of air power, Spaatz wanted to "lean a little on the side of understatement" to avoid false confidence at home and mistrust of superiors by the airmen who had to engage the German fighters supposedly destroyed by the AAF.[47]

Weigley also claims that "Spaatz was an airman genuinely troubled over the moral questions raised by aerial bombardment."[48] The USSTAF commander wrote in his diary after the dropping of the atomic bomb, "I have never favored the destruction of cities as such with all inhabitants being killed." In an often-quoted 1962 interview, however, he claimed, "It wasn't for religious or moral reasons that I didn't go along with urban area bombing."[49] One must be careful in interpreting this statement; Spaatz was emphasizing in the interview that the AAF bombed strategic military targets because that was the quickest way to win the war, not because the United States was morally superior to the British. From the beginning of the war, Spaatz condemned efforts to "belittle the RAF and their bombing effort" even though he was not "an enthusiastic supporter of all they do."[50] Spaatz had helped develop precision-bombing doctrine and pursued it doggedly in Europe. Although he did emphasize the efficiency of such tactics, he also continually expressed concern over civilian casualties caused by bombing. Richard Davis argues that Spaatz's devotion to precision bombing actually limited his ability to appreciate joint operations, and especially the difficulties and utility of ground operations. However, he did the best he could to develop a capable all weather force. As Davis writes of Spaatz, "He used the most modern radar, employed electronic countermeasures, took full advantage of ULTRA, and pushed his commanders and their men and machines to their limits in order to exploit all the force available to him. Once he had created this available force, it had to be employed." His dilemma was "how to wield an expanding force of limited accuracy against an opponent who had large reserves of manpower and machine tools without causing excessive or unnecessary collateral damage." Davis, like Schaffer, believes that Spaatz's use of so much blind bombing and his decision to relax bombing restrictions that protected German civilians departed from the doctrine and ethics he espoused, but Davis concedes, "To Spaatz, to most of his fellow soldiers, to his government, and to the people his government represented it was better to err on the side of excessive force by pulverizing the Reich, than to leave it the strength to resist and kill Allied soldiers."[51]

Spaatz's primary objective was to make the maximum contribution to winning the war in Europe. He cooperated with the ground effort when required, but he believed that precision bombing of economic targets, especially oil, made the best use of his bombers. His subordinate commanders supported his goals and AAF doctrine, though their attitudes demonstrated varying degrees of concern for morality, efficiency, and public opinion, depending on their background and training.

Lieutenant General Jimmy Doolittle, commander of the Eighth Air Force in 1944–1945, seemed to share Spaatz's attitude toward morality in strategic bombing. A famous air racer and aeronautical engineer before the war, Doolittle was not a career military man like the rest of the air commanders. Wartime biographers emphasized "his superb sense of fair play and his constant observation of the rules of human decency." He restricted his objectives to purely military targets during his famous Tokyo raid and carefully avoided religious shrines in his 1943 bombings of Rome, when he commanded the Northwest African Strategic Air Force under Spaatz. Doolittle wanted to be the first to bomb Berlin too, but he supported Spaatz in resisting obliteration attacks on that city.[52] In his autobiography, Doolittle remarked that in his opinion, the Americans who supported daylight precision bombing instead

Major General Jimmy Doolittle in the cockpit of his plane in 1943. He often flew his own aircraft to visit units under his command. Doolittle served under Carl Spaatz from 1942 until the end of the war in Europe and supported Spaatz in his efforts to restrict strategic bombing to precision targets.

of the night area attacks used by the British did so not because pinpoint methods were significantly more effective than RAF tactics but because "to us, it was the most ethical way to go."[53]

Despite earning the Medal of Honor for leading the daring raid on Tokyo, as well as the rest of his distinguished service, Dolittle remained humble and approachable throughout his life. At the age of ninety-six, he took the time to dictate a reply to a letter from a young schoolgirl asking about his own heroism and famous people he had known. His son, John, typed for him, "The General does not consider himself to be a hero. He always has done those things that he felt should be or had to be done." He opined that Winston Churchill was the greatest person he had ever known, and George Marshall the greatest American. Billy Mitchell, Hap Arnold, and Dwight Eisenhower were others whom he mentioned.[54]

Another of Spaatz's key subordinates was Major General Frederick L. Anderson, eventually USSTAF deputy commander for operations, who was a proponent of efficiency. He was young, a 1928 graduate of West Point, having risen from first lieutenant to brigadier general in less than six years, and unlike Arnold, Spaatz, Doolittle, or Eaker, he had no experience from World War I or the 1920s to draw on. He was, however, the AAF's leading bombardment expert. As a captain in 1939, he was put in charge of the bombardier school at the Air Force Technical School at Lowry Field, Colorado. He had not developed precision-bombing doctrine, but he trained bombardiers to put it into practice. When the AAF needed someone to evaluate crew training and bombsights in England in early 1942, Anderson got the assignment. He helped develop the justification for daylight bombing when it was questioned early in the war, emphasizing the efficiency of precision bombing and how it complemented British area bombing. Like Spaatz, Anderson was another strong proponent for an independent air force equal to the other branches. He believed "that for the efficiency of our fighting forces a reorganization is needed."[55]

Achieving an independent air service was also of paramount importance to Lieutenant General Ira Eaker, who commanded both the Eighth and the Fifteenth Air Forces at different times during the war and eventually became Arnold's deputy. Favorable public opinion was essential for this goal, and Eaker was deeply concerned about the AAF's image, both current and future. He warned the assistant chief of Air Staff for intelligence to keep criticism of operations out of official exchanges because "we have a mass of historians at both ends watching all this correspondence and these things cannot but creep into the official documents unless we are all on guard." He supported Arnold's drive for publicity about the importance of air power, promising, "We are making certain that every American newspaperman we can get our hands on has these facts hammered home to him."[56]

Eaker was extremely intelligent; he had a journalism degree and had taken some law courses at Columbia. Among the AAF leaders he came closest to being a true public-relations expert. After serving as the records custodian for Brigadier General Billy Mitchell's court-martial, he saw the dangers of confrontation and "deliberately set out to become army air's most persuasive spokesman." He worked hard to develop his writing and speaking skills, and his efforts paid off at the Casablanca Conference in January 1943. Plagued by a slow buildup of forces in Europe, lack of proper fighter escorts, and poor selection of target systems, American daylight bombers in 1942 had not been able to match the night efforts of RAF Bomber Command, which included 1,000 plane raids. Eaker made the presentation that convinced Churchill and others of the merits of a CBO involving round-the-clock bombing, thus preserving the AAF's chance to vindicate precision-bombing doctrine. Arnold also often sent Eaker to make presentations to the Joint Chiefs of Staff for the AAF. Eaker had written books and articles with Arnold, and the latter frequently asked his editorial advice. When an article criticizing daylight bombing appeared in *Reader's Digest* and caused a stir, Eaker wrote an official reply defending American air strategy that was released by the War Department.[57]

His comments to Arnold and other sources reveal that Eaker was not as committed to precision bombing as Spaatz or Anderson. He advised Arnold to put in a prewar *Saturday Evening Post* article that it was "probably uneconomical to bomb civil populations unless in extreme cases such as London or Paris, where it would be done for the morale effect in the hope for a short war." He admitted in a 1972 interview that he was not "completely sold" on daylight precision bombing when he took over the Eighth Air Force in England in 1942; he viewed his operations as a test of the concept, though he felt that Arnold and Marshall were "relying on him to make it work." If he had failed to save daylight precision bombardment at Casablanca, he was prepared to shift his forces to night bombing in three to six months after installing flame dampeners, taking out unnecessary machine guns, and retraining crews.[58] He proved quicker to fully embrace the new nonvisual bombing technology than Spaatz, which contributed to the Fifteenth Air Force's superiority in such missions while it was under his control as the commander of Mediterranean Allied Air Forces. In late 1944 General Spaatz criticized diversions of Eaker's Fifteenth Air Force from oil targets, but Eaker advocated dispersed attacks to destroy German morale, suggesting that such tactics might also pull defenses away from oil targets. When Eaker did oppose terror attacks in early 1945, his position was based on his fears about the political and historical ramifications of "throwing the strategic bomber at the man in the street."[59]

DIFFERENCES WITH THE BRITISH

The attitudes of American leaders committed to daylight precision bombing were bound to clash with the views of their RAF counterparts dedicated to

Eighth Air Force B-24 Liberators bombing harbor installations at Dunkirk, France, on 15 February 1943. Raids such as this one contributed to the dispute between American and British airmen over risks to civilians in occupied nations. (Special Collections Division, US Military Academy Library, West Point, NY)

"dehousing" German workers and obliterating whole cities. From the early days of the war, US military attaches in England had been sending reports criticizing the inaccuracy of night bombing, yet AAF personnel understood the rationale for RAF tactics.[60] They knew that aircraft capabilities and German countermeasures rendered British daylight precision attacks ineffectual, but public pressure demanded that the RAF strike back at Germany. Night raids on urban areas seemed the only viable alternative. If the British had possessed the long-range escort fighters that eventually made daylight bombing practicable, their campaign might have developed differently. But by 1942 AAF leaders realized that British aircraft, with their heavy bomb loads, inaccurate bombsights, and sparse defensive armament, were primarily adapted to night attacks and that the heavily armed American planes, with smaller bomb loads, good bombsights, and no flame dampers, were chiefly suited to daylight operations.[61]

Until they could prove the viability of their own tactics, AAF leaders were wary of criticism. British leaders or journalists who criticized daylight bombardment were often invited to go on American missions. Joint statements were issued to emphasize the complementary nature of RAF and AAF campaigns. Articles in the American press advocating night bombing also evoked nervous reactions, and a proposed film on RAF bombing exhibits in early 1943 was tabled because the AAF staff felt that "we should do nothing to stress night area bombardment to the American public."[62] Yet throughout the war, even after daylight bombing had proved successful, the Americans continually discouraged any public criticism of the British obliteration raids, believing that "odious" comparisons between bombing techniques only assisted German propaganda and caused resentment between the two Allies.

In private, however, sharp differences often existed over the bombing of civilians, especially about the attacks on countries conquered by Germany. From the onset of war, Spaatz was sensitive to civilian casualties in occupied areas. He was probably also aware of the strong anti-British feeling resulting from RAF raids on targets such as the Renault auto works in Paris. To avoid such reaction to AAF bombing, on 6 October 1942 a special broadcast to France was made on "America Calling Europe," warning the French that though the United States had "only the greatest sympathy" toward them, "all factories in France that are working for Germany are susceptible to being bombarded." Because bombs dropped from high altitudes often fell short of or beyond the target, "all those who live within two kilometers of factories working for Germany are advised to move." Even with this warning, casualties from a raid on Lille dismayed Spaatz; later in the month, to avoid similar results, he gave orders to his Eighth Air Force that if their primary military target was obscured, they could not attack Paris as an alternate objective.[63] The responsibility for political matters such as bombing in occupied countries was left to the British Air Ministry, and on 29 October their office issued a restrictive bombardment policy that limited targets in occupied countries to military objectives located far away from populated areas.[64]

The 29 October directive established a double standard that would exist throughout the war, allowing far more latitude for air attacks within Germany than in occupied zones. The policy presented no problems to the RAF because they were targeting German morale and cities. In contrast, confident in their own accuracy, chafing to attack the enemy and its support structures, and seemingly unappreciative that air power had "political as well as military" effects, the Americans were not happy with the restrictions that limited attacks against lucrative targets in occupied countries.[65] Such objectives were much closer to British bases, not as heavily defended as targets in Germany, and provided better opportunities to perfect daylight-bombing techniques with less risk.

Not only the airmen were unhappy. In March 1943 Assistant Secretary

General Carl Spaatz and General Dwight Eisenhower maintained a close relationship throughout the war in Europe even though they sometimes disagreed about the proper application of American airpower. Here Spaatz and his staff brief Ike on the initial deployment of the Eighth Air Force to England in 1942. Back row, left to right: Brigadier General Ira Eaker, Brigadier General Frank Hunter, Brigadier General Robert Candee; front row, left to right: Spaatz, Eisenhower, Major General Walter Frank.

of War Lovett had to explain to Judge Patterson, undersecretary of war who often did special work for Roosevelt, why the AAF was restricted to bombing "admittedly impossible targets" at submarine bases while "the RAF accomplishes the end result by bombing out the working community."[66] The next month saw an exchange of letters between Sir Charles Portal, Britain's chief of Air Staff and the Combined Chiefs of Staff chief agent for the CBO, and Major General Eaker, now commanding the Eighth Air Force and the senior American air commander in England while Spaatz was serving as commander in chief, Northwest African Air Forces, for Eisenhower. Spurred by complaints from the Belgian ambassador to the United States, the British again tried to restrict any attacks that could result in civilian casualties near targets in occupied zones. Eaker, with additional emphasis from Arnold, stressed that although the Allies had to avoid unnecessary civilian casualties and limit objectives in occupied countries to key factors in Axis strategy, all civilians employed "willingly or otherwise" in Axis industry were assisting the enemy and should accept the risks "which must be the lot of any individual who participates directly in the war effort of a belligerent nation." This policy applied to German workers as well as to the French and showed a consistency in thought independent of political considerations. Axis employees were no longer viewed as noncombatants, an important step in the escalation to total war. Yet it must be noted that this combatant status applied only to workers in factories being bombed; the AAF strategic campaign, unlike that of the RAF, did not target any laborers in their homes.[67] Although the British seemed willing to bomb any German, anywhere, the Americans wanted to target any Axis worker in any factory supporting that war effort. However, motivated largely by Winston Churchill's concerns about the backlash from bombing of occupied areas, in this case the British seemed more concerned about civilian casualties than the Americans.

One can only speculate whether Spaatz would have been more receptive to Portal's pleas than Eaker, but when Spaatz returned to England and was named commander of the newly created USSTAF in December 1943 he continued bombing precision targets near conquered cities. Also in January 1944 Doolittle, who had commanded the Northwest African Strategic Air Force, replaced Eaker as commander of the Eighth Air Force. Spaatz and Doolittle continued to debate the British over the issue of civilian casualties in occupied countries, this time concerning the air campaign to support the impending cross-Channel invasion.

As has been related earlier, civilian advisers to the British Air Ministry had studied operations in Italy and concluded that the best support for the invasion would result from mass attacks by all available air resources to completely disrupt the transportation system in Europe. The plan was supported by Deputy Supreme Commander Air Chief Marshal Tedder and Allied Expeditionary Air Force Commander Air Chief Marshal Leigh-Mallory. Spaatz's planners developed a counterproposal to attack the German oil industry, and the USSTAF position was also eventually favored by Bomber Harris. The Transportation Plan offered greater promise of "immediate effect on the success of OVERLORD in its initial period," and Eisenhower eventually adopted it. However, the plan also threatened considerable civilian casualties and evoked severe protest from USSTAF personnel.[68]

Spaatz resisted the Transportation Plan for many reasons. Because so much unused capacity existed in the rail system, damage to French and Belgian lines would really not restrict key troop movements. From his own experience in

Italy, Spaatz knew that the destruction of choke points such as tunnels and bridges was the best method to block movement and isolate the battlefield, and Anderson wrote letters to the British to recommend this course of action. USSTAF also believed that attacking oil targets promised the quickest way to cripple the German economy and end the war and made the most efficient use of strategic bombers. However, Spaatz, especially, complained most vociferously that the Transportation Plan would "jeopardize the good will of the French and Belgian people by the resultant loss of civilian lives in the attack of rail centers in populated areas and all for a very slight effect." This sentiment was shared by Churchill, who also worked hard to resist the plan and who succeeded in delaying its implementation for a while.[69]

Americans were completely left out of the planning and target selection for the Allied Expeditionary Air Force transportation attacks, and the USSTAF director of plans, Brigadier General Charles Cabell, believed that this was all part of a scheme by the British "to have some of the odium" for area bombing and indiscriminate air attacks shared by the United States. He and Spaatz feared that bombing the French might even jeopardize their support, needed for the invasion. The two airmen sent letters to Eisenhower and cables to the Joint Chiefs of Staff for "fact-finders" to ensure that the US government would "not accept any responsibility for that loss of friendly civilian lives, except with the best of knowledge as to its extent, with full understanding of its implications, and without any illusions as to the gain to be expected from it." When Spaatz's pleas were ignored and Eisenhower overrode any objections, the USSTAF commander did what he could to limit civilian casualties. He emphasized "very strongly" to his subordinate commanders that there was "great need for care in all operations against French targets." He directed that "the best lead bombardiers would be used, no indiscriminate bombing would be permitted, no H2X [radar] bombing permitted, and crews must be impressed with the need for air discipline in order to avoid needless killing of French personnel."[70] Through his efforts, civilian casualties were considerably reduced. Although the Americans may have accepted the killing of some French noncombatants in attacks on individual military and industrial targets of strategic worth, widespread attacks on transportation in occupied zones with vague objectives were not worth the ethical and political costs. Similar inter-Allied disputes would arise over Balkan targets as well, which will be discussed later in the book. Civilians in occupied zones appreciated Allied efforts to free them from Germans who claimed they were defending those areas, but understandably the civilians did not like suffering from errant bombs and bombing. The most notorious early terror raid of World War II was the German bombing of Rotterdam in May 1940 that killed an estimated 900 Dutch citizens in the center of the city. They were among the first of between 8,000 and 10,000 to die from air attacks in the Netherlands, ironically most from Allied attacks on Nazi targets. A prayer often recited there could have been said in France, Belgium, Norway, and many other countries throughout Europe, by any civilians enduring Allied bombing and German oppression: "Lord, please liberate us from our protectors, and protect us from our liberators."[71]

The attitudes of American leaders toward the bombing of urban areas were affected to varying degrees by concerns for ethics, efficiency, and public relations. Perhaps the best summary of a collective AAF approach appears in a letter titled "Suggested Reply to Letter Questioning Humanitarian Aspects of Air Force," composed in response to the letter from a concerned mother to the AAF commander (see appendix). It is impossible to determine who wrote the reply (it was probably composed by Lawrence Kuter on Arnold's staff), but it had traveled from Arnold to Spaatz to Anderson and been reviewed by each man. The letter combined the themes of public relations, ethics, and efficiency stressed by those leaders. It began by emphasizing that air warfare differs from more traditional forms only in its massive potential for destruction. "Law cannot limit what physics makes possible. We can depend for moderation only upon reason and humane instincts when we exercise such a power." It pointed out, however, that "the precision which is the keynote of America" was more efficient than terror bombing and at the same time more humane. By allowing reason and humanity to curb the "bestial instincts" released by "the awful weapon at our disposal," the AAF showed "that humanity pays and that Air Power is the most powerful urge for peace."[72]

None of these leaders professed to be moralists, yet all of them wrestled with the dilemmas resulting from good ends and bad means. They tried to strike a balance between the extreme views that war legitimizes all means or that suffering and death are absolute evils that can never be justified. Most of these men professed to be in favor of limiting "unnecessary" casualties and destruction, but they held different opinions as to what that qualification entailed. As the distinguished British historian Michael Howard has noted, "Those responsible for the conduct of state affairs see their first duty as being to ensure that their state survives; that it retains its power to protect its members and provide for them the conditions of a good life." When in doubt, leaders tended to do what was best to win the war and protect American citizens, whether those citizens were factory workers or bomber pilots.[73]

5. ATTITUDES AND PERCEPTIONS OF AMERICAN AIRMEN

> War shall yet be, and to the end;
>   But war-paint shows the streaks of weather;
> War yet shall be, but warriors
> Are now but operatives; War's made
>   Less grand than Peace,
>   And a singe runs through lace and feather.
>   —Herman Melville[1]

The more mechanical become the weapons with which we fight, the less mechanical must be the spirit which controls them.

                         —Major General J. F. C. Fuller[2]

In his influential work Men against Fire, S. L. A. Marshall wrote that "war is always an equation of men and machines. Efficiency comes of a proper balancing of the equation." There are limits, however, "to the uses of the machine in war," and ultimately its effectiveness depends on "the efficiency, intelligence, and courage of the relatively few men who must take the final risks of battle."[3] Many observers, though, would agree with Herman Melville that the technology of modern war has reduced the importance of soldierly qualities and produced an impersonal combat with no sense of humanity. One scholar argues that American airmen "were technicians and professionals who happened to be waging war" and that few saw themselves as warriors. They possessed an elite status and image, they were most concerned with mastering technique, and "their consuming goal" was completing their quota of missions. Their existence on the ground and in the air "created a curious sense of unreality and alienation" that also contributed to their sense of detachment from both the enemy and the real effects of AAF bombs. Other writers, however, acknowledge the risks airmen accepted and

85

lived with: "The constant presence of death was bound to affect the way air officers felt about killing people of enemy nations." Accordingly, airmen were fatalistic and hardened to losses, whether their own or the enemy's.[4]

The AAF did get preferential treatment at induction centers, especially earlier in the war, ensuring that their recruits generally scored higher on the Army general-classification test and mechanical-aptitude test than those soldiers sent to other branches. These test results were used along with more evaluations to classify candidates further into categories such as ground crew or aircrew. Standards for officers' positions such as pilots, bombardiers, and navigators were even more stringent. This process did reinforce a sense of the superiority of the AAF over branches such as the infantry, though the actual quality of air recruits diminished as the war went on because of the large numbers of men required by the expanded AAF. The airmen's perception of their elite status was also shaped by the greater proportion of officers and higher ratings of enlisted men who flew as well as by the recognition from the press and the general public of the courage and contributions of combat flyers.[5]

Yet the basic differences between infantrymen and airmen were environmental, not genetic. Most "grunts" of World War II would not have claimed to be warriors and were most concerned with completing a disagreeable job and going home; moreover, their attitudes about noncombatants were similar to those of the airmen. American servicemen tended to be much harsher with civilians of Axis nationalities than with those citizens of occupied areas, though soldiers and airmen usually found it hard to stomach the sight of any dead civilian. To maintain their sanity, infantrymen often rationalized such casualties by blaming enemy artillery. Aircrews rarely had to view dead or wounded enemy civilians, but many fliers would have agreed with a former World War II bomber pilot, later a Tulane professor, who claimed, "I don't believe that I could have faced seeing people killed close up." Airmen who returned from the first great fire raid on Tokyo and who had observed from low level the carnage they caused "handed in their reports with hands that shook, with shock and horror still reflected in their eyes."[6] Despite such reactions, B-29 crews carried out more incendiary raids because the airmen were convinced that such attacks were the only way to destroy strategic objectives and end the war quickly.

Although airmen did not face the constant exposure to danger experienced by frontline infantrymen, air combat was particularly intense, especially in Europe. On missions an aircrew was more concerned with survival than with technique; they fought many enemies. Aerial combat has been

Flak hits could be catastrophic. This unlucky B-17 had its nose shot off just after completing its bomb run on a target near Budapest, Hungary. Accompanying aircraft watched helplessly as it crashed and counted only five parachutes from its ten-man crew.

called "the most frightening warfare of all" because in the "unnatural habitat" of the air, one is "marooned aloft in an aluminum capsule" and cannot run or hide. Enemy fighters closed in to attack at speeds of up to ten miles per minute to deliver cannon fire, rockets, or bomblets. On the most widely used B-17, the G model, almost everyone except the pilots also served as machine gunners. In addition to enemy fighters, antiaircraft fire (flak) was a deadly threat; on deep-penetration missions it could last up to four hours.[7] During May and June 1944 almost 8,000 American aircraft were damaged and 300 more destroyed by flak alone. Crewmen who operated in a sitting position usually sat on one protective flak suit and draped another over their lap, "for the ultimate in physical and psychological protection." Not surprisingly, flak was a greater source of aircrew anxiety than enemy fighters, which could be shot down or outmaneuvered.[8] Weather and the elements also had to be endured. At bombing height, temperatures in B-17s and B-24s sometimes reached fifty degrees below zero, and even for airmen wearing heated clothing, severe frostbite claimed many casualties. Oxygen masks could freeze up as well. One bombardier wrote to his parents about his concerns regarding being wounded at high altitudes: "The pressure inside your body is so much greater than outside that you bleed profusely." Crewmen also worried about mechanical failures of their aircraft or human failures from fatigue.[9]

These factors affected bombing accuracy, focusing the airmen's attention on the airspace around them and not necessarily on the target. Commanders found, however, that the best way to bolster morale when the crew returned to base after the mission was to produce immediate photographic results of their attack to show the worth of the hell they had just been through. Personnel reporting to the Eighth Air Force in spring 1943 were told that B-17 and B-24 aircrews completed only an average of five and a half missions. A study done for Spaatz in early 1944 indicated that of 1,000 airmen assigned to the Eighth Air Force, only 216 could be expected to finish twenty-five missions. This figure may have been optimistic; data from the Office of the Air Surgeon for the European theater during the first half of 1944 revealed that AAF battle-casualty rates for heavy-bomber crews were 712 killed or missing and 175 wounded out of each 1,000 men who served for six months. This 89 percent casualty figure matches the finding of William Fili, a B-24 crewman in Europe, that only twenty-seven of the 250 men in his July 1943 gunnery class completed their quota of missions. The average airman's prayers consisted of a simple, constant repetition of the words, "Please God, I don't want to die."[10]

Because of the high casualty rate, American airmen in the European theater were critical of missions they believed were wasteful or that entailed risks beyond the perceived worth of the target. Indiscriminate attacks on cities with no clear objectives also violated the precision-bombing doctrine airmen had been taught. They especially criticized the long and dangerous raids on Berlin. Typical complaints in a June 1944 survey were that the city "is not a military target" and that it was bombed mainly for "headlines," and "I don't believe in spite bombing." Almost three quarters of veteran flyers stated they "occasionally" or "quite often" had gone on missions "not worth the cost."[11] Nor did airmen like humanitarian gestures that raised their risks, such as General Doolittle's April 1945 warning to workers at the Skoda works in Czechoslovakia of an impending raid in order to reduce civilian casualties. Although depleted defenses offered no resistance to the planes that dropped 500 tons of bombs on the factories, the disgruntled aircrews felt that their leaders had exercised "greater concern for the safety of civilian workers than their own."[12]

Combat conditions were not as severe in the Pacific. Only four of the crewmen on B-29s were gunners, and they fired their weapons by remote control. The rest of the eleven-man crew could concentrate on their own particular technical tasks. For the fire raids in 1945 LeMay even stripped out all the weapons and ammunition except that for the tail guns to allow a heavier bomb load. By that time the Japanese air force was no longer a threat, and antiaircraft fire over Japan never reached European intensities. Moreover, most of the long flight from bases in the Marianas to Japan, sometimes as long as eight hours one way, was over undefended waters. The B-29 also had a pressurized and heated interior lacking on other bombers, considerably increasing the crew's comfort.

On the other hand, the plane had been rushed into action before it was fully perfected, resulting in many technical problems, especially engine fires. The accident rate for the very heavy bombers was much higher than the AAF average. One pilot mused, "Sometimes we wondered whether the battle was with the Japanese or the B-29." As another result of the rush to get the bombers into combat, too few planes were available for training. Crews often did not get enough time flying the aircraft in the United States before deploying overseas and thus had to finish training on combat missions. An additional problem on the long flights to Japan was fatigue. A mission from initial briefing to final debriefing usually lasted twenty-four hours. Despite the liberal use of coffee and even amphetamines, some aircraft actually crashed because exhausted crews fell asleep. With fewer distractions from enemies and harsh cold and with much longer missions, airmen in the Pacific could have considered themselves as technicians more than as warriors, focusing on the mechanical problems of flying their aircraft and delivering their bomb load.[13] Though they witnessed the nightly conflagrations they caused, they might not have sensed what bombing cities really entailed; unlike airmen in England they could not go on pass and observe the results of the Blitz or of V-weapons firsthand or talk to air-raid victims.[14]

Unfortunately, few diaries or memoirs to verify these impressions were left behind by the crews who carried out the fire raids. Many reasons are possible for this scarcity of sources. The incendiary campaign was relatively short, lasting less than five months. In contrast, the American daylight-bombing offensive over Europe lasted almost three years. Possibly the shorter Pacific air campaign, with its more boring missions, did not provide the material or the inspiration for published memoirs, or perhaps B-29 crews were indeed aloof technicians and therefore less likely to express their feelings in writing. Another factor could have been the B-29 itself. Different crews often shared the same aircraft, and few airmen seem to have felt close to an airplane with so many technical problems. The best explanation, however, may be that the crews who carried out the fire raids did not want to remember them or had little pride in the destruction of Japanese cities and the deaths of Japanese civilians their bombs caused. LeMay wrote extensively about his recollections, but he never seemed to be bothered by the results of his campaign. On the other hand, Wilbur H. Morrison, another veteran of the Twentieth Air Force who has written about its experiences, relates that crews often watched the holocausts they had created "in utter horror."[15] The emphasis in LeMay's after-action reports that the object of the incendiary attacks "was not to bomb indiscriminately civilian populations" but to destroy "industrial and strategic targets" might have been intended to ease the troubled consciences of airmen sickened by the stench of death lingering in their planes.[16]

OTHER INFLUENCES ON ATTITUDES TOWARD BOMBING CIVILIANS

Just as varying factors of combat and technology in each theater could influence airmen's attitudes toward bombing civilians, so too could their individual training and position. Diaries and memoirs from the European air war support the contention that crew members' positions in the air were a primary factor in determining individual attitudes toward what happened when bombs hit the ground. The officers on the bombers in particular—pilots, bombardiers, and navigators—underwent considerably different training.

For example, when as a captain F. L. Anderson set up the curriculum for his bombardier school, he ensured that students received eleven hours of instruction on military law and the laws of war as well as classes on national policy and current events.[17] Technical training focused on targeting and accuracy; students practiced bombing day and night in order to achieve the average miss distance of 230 feet necessary for graduation. With this training and their responsibilities in combat, bombardiers seem to have been the crew members most concerned about the effects of indiscriminate bombing. This preoccupation was undoubtedly reinforced by the detailed bombardier briefing form required to be filled out after each mission, which described every aspect of bomb delivery. One man was able to keep his sanity only by following his chaplain's advice to "keep it impersonal" and not to focus on what happened on the ground. He rationalized that he was doing his best to hit military targets, helping to shorten the war and save lives in the long run. Yet he was still troubled throughout his tour by recurrent thoughts of an incident in which he had almost hit a city amphitheater with an errant bomb. Despite pleas from his nervous pilots, another lead bombardier took his wayward formation over most of Berlin through heavy flak to hit railroad yards when their primary target was obscured instead of dropping his bomb load onto a convenient built-up area of the city.[18]

On the other hand, the pilots who commanded the bombers concentrated most on what happened in the air. Fatigue, fear, and concern for their crew could wear pilots down quickly. In Lord Moran's classic study, *The Anatomy of Courage*, he found that more pilots broke from mental strain in Bomber Command than in any other section of the RAF.[19] The 1949 movie *Twelve O'Clock High* illustrates how the pressures and responsibilities of command could cause a nervous breakdown in the toughest air officer if he really cared about his men. John Muirhead, a B-17 pilot in the Fifteenth Air Force, saw many of his friends display the gaunt signs of fatigue or become comatose with the "clanks," their term for stress casualties. Muirhead tried to shield himself by ensuring that he did not know his crew or any other airmen. Psychiatric studies found that the loss of friends in aerial combat was the second most important source of stress (enemy activity was first), and Muirhead reasoned, "If I didn't know them, I would not grieve." Actor Jimmy Stewart, who rose to be chief of staff for an air wing after commanding a B-24 squadron, and who even flew a combat mission in Vietnam as a brigadier general in the Air Force Reserves, said in an interview that World War II airmen never talked about their odds of survival. "We all prayed a lot, though," he admitted. "I didn't pray for myself. I just prayed I wouldn't make a mistake" that could cost the lives of his crew. He thought about civilians on the ground, but he also remembered the defenseless civilians the Germans had been bombing throughout the war. Stewart won the first of his two Distinguished Flying Crosses for holding his formation together during a tough bombing run against Brunswick during the big attacks of February 1944. Later he lost some of his men during one of the bloody missions to Berlin. Badly shaken by the experience, he spent several weeks in the hospital and served the rest of the war in important ground duties. The memoirs of pilots like Philip Ardery are full of incidents in which pilot errors destroyed aircraft and crews. Haunted by the possibility of error, pilots did not seem concerned so much with the target they were attacking or with where bombs fell as with bringing their plane and crew back in one piece.[20] The best reason to hit a target right the first time, especially the tough ones, was to ensure it would not have to be attacked again.

Copilots shared the pilots' burdens. Locked into uncomfortable postures on long flights, they suffered physical and mental stress along with the pilots.

Squadron Commander Jimmy Stewart after receiving the French Croix de Guerre with Palm. Typical of pilots and leaders, Stewart worried about making a mistake that could harm the airmen under his command. (Northwest and Whitman College Archival Collections, Penrose Memorial Library, Whitman College, Walla Walla, WA)

Other crewmen could move around, but the pilot and copilot had to stay at the controls. They often had to switch positions during flight, especially while maneuvering into tight formations where the effects of vertigo could quickly interfere with the ability to coordinate controls properly. Most British bombers did not have copilots after 1942, increasing the psychological stress on their pilots even more.[21] Copilots lacked the overall command duties of pilots, but they felt responsible for their aircraft and could be especially frustrated if forced just to ride along while everyone else kept busy. Perhaps the best account of a copilot is found in *Serenade to the Big Bird* by Bert Stiles, who was killed in 1944 after transferring to fighters when he had completed thirty-five bomber missions in Europe. After his first bombing mission, he could think only about how fatigued he was, how lousy his flying had been, and how close he was to his crew, concerns that dominate his writings. Once he did muse about the "senseless ugliness" of bombing Berlin through overcast, questioning why the AAF wanted "to knock hell out of some city with the vague hope that some day that city will be rebuilt for some people we can get along with," but in general he seemed not to care about specific targets. After the D-day landings, his primary focus was to win the war "and win in a way so there is never another one."[22]

The most self-centered and individualistic aircrew officers seem to have been navigators. They plotted courses and kept a log of events; someone else flew the plane and dropped the bombs. The memoirs of Elmer Bendiner, a navigator on the Schweinfurt raids, differ from the accounts of pilots or bombardiers and resemble the image of the technician in combat. Bendiner writes less about the rest of the crew and more about his own experiences, noting that while planes fell all around him in combat he remained detached, "scribbling in the log the time, place and altitude of flak, of rocket bursts, of kills and fallen comrades, of headings and checkpoints." Surviving to complete "the magic number of twenty-five" missions was his primary goal. More cynical than most airmen, he believed that precision bombing was a "semi-fiction," but he also believed that any terror was permissible in response to German terror and that the Allies' just cause set them apart from the Axis, no matter what tactics were used. He surmised that Eighth Air Force crews would have attacked cities as did the British if trusted AAF leaders had said that in their judgment this was the best way to win the war and to get home safely. Yet like most of his comrades, he preferred "a surgical technique by which we could excise the vital organs of Nazi Germany without unnecessary bloodshed."[23]

Except for Stiles, however, in writing about their experiences these other airmen had the benefit of considerable hindsight in their judgments. A good example of a navigator's attitudes untainted by editing or rethinking can be found in the letters of Earle C. Cheek. He wrote to his girlfriend about every two weeks from March 1944 until his death near the end of the war, and his descriptions uniquely portray the European air war through a navigator's eyes. He constantly mentioned crews dying in crashes, even in training, and his consuming goal was to complete his quota of missions quickly and safely. He even arranged a transfer from the Fifteenth Air Force in the Mediterranean to the Eighth because it lowered his required missions from fifty to thirty. He showed little loyalty to any crew and was continually switching planes to get in more missions. For his thirtieth mission in April 1945, he hooked on as an extra navigator on a plane dropping supplies to British paratroops. He was killed when it was downed by ground fire.[24]

Cheek was a "technician and professional" more than he was a warrior. Trained on new radar navigational gear, he was extremely confident in its ability to see through overcast, and he eventually became a Pathfinder navigator leading missions. His letters rarely discuss the results of bombing, though "the high point of my combat tour" came when he led "the greatest raid of the war" on Berlin. When he did mention the effects of his work he emphasized precision bombing of factories, oil, and transportation. He wrote in March 1944 that "the only men who can be said to be fighting this war are the men who constantly face death," infantrymen in the front lines and "airmen flying combat missions." He changed his views, however, after meeting some infantrymen from Patton's Third Army, who had "nothing to look forward to except one action after another and living in the mud and cold. . . . They make me ashamed of any complaining I've done." Such admiration for ground troops was common among airmen. Cheek said of enemy flak and fighter attacks, "There isn't a thing you can do about it except fly through it at 30 degrees below zero with the sweat running off your face and freezing on your clothes and the exploding shells blowing the ship around like a cork in a stormy sea." Only once did he mention bombing civilians, after he had viewed bomb damage in London: "I suppose that in modern war civilians must suffer." But he rationalized what he was doing to Germany: "Civilians in countries under German occupation have endured much more than the English, of course."[25]

American doctors conducting psychiatric studies of World War II airmen found that bomber pilots, concentrating on safety and on accomplishing their missions, bore an especially heavy burden of responsibility. Researchers were surprised to find that, contrary to the image of unfeeling technicians indiscriminately dropping high explosives, heavy-bomber crews could not "tolerate well the guilt of killing" even though victims were "remote, almost abstract." Although fighter pilots who strafed ground targets were seldom affected by concerns for the casualties they caused, studies discovered that "many a bombardier tosses in his bunk at night to think what his bombs may have done to the civilians miles below his plane." The increased stress on bomber crews was alleviated somewhat by the "banding together" of combat crews and their reliance on each other, almost like the closeness of a family. The pilot was seen as a father figure and other crewmen as brothers, a feeling of camaraderie and teamwork that usually took between five and ten missions to develop. This process was especially evident in the Eighth Air Force, where command policies encouraged the consistent use of standard crews, and by the summer of 1944 it had received enough personnel to reach its authorized strength of two crews per aircraft. The Fifteenth Air Force had different practices and often seemed to expect airmen to perform like interchangeable parts as they were shifted between planes. The rationale for such actions may have been to lessen the effects on morale of death and wounds in close crews, but it was also a result of necessity because the Fifteenth not only had a higher casualty rate at that time but also had only one and a half crews assigned per plane. Thus it could not rotate complete teams and instead had to mix and match. The result was to increase the number of psychoneurotic casualties from stress. Flyers in the Fifteenth retained the peculiar burdens and attitudes of their positions on the crew without being able to rely on the strong bonds of comradeship existing among the members of a well-established combat team. Many Eighth Air Force airmen identified so much with their crew that they suffered more fear and tension "when they are on the ground and their crew is flying without them on a combat mission than when they are flying."[26]

AAF leaders became especially concerned about the morale of Eighth Air Force bomber crews after Doolittle's decision to release his fighters from strict escort duties and losses forced Spaatz to extend combat tours and even bring some crews back who had completed their quota. The battle for air supremacy between January and May 1944 cost USSTAF 2,351 heavy bombers in combat, and another 254 from accidents and unrepairable battle damage. In the summer of 1944 the number of crews and aircraft interned because of landing in neutral counties more than doubled over previous months, with eighteen in May, thirty-eight in June, and forty-one in July. B-24s from the 2nd Bombardment Division, most likely to be assigned deep missions because of their longer range than the B-17s, were most prone to get interned. Those statistics alarmed Arnold, as did the results of interviews with crews in Sweden conducted by US diplomatic personnel. Spaatz defended his airman in a heated exchange of messages with the AAF Commanding General, who eventually sent Lieutenant Colonel James W. Wilson to the United Kingdom to investigate the situation in August. He had instructions to determine if there was truly a "deterioration of combat crew morale." His report in September, based on over a thousand interviews with crew members, and the findings of a group of carefully selected USSTAF officers sent to Sweden and Switzerland to interview interned airmen, convinced Arnold and Spaatz that morale problems were exaggerated. Wilson concluded, "Not only were the airmen confident of their airplanes, their methods, and themselves, but they felt sure they were doing more to win the war than either the ground forces or the RAF." The internment controversy soon ended as the Allied advance in France, and later the Soviet move to the eastern borders of Germany, provided better safe havens for damaged aircraft seeking to land. Losses also declined, and personnel rotation policies relaxed a bit. Perhaps the most important reason for better morale was that all the previous sacrifice now appeared to be bearing fruit as Allied forces drove deep into Europe and prepared to destroy the Reich.[27]

Although more study of the attitudes of aircrews is warranted, my research indicates that navigators cared most about technique and finishing their mission quota, pilots about bringing their crews home safely, and bombardiers about accurate bombing. Like the American public, airmen in Europe probably would have tolerated bombing cities indiscriminately if they had thought it was necessary, but they believed in the precision doctrine that so many had died to prove. Some units even instituted lecture programs to reinforce the commitment to AAF doctrine.[28] If the leaders in Europe and in the Pacific had been more alike and if conditions in the two theaters had been similar, there would have been American fire raids on Germany. However, such similarities did not exist, and those intentionally indiscriminate and widespread attacks on enemy civilians did not occur.

One difference in attitude between the two theaters, however, disturbed American leaders: the feelings of AAF airmen about the enemy. Bombardment crews in Europe did not seem to hate the Germans enough; reports in Franklin Delano Roosevelt's files complained that US flyers had "no particular hatred of Germans." Surveys showed that almost three-quarters of heavy-bomber crews harbored no vindictiveness toward the German people and wanted only to punish their leaders. This feeling matched the attitude Stimson had complimented in Marshall. A commander wrote in an after-action

report, "Like every American who flies to Europe for combat duty, I regret-
ted my failure to get the desired crack at the Jap. I failed to possess any real
enmity toward Jerry and sensed a certain repulsion to European bombings
where non-combatant Axis life might be involved." He claimed that he soon
learned to hate the Hun, but others did not. Stiles wrote that he felt fighters
and flak were just "shooting at whole formations. There's nothing personal
in it."[29] Psychological studies of the Eighth Air Force during its first year of
operation revealed that only 29 percent of successful combat airmen had
any personal hatred for the enemy, including the desire to kill enemy fighter
pilots, and even then, "not always, but at least when they are in the air!"[30]

It was much easier to hate the enemy in the Pacific theater. Racism
played a part, as did the sneak attack on Pearl Harbor and reports of Japanese atrocities. Perhaps hatred would have been more intense in Europe
if more had been known about the concentration camps. When briefed on
the Malmedy massacre, Roosevelt said, "Well, it will only serve to make our
troops feel towards the Germans as they already have learned to feel about
the Japs." Airmen, however, again reflected the attitudes of society. Public
hatred was directed at Hitler and Mussolini rather than at their subjects, but
it was aimed against the Japanese people as well as the emperor. Ground
troops echoed public opinion too; officers and enlisted men in all theaters
expressed considerably more vindictiveness toward Japanese citizens. AAF
feelings toward the Germans were more a product of the home front than a
result of the aloofness of technicians. Such attitudes were reinforced by respect for enemy soldiers who seemed to be fighting hard but cleanly and who
treated AAF prisoners of war rather well, in accordance with the Geneva and
Hague conventions.[31]

LEADERS' PERCEPTIONS OF AIRMEN

AAF leaders realized that the attitudes of their airmen reflected those of society, but they perceived the public as abhorrent to any indiscriminate bombardment and supportive of precision doctrine. As with AAF press releases,
official AAF publications proclaimed a commitment to precision bombing
and also demonstrated its effectiveness. Probably the best source to illustrate
the perceptions of their soldiers that AAF leaders in Washington held and
to cover the course of the airman's war from combat photography is *Impact*
magazine. Assistant Secretary of War Lovett saw the publication as a way
to keep units informed of current developments, and General Arnold en-

dorsed it as a means to spread "knowledge of the technique and accomplishments of your fellow members of the AAF" and to provide "information of the enemies you are fighting." Arnold thought that photographs were the easiest form of information to absorb, and hence his emphasis on combat photography for newsreels and for filling 90 percent of *Impact.* With the assistance of Henry Luce, Lovett found some veteran *Life* editors to run the classified magazine, which was distributed by the assistant chief of Air Staff for intelligence to intelligence officers at AAF units around the world.[32]

Impact highlighted the effectiveness of precision-bombing doctrine; the text reflected Arnold's views by emphasizing efficiency and public relations, not ethics. "Expensive planes and highly skilled personnel" had to be used to attack the enemy's ability to wage war directly instead of being dissipated against area targets such as residential districts, "which are relatively unimportant from a military standpoint." An article touting the accuracy of Doolittle's bombing of Rome displayed the maps designating religious centers to be avoided, boasting, "It was a test of what our bombers could miss as well as what they could hit because of the crocodile tears Axis propagandists would be sure to shed if we had hit any religious edifice." Another article showed the military targets hit by the Doolittle raid on Tokyo to justify the "universal rage" over the execution of airmen captured on that mission. The avoidance of outright ethical statements might have been the result of the AAF's desire not to appear critical of the RAF. When British area bombing of cities was discussed, *Impact* emphasized that they "didn't invent [it,] nor did they start it. But it certainly taught the boys who did start it that they never belonged in the big leagues." By the end of the war, the magazine claimed that with British improvements in training, equipment, and tactics, the RAF night-bombing technique had become so accurate that it "no longer could correctly be called area bombing."[33]

From the editorial themes emphasized in *Impact*, one can deduce which beliefs and practices AAF leaders in Washington had decided needed reinforcement in the field. Americans have traditionally favored a strategy of annihilation and direct assault over indirect or partial approaches, and airmen seemed distrustful of any tactic that detracted from visually observed precision attacks on important military targets. The accuracy of radar-directed attacks through overcast was often touted with magazine captions such as "Radar Performed Miracles." The use of leaflets instead of bombs was explained at great length in articles supporting "psychological bombing." One article boasted that 77 percent of German prisoners captured in France "either carried leaflets in their pockets or had used them to surrender" (some units also used their lecture program to justify such tactics). Raids involving religious shrines were carefully explained as well. Besides the famous bombing of Rome, a raid on Florence was used to illustrate "the effort that is made to avoid hitting structures of historical or cultural interest." When the Mediterranean Allied Air Forces "yielded to the military necessity of bombing German troops from the famous Abbey at Monte Cassino," an article justified the action by explaining in detail that exploding ammunition and fleeing Germans demonstrated "that this was indeed a military installation."[34]

Impact mounted an especially intensive campaign to explain and support the fire raids on Japan. Coverage of the first such attack, on Tokyo the night of 9 March, was preceded by eighteen pages of articles describing Japan's economy and society, emphasizing that weather limited precision bombing and that concentrated industries and workers were more vulnerable to saturation raids. The proliferation of home industries, "small, feudal-type" family workshops creating "sub-contracting area complexes," necessitated area bombing to reinforce precision attacks by "interrupting the flow of components into final assembly." A common theme was that the fire raids were "destroying Japan's big industrial areas." Later issues of the magazine added that the low-level night raids were also safer for B-29 crews. When burned-out areas were shown, the destruction of individual factories was emphasized. One article pointed out 111 "small and medium-sized plants" ruined in one small area of Tokyo. In the summary of the campaign, *Impact* acknowledged that the objectives of incendiary attacks "were basically the same as those of British area bombing," but they were necessary to save lives and end the war. The fire raids were also legitimized as consistent with American practice and as increasing the effectiveness of precision attacks. Airmen were reminded that area bombing and precision bombing were both types of strategic bombing and were told, "Against Germany, the American doctrine was pinpoint precision bombing against key factories in key target areas. Against Japan, the American doctrine is the same plus the complementary incendiary program." Significantly, although the fire raids dominated actual B-29 operations during the last months of the war, precision attacks on Japan continued to receive equal coverage in the pages of *Impact*.[35]

The editors of *Impact* and the military bosses who approved their work obviously had an image of American airmen consistent with their view of the American public. Airmen were seen to support the precision doctrine taught in service schools and emphasized in unit lectures. Area bombing that did not concentrate on important targets and methods to bomb through overcast or at night when targets could not be clearly seen were suspect. Additionally,

AAF leaders perceived that airmen would not tolerate the indiscriminate bombardment of civilians or the destruction of targets with historical or religious significance—hence the lengthy explanations about Tokyo and Cassino, and even the justification and defense of RAF area bombing.

The view from Washington was partially correct. Airmen in general did believe in and support precision doctrine, and diversions from that accepted approach were suspect. General Doolittle confirmed that the morale of his personnel was adversely affected "by having to do a lot of things that they feel are not basically sound," such as using strategic bombers to attack tactical targets or bombing through overcast.[36] However, though many airmen had misgivings about bombing civilians and shrines, protecting their crews and winning the war were also important. When Doolittle said he would excuse any of his Catholic airmen from the mission to Rome who could not in good conscience bomb their Holy City, not one accepted his offer. Peer pressure, as well as confidence in the accuracy of precision bombing, was undoubtedly a factor, but the majority of those airmen concerned probably believed that their duty to their crews and the desire to gain the quickest possible victory outweighed any considerations of accidental damage to religious buildings.[37] Most Americans were not as callous as the officer who wrote after Cassino, "If the enemy intends to use Italian cities as fortresses, we should feel no qualms in using our Air Force to level them thereby saving countless lives."[38] Most airmen did feel qualms at one time or another, but they were convinced that their actions were the best means for winning the war and saving American lives, on the ground and in the air. And they believed that their bombing methods were the most efficient, and humane, possible.

6. THE LURE OF TECHNOLOGICAL INNOVATION: BOMBING AIDS

> We are becoming increasingly aware of our inability to achieve accurate bombing on some of our top priority targets. Leuna and Politz are two examples. When the weather is good, these are covered by a smoke screen which effectively obscures the target for visual bombing. . . . Our air war is becoming a radar war.
>
> —*Lieutenant General Carl Spaatz*[1]

Even during World War I, technology was perceived as the solution to the stalemate of trench warfare. Poison gas, heavy artillery, and tanks were developed and used in attempts to restore maneuver to the battlefield and bring victory. The airplane, too, was seen as a means to avoid such costly land warfare; thus, between the wars tactics and doctrine were developed to match the promise of aerial technology. It became apparent early in combat, however, that the tactics and technology of American precision bombing would need further refinement to realize its full potential.

Many critics of precision bombing have argued that it was too inaccurate to merit that title. Even Lieutenant General Spaatz agreed privately in 1944 that USSTAF precision had meaning "in a relative not a literal sense"; but that did not stop him from striving for the continuing development of bombs and bombsights and the training of bombardiers to achieve "pickle barrel" accuracy in all weather. General Arnold pushed his commanders by telling them, "Efficiency in winning the war is our goal, and, in bombing, efficiency and precision are synonymous." AAF equipment was capable of "precision beyond the fondest dreams of a few years ago," but this potential could not be realized without "tactics and techniques to match the equipment." The result of this combination would be increased accuracy, meaning more bombs on target, "one mission per vital target instead of two or three," and an "actual saving in lives and effort."[2]

Early in the war, improvements in bombing accuracy were mainly the result of improved tactics and techniques, not of technological innovation. American airmen had confidence in their equipment, especially their Norden bombsights, estimated to be six to eight times more accurate than the "simpler, less precise" Mark XIV bombsights used by the RAF. Only about 5 percent of the British bombs landed within a mile of their aiming point under combat conditions early in the war, but the cocky Americans expected 90 percent to get that close and 40 percent within 500 yards.[3] They had much work to do to refine their bombing methods, however. During the first half of 1943, the Eighth Air Force put only 14 percent of their bombs within 1,000 feet of their targets. Poor visibility, fighter attacks, inexperience, poor training, flak, and camouflage led to errant attacks. The rapid increase in the number of American airmen in Britain made training aircrews and maintaining their proficiency especially difficult. Sometimes bad luck contributed: The lead bombardier might be shot down or his bombsight could malfunction. Other problems resulted from the inherent difficulty of handling large bombing formations, as following groups always bombed with less accuracy than leading groups. Varying ballistics of incendiary and high-explosive bombs also caused errors. But by 1945 diligence, experience, refined tactics, and innovative techniques eventually brought accuracy up to 44 percent of all bombs falling within 1,000 feet of the target and 73 percent within 2,000 feet.[4]

These results were even better than the goals set early in the war and probably represented as much accuracy as could be expected from well-executed formation-bombing techniques with unguided bombs under combat conditions. Normally the twelve to eighteen planes of a squadron dropped their bombs simultaneously, on the signal of the lead bombardier, a tactic with many advantages. The best bombardiers could aim for everyone; the mass bombing operation would be carried out more rapidly than individual drops, lessening exposure to flak, and the groups could retain a tight defensive formation. The bomb impacts would be as dispersed as the formation, but commanders believed that a well-disciplined group could produce a tighter bomb pattern to smother any target more efficiently than several aircraft could while bombing on their own. Sometimes to ensure hitting a target, aircrews would use an intervalometer setting of 400 feet for a normal bomb load of twelve 500-pound bombs; thus bombs were released to impact 400 feet apart on the ground, producing a string of explosions 4,400 feet long for each plane. This technique offered more chances for hitting an obscured target or for inflicting greater damage to a large objective such as a marshal-

B-24s bombing Frankfurt through flak and clouds in February 1944. The plane in the foreground has dropped its bombs with a moderate intervalometer setting; the tight bomb pattern in the center of the picture shows no spread at all.

ing yard, but it also could result in widely scattered misses. In truth, such techniques made the difference between so-called area bombing and precision attacks less distinct—even more so when one considers that because of a scarcity of radar sets, especially in the Eighth Air Force, whole bomb groups of three or four squadrons usually dropped their bombs simultaneously with the lead bombardier in nonvisual H2X missions through heavy overcast. The large bombing footprint made by thirty-six to forty aircraft with a maximum intervalometer setting could cover close to a square mile. At the other extreme, some groups routinely achieved phenomenal results. Perhaps the best performance was by an eleven-plane squadron bombing submarine pens in Wilhelmshaven that used a combination of radar and visual sightings to put 90 percent of its bombs within a fifty-foot radius of the aiming point and the rest within 150 feet. Commanders really did not expect such tight bomb patterns, but the significant improvements in bombing accuracy achieved by the AAF in Europe through training and experience between 1943 and 1945 reinforced the faith that airmen had in precision-bombing capabilities.[5]

Yet General Arnold warned his commanders not to "complacently tell ourselves that our methods and efforts have begun to reach a peak of perfection beyond which we cannot go." Jealous of the impressive tonnage dropped on Germany by Bomber Command, he began very early to push his commanders in Europe to find ways to increase their number of missions. Considering the European weather, especially in fall and winter, an increase meant that methods had to be devised to bomb through overcast.[6]

RADAR AIDS TO BOMBING

The problem of overcast was countered primarily by using various forms of radar, either to guide aircraft to targets or to allow bombardiers to see their objectives through the cloud cover. Most of the devices were developed by the British to assist in their night area attacks. Navigational aids came first. GEE appeared in 1941, a system by which a navigator could determine his position by calculating the time it took to receive pulse signals from three different ground stations in Britain. German jamming negated its usefulness by late 1942, and it was replaced by OBOE, a radar pulse sounding like that musical instrument. Variations from course caused recognizable changes in the pulse; a second signal then told the bombardier when to release his bombs. These systems were limited in range, however, because of the curvature of the earth.[7] For deep-penetration missions, the Americans had to rely on radar scanners that could be carried in their aircraft to present a picture of the ground below.

Spaatz and Major General Ira Eaker had begun experiments to circumvent overcast conditions in late 1942 but became frustrated by limitations in GEE and OBOE. By March 1943 the Eighth Air Force had turned to H2S, "a self-contained radar device transmitting a beam which scanned the ground below and provided a map-like picture of the terrain on its cathode ray tube indicator." Eaker boasted to the Joint Chiefs of Staff that with these new devices the notorious English weather "would actually become an aid rather than a hindrance" because it would enable Allied bombers to exploit conditions that severely hampered enemy defenses. Much of this enthusiasm was fueled by optimistic reports on H2S from military attaches in London. American versions of this device were called H2X; by fall 1943, enough were available to mount the first major raids to test the radar's effectiveness. Considering the continuing focus on eliminating capacity, as well as some signal successes, it is unfair, as Ronald Schaffer and Richard Davis have, to call the use of these nonvisual bombing methods "tantamount to urban area attacks," but USSTAF planners did recognize that these techniques involved some compromise with precision tactics. Targets had to be carefully selected. At first leaders picked objectives in city areas on coastlines or estuaries because of the verifiable distinction between water and land on radar screens. This technique allowed a large increase in raids during the testing period in late 1943 and early 1944 and thereby relieved much of the intense pressure Arnold applied for maximum bombing.[8]

The first H2X mission on Wilhelmshaven in October 1943 proved a resounding success, and in December the Eighth Air Force announced in a press release the "development of a new day bombardment technique employing latest scientific devices enabling bombing through solid cloud cover. . . . While accuracy is not equal to that usually attained in high altitude attacks when the target can be seen, . . . accuracy is satisfactory and gives promise of improvement. . . . The new technique is regarded as a logical outgrowth of American bombardment doctrine made possible by scientific advances and does not involve any basic change in the American conception of bombardment."[9] Presumably a public that seldom questioned such military pronouncements accepted this position, but the release also seemed to be an accurate representation of Eighth Air Force beliefs.

Arnold, however, was not initially convinced of the effectiveness of such techniques. His staff advised him that radar bombing had not been tested thoroughly and that much training and experimentation were still needed. Ever mindful of the AAF image, Arnold particularly feared that the term "blind bombing" then in use would create the wrong impression, and he directed the Eighth Air Force to drop that phrase. Press censors in Europe had already begun stopping any news items implying deviations from precision bombing, ostensibly to keep the Germans from finding out that the Allies had new bombing equipment. When Brigadier General Curtis LeMay, who had led the pioneering raids, came to the United States on a public relations tour, he was prohibited from even mentioning overcast bombing.[10]

Eaker, then commanding the Eighth Air Force, was especially enthusiastic about the nonvisual attacks. Never as committed to the idea of precision-bombing doctrine as Spaatz, he saw great possibilities for H2X and worked hard to persuade Arnold of the rightness of his views. Coast ports were easy to recognize, and destroying them through overcast would lower enemy morale and force the Luftwaffe out to defend them. He broadly justified his assaults on lower-priority targets: "The material destruction by these overcast attacks in workmen's homes and in harbor facilities and allied war industries is considerable and is certainly alone worth the effort." At this point in the development of radar bombing tactics and procedures, Eaker was willing to compromise precision targeting in order to keep pressure on the enemy, but through "experiment and test and trial," he was confident that eventually small point targets would also be attacked successfully using radar techniques. In correspondence to both Arnold and Lovett, Eaker emphasized the increased number of raids resulting from the ability to bomb nonvisually. This last argument in particular eventually swayed Arnold to wholehearted support of the continued development and use of such methods.[11]

The first nonvisual missions on recognizable docks and shipyards in coastal cities such as Wilhelmshaven and Kiel encouraged the believers in radar bombing and converted the doubters, but the early successes turned out to be beginner's luck. They "gave an unfounded hope of potential accuracy; and it may therefore have contributed to an unfortunate tendency to treat H2X as a rival of visual bombing rather than a supplement to it." The successes may also have helped to make the Eighth Air Force complacent about the increased rate of operations that the new equipment made possible through the winter. However, by early 1944 it was evident that new training and equipment would be necessary to achieve acceptable accuracy.[12]

DEVELOPMENTS CONTINUE

In late December 1943 Spaatz returned to Britain from the Mediterranean. A disappointed Eaker, replaced by Doolittle, was reassigned from his beloved Eighth Air Force to command all air forces in the Mediterranean, including the strategic bombers of the American Fifteenth Air Force. Along with policies concerning the bombing of civilians in occupied countries, Spaatz inherited Eaker's and Arnold's commitment and program to pursue nonvisual bombing. Initially Spaatz was enthusiastic about the performance of H2X Pathfinder aircraft in leading bombing missions, calling them "the

Beginning in 1944, Lieutenant General Carl Spaatz and Major General James Doolittle often pleaded with General H. H. Arnold for better radar equipment to replace their H2X sets, but the priority for the improved APQ-7 Eagle radar remained with the B-29s in the Pacific. Here radar operator Sergeant W. C. Yoder of the XX Bomber Command searches for targets on his Eagle scope over Omura, Japan, on 21 November 1944.

most critical need of the Strategic Air Forces." In January he successfully defeated attempts by the Combined Chiefs of Staff to force him to cut back on radar attacks before OVERLORD, arguing that it would be "wasteful" not to use radar methods if cloud cover prevented visual bombing. He admitted in a March press conference that radar attacks were primarily made on "area objectives" but stressed that they had "resulted in considerable pressure on the German Air Force, combined with the destruction of a number of his vital factories."[13] For USSTAF, area objectives meant concentrations of factories, shipyards, or marshaling yards, not residential zones hit in RAF raids. Unlike Eaker, Spaatz did not consider workers' houses suitable targets. Yet the use of less accurate nonvisual bombing techniques in urban areas resulted in an increase in the risk to civilians in targeted cities.

By April Spaatz's enthusiasm for current radar technology and tactics had begun to wane. He complained to Arnold that "the inherent accuracy and presentation of H2X equipment is not satisfactory enough for precision bombing of high priority strategic targets." Sparked by complaints from Doolittle that the radar pictures needed more detail, Spaatz asked for new radar equipment; Doolittle and Spaatz would continue such pleas until the end of the war. The new Eighth Air Force commander had little faith in radar bombing and waited for good weather instead of using nonvisual methods during his Big Week attacks in February that began the process of breaking the back of the Luftwaffe.[14]

After six months of nonvisual raids, problems were apparent with both personnel and equipment. Daily USSTAF intelligence summaries reveal that the results of most nonvisual raids remained unobserved; the same poor weather that limited accuracy and visibility also limited damage assessment. When results were readily available, they were sometimes embarrassing. On 1 April 1944 the Second Bombardment Division mistakenly bombed Schaffhausen, Switzerland, in "particularly unfavorable" weather conditions. An investigation revealed that "the advent of GEE and H2X had caused a letdown in the standard of dead-reckoning navigation because of a misconception that these aids to navigation constituted in themselves a means of navigation." After completing his training course on these radar aids, navigator Earle Cheek wrote, "There is very little error with this equipment and it makes no difference to the navigator whether the ground is visible or not." The Schaffhausen incident proved that judgment wrong. Classes were instituted throughout the Eighth Air Force to highlight each crew member's specific tasks with radar and to prevent any more decline in visual bombing skills.[15]

Meanwhile, coverage of radar bombing in *Impact* emphasized that the new methods allowed the Eighth Bomber Command to drop a record tonnage of bombs in November 1943, ordinarily a month of bad weather and few missions, and showed pictures of damage to Wilhelmshaven. Articles pointed out to airmen that the cloud cover also improved the crew's safety by providing protection from flak and fighters. The *Official Guide to the Army Air Forces*, printed for the public in spring 1944, proclaimed, "Accurate high level bombing has been accomplished through more than 25,000 feet of overcast."[16] Apparently Eaker's early enthusiasm and bomb-tonnage figures had convinced the Air Staff in Washington of the usefulness of bombing through overcast. Although Spaatz and Doolittle did not share this optimism about the strategic effectiveness of nonvisual methods, the coming of OVERLORD focused their attention on tactical applications for the new technology. Placed under the direction of General Eisenhower for the Normandy campaign, the airmen now had to consider ways to support the ground troops and the land campaign directly with heavy bombers in addition to the usual lighter tactical aircraft.

The lessons learned in trying to perfect nonvisual bombing for strategic bombers paid dividends in tactical applications and in support of the invasion. Using H2X on D-day, 1,365 Eighth Air Force bombers dropped 2,798 tons of bombs nonvisually behind the beaches thirty minutes before the landing, with more raids during the day. Concerns for safety meant that many bombs fell up to three miles inland, but the air bombardment did help the assault on Utah Beach especially and caused no friendly casualties. Effects on the morale of German troops were significant.[17] Ground forces were disappointed with the results of the bombing because a deliberate delay of several seconds in releasing bombs, ordered by Doolittle to prevent damage to assault craft, also meant that beach defenses were spared. Only later was it apparent that the heavy bombing had destroyed important minefields and rocket pits and that the damage caused behind the beaches had severely restricted the movement of reinforcements.[18]

With the troops ashore, radar bombing tactics, techniques, and procedures initially developed for the strategic air campaign soon became essential to support the ground drive across Europe. The Ninth Air Force, concerned with tactical missions, pioneered numerous advances in the use of radar to guide in air strikes, eventually using microwave early warning stations (MEWS) and SCR-584 control radars at forward director posts to lead planes to their targets. These techniques, combined with GEE and SHORAN, the latter a new directional guidance system from ground stations, enabled light and medium bombers to provide ground support even in winter weather. Because of developments in radar and tactical improvements, Ninth Air Force planes operated in support of the advancing armies for 139 days between 1 October 1944 and 9 May 1945. Accuracy increased, and friendly casualties from bombs dropped short of targets were lessened. Tactical instrument bombing, based on many of the lessons of strategic attacks, allowed increased and sustained air support for the successful Allied ground campaign.[19]

The crews of the heavy bombers, however, did not like hitting tactical targets. The men were not suited to such a role, having had training in organization, tactics, techniques, and procedures that differed from that of the light- or medium-bomber units. The heavy crews did not like bombing through overcast either. General Doolittle claimed that his airmen considered those missions "not basically sound." They wanted to get back to bombing Germany, visually observing their bombs destroying key military and industrial targets and thus shortening the war.[20] By fall 1944 the heavy bombers were released from Eisenhower's direct control and had more free-dom to hit strategic objectives. However, because of typical German fall and winter weather, nonvisual bombing remained an essential part of the USS-TAF air campaign.

Spaatz relied heavily on a team of advisers on radar bombing methods sent out by Arnold to prepare for the coming air campaign. He asked for ad-vice on the use of new beacon systems arriving in October 1944 and received details on advances in nonvisual aids used by B-29s. He pushed Doolittle to use "originality and initiative" in order "to take advantage of the fleeting opportunities for bombing during the winter season." With the German air force broken and Allied armies advancing, Spaatz wrote, "We cannot allow the advantages gained by the very successful operations during the past summer to slip out of our hands during the winter season."[21] Much of the impetus for increased radar bombing at this time came from General George C. Marshall, who visited the European theater in October 1944 to formulate plans to bring about the defeat of Germany by 1 January 1945. The chief of staff was not satisfied that the air effort was exerting full pressure in the right places, and he therefore suggested that USSTAF abandon its long-range ob-jectives in favor of an all-out effort to force an early surrender. As a result of this prodding, Doolittle, who had a strict policy prohibiting secondary or last-resort attacks on German towns or cities without identifiable military objectives, modified his directive to allow secondary overcast-bombing at-tacks on "towns and cities large enough to produce an identifiable return on the H2X scope" because they generally contained appropriate military targets. This move was a departure from USSTAF's record on avoiding indis-criminate bombardment. Spaatz and Doolittle were not pleased with their options, but they agreed that pressure had to be maintained on Germany through winter weather, and they wanted to comply with Marshall's intent to end the war as soon as possible.[22] During this period, the USSTAF staff was also working on other operations to end the war with a blow from the air that involved yet more compromise of precision doctrine. These plans will be discussed later.

RESULTS OF RADAR BOMBING

Approximately 80 percent of Eighth Air Force missions during the last quar-ter of 1944 used some type of radar bombing devices, either for navigation or targeting. Although winter raids did prevent sectors of German industry and the Luftwaffe from getting any respite, accuracy was disappointing. Analysts estimated that about 50 percent of blind missions were "near failures or worse." The Eighth Air Force Operations Analysis Section estimated that bombing under good visual conditions was six times more accurate than with GEE or with a beacon combination with H2X called Micro-H or Gee-H and 150 times more accurate than with H2X through complete overcast. Poor results stemmed from false returns from cloud static, increased crew fatigue from adverse weather conditions, and the difficulty of briefing radar missions.[23] The USSTAF staff was also concerned with the difficulty of getting any poststrike photo reconnaissance of targets after attacks because cameras, unlike radar, could not see through overcast; without good pictures, the value of attacks could not be assessed. Major General F. L. Anderson proposed using smaller formations or single aircraft, but there were too few trained crews and radar sets for that. Moreover, Doolittle complained that the bad-weather operations were producing more accidents and safety hazards. In December 1944 Spaatz again pleaded with Arnold for new and better radars, whatever the cost: "We are . . . willing to pay the high price of introduction of new and complicated apparatus because the return is proportionately high."[24]

Perhaps the Eighth Air Force's poor record was to some degree a self-fulfilling prophecy. Strategic Mediterranean Allied Air Forces bombers under Eaker, an enthusiastic supporter of nonvisual bombing from the beginning, performed more successfully during this same period under similar weather conditions. For the last three months of 1944 the percentages of Eighth Air Force bombs falling within 1,000 feet of the target were 38, 25, and 25; for the same months the Fifteenth Air Force in the Mediterranean achieved percentages of 40, 36, and 36. The latter continued with a better record throughout the war. The Eighth Air Force tried to equip two bombers in every group as H2X Pathfinders to lead blind missions; the Fifteenth assigned four each to half its groups. Not only did this distribution allow more backups in case of mechanical failures, it also allowed Fifteenth groups to split up to bomb in smaller formations with tighter bombing footprints. These specially equipped groups carried out deep attacks on Germany and flew overcast missions, and the remaining groups bombed visually closer to Italian bases—specialization that seemed to pay off in greater accuracy. Eaker also sustained pressure on the enemy with lone-wolf raids by single bombers or small groups (as Anderson had proposed) and was especially successful with attacks on oil refineries. His surprise attacks, often at night and in bad weather, "hit the refineries when they are working and more vulnerable."[25]

Eaker proclaimed his successes to USSTAF and Washington, whose attitudes he thought were too "gloomy" about radar bombing. He pointed out that during ten days of bad weather, Lieutenant General Nathan Twining's Fifteenth Air Force had shut down all synthetic oil refineries within its range. He admitted that his Pathfinder techniques were not as accurate as visual bombing; "However, enemy smoke screens are becoming increasingly effective making blind bombing attacks mandatory even in good weather." Such concealment was especially effective on a target such as an oil refinery or an important factory. Eaker gave the credit for his success to "an emphasis on training that it does not appear has been duplicated elsewhere." His commanders at all levels were "absolutely enthusiastic about this technique and their ability to do a worthwhile job employing it." Neither this training nor this faith in nonvisual techniques seemed to exist in the Eighth Air Force, with the possible exception of Curtis LeMay's Third Bombardment Division.[26]

The Army also apparently had faith in nonvisual bombing, perhaps because of Ninth Air Force successes. The ground forces also remembered the contributions of heavy bombers to the breakout from Normandy during Operation COBRA. Though Spaatz was no longer under Eisenhower's direct control, the airman preferred working with Ike to the British, and there were abundant air assets available to support Supreme Headquarters, Allied Expeditionary Forces, when called upon. Arnold also wanted to stay friendly with the ground forces so that he could count on their support in his drive for an independent service. Airmen sometimes had to restrain soldiers from calling for blind attacks on impossible targets, such as the time when General Jacob Devers demanded that Brissac and its bridge be heavily bombed, "blind or otherwise." Spaatz's deputy chief of staff had to go to the deputy supreme commander to keep the target's priority for visual bombing only. Usually, however, USSTAF supported ground demands, and Doolittle complained to Washington that he "desired better aids from radar for bombing thru the overcast at front lines. At present we are killing too many of our own men."[27]

The correspondence to Washington had some effect. Spaatz was sent a few new APQ-7 Eagle radars, but priority remained with air units assigned to bomb Japan. Lieutenant General Barney Giles, Arnold's deputy commander and chief of Air Staff, cautioned Spaatz, however, that new radars probably would not solve his problems. The Air Staff knew that the Fifteenth Air Force was performing much better than the Eighth, and Giles told Spaatz to look internally for "the cause of the large errors in your present H2X bombing." To assist in lowering the risk to ground troops in bombing near their lines, Giles suggested that Spaatz look at SHORAN, another line-of-sight beaconing system that had been tested in Italy and that had been called "the real precision blind bombing system."[28]

Spaatz accepted the advice. He soon acknowledged the superiority of SHORAN in bombing efficiency over self-contained units such as the APQ-7 Eagle. During the Korean War, the Circular Error Probable for SHORAN missions approached a remarkable 600 feet. Bombing accuracy increased significantly from February to May 1945, resulting from "improvement in weather, defeat of the German Air Force, greater exploitation of fighter escort, bombing by smaller forces, and further improvement in technique and equipment." USSTAF training improved so much that Brigadier General Lauris Norstad of the Twentieth Air Force requested that Spaatz send some radar lead crews to the Pacific to train and guide missions there.[29]

The contention that American nonvisual bombing was the equivalent of area bombing is not supported by the record of European air operations. During the early RAF night attacks on the Ruhr, less than one-tenth of British bombs fell within five miles of the aiming point. By the end of the war, the average error for the most accurate RAF raids, using OBOE, was a little over 2,000 feet; Eaker's airmen actually had a better record using only H2X. However, the key difference between the two air forces lay in their targets. RAF area attacks aimed at the center of residential districts; American H2X attacks, the most inaccurate nonvisual method, usually targeted docks or marshaling yards that operators could detect on radar scopes. There was a large difference between the RAF and the AAF both in intent and effort as to the number of civilians killed. Exceptions occurred, such as LeMay's attack on Munster and raids on Berlin, which will be discussed later, but generally the Americans consciously avoided indiscriminate nonvisual assaults that airmen considered wasteful.[30] Yet it is undeniable that USSTAF's extensive use of radar bombing was a departure from the spirit of precision bombing and implied the acceptance of greater civilian casualties to achieve strategic objectives. As the war continued, such a trend would become more evident, and the description of actual missions in chapter 3 demonstrates how much USSTAF relied on nonvisual techniques in the first quarter of 1945.

Perhaps the most important contribution of radar bombing to the war was in Ninth Air Force tactical support for ground troops, but there were significant strategic benefits as well. An assessment of Eighth Air Force operations concluded that nonvisual methods permitted many extra visual missions by guiding aircraft through overcast to targets, that these methods were fairly accurate when H2X was combined with some visibility and beacon

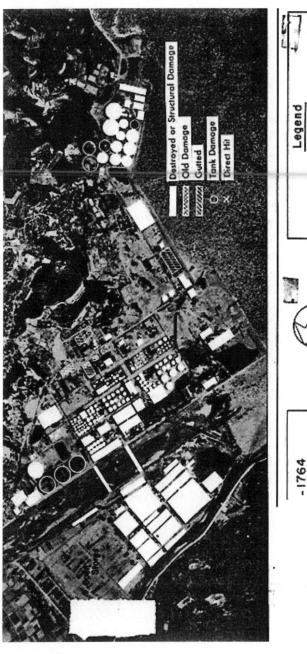

-1764

MARUZEN OIL REFINERY
Missions 245 & 255, 2 & 6-7 July 45
Damage Assessment Report 142
C.I.U. 20 Air Force
CONFIDENTIAL

Destroyed or Structural Damage

Gutted

Old Damage

○ Tank Damage

✗ Direct Hit

APPROX SCALE IN FEET
500   0   500

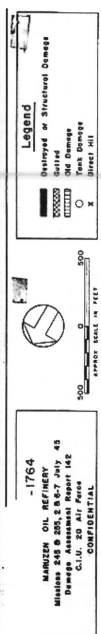

Legend

Destroyed or Structural Damage

Old Damage

Gutted

Tank Damage

Direct Hit

○

✗

This photograph for bomb-damage assessment shows the potential of perfected nonvisual bombing methods. Using Eagle radar techniques, the B-29s of the 315th Wing destroyed 95 percent of the oil refinery at Maruzen, Japan, in only two raids in July 1945.

guidance, and that the technology permitted bombing of targets through total overcast or smoke screens that would otherwise have gone unbombed. Even the poorest H2X missions against isolated oil plants like Leuna eventually produced significant results that airmen felt were worth the many wasted bombs. In addition, operating in bad weather caused severe problems for responding German fighters, which had no instruments for blind flying, no cockpit deicers, and little training for such conditions. Adolph Galland, general of the Luftwaffe fighter arm, admitted that his winter losses were "appalling." Hitler himself attributed Allied air superiority to the development and use of radar. The H2X campaign against marshaling yards did have a major impact on the German economy, especially regarding coal transportation. Developments in Europe also contributed significantly to strategic successes in the Pacific. Equipped with new Eagle radars and using special training learned from missions over Germany, the 315th Wing managed to obtain results with nonvisual bombings on Japanese oil refineries that were 98 percent as accurate as visual bombings.[31]

Yet the use of nonvisual techniques did contribute to the escalation toward total war that would culminate in the Pacific. Although Spaatz and Doolittle did not like radar bombing, they acknowledged the need for it to keep pressure on the enemy and to win the war. Accepting less accurate bombing methods also meant accepting increased risk for civilians. While in Europe the majority of American strategic air attacks were still in daylight under visual conditions, in Japan the opposite would be true. B-29 crews deployed to the Pacific were trained in night radar-bombing methods supposedly perfected in Europe, and it proved difficult to revert to daylight precision methods.[32] Eventually LeMay would devote his main effort to night fire raids on cities portrayed on radar scopes and marked by radar Pathfinders. Whereas the adoption of nonvisual bombing techniques in Europe signified that civilian casualties were a matter of decreasing concern, by the time such methods were applied against Japan, civilian casualties were of no concern at all.

7. THE LURE OF TECHNOLOGICAL INNOVATION: BETTER BOMBS

It seems to me that this whole project [APHRODITE] is put together with baling wire, chicken guts, and ignorance.

—*Lieutenant General Jimmy Doolittle*[1]

Developing better techniques for more accurate bombing was not the only way to improve bombing effectiveness. Research on better bombs with more accurate guidance or with greater destructive power was also pursued in a series of projects that would climax in World War II with the development of the atomic bomb. Except for nuclear developments, however, and to some extent incendiary bombs, these projects did not contribute significantly to the escalation to total war. Examining them in detail emphasizes the persistence of the belief in precision bombing among USSTAF leaders and how that commitment sometimes clashed with the attitudes of leaders in Washington. They also reveal much about the roots of contemporary drone programs and precision-guided munitions.

According to Ronald Schaffer, one of the programs that "appeared to conflict with the official policy against indiscriminate air attacks" was the War-Weary Bomber project, a plan involving the use of explosives-laden, worn-out aircraft as guided missiles against European targets. "AAF leaders recognized that War-Weary planes would fall on the Germans indiscriminately," but the leaders wanted to use them anyway. Indeed, only British fear of retaliation stopped the program.[2] The AAF official history acknowledges that the project was a sign that "opposition in the AAF to area bombardment had actually weakened" by early 1945.[3] These observations are generally accurate if one considers only the attitudes of leaders in Washington, but an examination of the actual testing and use of the war-wearies in Europe provides more evidence that the belief in precision bombing remained strong at both the operational and tactical levels.

It is not surprising that the main force behind the project was General Henry "Hap" Arnold. Along with his interest in new gadgets, he was intrigued by the idea of pilotless flying bombs like the German V-1s. During World War I, Arnold had been closely involved with the testing of the Kettering Liberty Eagle, a rather primitive and flawed pilotless bomber.[4] He retained his interest in such weapons, and according to his memoirs by December 1941 an American radio-controlled model had been developed with a range of 200 miles. Attracted by their inexpensive price tags—he claimed that 500 of them could be purchased for the price of one B-17—Arnold believed that their range and accuracy were capable of rapid improvement. Nonetheless, despite the additional appeal that these "Bugs" might save the lives of many aircrews, he abandoned the project when the war started because with Britain as a base, "we could not get at the real heart of our enemy—interior Germany itself." His recollections are inaccurate, however. The Bug program actually lasted until 1943 but even then never showed much promise.[5]

Predictably, Arnold reacted enthusiastically to Spaatz's request on 20 June 1944 to provide support for a special project to destroy hardened German V-1 launching sites that were "practically invulnerable to normal bombing attacks." Spaatz mentioned special bombs or radio-controlled aircraft as possibilities and asked that the AAF Proving Ground Command at Eglin Field, Florida, select and test some methods. At the same time, he reported that his units were initiating a program to equip war-weary B-17s with radio-control equipment "for the purpose of carrying a heavy explosive load and diving it into the target."[6] Spaatz was convinced that his heavy bombers were being wasted in attacks on the V-1 sites, code-named Operation CROSSBOW, and was searching for a more effective method to destroy them.[7] The difficulties experienced by American airmen hunting missile launchers in Europe in 1944 foreshadowed similar problems encountered by their successors seeking Scuds in the Iraqi desert in 1991.

Response in Washington was swift, and the Navy also immediately offered men and equipment. Soon special units from the US Navy's assault-drone station at Traverse City, Michigan, and the Army Air Corps Signal Division's CASTOR unit at Wright Field, Ohio, arrived at the secret staging field at Fersfield, England.[8] The AAF chief of staff also informed his subordinate field commanders of Spaatz's plan, which to Arnold suggested "an effective method of disposing of our great and growing numbers of war weary aircraft of all types in all theatres" because they could be expended against targets in the Far East as well as in Europe. From the Mediterranean Eaker replied that if the Germans retired within a heavily defended "inner ring," then "one of our most effective weapons . . . would be masses of pilotless aircraft with sufficient range."[9] Perhaps the most enthusiastic reaction came from the innovative Lieutenant General George Kenney, commanding the US Far East Air Forces and the Allied Air Forces, Southwest Pacific Area under Douglas MacArthur, who pledged "100% cooperation" if Arnold would send him the engineers and equipment to take advantage of his area's "many suitable targets . . . for high explosive war-weary B-24's."[10]

In Europe Spaatz gave the responsibility for the project, now code-named APHRODITE, to Doolittle's Eighth Air Force. Beginning in July 1944, nine old B-17s in Britain were loaded with ten tons of TNT and one B-17 with ten tons of jellied gasoline. By then the Allies had already lost 2,900 men and 450 aircraft trying to knock out the rocket sites, and pressure for results was intense. As the more technically advanced Navy and CASTOR units prepared their equipment, an Eighth Air Force team under Major Henry James Rand was already prepared to go. They flew the first missions with a rather primitive double-Azon (azimuth only) control system, with an operator on a mother ship flying the pilotless aircraft much like a radio-controlled model airplane. A two-man crew had to get the robots into the air, set their controls, and then bail out. The AAF flew six Azon aircraft missions against missile-launching sites in early August but managed only two ineffective attacks on targets, the nearest hitting about 500 feet away. One enterprising controller, finding that he could not dive his robot, flew it around an unsuspecting German flak battery until a direct hit destroyed both the war-weary and the battery. One of the robots went out of control and disappeared but was found circling the English town of Ipswich; a frantic controller barely managed to dump it into the North Sea. The missions were especially hard on bail-out crews; one pilot was killed in a crash, and seven others were hurt in jumping. When Doolittle, who surveyed each mission in his personal fighter, saw the results and the casualties of the double-Azon sorties, he stopped those missions and released Rand's team.[11]

The Navy was also involved in APHRODITE, initially with one PB4Y robot (a Navy B-24) and two PV-1 Ventura control aircraft. The Navy assault-drone contingent, now dubbed Special Attack Unit 1, had been working on remote-controlled aircraft since 1937. They had a more sophisticated system, involving FM equipment, a block to better handle the robot's controls, and a TV camera and monitor to enable the operator to aim the B-24 he was controlling more accurately. Their first mission, on 12 August 1944, ended in

AZON TAIL FOR 1000 lb. BOMB

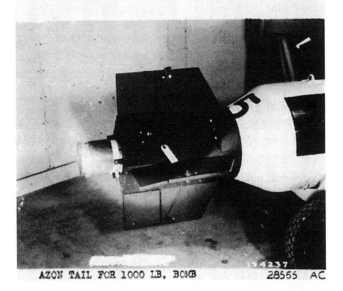

AZON TAIL FOR 1000 LB. BOMB   28565   AC

The Azon system initially used on APHRODITE was derived from a
similar method for controlling bombs. These diagrams illustrate the
workings of this rather crude but pioneering guided munition, which
foreshadowed a similar mechanism to control modern laser-directed or
inertially-guided bombs.

disaster when the robot disintegrated from a premature explosion, probably from a faulty electrical arming panel. One of the pilots killed was Lieutenant Joseph P. Kennedy, and fears of his father's reaction caused much consternation at many military headquarters. The Navy then suspended its project in order to find another drone and perfect its equipment; among other things the faulty electrical detonators were replaced with manual arming. By the time the unit was ready to go again, the Germans had abandoned hardened launch sites in favor of mobile ramps, and the primary targets for the project now became submarine pens at Heligoland. The next mission went well until it was close to the objective, but the block operator misidentified his target and then lost his picture because of a flak hit.[12]

After the initial failures, Spaatz began to lose his enthusiasm for the use of war-weary aircraft, informing Eaker of his belief that RAF 12,000-pound bombs were more promising as a method to eliminate the missile sites. After the Germans switched to mobile launchers, Spaatz stopped the procurement of worn-out aircraft and released the naval unit. Apparently the only reason for keeping the project going was the knowledge that, in the words of one disgruntled officer, "this is the Old Man's baby," referring to General Arnold's continuing interest. General Doolittle of the Eighth Air Force had already collected eleven planes for the missions, and Spaatz directed him to use them up and file a report with any recommendations for their use. The AAF now had the use of its CASTOR control equipment, similar to the Navy system, and results improved. Seven robots were flown against docks, sub pens, and an oil refinery, with the first two hitting very close to their targets, though bad weather spoiled the other sorties. One lost war-weary exploded in southern Sweden, but Swedish military authorities just sent a polite note with regrets that they could find no trace of any crewmen. Spaatz directed Doolittle to expend the last four aircraft "in attacks on industrial objectives in large German cities as far inland as practicable" to test their effectiveness on deep-penetration missions against softer targets more susceptible to the weapon's blast effects. These aircraft were used against marshaling yards at Herford and the thermal-power station at Oldenburg in December and January, but bad weather again negated their effectiveness. The main result of these deep missions was to cause fears that the program had been compromised when carburetor icing forced one robot down intact behind enemy lines. For three weeks fighters and bombers went back to find and destroy the plane, but not until after the war did Allied intelligence learn that a German infantry patrol had destroyed the robot, and themselves, battering in the plane's door.[13]

The final report on the APHRODITE project was quite critical; the "Weary Willies" were a failure as a strategic weapon. They were ineffective against heavily defended targets and severely hindered by adverse weather, and the few allotted radio frequencies limited the number of "Willie Mother" and "Baby" aircraft that could go on a mission. The report concluded that if the weapon was to be used in Europe, "it should be used as a tactical rather than a strategic weapon with its launching base well forward." In November 1944 the Ninth Air Force had begun to test this concept in Project WIL-LIE ORPHAN. During this operation, the aircraft was to be flown to within thirty-five to fifty miles of the front lines, where the pilot would bail out and a ground-control station would then guide the robot onto its target. Encouraged by preliminary tests against area targets at Eglin Field, Arnold sent personnel to Europe in mid-November to support this phase of testing. Despite advice to the contrary, Spaatz accepted the project, telling Arnold that he envisioned the use of the Weary Willies "against fortified German cities or other suitable area targets" that would supplement the tactical air forces' ground-support effort.[14]

However, the commander of the Ninth Air Force viewed things differently. Shortly after Spaatz took the project, Lieutenant General Hoyt Vandenberg notified him that the weapon was "not sufficiently accurate when controlled from the ground to be effectively employed against normal precision tactical targets." He maintained that his unit could not afford to waste time with a weapon "still under development" and requested that the Eighth Air Force fly some airplane-guided missions to learn if that was a more accurate technique. Some ground commanders also had misgivings, fearing that there was more danger to friendly troops along the worn-out aircraft's flight path than to any enemy in the target area. In December General Eisenhower told Arnold that he would give WILLIE ORPHAN a limited try, but only after more training on safety checks to ensure that no accidents would occur over friendly territory.[15]

Meanwhile the Joint Chiefs of Staff (JCS) were developing their own concept of a plan to use the Weary Willies, a move highlighting the lack of communication between Washington and the field. While all this rather dismal testing was going on in Europe, Arnold had already announced to the JCS that the AAF was preparing a plan "for the launching of over 500 loaded war-weary US bombers against large industrial target areas in Germany." This project involved a weapon similar to Arnold's Bugs, far different from Spaatz's original concept. The AAF commander did not even mention television or radio control, and when the British chiefs inquired about it, the

Americans replied that any possible improvements in accuracy by using such controls "did not justify the additional time and personnel which would be required in further research or in the movement to the theater of specialized technicians and equipment." The JCS envisioned the project not as precision bombing but "as a means of requiring continued mobilization of enemy civilian defense services, interrupting industrial production and producing economic-industrial disruption." Fearing retaliation with similar weapons from the Germans, in January the British announced that they could not agree to such a proposal, and all further testing in Europe was halted.[16] There was some justification for British fears; the Germans had already used their own explosives-laden, war-weary Junkers 88 bombers in attacks on shipping. These robot bombs were guided strictly by automatic pilot, but captured Allied technology could have been used to improve their performance. When Major General Lawrence Kuter assailed Sir Charles Portal for "Indian giving," the British airman blamed "politicoes" for the decision against using the Weary Willies.[17]

A few weeks after presenting his plan to the JCS, Arnold sent a preliminary report to Spaatz on the results of war-weary tests at Eglin Field. He seemed to ignore the outcome of Spaatz's tests and gave a general outline of his plan to use the Weary Willies "as an irritant and possibly a means of breaking down the morale of the people of interior Germany." Arnold saw "very little difference" between this operation and British night area bombing (as if that were a justification for the project) and asked for the USSTAF commander's reaction to the proposition. In his reply, Spaatz was diplomatic but presented his position clearly. He described the problems of APHRODITE and concluded that the use of the robots for strategic deep-penetration raids "had good chances of success against Japanese targets" despite their failure in Europe, presumably because of better weather there and because long flights could be made over open, undefended waters. As for WILLIE ORPHAN, Spaatz wrote that he could "see no reason why we should not attack towns if they have military targets or industries associated with them." However, he was referring to robots guided by ground stations of limited range into targets near the front, a tactic to assist the ground advance and not necessarily to attack civilian morale. He argued that limitations on aircraft and trained personnel would prevent any volume of war-weary aircraft from being launched and that the AAF had to "be reasonably sure of hitting the target" to achieve any significant effect. Arnold's plan to "turn them loose to land all over Germany" would therefore be impossible to support and a waste of effort.[18]

It is difficult to know the effect of Spaatz's letter on Arnold, but after the

British rejected the use of Weary Willies, Arnold changed his position somewhat. In February Arnold instructed Eglin Field to send a letter to Spaatz explaining all the control techniques that had been developed for the robot aircraft, and at a JCS meeting the AAF tried to reopen the issue with the British.[19] Major Generals Laurence Kuter and Frederick Anderson argued that there had been a "misunderstanding on the part of the British as to the employment of the weapon" and that the AAF never intended to launch the robots indiscriminately against Germany. Recent developments in guidance had now proven that "explosive-laden aircraft could be directed against military targets with considerable accuracy." Their arguments must have been persuasive because they convinced Admiral William Leahy, a staunch opponent of indiscriminate bombing who had considered the war-wearies "an inhuman and barbarous type of warfare with which the United States should not be associated," that the missiles "could be usefully employed."[20]

Eventually the JCS persuaded President Roosevelt to intervene with Churchill after Leahy wrote Roosevelt a memo describing the improvements and arguing that the "highly concentrated areas of the Japanese homeland" were especially vulnerable to the Weary Willies if enough combat experience could be gained in Europe. The president used the same logic in his letter, but by the time Churchill reluctantly agreed, Roosevelt was dead and the war in Europe was almost over. "Due to the tone of the message [from Churchill] and the circumstances on the Western Front," Truman directed that the project not be "pressed further" in Europe. Arnold's staff continued experimentation in the United States, but nothing came of it.[21] Kenney never did get the support he had requested for the Pacific, but the plan JAVAMAN was later devised using Weary Willy technology to guide robot boats with B-17s. The boats were designed to destroy the Kammon tunnel in Shimonoseki Straits in September 1945, isolating the area in Japan to be invaded, but of course they were not needed.[22]

AMERICAN GLIDE BOMBS AND BUZZ BOMBS

The record shows a considerable difference between the views of General Arnold and the opinions of his field commanders in Europe on the employment of Weary Willy. Their intent was to use the war-weary aircraft as a tactical or strategic missile of some precision, not as an indiscriminate weapon of terror. A similar gap between Arnold and his field commanders can be seen in his other attempts to force new weapons particularly on Spaatz, be-

Two GB-1 glide bombs slung under a B-17 for testing. The results of experimental attacks on Cologne with these munitions in 1944 were disappointing, and the GB-1s were never used in combat again.

ginning as early as 1942 when the AAF chief of staff tried to get Spaatz to use a new "stabilized glide bomb" that could hit "an area the size of Dayton, Ohio, from 25,000 feet" while the bomber stayed out of flak range. Unimpressed with the new weapon's accuracy, Spaatz declined. Even Kuter, who worked for Arnold, believed it was "a bomb to do indiscriminate bombing the hard way." Yet during Eaker's command of the Eighth Air Force in 1943, he arranged with Arnold to test it. When Spaatz returned, the trials were discontinued. Eventually, despite protests from Doolittle and Spaatz, "chairborne" leaders in Washington insisted that the Eighth Air Force test the GB-1, an unguided and unpowered 2,000-pound bomb with stubby wings. On 28 May 1944 the 384th Bomb Group launched a strike with the glide bombs against targets in Cologne. None of the GB-1s even hit the city, and the only significant effect of the attack was to increase the confidence of German flak gunners who were sure that the glide bombs exploding throughout the countryside were really downed B-17s. Engineers at Wright Field in Ohio continued to work on improving the GB-1, but the Eighth Air Force never again had to test them.[23]

Eaker retained his interest in such technology, which eventually produced a bomb guided in azimuth by radio, a system used in APHRODITE. A transmitter emitted signals that varied the pitch of the bomb's stabilizing fins, allowing the bombardier to reduce deflection errors. In May 1944 Eaker arranged for a test raid on the narrow Avisio Bridge, a difficult target that bombs usually straddled but key in the Brenner Pass rail system. Four special B-17s dropped twenty-four 1,000-pound Azon bombs and took out a seventy-foot stretch of the bridge with four direct hits. There was some dispute about these results, however, and European tests were generally disappointing. Kenney also used these weapons in the Pacific, and the 7th Bomb Group in the China–Burma–India theater destroyed about forty bridges with them, estimating that Azon bombs were ten times more effective than conventional munitions against such targets. Azon bombs were not widely used in World War II because the technology was limited in availability and reliability and because pilots did not like the requirement to fly straight and level after bomb release so that bombardiers could guide the Azons to the target, a particularly dangerous tactic against heavily defended objectives such as important bridges. Even with limited use, the Azon bombs showed some promise, especially in Burma. Further development was neglected after the war, however, and American airmen would not get effective guided bombs until late in the Vietnam War. These World War II weapons can be seen as the predecessors of the "smart bombs" perfected in Vietnam and that received such glowing publicity during DESERT STORM.[24]

Arnold continued to pursue new weapons, and his fascination with the German V-1 culminated in a project to copy it. During a trip to England in June 1944 he calculated that "if the Germans were as efficient as we were" they would be able to launch as many as 1,440 cheap V-1s per hour, to "cause consternation, concern, and finally break the normal routine of life in Britain and dislocate the war effort."[25] He also examined salvaged V-1 parts, and on 12 July 2,500 pounds of them were shipped from Great Britain to Wright Field. Within three weeks the AAF had completed its "Jet Bomb 2," a "Chinese copy" of the V-1. An attempt to develop a purely American-designed flying bomb, the JB-1, was initiated at about the same time, but that project never made much progress.[26]

During the first few months of the project, Arnold was engaged in a battle with the Ordnance Corps and Army Service Forces over control of research and development of guided missiles. The ground services wanted a weapon with missile range and artillery accuracy; Arnold did not seek such precision. In January 1945 Arnold won his victory when Marshall gave the AAF sole responsibility for developing the JB-2. That same month, *Impact* announced the existence of the new weapon.[27]

Spaatz and Eaker had been told about the weapon in October in a message admitting that plans for accurate guidance were "proceeding slowly" but asking that the European commanders cable their estimated monthly requirements for the new missile. Twice Spaatz "reiterated his lack of immediate interest" before Arnold sent an emissary to change his mind. The Air Staff in Washington thought that the JB-2 could be effective only "against a large urban area" like the Ruhr and only in great quantity, an opinion that assuredly contributed to Spaatz's lack of enthusiasm. To appease Arnold, in December the USSTAF staff finally sent him an estimated need of 1,000 missiles per month but added that the project should have no special priority. In other words, they really did not want the missiles.[28]

About the same time, probably at Arnold's urging, Marshall sent Eisenhower a cable on the JB-2. The chief of staff admitted that with current inaccuracy it was a "terror weapon when used on a small scale," and for any decisive strategic effect 500 to 1,000 per day would have to be launched at a major target like the Ruhr. He was concerned that such usage would be prohibitive in cost, might cut into artillery ammunition production, and would tie up too much shipping. Marshall added, however, that possible radar control to improve accuracy would lower the launch rate and make the weapon useful on strategic and tactical targets. He asked Eisenhower for his opinion. In Marshall's view, the main problems with using the JB-2 were "logistical not tactical"—and seemingly not moral either. Eisenhower proposed a plan to produce 100 JB-2s a day and to launch 300 a day, ten days a month. Arnold's staff called this wasteful of manpower on idle days and developed a counter plan to fire 300 every day of the month; this increased possible conflicts with other production, however. The Air Staff's final plan proposed the expenditure of 1,000 JB-2s per month.[29]

Meanwhile, Lieutenant General Barney Giles, Arnold's chief of Air Staff, wrote to Vannever Bush of the Office of Scientific Research and Development to garner support for the AAF plan and rightly prophesied, "We believe the JB-2 to be representative of a new family of very long range weapons whose capabilities will profoundly affect future warfare." But he still could not overcome the office's "lack of interest" in the project.[30]

Arnold's and Lovett's scientific advisory group in Europe was slightly more successful. They presented a paper to Spaatz explaining their plans to

The American JB-2 buzz bomb, set for launching from a rail system. It closely resembled the German V-1 that inspired it. Though the JB-2 was built and tested, it was never deployed in the field for a number of reasons.

apply Weary Willie control technology to the JB-2 along with ground control by SCR-584 radars,[31] which would bring the weapon "into the class of very flexible, extremely long range artillery." When Spaatz found out that JB-2s could not be deployed until September, he agreed to support the program then. This shift did not signify any weakening on his part; rather, he reasoned that if the war was still going on in Europe in September it would be because "some new developments by the Germans have made it impossible for us to continue to operate the VIII Air Force on the present scale." If that were the case, drastic measures such as the JB-2 might be needed, but he did not really believe this would happen. His acquiescence in a later date was also a convenient way to appease Washington at no real cost. Ground commanders Omar Bradley, Courtney Hodges, and George Patton agreed with Spaatz that the weapon had great possibilities for siege warfare, but they were also "affected by an undercurrent of conviction that the war would be over before these weapons could be brought into operation." Leaders at Supreme Headquarters, Allied Expeditionary Forces (SHAEF), remained skeptical about the weapon, believing that it was unsuitable for both strategic precision use and tactical bombardment; however, that position was subject to review as more test data became available.[32]

As the European field commanders had foreseen, the JB-2 was never needed there. A month after V-E Day in 1945, the Air Staff cut back its order of weapons to 7,000 for development, training, and combat testing and continued its procurement of auxiliary equipment to set up one special weapons unit to fire them. At the same time, Eaker, now Arnold's deputy commander, approached Kenney about putting the JB-2 into operation in the Pacific. If Kenney's response to Weary Willies was any indicator, he would have been an avid supporter of the new project, but the war ended before the American buzz bomb could be used in combat.[33]

GAS AND INCENDIARY BOMBS

Giles's prediction that guided missiles could revolutionize future warfare was correct. Today such weapons are especially deadly because of the nuclear, biological, or chemical warheads they can carry. These extreme methods of warfare were all available in World War II as well, the use of any of them signifying a new escalation in the move toward total war, but they were never viable options for field commanders in Europe. Of course the atomic bomb was not ready before V-E Day, and apparently Spaatz and his subordinates were not aware of the biological warfare program spurred on in Britain and the United States by fears of Axis developments in that area.[34] They did get involved in the issue of chemical warfare, however.

The main impetus to use gas warfare in Europe came from the British, especially Winston Churchill. Roosevelt's known opposition to such weapons contrasted sharply with his British counterpart's attitude, especially after German V-weapons began raining down on England in 1944. As early as January of that year, Brigadier General Charles Cabell of the USSTAF staff had participated in meetings of the British War Cabinet Inter Service Committee on Chemical Warfare. Committee members agreed that "the destruction of an industrial city or area by incendiary or high explosive attack offers a more direct and lasting diminution of Germany's capacity to make war than the more or less temporary contamination of the same locality . . . with . . . gas." The group did propose a contingency plan for retaliatory use of gas, however, involving "six major area attacks with Mustard Gas and two with Phosgene Gas per month."[35]

Arnold had already directed the preparation of such plans for retaliation against Japan, and he kept Spaatz informed about new developments in chemical bombs and agents.[36] The USSTAF commander had first seen British plans for gas attacks by air on Germany in December 1943 and at that time had generally indicated that he was willing to use such tactics if the Germans did it first. By May, when he was asked to provide recommendations to SHAEF on this course of action, Spaatz had considered his position in more detail. He advised Eisenhower that despite governmental threats, "we should assume no *obligation* to conduct retaliatory gas attacks." Even if the Germans used gas, the most effective response would be determined by the "situation at the moment." Spaatz believed "a strong effect on morale could be obtained through the continuance of the threat alone. Punishment might be meted out more strongly through other bomb loads." With the number of strategic targets he had to hit and the few good bombing days he had available, Spaatz did not want to waste missions on relatively ineffective gas attacks on cities. His logic was not completely pragmatic because he strongly emphasized that the use of gas by the Germans "on military personnel does not justify our unrestricted use of it" on civil populations. He was especially adamant about the use of gas in occupied areas: "The repercussions of gas use against satellite populations would outweigh the slight advantages to be gained." He did acknowledge, however, that a threat of use in those areas might tie down defensive equipment. It is clear from Spaatz's recommendations to SHAEF that he did not favor gas warfare, and because Hitler never resorted to it and Churchill's military advisers forced him to yield on his plans for first use, the USSTAF commander never had to face a challenge to his convictions.[37]

Only one aspect of the search for better bombs in Europe actually contributed to the escalation toward total war in World War II, and its effects would come to fruition in the Pacific: the development and use of incendiary bombs for American strategic bombing. Ironically, the impetus for this new bomb can be traced to Colonel Crawford Kellogg, head of the Eighth Air Force chemical section, who was initially responsible for ensuring that his units had sufficient protection against German gas attacks. Once this mission was completed in summer 1942 he turned his attention to expanding the role of the Chemical Warfare Service (CWS) in the impending American air campaign against the Axis. Considering the US position on the use of gas, he realized that the only hope for any CWS contribution would be through the use of incendiary bombs controlled and developed by the chemical branch.[38]

After ensuring that the CWS supply division at Edgewood Arsenal had enough incendiaries to supply his expected needs, Kellogg enlisted the help of the British to persuade American airmen in England to use these bombs. The British were enthusiastic and provided demonstrations in England and reports for distribution to the War Department in Washington. Initially Arnold and his staff were not convinced of the usefulness of incendiaries, agreeing with the views of most American airmen that demolition bombs were more effective for precision bombing, especially when resources were limited. Incendiaries worked well for mass-area raids of 1,000 aircraft but not for pinpoint bombardment with smaller numbers of planes.[39]

By April 1943 Arnold saw three uses for Eighth Air Force incendiary raids: to burn down precise industrial objectives that could not be damaged as effectively with an equivalent tonnage of high-explosive bombs, to start fires to act as night beacons for the RAF, and to burn down cities "when the occasion warrants." He directed his staff to determine the effectiveness of incendiaries on industrial targets, and they provided a rather dismal assessment of the bombs' capabilities against German factories. However, research and development went into high gear, motivated especially by the CWS, which built a five-square-mile complex of German and Japanese towns at Dugway Proving Ground that included authentic furnishings. Dropping bombs on this site led to the development of special incendiaries that could penetrate German roofs. A small, delayed-action incendiary called a Braddock was even invented, designed to be dropped into Germany and used for sabotage by disgruntled workers. Thousands were dropped, along with leaflets advertising them, but their main contribution to the war effort seems to have been in keeping Nazi security forces busy picking them up.[40]

The most innovative use of incendiaries, or the most bizarre, depending on your perspective, was Project X-RAY, the bat bomb. It was the brainchild of Lytle S. Adams, a practicing dentist from Pennsylvania who also dabbled in aerial inventions. He was also president of Tri-state Aviation, which eventually became US Airways. He had acquaintances at high levels of government, including Eleanor Roosevelt, whom he had flown around to demonstrate a rural air mail pickup system. She delivered a letter to the president from Adams in January 1942 that proposed bats could be used to deliver firebombs in vulnerable Japanese cities that would sow terror and cause great destruction. Roosevelt sent a note to his coordinator of information, Colonel William "Wild Bill" Donovan that actually began with the words, "This man is not a nut," and encouraged support for the idea. Although that personnel evaluation could be questioned, eventually the project was picked up by the CWS and the AAF. Initial experiments to determine the load-carrying capabilities of Mexican free-tailed bats seemed discouraging until it was discovered that the test subjects were pregnant females. Further work revealed that healthy bats could carry between fifteen and eighteen grams of extra weight, and Dr. Louis F. Feiser, distinguished Harvard chemist and the father of napalm, produced an incendiary device for them. In the meantime, Adams was driving his old Buick around the Southwest with a bunch of impressed draftees from local universities and laboratories, and they found millions of the right kind of bats in caves near Bandera, Texas.

The next step was to determine how best to get the bats to deliver the ordnance. The team found that freezing the bats made them hibernate so the bombs could be attached, but the frozen bombardiers did not thaw out quickly enough when dropped out of airplanes. Eventually a device was developed that was dropped by parachute. The bats were put in trays that would pop open as the contraption floated down. As they warmed up, they flew off to roost under eaves and in attics until their devices ignited. Tests at Dugway Proving Ground in December 1943 proved that one load of bat bombs would start between eleven and twenty-nine times as many fires as the same weight of typical incendiaries. However, by then enthusiasm for X-RAY had waned. The AAF lost interest in mid-1943 after some errant bats or devices displayed for publicity efforts burned down Carlsbad Auxiliary Army Airfield. The Navy then took over the project, but killed it early in 1944 because it was not expected to be available before the end of the war, and the money would be more useful expended on a more promising enterprise called the MANHATTAN Project.[41]

Despite CWS efforts and British successes such as the fire storm at Hamburg in July 1943, American strategic air forces in Europe never embraced the incendiary as a replacement for high-explosive (HE) bombs. Airmen complained about wasted space in bomb bays that reduced the destructive power they could carry and about the difficulty of aiming the new bombs. Ballistic problems plagued the lighter munitions. Incendiaries also proved vulnerable to damage in shipment. The CWS solved these problems with aimable clusters and improved packaging procedures by 1944, even claiming in official histories that the AAF in Europe "began to scream for incendiaries," an assertion not borne out by the record, however. Colonel Kellogg did persuade Curtis LeMay to use them in quantity and the British continued to push for increased use, but the Eighth and Fifteenth Air Forces dropped HE bombs predominantly, 87 percent and 98 percent of their total tonnage, respectively. In Europe, incendiaries remained supplements to HE bombs that could at times increase damage and presented a different threat to enemy efforts to protect strategic precision targets. Even in raids on the center of Berlin, the AAF chiefly used HE bomb loads. The full effect of new developments in incendiaries would become evident only when they were used in mass-area attacks on Japanese cities. Approximately two-thirds of the bomb tonnage dropped by the Twentieth Air Force in the Pacific would be incendiaries. Although Feiser mourned the demise of Project X-RAY in his memoirs, imagining that the winged warriors would have panicked and devastated Tokyo, he conceded that the M-69 incendiary gel bombs he helped develop did the job just as effectively.[42]

The fire raids on Japan would set the stage for the use of the atomic bomb, the culmination of World War II technological innovation. That weapon also promised to achieve the dream advocated by airmen from Douhet to the writers of AWPD/1: to end the war in one final deathblow from the air, thus realizing the potential of technology by preventing a costly stalemate on the ground.

8. THE LURE OF THE
DEATHBLOW IN EUROPE

Timeliness of attack is most important in the conduct of air operations directly against civil morale. If the morale of the people is already low because of sustained suffering and deprivation and because the people are losing faith in the ability of the armed forces to win a favorable decision, then heavy and sustained bombing of cities may crush that morale entirely. . . . It is believed that the entire bombing effort might be applied toward this purpose when it becomes apparent that the proper psychological conditions exist.

–AWPD/1[1]

The vestige of Douhet's theory that remained in AWPD/1 lingered in the minds of ground and air commanders in Washington and in the European theater of operations. Army leaders hoped to save the lives of their men by bombing the Germans into capitulation, and the AAF hoped to bolster their postwar position by bringing the war to an end with victory through airpower. Once the Allies were firmly established on the Continent, these desires produced a number of plans for an aerial *Todestoss* that increased pressures to stray from the doctrine of precision attacks against German capacity and established precedents and a state of mind that would influence the air war against Japan.

These plans were also fueled by leaders' perceptions of the results of similar air attacks aimed at breaking morale in the Mediterranean theater, especially against Italy, where Douhet's theories about the effects of air bombardment on morale seemed particularly applicable to his own countrymen. The surrender of the Italian garrisons on the islands of Pantelleria and Lampedusa in June 1943 was due almost completely to intensive bombing of military installations there, and this victory caused some airmen to assert that no place and no force could hold up under a concentrated aerial bom bardment. Future operations would show this claim to be false, but ground commanders such as George Patton continued to resort to intensive air attacks against stubborn enemy strongholds throughout the war.[2]

More significant were the effects and perceptions resulting from Doolittle's July 1943 attack by the Northwest African Strategic Air Force on Rome. The marshaling yards there were the key bottleneck for Axis supplies flowing south, but many leaders feared the backlash from Catholics, artists, architects, and other concerned parties that might result from attacking the Holy City. The British had been itching to attack the city since October 1940 but realized that the time for such an operation had to be carefully selected. Roosevelt and Stimson wanted Rome declared an open city, not to be bombed, but the Italians procrastinated. Churchill believed that the decision to mount a daylight attack should be left to Eisenhower, and Arnold supported that view, recommending that Ike "should not be influenced by religion or politics" in his decision. Eventually the JCS persuaded the president to allow the mission, and it was scheduled for 19 July 1943.[3]

Italy seemed particularly vulnerable to being bombed out of the war. The nation had no organized structure or mind-set for civil defense. RAF Bomber Command had started attacking Italian cities in the autumn of 1942. Turin and Genoa were especially hard hit, producing mass evacuations and resulting protests. By the spring of 1943, British intelligence and the American Office of Strategic Services had received many reports about the fragile state of Italian civilian morale. The tactical US Ninth Air Force contributed to the campaign by dropping sixty-four million leaflets during the first eight months of the year that prodded the populace to "refuse to fight the war of Hitler and Mussolini," while warning that continued resistance risked innocent suffering.[4]

In accordance with the views of both Churchill and Roosevelt, crews were carefully briefed on the location of historic and religious sites in Rome. Press releases were prepared for quick issuance to get information out before enemy propaganda could exploit the attack, and warning pamphlets were dropped on 3 and 18 July. The airmen fully understood the importance of their mission. "I never briefed crews quite as carefully and flew a bombing run through flak as meticulously as on this raid," one group commander wrote.[5]

The immediate effect of the attack brought Italian rail traffic to a standstill; the yards were demolished by 1,000 tons of bombs. The Vatican protested, but only one shrine, the Basilica of San Lorenzo, was significantly damaged. Spaatz even reported to Arnold that the raid was "too easy"; there

A sample of the destruction caused by Doolittle's attack on the marshaling yards near Rome. The undamaged building in the left background is a result of careful targeting and precision bombing.

was little opposition. The long-term results of the attack were even more important. Factory workers fled or failed to report for work, producing a noticeable decline in war production and clear evidence that the civil populace was tired of war. The air strike influenced King Victor Emmanuel to desert Mussolini a week later, and the Fascist Grand Council deposed him. Seven weeks later, in early September, a new Italian government signed a peace treaty. Diplomats and commanders recognized that the bombing of Rome had contributed directly and significantly to the Italian surrender. Richard Overy asserts that the extensive bombing of Italy that preceded the Rome raid in 1943, with twice the tonnage dropped on Britain during the Blitz, and included attacks on ports and much collateral damage around other targets such as airfields and rail yards, created popular disillusionment with a regime that could not seem to handle the resulting destruction and dislocation. For him, the Rome attack was just one of many aerial blows that brought down the government.[6]

BOMBING THE BALKANS

The easy elimination of Italy led planners to consider the vulnerability of Balkan targets. In October Major D. Dalziel, deputy assistant chief of staff for Spaatz's Northwest African Air Forces, submitted a plan to knock Bulgaria out of the war. Basing his claims on interviews with a Yugoslavian officer, Dalziel argued that the Bulgarian people were not afraid of any ground advance but that "the very possibility of air attack by US Forces has them practically terrified." He proposed that the capital, Sofia, should be "bombed in its entirety" by day and by night, which would probably cause the collapse of the country. Within five days after successful completion of these attacks, Bucharest, Romania, would receive the same treatment.[7]

There is no evidence that Dalziel's plan received any consideration from Spaatz, but similar operations were being developed at higher levels. The Joint Planning Staff of the British War Cabinet had studied the problem of forcing the German Balkan satellites out of the war and had also decided that Sofia was the best target. Support of the land campaign in Italy and the Combined Bomber Offensive would retain priority over attacks on Balkan capitals, but the Northwest African Air Forces could mount such raids during bad weather or lulls in other campaigns. Psychological warfare operations would be launched to "unnerve Bulgarian opinion," along with a propaganda campaign to emphasize the military importance of Sofia because military and communications targets were "so small and so situated within the town that their attack would result in the destruction of the city proper." Instructions to propose this plan to the CCS were transmitted to the Joint Staff Mission in Washington.[8]

As a result, the CCS directed Eisenhower to pursue the Balkan attacks when sufficient resources were available. Ronald Schaffer in particular criticizes the raids: "American flyers were expected to terrorize Balkan civilians without appearing to use terror tactics," and he cites the acceptance of these attacks by leaders as an important step in the escalation to total war.[9] Yet airmen always expected some psychological impact from any air raid, whether on ground troops or factory workers, and valid military reasons existed for bombing Balkan communication centers, especially as the Russians moved closer. If secondary effects on morale could be obtained from precision attacks, as in Rome, and if bombing Bulgarian marshaling yards could influence that government to leave the war, then so much the better. Still, American airmen in Europe resisted such attacks when they were seemingly targeted primarily at morale and saw the Balkan city missions as a diversion from more important targets, such as the oil refineries at Ploesti. This AAF position was bound to produce friction with the British, who were determined to exploit the political possibilities of bombing cities such as Sofia and Bucharest.

Sir Charles Portal had the authority to set priorities for strategic air forces on behalf of the CCS, and he continued to emphasize the Balkan raids while the Americans tried to establish a stable chain of command for European air operations. In early 1944, the American air command structure in Europe was in some turmoil as Spaatz and Doolittle moved to England and Eaker settled in as commander of Mediterranean Allied Air Forces. In January Anderson told the USSTAF director of intelligence to prepare a policy directive covering the bombing of Balkan cities "similar to that used by forces operating from the United Kingdom . . . applied to cities in the occupied countries." The next month Budapest, Sofia, Bucharest, and Vienna were listed as a secondary priority for "over-the-cloud" area bombing. However, few such raids were mounted because Spaatz and Anderson resisted the diversion of strategic bombers to "the intangible attempt to break civilian morale."[10]

The British, however, continued to press for more Balkan attacks. The Air Ministry provided tempting intelligence reports describing Bulgarian offers of surrender and intimating that one or two more raids might knock them out of the war. Other reports promised Russian diplomatic pressure and emphasized the assistance to Operation OVERLORD that would be provided if the Germans had to garrison the Balkans.[11] Portal also tried to bypass the recalcitrant USSTAF headquarters by having the commander in the Mediterranean theater, General Sir Henry Maitland Wilson, give "strategical directions" to the Fifteenth Air Force, a move that brought strong protests from Spaatz, who possessed that authority as commander of USSTAF. Portal apologized to Spaatz and Arnold, but he also strongly urged the AAF commander to support more attacks on the Balkans. At this time the JCS was also doubtful whether attacks on Bulgaria would achieve the desired effects. Arnold cabled Spaatz that the CCS had approved attacks on political targets in Southeastern Europe, "when highly important results might be expected and the situation warrants it" but did not tell Spaatz to make them a priority.[12]

Spaatz continued to clash with Portal over the choice of Balkan targets, repeatedly asking to adjust strategic priorities to emphasize the oil refineries at Ploesti instead of the marshaling yards in cities. The USSTAF staff complained bitterly that when the issue was referred to the CCS, they left the decision in Portal's hands. "Accordingly . . . Portal enforced his own" desires.[13] Because Spaatz could not ignore Portal completely because of his CCS influence, the USSTAF commander apparently employed the assistance of the American ambassador to Great Britain. Ambassador John Winant informed the president in April that the attacks being forced on United States air commands in the Balkans were militarily unsound, creating ill will against the Americans and helping the Russians politically. He complained that targets were being selected by the Joint Intelligence Committee, which had no US representation, and forwarded by Portal. Decisions were based on British political judgment and "not subject to political review by us although carried out by United States Military Commands." Winant concluded, "I believe that British political considerations are integrated in military decisions and that they do not conform necessarily with United States long term interests." Roosevelt referred the problem to his advisers; the Department of State and the JCS agreed that the AAF should not have to make such politically oriented attacks and proposed to the CCS in July that "strategic priorities for bombing operations in the satellite countries (Hungary, Bulgaria, and Romania) will be strictly limited to military objectives." The British tried to amend the policy to allow Portal and Wilson to designate political targets as well, but the CCS adopted the American proposal. The British may have given in so easily because Romania had already surrendered and Bulgaria was also about to defect from the German orbit. Some American raids were launched on Balkan marshaling yards after this, but they were designed to assist the advancing Russians or to tie in to systematic assaults on Axis transportation. The British continued to express interest in Balkan operations throughout 1944, including recommending a landing there to support OVERLORD instead of in southern France.[14]

Some international agencies also complained about the air attacks on Balkan cities. In September 1944 the International Red Cross protested AAF bombing attacks on Romanian civilians in Bucharest. Eaker had already visited the city and discovered that as a result of a series of unforeseen occurrences, 12,000 people had been killed in one attack. Six thousand foreign workers had died in trains passing through the marshaling yards, and many Romanians had ignored air-raid sirens because of an advertised practice drill shortly before the raid. Surprisingly, the people showed no resentment toward the Americans, perhaps because of recent German dive-bombing attacks on city streets. Romanians and Russians described American bombing accuracy as remarkable and obviously "after purely military objectives." Eaker's perceptions were seconded by his inspector general and incorporated into Stimson's reply to Secretary of State Hull concerning the Red Cross charges. The secretary of war expressed his regrets over any civilian deaths and reiterated his assurances "that the Army Air Forces has not condoned, and will not condone, any wanton slaughter of non-participants in the war."[15]

The 1944 attacks on Balkan cities did not influence American airmen to adopt terror tactics. Though the campaign was perceived as a British attempt to divert valuable strategic bombers to attain questionable political objectives, the AAF believed that it had attacked primarily military objectives with the maximum precision possible. The only legacy from these attacks for future operations was the reinforcement of the belief that marshaling yards in cities were viable precision targets.

PURSUING A DEATHBLOW AGAINST GERMANY

Meanwhile, other plans to deal an aerial deathblow to the Axis were being pursued against Germany. The Americans had been reluctant participants in such operations in the Balkans, but they could not resist the temptation to try to end the war against the Nazis. Although Omar Bradley and other ground commanders had hoped that air bombardment might defeat the Germans as early as winter 1943, AAF leaders did not really pursue a systematic *Todestoss* until mid-1944, after the Allies were firmly established on the Continent and the enemy appeared close to collapse.[16]

In August 1941 President Roosevelt had proposed that the British could demoralize the Germans by bombing small towns across the nation. In December his coordinator of information, William J. Donovan, who worked on special projects against the Nazis with the British, completed a study of German morale predicting that the universal realization "that ultimate defeat is inevitable" would bring national collapse, unless the propaganda ministry could instill a sense of "last-ditch defense" in the face of adversity.[17] Colonel Edgar Sorenson, Arnold's assistant chief of Air Staff for intelligence, concluded in a report two years later that although "present evidence indicates that air bombardment alone cannot decisively reduce the morale of the civilian population," the indirect results of air bombardment or impending military catastrophe might push the German army or the industrialists to "revolutionary action" against the Nazis to preserve the existing social order from irreparable damage.[18]

A more realistic view of the chances of ending the war through aerial attacks on morale was expressed by Spaatz in his exhaustively documented plan submitted in March 1944 to counter the Transportation Plan in support of OVERLORD. It recognized how completely the Nazis controlled German society and that even refusal to work would just result in resisters being shot. The army was the only group with the potential to challenge the Nazis, and it was more concerned with factories than with workers. The report concluded, "Attacks on industries of direct military importance, therefore, are far more capable of producing significant effects on Army political moves than attacks on non-industrial areas."[19] At the same time, Spaatz directed the Eighth and the Fifteenth Air Forces to prepare operations to attack profitable and relatively undefended industrial targets throughout Germany, an idea he apparently adopted from a rather informal 1942 letter sent to him by a Londoner named E. Frey. Spaatz expected to spread or avoid German ground defenses, extend operational days, and improve accuracy by bombing targets at lower altitudes. He also saw the opportunity to overcome external censorship and impress people and officials throughout Germany with "the fact of Allied air mastery and its impact." He cautioned his commanders, however, that official or civilian morale was "not worthy of being the primary objective" of these operations, which would mainly increase "chances for drawing extra dividends from our regular target systems." The assignment of USSTAF to SHAEF's control for the duration of OVERLORD prevented these "bomber sweeps" from being carried out at that time, but Spaatz continued to refine his concept.[20]

With the successful invasion and the lodgment at Normandy in June 1944, air commanders in Washington and Europe began seriously to consider ways to achieve victory through airpower over Germany. For many leaders, the time seemed right for an aerial *Todestoss*. Three weeks after the landings, a captain at USSTAF headquarters, probably inspired by the deputy director of intelligence, Colonel Lowell Weicker, submitted a plan to the USSTAF director of intelligence to break military and civilian morale by bombing 100 German cities in one day. Attacks would be made by heavy bombers on government buildings, transportation facilities, or minor industries "to free such an operation from the stigma of being merely retaliatory terror bombing"; but psychological warfare through leaflets and broadcasts would also be used to emphasize the defenselessness of the Reich to air attack. The plan, Operation SHATTER, was analyzed in detail by Colonel Charles R. Cabell, USSTAF director of plans. He thought that attacks against "priority non-morale targets" of a military or economic nature held more promise and that obvious terror attacks would assist German propaganda, while the effect on world opinion "would be detrimental to the interest of the AAF and the US government." Cabell did not recommend the plan.[21]

In July Cabell was promoted and sent to head the Operations and Intelligence Section for the Mediterranean Allied Air Forces under Eaker. Cabell's successor, Colonel Charles G. Williamson, immediately became embroiled in a bitter dispute within USSTAF headquarters over plans like SHATTER coming from the Office of the USSTAF Director of Intelligence. Although Brigadier General George McDonald signed the proposals, his deputy, Colonel Weicker, was responsible for them, and he was opposed by the chief of his own target section, Colonel Richard Hughes. Hughes was a former British army officer who became an American citizen in the 1930s. He has been described by one of his subordinates as "one of those selfless men, of high intelligence, integrity, and dedication, who play major roles in great enterprises but, operating at a middle level of authority, leave little trace in the formal records of history." Hughes argued that Weicker based his proposals on questionable assumptions and that his plan pursued the same "Will of the Wisp" of morale that had been sought so long in the Balkans, deviated from fundamentally sound doctrine and diverted resources from more important objectives. He also devoted great attention to morality:

> Hypocritically sometimes, Polly Anna–ishly frequently, but yet none the less fundamentally rightly, America has represented in world thought an urge toward decency and better treatment of man by man. Japs may order our prisoners to be shot, but we do not order the shooting of theirs. Hot blood is one thing—reason and the long view is another. As Mr. Lovett stated very strongly the other day, silly as it may seem to some of us realists here, there is definite and very genuine concern in both the Senate, Congress, and the country about the inhumanity of indiscriminate area bombing, as such.[22]

Weicker replied that Hughes had "a closed mind and a prejudiced point of view." The deputy director thought the target selection was based on an orderly system of military requirements and necessity. He agreed that Americans wanted to use "Marquis of Queensberry's rules" to protect civilians, but this approach was not feasible against the brutal Nazi regime. His program was not a new way to kill women and children, he contended, but a method to press home fundamental ideas to the German people about their defenselessness that could end the war. He did argue, however, that if his program saved a few Allied lives, any price paid by the enemy should "not be a factor of sober and practical consideration." When Colonel Charles Taylor, Williamson's deputy, saw Weicker's plan and the attached arguments, he agreed with Hughes, adding that it went against his own perceptions of General

Arnold's desires as well. Williamson agreed, and Taylor penned "Never sent, Thank God!" on the proposal that was to be submitted to Air Chief Marshal Sir Arthur Tedder, SHAEF deputy supreme commander. One week later Taylor killed another psychological warfare plan that proposed to destroy "Nationally Famous Monuments of Industry" to sap morale and to attack the power and transportation infrastructure in 116 cities. His comments, reflecting his growing irritation with such plans, noted that the proposal "leaves the door open for civilian bombing and the needless destruction of industrial monuments." If the "industrial monument" was "a major factor in keeping Germany in the war," it would be destroyed anyway as part of the strategic-bombing campaign. He concluded testily that if the target was not that important, "then to hell with it. Let's get on with the war."[23]

Contrary to Taylor's perceptions of the AAF commander, Arnold was indeed considering *Todestoss* at this time. By mid-July he began to believe that a well-timed strike by ground or air units would destroy the "increasingly shaky structure" of German resistance. Although he and Kuter, now the assistant chief of Air Staff for plans, saw some promise of weakening German morale with air attacks concentrated on one or two cities, Spaatz and Anderson, USSTAF deputy commander for operations, envisioned widely dispersed raids similar to Spaatz's earlier ideas for bomber sweeps.[24]

Meanwhile, the British Air Ministry circulated a memorandum entitled "Attack on German Civilian Morale" that proposed to break the morale of the army and the civil population primarily with an intensive bombardment of Berlin, concentrated on the administrative center of the city and continued "without respite so long as operational factors permit." Clearly they wanted to replicate the urban destruction and civilian dislocation of the July 1943 raids on Hamburg. Approximately 45,000 people had died there, the vast majority from the devastating RAF firestorm of the night of 27 July, the first such conflagration caused by bombing. Most of the dead had heeded the advice of local authorities to stay in basement shelters, where they were asphyxiated by carbon monoxide or crushed by collapsing buildings. However, those who took to the streets sometimes died even more horribly, sucked into fires by high winds or caught in molten asphalt. The Eighth Air Force made two daylight raids on precision targets as part of the series of attacks on the city. They were responsible for less than 1 percent of civilian casualties but achieved poor bombing results because targets were obscured by smoke from fires induced by RAF incendiaries. Because of this experience, the Americans learned that they could not follow Bomber Command in attacking a target, a lesson seemingly forgotten by the time of the Dresden raid in February 1945.[25]

The Americans were generally disappointed with their performance against Hamburg; bomber losses were heavy, and bombing accuracy was poor. Eaker was evidently impressed with the destruction of the RAF attacks, however. He rightly believed that the fear of another Hamburg "apparently has the Germans in a great dither," and he wanted to exploit the situation with a similar attack on Berlin with the RAF. Some American command-ers perceived that Hamburg had affected the will of the German people and wanted to mount spectacular precision raids to further demonstrate Nazi weakness. Anderson, then commander of Eighth Bomber Command, thought an American daylight attack on the capital would increase German panic and demonstrate the power of the AAF in the European theater. Yet the mass raid on Berlin did not occur. During the remainder of 1943 Eaker and Anderson mainly focused on other ways to prove the worth of preci-sion daylight bombardment, and Eaker was reassigned to the Mediterranean by the end of the year. Arnold's emphasis remained on precision attacks, especially on German aircraft factories and facilities. Spaatz and Doolittle had been engaged in Sicilian operations at the time of the Hamburg attacks and seemingly took little notice of them. Hamburg did not move the AAF toward carrying out similar attacks on civilian morale; key leaders in the European air war remained committed to the ideas of precision-bombing doctrine against enemy capacity.[26]

This commitment was evident in the response of American air leaders to the British proposal to attack German civilian morale. It produced "di-verse reactions," but most of them at AAF headquarters in Washington were negative. Kuter echoed Spaatz's fears when he wrote to Anderson that "we should consider whether the recent buzz-bomb attacks have not instilled in the British government a desire for retaliation in which American air units will be called upon to share with RAF Bomber Command the onus for the more critical features of night area bombing." He reiterated that it had been American policy to bomb military and industrial targets in accordance with the precision doctrine he had helped develop. Apathy and discouragement resulting from morale bombing "are not the qualities to pressure revolt," and people in the Nazi police state were not in a position to influence national will as much as in a democracy. "Furthermore," Kuter added, "it is con-trary to our national ideals to wage war against civilians." AAF headquarters found several other aspects of the British plan unacceptable. Contrary to Anderson, Kuter thought that "attacks against impressed labor of non-German origin are unsound." In regard to strikes against civilians he emphasized, "We do not want to kill them—we want to make them think and drive them to action."[27] Kuter told Williamson, visiting Washington, that the AAF had been and would continue to be "employed exclusively against military objectives until the time when it is broadly accepted that morale attacks including the killing of German civilians will tip the scales causing the cessation of hostilities." The decision to make such an attack "would be the unquestioned prerogative of the commander in the field." Even someone as devoted to precision doctrine as Kuter was willing to depart from it for *Todestoss* and conceded that such a course of action should be based on operational, not policy, concerns. Though Williamson believed that the adoption of civilian morale as a primary target would be "regrettable," he thought that Spaatz's ideas on the subject were more "acceptable" and more "likely to succeed" than British proposals. Williamson managed to get Arnold's concurrence for USSTAF to prepare a plan based on Spaatz's concepts that would entail an "all-out, widespread attack, of perhaps six or seven days duration." Arnold did not yet favor obliteration attacks, even on Berlin. No one in the AAF thought the time for *Todestoss* had arrived, but everyone agreed that contingency plans should be prepared.[28]

The time for executing these plans would soon arrive. As the war in Europe dragged on through 1944 and into 1945, the temptation to end it with the aerial deathblow against morale envisioned in AWPD/1 became almost irresistible. For Arnold, that would demonstrate the decisiveness of airpower and virtually ensure his dream of an independent air force. For members of the JCS and other leaders in Washington becoming increasingly anxious about the will of the American people to sustain the war, a swift *Todestoss* against Germany was essential to facilitate the timely shifting of emphasis and resources to Japan. For ground commanders facing a seemingly revitalized German army, any victory through airpower would save many lives, an argument that even the most devoted advocate of precision bombing had to consider. Arguments about the inefficiency of area bombing of cities could be waived for this special case, in which a set of unique circumstances, however vaguely defined, promised decisive results from an attack on civilian morale. Some leaders who retained strong scruples against killing civilians, such as Spaatz, would try to develop and execute a plan capitalizing on the inherent psychological shock effects of air attacks, designed to terrorize without killing by collapsing enemy morale through a widespread assault on military or economic targets. Other leaders less committed to precision doctrine would go to almost any lengths to end the war and still be comforted by the belief that any expedient against civilians at this critical phase of the conflict would save many more lives in the long run. Once the precedent for such attacks was established in Europe, *Todestoss* inevitably would be sought against Japan as well.

9. DELIVERING THE DEATHBLOW TO GERMANY

If the time ever comes when we want to attack the civilian populace with a view to breaking civil morale, such a plan as [CLARION] is probably the way to do it. I personally, however, have become completely convinced that you and Bob Lovett are right and we should never allow the history of this war to convict us of throwing the strategic bomber at the man in the street.

—Lieutenant General Ira Eaker to Lieutenant General Carl Spaatz[1]

The reactions of the people of Berlin who have been bombed consistently will be very different from the people of London who have not experienced a heavy raid in years. Terror is induced by the unknown. The chances of terrorizing into submission, by merely an increased concentration of bombing, a people who have been subjected to intense bombing for four years is extremely remote. We will, in what may be one of our last and best remembered operations regardless of its effectiveness, violate the basic American principle of precision bombing of targets of strictly military significance for which our tactics were developed and our crews trained and indoctrinated.

—Lieutenant General Jimmy Doolittle to Lieutenant General Carl Spaatz[2]

Your comments on the decisiveness of results achieved by air power lead me to believe that you might be following the chimera of the one air operation which will end the war. I have concluded that it does not exist.

—Lieutenant General Carl Spaatz to Gen. H. H. Arnold[3]

While Americans in Washington discussed contingency plans for *Todestoss*, the British in Europe were pushing their own proposals. They developed a new plan for a combined effort to destroy the Ruhr, Operation HURRICANE, to go along with Operation THUNDERCLAP, the attack on Berlin. The name Hurricane caused some confusion because Spaatz had chosen the same designation for the plan he was developing. As a result, the operations were initially known as HURRICANE I (British) and HURRICANE II (American) until the Americans changed theirs to CLARION late in 1944.[4]

146

The detailed plan for Thunderclap came out on 20 August, and immediately USSTAF commands complained. Cabell wrote a scathing letter to
Hughes, sarcastically calling the plan "the great opus" and "a combination
of retaliation and intimidation for the future." Cabell thought that German
morale was still very strong but realized that USSTAF needed its own "morale
plan ready to offset the baby killing schemes." He proposed that widespread
objectives be selected for attack that were symbolic of German industrial,
economic, or military strength. Reflecting his subordinates' concerns, Spaatz
wrote to Arnold outlining his own opposition to the British proposal: "I feel
that a case may be made on the highest levels for bombing of the city of Berlin." Any deviation from policies of precision bombing of military objectives,
"even for an exceptional case," would be "unfortunate" because "there is no
doubt in my mind that the RAF want very much to have the US Air Forces
tarred with the morale bombing aftermath which we feel will be terrific."
Spaatz also pointed out that his position "so far has been supported by Eisenhower," who still had overall direction for strategic air forces.[5]

Spaatz informed Eisenhower about THUNDERCLAP on 24 August, stating
that he opposed the operation as it was planned. He was willing to partic-
ipate in an attack on Berlin but would "select targets for attack of military
importance." Eisenhower's mixed reply must have alarmed Spaatz: "While
I have always insisted that US Strategic Forces be directed against precision
targets, I am always prepared to take part in anything that gives real promise
to ending the war quickly." Ike told Spaatz not to change current operational policies yet but to bring the paper to SHAEF for a discussion. When
they conferred on 9 September the military situation was at a critical stage.
The Germans were broken and fleeing across France, but the Allied pursuit
had ground to a halt during the first five days of September. Transportation was not adequate to keep the fast-moving columns supplied, and logistical shortages threatened the victory that seemed so close. This dilemma
must have influenced Eisenhower to favor operations such as THUNDERCLAP,
which promised to exploit the recent successes on the ground by breaking
the apparently crumbling German morale from the air. Ike directed that the
Eighth Air Force be prepared to bomb Berlin "at a moment's notice." Following this order, Spaatz told Doolittle "that we would no longer plan to hit
definite military objectives but be ready to drop bombs indiscriminately on
the town." USSTAF was now officially committed to THUNDERCLAP.[6]

The idea of a devastating attack on Berlin to shatter German morale was
not new to American leaders. In 1943 Eaker had wanted to mount a three-
day combined operation with the RAF against the city to compound the

effects of the firestorm on Hamburg; in early 1944 Arnold's staff had prepared an inconclusive study of the effects on morale of bombing the enemy
capital.[7] Berlin was a unique target with much symbolic value. Seversky's
predictions of the possible benefits of bombing cities had been realized
in Berlin; daylight attacks on the enemy capital harmed German prestige,
forced the Luftwaffe to defend it, and demonstrated Allied might. American
planes had participated in a giant raid on Berlin as recently as 21 June 1944.
(The British also were supposed to provide heavy bombers but withdrew
because of insufficient fighter support.) The British intended the attack to
achieve the goals of THUNDERCLAP, which was still being developed; but with
Eisenhower's support, Spaatz targeted only military objectives: aircraft factories, railroad facilities, and government areas. Forty-four bombers were lost, a
high casualty rate typical of such deep-penetration raids. Resistance to THUN-
DERCLAP from the rank and file of USSTAF was bound to be fierce. Eaker was
in the minority with his enthusiasm for such attacks. Airmen did not like the
long and dangerous Berlin raids, and most agreed with the commander who
said, "[Hitler] has made the morale of the German civil population highly
invulnerable to either propaganda or morale attacks." Part of the opposition
of American air commanders in Europe to THUNDERCLAP stemmed from the
realization that their subordinates had no desire to attack such a dangerous
target for the vague and probably unachievable objectives of breaking morale
and destroying the German will.[8]

The plan was also causing a stir in Washington. In mid-September the
Combined Chiefs of Staff deferred a British proposal to endorse morale
bombing after Admiral William Leahy, Roosevelt's chief military adviser,
said it would be a mistake to "record" such a decision,[9] an apparently diplomatic way to avoid offending the British and endorsing a distasteful proposition. However, pressure for THUNDERCLAP began to mount after the Battle of
the Bulge in December. General Marshall, already concerned with American
staying power for the war with Japan still ahead, began "pressing for any and
every plan to bring increased effort against the German forces for the purpose of quickly ending the war." He suggested that Munich also be bombed
as part of THUNDERCLAP, to demonstrate to civilians evacuated to that city
"that there is no hope." By the end of January, Bradley's headquarters staff,
facing a bloody assault into Germany, were also pressing for THUNDERCLAP.
Arnold acknowledged that these pressures were causing him to stress "some
very marginal projects," but "we will not know just where the breaking point
may be."[10]

With improving weather and the availability of more fighter escorts, a reluctant Spaatz could delay no longer. Acceding to Marshall's and Eisen-hower's desires, he scheduled the operation for 3 February 1945. He also ordered the Fifteenth Air Force to plan to bomb Munich, as Marshall had wanted.[11] Though without British participation the operation was techni-cally not THUNDERCLAP, that is how the Eighth Air Force perceived it, and they would have executed the same mission with the RAF. Leaders in Wash-ington also used that term to describe the coming operation as late as 2 Feb-ruary. True to form, Doolittle resisted to the end. On 30 January he sent a long message to Spaatz explaining his reservations. Besides the dangers to his crews, he complained, there were few "important strictly military targets in the designated area." He argued that the chance of terrorizing Berliners was remote because they had been subjected to intense bombing for four years and were used to it. What would be "one of our last and best remembered operations" violated American doctrine and principles, and American crews were not trained for such area bombing. Doolittle pleaded with Spaatz to let the RAF hit the city while the Eighth Air Force bombed precision targets that would ensure effectiveness and lower losses. Spaatz cabled back some partial replies, emphasizing the priority of visual oil targets and redefining the purpose of the operation by telling Doolittle to stress in news releases the "effort to disrupt reinforcement of Eastern Front and increase adminis-trative confusion."[12] Not satisfied, Doolittle sent another message: "Is Berlin still open to air attack? Do you want priority oil targets hit in preference to Berlin if they definitely become visual? Do you want center of City in Berlin hit or definitely military targets, such as Spandau, on the Western outskirts?" Spaatz replied that Doolittle should hit oil targets if good visibility existed for them; otherwise, the center of Berlin would be the target. Spaatz would carry out his assigned operation but only when it would not interfere with his oil campaign.

Just as Spaatz was interpreting his orders as he saw fit, so did Doolittle. He bombed the center of Berlin as he was told, but he still had his crews tar-get transportation facilities and government areas more in keeping with his concept of how Americans should bomb. Accuracy was fairly high, though aircraft did have to evade murderous flak that downed twenty-one heavy bombers. Nevertheless, the density of that part of the city led to reports of up to 25,000 civilian casualties, and because the raid coincided closely with the attacks on Dresden, it contributed to the ensuing controversy over whether the AAF was adopting terror tactics. In reality, however, the attack by 937 of Doolittle's bombers killed less than 3,000, more a tribute to his restraint than evidence of indiscriminate slaughter.[13]

OPERATION CLARION

Spurred by a sincere desire to end the war and by the realization of the need for an alternative to THUNDERCLAP, USSTAF leaders continued to work their own plan for *Todestoss* throughout late 1944 and early 1945. On 1 October 1944 Spaatz wrote to Lovett that he had "started the development of a plan for the full-out beating up of Germany with all the Air Forces at our disposal." He believed it represented the only means to end the war that year since the weather would limit operations by November. In a similar message to Arnold, he explained that HURRICANE would use bombers and fighters to attack "the most critical target system or targets inside Germany within the tactical capabilities of the forces involved" and was designed "to impress the German High Command with the might and destructive power of Allied Air Power."[14]

At the same time, Anderson was attending a conference on HURRICANE at the British Air Ministry, along with Hughes and Colonel Alfred Maxwell, USSTAF director of operations. The British expected the Americans to present a plan based on SHATTER; instead they proposed a widespread attack on oil targets. USSTAF conceded that the best objectives for tactical forces would be rail targets but even those attacks would facilitate the oil campaign by forcing more use of motor transport. The British offered to let USSTAF bomb oil targets in the Ruhr as part of their own operation. The meeting concluded with both parties committed to both concepts, HURRICANE I, the British plan to obliterate the Ruhr, and HURRICANE II, the American plan for widespread attacks on oil targets. Meanwhile Arnold had replied to Spaatz's cable, which had been inspired by Anderson. Though USSTAF still willingly took direction from Eisenhower, it was now technically under the supervision of Arnold as the agent for the Combined Chiefs of Staff, and his support would help in executing the American plan. Arnold endorsed it wholeheartedly, though he believed that "everything with military importance," no matter how small, should be attacked, because "all sections of Germany should have opportunity to be impressed by overwhelming superiority and destructive power of Allied Air Forces." He rebuked the British for their plan: "I will not condone attacks on purely civilian objectives."[15]

The plans Anderson brought back were circulated among the USSTAF staff. Maxwell criticized the British proposal for ignoring the "dividends of wide-spread fighter strafing" and for selecting targets for US air forces that could be knocked out at any time, not just during a special operation.[16] Hughes's Target Section was even more critical of HURRICANE II, conclud-

The shadow of a B-24 over the shattered marshaling yard in Munich. Such transportation objectives were included in AWPD/1 and targeted as a means to weaken the German economy, but their location within urban areas meant increased risks for enemy civilians. (Northwest and Whitman College Archival Collections, Penrose Memorial Library, Whitman College, Walla Walla, WA)

ing that only oil objectives offered "ample targets suitably geographically located" and also "immense, quick, military returns"; rail transportation and morale were not suitable target systems for such an operation. Despite this recommendation, the section was told to prepare a plan to attack German transportation. Using SHATTER as a guide, they looked at 100 cities with transportation targets to destroy but again presented objections, emphasizing that transportation was best disrupted through attacks on oil. Such an attack on so many cities "might subject our commanders to the criticism of having espoused a combination of morale and terror bombing."[17]

There were many forces at work that would produce the final American plan, Operation CLARION. The realization of the limitations of tactical fighters and of Bomber Command focused USSTAF's attention on transportation. Although transportation systems had been low on the list of precision-bombardment objectives, many leaders in SHAEF believed that widespread attacks might collapse the German economy and assist the ground forces as well. Tedder emphasized that the biggest dividends were to be gained by bombing small railroad stations because of the effects on railway personnel and the signaling system. Major General Elwood Quesada of the Ninth Tactical Air Command had also impressed the Advisory Specialists Group with his plans to loose fighter-bombers across Germany, an idea transmitted to the War Department. Lovett became an especially avid supporter of these "Jeb Stuart" units. Transportation targets such as trains were especially vulnerable to strafing.[18]

"The General Plan for Maximum Effort Attack against Transportation Objectives" was published by USSTAF on 17 December. It was designed to disrupt the enemy's lines of communication and transportation system, thereby assisting the ground forces, depleting oil supplies for motor transport, and perhaps even precipitating a crisis among railway workers. As a secondary benefit, the attack would bring home the effects of the war to German industry and the people to push them "over the brink," and perhaps cause the Germans to further spread their flak defenses. Targets included bridges, marshaling yards, railway stations, signaling facilities, and locks. Undefended or lightly defended targets were to be selected, and they were to be attacked with bombs, machine guns, and napalm. Actual "development of a scheme which will insure a maximum efficiency in the use of forces" was delegated to air force commanders. It was hoped that RAF Bomber Command would attack the Ruhr, but they would not participate directly in the operation. The Americans and the British were now pursuing their ideas of *Todestoss* independently.[19]

The plan raised violent objections from USSTAF commands, especially from key officers in the Mediterranean Allied Air Forces. Though in October Cabell had proposed his own plan to cause German collapse by attacking their rail system, he penned on his copy of CLARION, "This is the same old Baby killing plan of the get-rich-quick psychological boys, dressed up in a new kimono. It is a poor psychological plan and a worse rail plan." Lieutenant General Nathan Twining, commanding the Fifteenth Air Force, was confident that he could execute the plan, but he thought that low-altitude bombing and strafing by valuable heavy bombers was dangerous and unsound. He also was concerned with "how the enemy and our own people will react to our attacking these types of targets and the resultant heavy losses to the civilian populace." Eaker echoed these concerns in a personal letter to Spaatz, adding that the attack would convince the Germans that the AAF were "barbarians" because 95 percent of those people killed would be civilians. Eaker did think the plan was the best way to attack civil morale, if such a plan were needed, but he was now convinced "that you and Bob Lovett are right and we should never allow the history of this war to convict us of throwing the strategic bomber at the man in the street." Eaker's apparent softening on such attacks might have resulted from working with Cabell, or possibly he decided that with the war almost won, the AAF should not risk tarnishing its image.[20]

Doolittle expressed similar objections to CLARION, adding that outraged German civilians might take out their anger on Allied prisoners of war. He was also concerned that the plan risked heavy losses of low-flying aircraft "to attack objectives with results of such uncertain permanent value." The Ninth Air Force offered some minor suggestions, though no air force said it could not accomplish the mission if so ordered. The British Air Ministry added to the cacophony of complaints, its greatest concern being that diverting resources to CLARION might affect the fulfillment of the plan to destroy oil supplies![21]

Before the execution of CLARION, Spaatz moved to alleviate his subordinates' concerns. He not only understood the validity of their arguments but also had lost faith in the possibility for *Todestoss*. In January he wrote Arnold that Germany was far from ready to crack, and on 5 February he announced to his chief that he had given up "following the chimera of the one air operation to end the war." He now expected that the attack would paralyze German transportation for only a few days. The same day he sent a message to his subordinate commands concerning their questions about the operation. Explaining that the plan they had seen was but a guide and that it was up to them to balance risks against the objective to attack widespread communication facilities, he delegated the resolution of all questions back to the units that had asked them. In effect, he left the complete execution of CLARION to his field commanders and abandoned any concept of a concerted attack aimed at morale. To ensure that his intent was understood by his own units and by outside agencies, and to prevent any public perception that the AAF was engaged in terror bombing, he cabled all commanders on the night before the operation, directing them to emphasize the military nature of targets and not to give the impression in any releases "that this operation is aimed at civilian populations or intended to terrorize them."[22]

On 22 February the weather cleared enough to leave most of Germany vulnerable to air attack, and for two days strategic and tactical bombers pummeled German railroads, primarily. Ronald Schaffer argues vehemently that CLARION was a terror attack, citing among other items instructions to a briefing officer emphasizing that the attacks, striking throughout Germany, would "provide a deterrent for the initiation of future wars."[23] Yet deterrence was considered a side effect by the officers involved, and the units engaged in the attack did not purposely target morale in any way. The subject was not covered in lower-level plans, and no information on it was available in poststrike air force intelligence assessments. Even fighter-bomber pilots were briefed to stick to communications targets for bombing or strafing. Reports from participating units concentrated on the destruction of railways and rolling stock. Situation maps in Roosevelt's war room primarily highlighted bridges and marshaling yards.[24] German observers stated after the war that the February air attacks "had been indistinguishable from any others."[25] Reports on the operation were mixed; even today studies differ radically in their assessments of CLARION. Not surprisingly, Portal and the British Joint Intelligence Committee perceived little serious damage and recommended total suspension of such operations. SHAEF was pleased and the USSTAF summary called it "a spectacular success." Doolittle made a film showing that CLARION "materially aided in the break-through of the armies to the Rhine." The official American history claims Spaatz also thought CLARION was useful, but when the operation was scheduled again for 3 March, he personally stopped it.[26]

THE RAID ON DRESDEN AND ITS AFTERMATH

The basic focus of CLARION—attacks on enemy transportation—was not a departure from precision-bombing doctrine. Even AWPD/1 planned to attack transportation objectives but recognized that large facilities such as marshaling yards, because of their dispersed nature and easy reconstruction, required a type of repeated area bombing. The American method of area bombardment differed significantly from RAF attacks on major residential zones. Still, the selection of such a large objective within a city usually resulted in predictably increased civilian casualties, as evidenced in the earlier raid on Bucharest. As explained in chapter 6, American formation-bombing techniques often covered a wide zone, a tactic that kept formations tight for defense and increased chances of hitting the objective but that also produced a bomb pattern dispersed according to the arrangement of aircraft and spread out by varying intervalometer settings. Planners and commanders reasonably expected that most bombs would fall on or near the target,

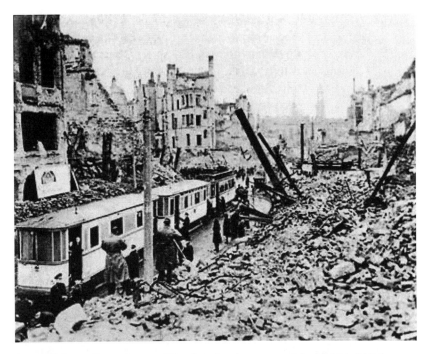

Ruins of Johanne Strasse in central Dresden after the controversial raid of 14–15 February 1945. This picture was taken more than a year later, reflecting not only the interest of the press in the bombing of the city but also Russian and German desires to exploit the destruction through propaganda. (Special Collections Division, US Military Academy Library, West Point, NY)

but results, as air force leaders knew, were never as precise as articles on the home front claimed. Rail centers were also popular nonvisual targets because large marshaling yards could be discerned on H2X radar screens. As large industrial targets were destroyed or dispersed and more heavy bombers became available, strategic attacks on transportation objectives increased significantly. Such air strikes also helped the rapidly advancing Russians. Alfred C. Mierzejewski argues convincingly that the bombing of marshaling yards was actually the decisive factor in creating a "moribund" economy in Germany by the end of the war. Disrupting marshaling "severed the coal/transport nexus, demolished the division of labor, and contributed heavily to the disorganization of [Albert] Speer's administrative system."[27]

An example of the deadly effect of formation bombing on such a target within a major city occurred a week before CLARION during the 14–15 February American raid on Dresden, planned in conjunction with massive British night area bombardments. Poor visibility over the target, in part the result of the many fires started by the RAF, compounded the errors. US bombing was good the first day but very poor later, after targets were obscured by smoke.[28] The lessons of Hamburg concerning the problems of hitting precision targets after RAF fire raids seem to have been forgotten. The majority of the 25,000 to 35,000 people killed in Dresden died from inhaling hot gases or carbon monoxide in the tornado of the firestorm caused by RAF incendiaries, though inaccurate USSTAF bombing of marshaling yards in the city probably contributed to the casualties to some degree. British tactics were especially deadly because they mounted a follow-up attack with mostly high-explosive bombs just as the firestorm burned itself out and before citizens could flee from their cellars to surrounding suburbs. For years after the raid, German and Russian propaganda estimated deaths as high as 135,000 and contributed to the horror associated with the raid.[29]

The best studies dealing with the attack lay much of the blame on Churchill and the confusion over Russian desires for support. In preparing for the Yalta Conference in late January 1945, the British prime minister prodded his air commanders at Malta to come up with an operation to aid the Soviet advance and impress them with the contributions and might of Anglo-American airpower. Harris and Portal came up with a list of four cities to attack that would cause great chaos in the movement of both military forces and refugees, then persuaded Spaatz to go along. At the Yalta Conference on 4 February, General Antonov and Marshal Stalin asked for Allied air attacks on communications centers to prevent the shifting of German troops to the Russian front; this request meshed with Churchill's plan and led directly to the bombing of Dresden. Antonov specifically mentioned the junctions of Berlin and Leipzig, but Allied planners also had identified Dresden and Chemnitz as other appropriate objectives to meet the Russian needs. On 8 February SHAEF instructed RAF Bomber Command and USSTAF to prepare an attack on Dresden because of its importance in relation to movements of military forces to the eastern front. Contrary to later reports, the city did contain important industrial and transportation targets worth destroying.[30] Like the intelligence summaries, newspaper accounts emphasized the communications and industrial features of Dresden and the support the attack gave the Russians, though military reports did not ignore the residential devastation. General Doolittle was quite disturbed about the destruction from the raid, telling assembled SHAEF air commanders with the "greatest reticence" that smoke from the burning city rose to 15,000 feet.[31]

The targeting of Dresden fueled two contemporary controversies, one involving SHAEF, USSTAF, and AAF headquarters before the actual attack and another that included the media and War Department afterward. When control of the strategic air forces reverted to the Combined Chiefs of Staff in September 1944, directives governing the operations of USSTAF and Bomber Command were drafted by Spaatz and Air Marshal Bottomley, delegates for Arnold and Portal. Oil was the main priority of Directives 1 and 2, and in October 1944 transportation was elevated to second place in Directive 2. These remained basically as the top two priorities for Directive 3, issued on 12 January 1945. Though Spaatz was pleased that oil retained its importance, in reality air force commanders still possessed great latitude in choosing their targets. Weather was often the main arbiter in deciding whether to bomb an oil refinery, a marshaling yard, or a tank factory. The situation was muddled even more when the Allied air leaders meeting at Malta, prodded by Churchill while anticipating Russian needs and requests at Yalta, and with the approval of General Marshall, revised the directive on 30 January, as explained above. Second priority became "Berlin, Leipzig, Dresden, and associated cities where heavy attack will cause great confusion in civilian evacuation from the east and hamper reinforcements." Attacks on communications came third.[32]

Kuter was visiting Eaker at the Mediterranean Allied Air Forces and immediately sent a copy of the directive to Arnold. Bottomley claimed correctly that Spaatz had agreed with the plan, and Kuter, another architect of precision doctrine, was troubled by USSTAF's apparent shift to city bombing. In response to Kuter's cable, Giles sent a message expressing concern over the high priority given the bombing of cities and supporting Kuter in his queries to Spaatz on the issue. In reply, Spaatz assured Arnold, who was recovering from his fourth heart attack, that USSTAF was continuing to follow Directive 3 and that he had not issued a revision of it because he felt none was necessary. The Malta message basically "reflected the differences in capabilities" between the RAF and USSTAF and was more in accordance with operations that Bomber Command could actually carry out. USSTAF continued with business as usual. Arnold said he was satisfied, though he emphasized that he would not accept "the promiscuous bombing of German cities for the purpose of causing civilian confusion"; it was acceptable to bomb transportation targets in those cities, however.[33] The same attitude was evident on the USSTAF staff. Brigadier General George McDonald, director of intelligence, published a memorandum for Anderson, "Target Value of Berlin, Cottbus, Dresden, Chemnitz," on 19 February, stating, among other points, that Dresden was an important railway center and military supply point and therefore a valuable target. Yet two days later, after reviewing the interim directive from Bottomley, he protested strongly that its emphasis on bombing cities to cause civilian confusion would be ineffective or counterproductive, as it had been in the Balkans, and linked USSTAF "to indiscriminate homicide and destruction." He argued that if the air forces were to adopt such a strategy, then "it follows as a corollary that our ground forces, similarly, should be directed to kill all civilians and demolish all buildings in the Reich."[34]

Arnold's concern intensified even more when, as the result of a press conference after the Dresden attacks, nationwide headlines appeared such as "Terror Bombing Gets Allied Approval as Step to Speed Victory." Howard Cowan, an AP reporter, based his story on a briefing in Paris by Air Commodore C. M. Grierson of the SHAEF Air Staff. Grierson did not mention morale attacks by name but pointed out that recent heavy-bomber attacks on population centers such as Dresden had caused great need for relief supplies and had strained the economic system. Arnold was appalled at the negative publicity and immediately demanded an explanation from Spaatz. Spaatz was in the Mediterranean, but Anderson replied that the report had exaggerated the briefing officer's statements and had never been cleared by censors. He reiterated that USSTAF's mission remained to destroy Germany's ability to wage war and that the Air Force did not consider attacks on transportation centers terror attacks: "There has been no change in policy, . . . there has been only a change of emphasis in locale." Anderson also wrote to Kuter and told him that because an RAF officer had caused the trouble, it had "led some people to say that it was intentional in an effort to tar us with the same brush with which British Bomber Command has been tarred." Anderson disagreed: "I believe it was a shear [sic] case of absolute stupidity by an incompetent officer." Eisenhower confirmed that the briefer had gone beyond his knowledge and authority.[35]

Spaatz's cable to his commanders on the eve of CLARION was probably also inspired by concerns over the adverse publicity after the Dresden raid. Despite AAF fears of US public reaction to the announcements of terror bombing, none came. Arnold was satisfied by 20 February that "the whole matter is now definitely in hand," but on 5 March the secretary of war asked for an investigation of Dresden: "An account of it has come out of Germany which makes the destruction seem on its face terrible and probably unnecessary." He did not want Dresden destroyed because he hoped the capital of Saxony could be "a portion of the country which can be used to be the center of a new Germany which will be less Prussianized and be dedicated to freedom." Typically, Stimson found out about the incident long after the fact and probably not through regular channels. He seems to have read the accounts of Grierson's briefing in the press. Arnold, recuperating in Florida from a heart attack, was perturbed when informed that Stimson was concerned about the raid. Reflecting his exasperation with everyone who questioned AAF bombing policies, Arnold scrawled on a message from his headquarters dealing with Stimson's request, "We must not get soft. War must be destructive and to a certain extent inhuman and ruthless." However, the resulting AAF report by Arnold's staff was not so callous and correctly blamed RAF incendiary bombs for most of the damage in Dresden. Trustful of his military advisers, Stimson seemed satisfied, and he let the matter drop. The whole controversy caused Arnold considerable strain and contributed to his declining health and numerous convalescent leaves and trips.[36]

Partly as a result of this controversy and partly because of the accidental bombing of Swiss territory during CLARION, a new bombing policy was issued to USSTAF on 1 March. It emphasized that only military objectives could be attacked and was especially restrictive about attacks in occupied areas. As the number of strategic targets continued to diminish, operations became "more and more of a tactical nature," designed to "help keep the break-throughs rolling." On 9 April Portal sent a message suspending area bombing on "remaining German industrial centres" because the full effects would not be felt before the end of the war and requesting that bombing avoid the destruction of "housing and other facilities which will be needed for the accommodation of our occupying forces." Attacks on built-up areas were still allowed to help ground assaults. When Arnold cabled Spaatz for comment, Anderson wrote a testy reply emphasizing that the USSTAF "have not at any time had a policy of making area attacks upon German cities." Anticipating such directives, USSTAF had already cut back operations on 15 March and was concentrating on oil targets, oil-supply routes, and German airfields and training installations. The AAF also assisted ground troops, though the Army continued to request attacks that the airmen considered excessive. Spaatz maintained that a town would be bombed only "when the Army specifically requires the action to secure its advance and specifically requests each town as an individual target in writing." Major General David Schlatter, deputy chief of Air Staff for SHAEF, noted that Spaatz's policy was so restrictive because "he is determined that the American Air Forces will not end this war with a reputation for indiscriminate bombing."[37]

The search for the single aerial deathblow against Germany was unsuccessful. USSTAF's heart was never really in the effort, mainly because of the attitudes of its commander, Lieutenant General Spaatz. The Americans had resisted getting involved in the attempt to bomb Balkan cities, and Spaatz's Operation CLARION evolved into an attack on transportation and not on morale. He had acquiesced in Eisenhower's desires and permitted THUNDER-CLAP, but Doolittle managed to direct that attack at military targets as best he could. The increased emphasis on transportation attacks, especially on marshaling yards in German cities, did signify a relaxation of the standards limiting civilian casualties. The larger the target, the more widespread the bomb spillover would be. With the diminishing number of good strategic targets, the large number of available bombers, and the constant pressure from the ground forces, such a shift was inevitable. As Tami Biddle notes, during the month of February that included the raid on Dresden and preceded the launching of the incendiary campaign against Japan, *Time* magazine reported US casualties on all fronts numbered 49,689 killed, 153,076 wounded, 31,101 missing, and 3,403 prisoners. The war was far from over.[38] However, USSTAF did resist the temptation to attack morale directly and to kill civilians to attain that end.

The lack of *Todestoss* in Europe had important repercussions in the Pacific. The momentum for such an operation continued, and advocates for an independent air force saw their last chance to prove its value against Japan. The Twentieth Air Force had the opportunity to bring about enemy surrender there almost completely on its own. This emphasis on the Pacific was clear to Spaatz as early as November 1944, when he became disturbed over the increasing diversion of strategic air units to the Pacific to the neglect of Europe. Lovett explained, "It seems to me that we ought to be shot if we don't have more than we can deploy in the Pacific and not try to balance the thing out to the last penny, thereby losing the possibility of exerting such overwhelming air power on the enemy as to give us a chance to find out whether air power can bring a nation to its knees or not. I don't see how we can make a bear rug until we have killed the bear."[39] Many Japanese civilians would be killed as well.

10. TORCHING JAPAN

From the practical standpoint of the soldiers out in the field it doesn't make any difference how you slay an enemy. Everybody worries about their own losses. . . . But to worry about the *morality* of what we were doing—Nuts. A soldier has to fight. We fought. If we accomplished the job in any given battle without exterminating too many of our own folks, we considered that we'd had a pretty good day.

—*General Curtis LeMay*[1]

What was criminal in Coventry, Rotterdam, Warsaw, and London has now become heroic first in Dresden and now in Tokyo.

—*Oswald Garrison Villard*[2]

As the air campaign in Europe drew to a close, the focus shifted to the Pacific. The same forces and precedents involved in the assault on Germany influenced the aerial bombardment of Japan, but more than just geographical distance separated the two theaters of operations.

Americans perceived the Japanese and the Germans differently, and many saw the "Japs" as a primitive, cruel race deserving no quarter or compromise. As mentioned in chapter 7, President Roosevelt even approved a project in which bats carrying small incendiary bombs would attack Japan; planners thought this approach would be effective against bamboo houses as well as the superstitious natures of their occupants.[3] As John Dower points out, racism was evident on both sides in the Pacific. The Japanese were often portrayed as less than human in the American media, and polls showed that 10 to 13 percent of the public favored their annihilation as a people.[4] Roosevelt, who thought the evil of the Japanese might be a result of their less-developed skulls, was convinced that Americans felt much more hatred toward the Japanese than the Germans. He carefully controlled the release of

161

information on Japanese atrocities in order to keep a strong public reaction from threatening the "Germany First" strategy and to prevent retaliation against American POWs.[5] Release of these stories began in late 1943, and they inflamed passions to an even greater degree. The information campaign climaxed in 1944 with the movie *The Purple Heart* dealing with the fictionalized trial and execution of captured airmen from the Doolittle raid. As one character, played by Dana Andrews, is led away to his death, he proclaims:

> It's true we Americans don't know very much about you Japanese, and never did—and now I realize you know even less about us. You can kill us—all of us, or part of us. But, if you think that's going to put the fear of God into the United States of America and stop them from sending other fliers to bomb you, you're wrong—dead wrong. They'll blacken your skies and burn down your cities to the ground and make you get down on your knees and beg for mercy. This is your war—you wanted it—you asked for it. And now you're going to get it—and it won't be finished until your dirty little empire is wiped off the face of the earth.[6]

Fanatical, savage fighting characterized war in the Pacific theater. The Japanese military committed numerous atrocities. Japanese soldiers and civilians usually committed hara-kiri rather than surrender and thought it shameful for their enemies to surrender. Americans retaliated when the Japanese mutilated and killed captives; "not since the French and Indian War had American troops been so brutal." Air commanders such as George Kenney feared that people back at home, including those in the War Department, were underrating the enemy. He wrote Arnold that the Japanese "national psychology" was "to win or perish"; their soldiers were "undoubtedly a low order of humanity," but they knew how to fight, and being in the army let each soldier "indulge in his Mongol liking for looting, arson, massacre, and rape." They could live on almost nothing and were guaranteed a place in paradise for dying in the service of the emperor. Those who thought the Japanese would be a "pushover as soon as Germany falls" were due "for a rude awakening." Kenney predicted that it would take a "crusading spirit or religious fervor" to win and that there was no time to train gradually for such an effort. "There are no breathers on this schedule. You take on Notre Dame every time you play."[7] Japanese civilians on the home islands were seen to be just as fanatic as their soldiers; everyone supported the war effort. In contrast to commonly held views on Nazi Germany, Japan was not perceived as a police state or as a society containing impressed workers.

The Japanese were also regarded as a direct threat to the continental United States. Early in the war, Californians feared that San Francisco could be firebombed into a conflagration such as the one caused by the 1906 earthquake, a fate destined for Tokyo instead. Authorities in Washington worried that any actual air raids on the Pacific Coast could bring a public outcry to divert more assets into continental air defense.[8] The Japanese did in fact drop incendiaries on the United States Pacific Northwest as a seaplane launched from a submarine unsuccessfully tried to start forest fires in Oregon in September 1942. Somewhat more dangerous was the A-Go project, balloons carrying small bombs launched into the jet stream from Japan. One killed a family in Oregon, and others exploded as far east as Texas. Arnold expected the Japanese to use the balloons for biological warfare.[9]

Other pressures toward escalation in the Pacific did not exist to the same degree in Europe. American leaders feared that the public could not sustain its war fervor for a long conflict and became particularly apprehensive as V-E Day approached. Admiral Ernest King typified the attitude of the JCS when he told reporters privately that he was afraid "the American people will tire of it quickly, and that pressure at home will force a negotiated peace, before the Japs are really licked."[10] This pressure to do anything to end the war was exacerbated by the confused lines of authority in the theater itself. Ronald Spector has argued that the two-pronged advance across the Pacific led by Nimitz and MacArthur was not the "sensible compromise solution" many scholars claim but the result of interservice rivalries that caused much conflict over resources and strategy. The Japanese never did take full advantage of the opportunities this divided command offered, but the AAF did.[11] When Curtis LeMay took command of the XXI Bomber Command of the Twentieth Air Force he generally did as he pleased. Like Spaatz, he dealt directly with Arnold for strategic priorities; unlike Spaatz, LeMay had no close relationship with any other theater commanders. Although competing British strategies forced the Americans in Europe to unite behind a common course of action, the British played a subordinate role to the United States in the Pacific. Because of the long range of the B-29s, the AAF could focus directly on striking at the fortress of Japan and avoid dealing with the incremental island-hopping Nimitz and MacArthur faced.

It is interesting to speculate about the course events might have taken if LeMay had been controlled by MacArthur, who adhered to the most restrictive bombing policy concerning civilians. The prime minister of Australia inquired in 1943 about MacArthur's policies covering the bombing of villages in enemy-occupied Australian territory, and the general assured him that

The "planner" and the "operator." Brigadier General Haywood Hansell Jr. (above), pictured here in Washington shortly before leaving for the Pacific, helped develop precision doctrine and AWPD/1. When his methods did not produce effective results against Japan, General H. H. Arnold replaced him in January 1945 with the innovative Major General Curtis LeMay (opposite), who initiated mass incendiary raids on Japanese cities in March.

missions were limited strictly to military objectives. When punitive bombing was carried out to ensure the safety of coast watchers, only one or two bombs were used, and only with MacArthur's approval. He continued stringent control of air bombardment when he returned to the Philippines. The attack of any target "located within inhabited areas of cities and barrios or sufficiently close thereto to endanger such areas" had to be cleared through MacArthur's headquarters. He sent a message to all air and naval forces under his command explaining his policy, emphasizing that the Filipinos "will not be able to understand liberation if it is accompanied by indiscriminate

destruction of their homes, their possessions, their civilization, and their lives." He contended that this position was dictated by "humanity and our moral standing throughout the Far East."[12]

MacArthur maintained his standards even when they hindered his subordinates. He refused General Walter Krueger's request to bomb the Intramuros District during the retaking of Manila even though such air support "would unquestionably hasten the conclusion of the operation." MacArthur maintained that "the use of air on a part of a city occupied by a friendly and allied population is unthinkable." He also respected the laws of war in raids on Japanese targets. When authorities on Rabaul complained that an air raid had destroyed a hospital there, MacArthur ordered a full investigation, which revealed that planes were attacking an antiaircraft position right next to the hospital. A detailed report with maps was furnished to the Japanese government through the Spanish embassy.[13]

MacArthur did not deal directly with the issue of bombing Japanese civilians during his operations, though a staff study done for him in 1944 concluded that they were too adaptable and inured to hardship to be affected by such tactics. In June 1945 one of his key staff aides called the fire raids on Japan "one of the most ruthless and barbaric killings of non-combatants in all history." This judgment probably represented the ethical views of an old soldier like MacArthur, who, in his speech at the formal surrender, emphasized the "spiritual recrudescence and improvement in human character" necessitated by the development of the atomic bomb. As will be discussed later, MacArthur's air commander, George Kenney, who was also enthusiastic about using war-weary bombers, did conduct three fire raids of his own in August against Kyushu, but it is doubtful his boss, absorbed by planning to invade Japan, was aware of them. Perhaps if Kenney had made a strong argument about the necessity of such attacks to support the invasion, MacArthur would have approved them. During the Korean War, he had eventually allowed Far East Air Forces (FEAF) commander George Stratemeyer to firebomb North Korean cities in early November 1950 after the airman asserted that was the only way to deter or limit possible Chinese intervention.[14]

MacArthur's naval counterpart, Admiral Chester Nimitz, commander of the Central Pacific theater, also demonstrated a more restrained view of the role of strategic bombers. He diverted considerable B-29 assets during April and May 1945 to conduct tactical missions against Japanese airfields and kamikazes threatening Okinawa. When naval and surface forces were in position to strike the enemy homeland in force, Nimitz ordered his units to "attack Japanese naval and air forces, shipping, shipyards and coastal objectives," including shelling iron works at Kamaishi and bombing military targets in Tokyo.[15]

If LeMay had been under MacArthur's or Nimitz's control, the feisty air commander would have been required to work very hard to justify his tactics. However, LeMay was not responsible to anyone except Arnold, and even that long link was tenuous, especially after the AAF chief had his fourth heart attack in January 1945. The XXI Bomber Command was headquartered on Guam along with the Central Pacific theater staff, but except for squabbling over resources and coordinating support for the invasion of Okinawa, LeMay and Nimitz rarely communicated.[16] The Army and the Navy each had a hero, a campaign, and a strategy to pursue the war against Japan; so did the AAF.

LEMAY AND THE FIRE RAIDS

Curtis LeMay was probably the most able and innovative air commander of World War II. His background was considerably different from that of most AAF leaders, with his commission from Ohio State Reserve Officer Training Corps and his lack of any previous war or barnstorming experience. He had little interest in theory or strategy and did not learn much from his courses at the Air Corps Tactical School. He was suspicious of geniuses because they were "inclined to forget about the rest of the team" and preferred "a group of average individuals who were highly motivated." In addition to his flying instruction, LeMay had received special training as a navigator, and he was always looking for a better way to do things. Like Arnold, he was willing to try new ideas. In Europe he had developed staggered formations to increase defensive firepower, designed the non-evasive-action bomb run to improve bombing accuracy, and initiated the training of selected lead crews to specialize on important targets. Known to his men as "Iron Ass," he was tough but fair and insisted on going on missions to share the risks. He had great respect and admiration for his men and hated to lose them. He was an accomplished navigator and pilot who also knew all about bombardment. As one subordinate stated, "He knew what to expect, what to demand, and how to get it."[17]

Some of his actions in Europe foreshadowed the course he would follow in the Pacific. He pioneered in the use of nonvisual bombing techniques and developed a great interest in the utility of incendiary bombs. In October 1943 he led an area raid targeting the center of the city of Munster that destroyed four hospitals, a church, and a museum, along with other targets. His subordinate commanders realized that "the RAF had been doing that sort of thing for a long time," but his superiors and the press took little notice of the Munster raid because it was overshadowed by the epic and costly attacks on ball-bearing plants at Schweinfurt that same week. Whether LeMay was trying to evade effective fighter and antiaircraft defenses that shot down 29 of his 119 bombers or just trying out a new bombing technique is unclear. He may have been experimenting with tactics used by the British in their devastating bombardment of Hamburg. Mission briefings from his intelligence personnel stressed that both primary and secondary target areas were "densely populated areas" where all the workers lived, "and the idea was to wipe out the built up areas and disrupt the people as much as possible." A remark in the intelligence briefing material that stated, "This is definitely an area bombing job instead of a precision target job" was crossed out—by whom and when is unclear. Someone in authority obviously did not want such a policy openly admitted. Such purposeful area attacks on city centers solely to "wipe out the built up areas" and "disrupt people" were not repeated by the AAF in Europe, but LeMay would make such objectives more commonplace in the fire raids against Japan.[18]

The vulnerability of Japan to firebombing was common knowledge. In 1939 an Air Corps Tactical School course taught that "large sections of the great Japanese cities are built of flimsy and highly inflammable materials. The earthquake disaster of 1924 bears witness to the fearful destruction that may be inflicted by incendiary bombs." In June 1941 the US government agreed to provide the Chinese with some bombers to attack "Japanese industrial areas," and Arnold told Lovett that the Chinese planned to use incendiaries to maximize the damage.[19] Shortly before the Japanese attack on Pearl Harbor, General George Marshall threatened to send Flying Fortresses "to set the paper cities of Japan on fire," though whether this was actually planned or just a remark to deter Japanese aggression is unclear. Articles in the press at that time conjectured about air operations against the home islands from the Philippines, Guam, the Aleutians, and Siberia.[20]

Once the war began, planners in Washington did not take long to focus on targets for incendiaries in Japan. By February 1942 Arnold's staff had prepared target folders on Japanese objectives that included areas of Tokyo ranked in order of "vulnerability to incendiary attack." The AAF chief maintained on file a copy of a 1942 *Harper's* article emphasizing that Japan's main weakness was its concentration of industry in cities vulnerable to "the easiest and cheapest type of bombing—the broad-casting of many small incendiaries over a comparatively wide area." The piece pointed out that ramshackle and combustible buildings sheltering small, dispersed industries would create conflagrations beyond the capacities of fire departments to control. It also conceded that the suffering in some areas that would result from incendiary attacks "is terrible to contemplate," a point that future planners seemed to ignore but that aircrews often could not. With Arnold's penchant for new ideas, it is not surprising that he continued to pursue this idea of Japan's vulnerability.[21]

In early August 1943 Kuter called for the convening of a group made up of Seversky and "other avowed civil air power experts" to develop "a purely air plan or plans to defeat Japan without the limitations of practical realities as seen by conventional planners."[22] The problem was also being examined by the Committee of Operations Analysts, a group of military and civilian experts on industrial intelligence and target selection that produced special studies for Arnold, and by planners involved in the B-29 Very Heavy Bomber program. From these efforts, Arnold prepared "An Air Plan for the Defeat of Japan," which he presented at the Quebec Conference later that month. He claimed in a wordy and convoluted passage purposely avoiding any clear reference to killing civilians that a heavy and sustained bombing of concentrated urban industrial areas would produce "the absorption of man-hours in repair and relief, the dislocation of labor by casualty, the interruption of public services necessary to production, and above all the destruction of factories engaged in war production." Arnold's statement, with its emphasis on destroying industrial capacity and its neglect of any consideration for noncombatants, foreshadowed the pattern that would be used to develop and evaluate the fire raids. In November, the Committee of Operations Analysts produced its report, which recommended targeting merchant shipping, steel production, urban industrial areas vulnerable to incendiary attacks, aircraft plants, the antifriction bearing industry, and the electronics industry, with no designated priorities.[23]

During 1944 theory began to be put into practice. Arnold had the AAF board construct some "Little Tokios" at Eglin Field to estimate the effect of incendiaries and fire tactics on Japanese cities. These tests were similar to those carried out by the Chemical Warfare Service at Dugway on simulated German targets, and they demonstrated how potentially destructive fire raids could be. While these tests were being conducted, Arnold sent an outline of his views to the president, which emphasized that "1,700 tons of incendiaries will cause uncontrollable fires in 20 major cities," thus destroying numerous war industries.[24] However, it is significant that he never made these opinions known to his field commanders and that the real impetus for the incendiary campaign would not come from Washington.

In December 1944 another innovative air commander, Major General Claire Chennault, persuaded General Albert Wedemeyer, commanding American forces in the China–Burma–India theater, to order an incendiary attack by B-29s on supplies in Hankow. XX Bomber Command had been operating out of bases in India and China since June 1944 as part of Operation MATTERHORN. Its first leader, Kenneth Wolfe, who had organized and trained the first B-29 units, had been fired by Arnold after only a month of disappointing failures. LeMay, commander there since August, was reluctant to comply with Wedemeyer's request, believing that it was not his mission to attack such a limited objective. The operation was a resounding success, however, and LeMay would not soon forget the results.[25]

The Hankow raid was also notable as one of the few successes of early B-29 operations in the Pacific. Operation MATTERHORN, which had been inspired both by AAF desires to get the new B-29s into the war and a perceived need to shore up the faltering Chinese, had run into much resistance from joint planners, and their concerns proved prescient. The XX Bomber Command's bases in India were too far from Japan to strike targets there, and its bases in China were vulnerable to ground offensives as well as difficult to supply with fuel, which had to be flown over the hump route across the Himalayas. During the ten months it operated in the China–Burma–India theater, XX Bomber Command mounted only forty-nine missions. Combined planners had always realized that the Mariana Islands would be a much better platform to launch bombing operations against the home islands as part of a still ill-defined strategy to defeat Japan, and once the JCS decided in March 1944 to move up the invasion of Saipan to June, MATTERHORN's utility and priority was considerably reduced.[26] Along with the rest of the JCS, Arnold expected the main strategic attacks on Japan to come from Brigadier General Haywood "Possum" Hansell, who took command of the XXI Bomber Command in the Marianas about the same time LeMay arrived in India. Hansell had long been a planner for Arnold and was one of the primary architects of precision doctrine. Hansell's XXI Bomber Command had better logistics and more secure fields, and was closer to Japan than LeMay's XX Bomber Command and could concentrate its firepower against the heart of the enemy home islands. Arnold had high hopes that Hansell could exert decisive airpower against Japan's homeland fortress and prove the worth of an independent air service. The AAF chief had staked a lot on the Very Heavy Bomber (or Very Long Range Bomber) program, and it looked as if it was finally going to pay off.

However, Hansell faced significant problems, many of them stemming from the haste with which the B-29s had been rushed into combat. It was the largest and most complex aircraft built in any quantity by any belligerent in World War II. The weapons system still had many flaws, and the Wright R-3350 engines especially were prone to failure, resulting in a high abort rate and many accidents. LeMay later remarked, "B-29s had as many bugs as the entomological department of the Smithsonian Institution." Training was also a major concern. XX Bomber Command was thought to be too small to fight its way through Japanese defenses in daylight. Because the first elements of XXI Bomber Command had originally been scheduled to go to China as well, crews were supposedly prepared to bomb primarily at night by radar, but operators had received inadequate training in the United States "due to a shortage of equipment and early commitment dates." Most of the strategic targets in Japan assigned to XXI Bomber Command were not suitable for radar-directed bombing anyway because of terrain that provided poor scope contrast. Hansell planned to get around this shortcoming by bombing visually by day in accordance with precision doctrine and Arnold's directives, but the shift in tactics necessitated that all crews be retrained. And no amount of training could prepare the crews for the weather over Japan, which made high-altitude precision bombing almost impossible.[27]

Towering cloud fronts off the Japanese coast broke up formations and increased their vulnerability to fighters. Even if planes arrived safely over the target, wind speeds exceeding 230 knots at bombing altitude created conditions that surpassed the capabilities of bombardiers and bombsights. Bombing tables were not designed for the 550-knot ground speeds that tailwinds produced, and B-29s fighting headwinds were sitting ducks for antiaircraft fire. Wind speeds were highest from December to February but still excessive in other months, and during those periods with the lowest incidence of high winds, the cloud cover increased.[28]

As 1945 began, bombing results of XXI Bomber Command remained dismal and abort rates high. B-29 crews were losing faith in their planes and their tactics. Their precision attacks had little effect on Japanese industry because of the dispersion of cottage industries as well as the woeful inaccuracy of high-explosive bombs dropped from high altitude. Hansell seemed unable to produce timely improvements, and Arnold needed results, not only to prove the worth of airpower and the B-29s but also to keep from losing control of them to MacArthur or Nimitz or even to Lord Mountbatten in the China–Burma–India theater. Hansell also did not help matters by admitting in a lengthy statement published in American newspapers in late December 1944 that his organization still had "much to learn and many operational and other technical problems to solve." In late December Arnold decided to remove XX Bomber Command from China and India and consolidate all B-29s in the Marianas under one commander; as part of the reorganization he awkwardly relieved Hansell and replaced him with LeMay as the new year opened. Brigadier General Lauris Norstad, responsible for B-29 operations as Twentieth Air Force chief of staff under Arnold, was sent to Guam to supervise the change of command. Norstad later said of the changeover, "General Arnold—and all of us, including, I think, Possum—now know that this LeMay is the best man for this particular job, the job of carrying out what Possum and the rest of us started. LeMay is an operator, the rest of us are planners." Now it was this operator's job to vindicate AAF planning in the Pacific.[29]

LeMay began with a total shake-up of personnel. The staff was "practically

B-29s dispersed at one of their bases at Isley Field, Saipan. Incomplete facilities had plagued Brigadier General Haywood Hansell's efforts to improve his operations, and one of Major General Curtis LeMay's first projects in the Marianas was to finish building adequate airfields.

worthless," and he needed to change some group commanders as well, so he brought over some of his people from China. Incomplete facilities and bases significantly hampered training, and he exerted pressure to complete them. He set new training programs in motion, especially concerning radar. For further assistance in operations and training, Norstad procured some radar lead crews from Europe. LeMay established a better maintenance program that put more planes in the air and lowered the abort rate. He even tried breaking the Russian codes to get their weather reports. The staunchly anti-communist LeMay also sent medical supplies to Mao Tze-tung in exchange for the right to establish a radio station in Yenan that provided information on weather and downed airmen. Crew morale rose and performance improved, but the results of daylight precision attacks remained disappointing. LeMay knew that he too could be relieved and began to search for a better way to accomplish his mission.[30]

Some planners on Arnold's staff, wishing to exploit the psychological effects of the loss of the Philippines and further demoralize the Japanese people, recommended that the time was ripe for an incendiary assault on urban industrial centers. However, pinpoint attacks on aircraft-engine factories retained first priority in Arnold's directives. Hansell claims he was unaware of General Arnold's "lively interest" in incendiary raids and was prepared to carry out urban area attacks only as a last resort. LeMay also believed that the AAF chief desired a continuation of precision-bombing methods and asked Norstad if Arnold, recuperating from another heart attack, ever went for a gamble. Norstad seemed to imply that being unorthodox was acceptable to the AAF chief but would not "stick his neck out" with anything more definite, despite the fact he had encouraged disappointing experiments with high-altitude incendiary raids in February. With a sense of uncertainty, Le-May decided to switch his tactics without informing Arnold of the details. LeMay claimed that he did not want any of the responsibility for failure laid on Arnold, giving him a free hand to put in a new commander, if necessary, to salvage the B-29 program. LeMay did eventually send Washington notice of his rather radical plans on 8 March, but he knew that both Arnold and Norstad would be out of town that day.[31] There is no evidence that LeMay feared any moral indignation from Washington over the firebombing; he never seemed to worry about ethical considerations anyway. He may have been afraid, however, that AAF headquarters would interfere in an attempt to change his tactics if they discovered that he was about to risk such valuable aircraft in dangerous attacks at low altitude with reduced defensive armament. Given the dismal results of the air campaign so far, LeMay probably believed he had nothing to lose by trying something new.

Many tactical reasons supported LeMay's adoption of low-level night incendiary raids, though the crews feared having to engage more fighters or lacking enough altitude to ditch after a mechanical failure. Many on his staff have tried to claim credit for coming up with the idea, but their boss had to make the decision to implement it. His experimental raids in February with high-level firebombing, both in daylight and at night, had been failures. Planes at lower altitudes normally encountered winds of only twenty-five to thirty-five knots and fewer clouds; scope definition on radar was better also. Such attacks took advantage of the lack of effective Japanese night fighters or low-level antiaircraft fire. These factors all improved bombing accuracy. Additionally, low-altitude flying reduced engine strain considerably so that less maintenance was required and there were fewer aborts. With the elimination of the need to climb to high altitudes or to fly in formation, less fuel was needed, and a greater bomb load could be carried with the bomb bay gas tanks removed. To increase the bomb load further, LeMay also dispensed with all defensive weapons and ammunition except for the tail guns, and only one or two gunners instead of four went on the mission. Selected urban target areas contained numerous industrial objectives. Mission reports emphasized that "it is noteworthy that the object of these attacks was *not* to bomb indiscriminately civilian populations. The object *was* to destroy the *industrial and strategic targets* concentrated in the urban areas." This wording could have been designed to counter any criticisms of the fire raids or perhaps to strengthen the resolve or to ease the troubled consciences of airmen who might have questioned the value of the missions or who felt guilty about the stench of charred flesh that lingered in their bomb bays. That line of argument was reinforced by messages from Washington concerned about editorial comments referencing "blanket incendiary attacks upon cities." It also emphasized again the AAF focus on destroying enemy capacity to resist.[32]

RESULTS OF THE FIRE RAIDS

That objective of American bombardment was not evident to people in targeted Japanese cities, particularly in Tokyo, during that first massive fire raid, code-named Operation MEETINGHOUSE, on the night of 9 March 1945. The selected zone of attack covered six important industrial targets and numerous smaller factories, railroad yards, home industries, and cable plants, but it also included one of the most densely populated areas of the world, Asakusa Ku, with a population of more than 135,000 people per square mile. This fact was noted in the Bomber Command Target Information Sheets, which acknowledged, "Primary purpose of this type of attack is to capitalize on the fact that many of Japan's industrial and transportation facilities lie within or immediately adjacent to known highly inflammable sections of her principal cities."[33] Despite these claims, it appears that another consideration for this first raid of the new air campaign was to attack an especially dense urban area to provide the best possible chance for a spectacular result.

That would be achieved. Before Operation MEETINGHOUSE was over, between 90,000 and 100,000 people had been killed. Most died horribly as intense heat from the firestorm consumed the oxygen, boiled water in canals, and sent liquid glass rolling down the streets. Thousands suffocated in shelters or parks; panicked crowds crushed victims who had fallen in the streets as they surged toward waterways to escape the flames. Perhaps the most terrible incident came when one B-29 dropped seven tons of incendiaries on and around the crowded Kokotoi Bridge. Hundreds of people were turned into fiery torches and "splashed into the river below in sizzling hisses." One writer described the falling bodies as resembling "tent caterpillars that had been burned out of a tree." Tail gunners were sickened by the sight of hundreds of people burning to death in flaming napalm on the surface of the Sumida River. A doctor who observed the carnage there later said, "You couldn't even tell if the objects floating by were arms and legs or pieces of burnt wood." B-29 crews fought superheated updrafts that pasted crews to seats with violent g-forces while destroying at least ten aircraft, and wore oxygen masks to avoid vomiting from the stench of burning flesh. Assigned by LeMay to observe the raid, Brigadier General Thomas Power of the 314th Bomb Wing and his intelligence officer circled the city and sketched the growing conflagration, noting that smoke rose over 25,000 feet and "the glow from the fires was clearly visible 150 miles away." By the time the attack had ended, almost sixteen square miles of Tokyo were burned out, and over one million people were homeless. Survivors of the city remembered that terrible night as "The Raid of the Fire Wind."[34]

Newspaper accounts of the incendiary attacks, mirroring Air Force intelligence on bombing results, concentrated on physical damage rather than on civilian deaths. Articles on the Tokyo raid were typical. They noted the heavy population density but emphasized that in the area destroyed, "eight identifiable industrial targets lie in ruins along with hundreds of other industrial plants." One account, quoting LeMay, mentioned thousands of "home industries" destroyed, and another claimed that the raid's purpose was realized "if the B-29s shortened the war by one day." Accounts did not estimate civilian casualties, but they did proclaim that the many thousands made homeless posed an immense refugee problem for the Japanese government. Deaths were not mentioned, and of course there were no pictures of the destruction, just maps of the destroyed zone.[35] The lack of reference to noncombatant casualties by the press resulted from a similar oversight in

AAF accounts of the incendiary attacks. This omission was not an example of AAF censorship because the mission reports also neglected such statistics; such figures were difficult to determine even by civil defense authorities on the ground and were not normally included in AAF intelligence assessments that relied primarily on aerial photography.

The resort to fire raids marked another stage in the escalation toward total war and represented the culmination of trends begun in the air war against Germany. Although target selection, especially of transportation objectives, late in the European campaign showed less effort to avoid civilian casualties, LeMay's planning ignored such considerations even more. His intelligence officers and operations analysts advised him that massive fires were essential in order to jump the fire breaks around factories, and residential tinder fed those conflagrations. Precision bombing was no longer more effective than urban area bombing when applied to combat conditions over Japan; concerns for humanity could not override the desire for efficiency. Noncombatant deaths were unavoidable in order to destroy Japanese industry and forestall an invasion of Japan, which LeMay feared would cost many American lives. The success of the new tactics at producing obvious results also "salvaged the morale and fighting spirit" of LeMay's crews and proved to them that the B-29 was "an efficient and reliable combat aircraft."[36] Although areas of industrial concentrations remained primary targets, the concept of workers as belligerents that had surfaced in European combat once again justified civilian casualties. In addition, all Japanese were perceived as manufacturing for the war effort, often in their homes. LeMay defended burning Tokyo:

> We were going after military targets. No point in slaughtering civilians for the mere sake of slaughter. Of course, there is a pretty thin veneer in Japan, but the veneer was there. It was their system of dispersal of industry. All you had to do was visit one of those targets after we'd roasted it, and see the ruins of a multitude of tiny houses, with a drill press sticking up through the wreckage of every home. The entire population got into the act and worked to make those airplanes or munitions of war . . . men, women, children. We knew we were going to kill a lot of women and kids when we burned that town. Had to be done.[37]

LeMay also emphasized that, whenever possible before later incendiary raids, populations were notified to evacuate. As with Doolittle's warnings to Czech workers, aircrews did not like such tactics, fearing defenders would be likewise forewarned and therefore forearmed.[38] LeMay's intent was to capitalize on the fear generated by his firebombing to disrupt industry and the social infrastructure without killing everyone. Refugees clogged the roads and caused the Japanese government immense relocation problems. The leaflet design was carefully chosen. "Objectionable" pictures that demeaned the Japanese were rejected by the AAF; instead, their leaflet depicted a B-29 dropping incendiaries with the names of eleven cities printed around the plane. The text emphasized that air attacks were aimed only at military installations, "to destroy all the tools of the military clique which they are using to prolong this useless war. . . . But, unfortunately, bombs have no eyes. So, in accordance with America's well-known humanitarian principles, the American Air Force, which does not wish to injure innocent people, now gives you warning to evacuate the cities named and save your lives." The leaflet proclaimed that America was not fighting the Japanese people, only the military group that had enslaved them, and encouraged the populace to demand "new and good leaders who will end the war." It concluded with the promise that at least four of the named cities would be attacked but also noted that unnamed others could be hit as well. This psychological warfare campaign was quite successful, and at its height, more than eight and a half million Japanese were leaving their cities. The government had been trying to get people to disperse from the hard-to-defend cities, but the fire raids actually convinced more than one-seventh of the Japanese population eventually to flee to the country.[39]

George Kenney followed suit. Completely trusted by MacArthur, Kenney had a free hand to conduct FEAF operations, and he built upon LeMay's psychological warfare with his own. FEAF initially dropped leaflets on Kyushu that exploited the results of the B-29 raids, then followed with warnings to its three targeted cities seventy-two hours before the bombers arrived, proclaiming, "We want you to see how powerless the military is to protect you." Civilians were urged to evacuate, and also to overthrow their government "to save what is left of your beautiful country." After the attacks, which did have industrial target objectives, including factories reported to be manufacturing rocket suicide planes, follow-up leaflets again urged a regime change while comparing American might to feared forces of nature: "The military forces of Japan can no more halt the overwhelming destruction of the United States Air Force than the people can stop an earthquake." These campaigns to exploit civilian morale incorporated a scheme that had been proposed and rejected in Europe—another sign of the intensification of the war in the Pacific.[40] Indeed, this use of psychological warfare made the generation of terror a formal objective of the fire raids. Though no American

An area of Tokyo in flames near the Imperial Palace, bombed on the night of 26 May 1945. A few days after this raid, a troubled Henry Stimson questioned General H. H. Arnold about the justification for the mass incendiary attacks on Japanese cities.

leader would publicly admit it, the AAF was now engaged in area attacks against Japan similar to those raids that RAF Bomber Command had conducted against Germany. Moreover, LeMay's XXI Bomber Command was more efficient than the RAF and Japanese cities were much more vulnerable than German ones. While he was destroying the enemy's industrial and military infrastructure in accordance with precision objectives, LeMay was also mounting mass assaults on civilian morale, though that was his secondary objective—his "destruction bonus," not his main goal. He still expected to achieve victory primarily by destroying enemy capacity to resist.

AAF headquarters in Washington was ecstatic about the incendiary attacks, and planners quickly constructed a new list of industrial sectors within cities for priority targets. Twentieth Air Force headquarters assured LeMay that except for aircraft engine plants, there were no real strategic bottlenecks in Japan suitable to attack, but "Japanese industry as a whole is vulnerable to attacks on the principal urban industrial areas." LeMay received congratulatory letters from Arnold, Norstad, and Giles. Among leaders there, only Stimson seemed troubled. Typically, he apparently learned the details of the raids later and then from press accounts, probably after LeMay gave a briefing on Guam about the fire raids on 30 May that produced stories claiming it was possible that "1,000,000, or maybe even twice that number of the Emperor's subjects" had perished in the conflagrations. On 1 June Stimson told Arnold that Lovett had promised that only precision bombing would be used against Japan. Arnold explained that because of Japanese dispersal of their industry, "it was practically impossible to destroy the war output of Japan without doing more damage to civilians connected with the output than in Europe." Arnold did promise that "they were trying to keep it down as far as possible." Having no other information, Stimson seems to have believed Arnold. In a later meeting with President Truman, the secretary of war repeated Arnold's arguments. Stimson was anxious because he did not want his country to "get the reputation of outdoing Hitler in atrocities." Paradoxically, he also was afraid that the AAF would leave Japan "so thoroughly bombed out" that no suitable target would remain to demonstrate the atomic bomb.[41]

PLANS TO END THE WAR

Stimson may have had misgivings about the moral implications of the fire raids, but he was even more concerned with the war weariness of the American people. Military leaders feared that victory in Europe would bring "a general let-down in this country" and that perhaps public opinion would demand the return home of forces from Europe instead of allowing them to be deployed in the Pacific. The JCS was alarmed by reports of unrest, irritability, and ignorance about the continuation of the war, fears shared by President Truman. In Europe it had been fairly obvious when the end of the war approached and targets disappeared, but air attacks on Japan had to continue in preparation for the invasion of the home islands. The Japanese had never been forced to surrender to a foreign power, and planners had no way to predict their behavior. Resistance seemed fanatic; the Japanese people appeared to be prepared to die for their emperor. When the Japanese organized a People's Volunteer Corps, making all men from fifteen to sixty and all women from seventeen to forty liable for defense duties, the Fifth Air Force intelligence officer declared, "There are no civilians in Japan," a policy that contributed to at least two cases of fighters strafing civilians. American battle casualties in the Pacific increased dramatically as the average monthly rate of deaths quadrupled to nearly 13,000. The desperate fighting on Okinawa during the spring and early summer foreshadowed the consequences of invasion and increased doubts as to whether the American people had the stamina and will to achieve unconditional surrender.[42] Grim G-2 estimates predicted that 200,000 regular troops and 575,000 reservists would defend Kyushu, and Japanese reinforcements might be able to overcome planned American local superiority. Intelligence experts expected 350,000 regulars and up to 600,000 reservists to resist subsequent operations on the Kwanto Plain of Honshu.[43]

In this atmosphere leaders pursued any idea that held hope of speeding victory and reducing losses and believed that the public expected them to do so. The tortured ethical calculus involved in deciding the conduct of the war and leading to the use of the atomic bomb could also be applied to enemy casualties. A successful siege could avoid the costs of assault for the Japanese as well as for the Americans, though considerations of friendly losses were far more important to decision makers and bomber crews. LeMay wrote in April 1945 that he believed he had the resources to destroy the enemy's ability to wage war within six months. This was Clausewitzian calculus at its most brutal; with no capacity left in the equation, resistance had to go to zero. When Arnold visited Guam in June, LeMay's staff presented a briefing describing how their bombers could bring Japan to the brink of defeat by destroying all industrial facilities by 1 October. Arnold was skeptical but wrote in his journal, "We did it in Germany with much more difficult targets and much more intense antiaircraft. Why not in Japan? We will see." Arnold had already received a message that President Truman wanted to meet with the JCS to discuss the invasion of Japan and whether the AAF could really win the war by bombing; and the AAF chief decided to send LeMay back to Washington to assist Eaker, now Arnold's deputy, in presenting the Air Force's position. Arnold saw this effort as "another opportunity to make military history." LeMay's staff went with their commander and repeated the briefing they had just given Arnold to the JCS. General Marshall slept through most of the presentation, and LeMay came away convinced that leaders in Washington were fully committed to invading Japan just as they had invaded Europe.[44]

Among the points that Arnold had wanted his staff to emphasize to the president and the JCS were the increased use of psychological warfare and the use of poison gas. Arnold had ordered the preparation of AAF plans for the retaliatory use of poison gas against Japan as early as 1943, and he was not alone in his advocacy of first use of the weapon in 1945.[45] Joseph Stilwell and Douglas MacArthur both favored the gassing of enemy troops to assist the invasion of the home islands.[46] So did Marshall, in keeping with his tendency to favor more drastic measures to end the war as the conflict dragged on. He emphasized that the gas did not have to be the most potent, just enough to sicken and weaken enemy soldiers. The weapon would not be used "against dense populations or civilians," but the matter of public opinion would still have to be considered.[47] In June Marshall presented a study to Admiral Ernest King proposing that the JCS issue instructions to build up stockpiles of gas for the invasion of Japan and that "the question of the acceptance of the principle of initiating gas warfare against the Japanese . . . be informally discussed with the President." If Truman approved, he could then take up the matter with Stalin and Churchill. Marshall believed that if faced with the possible costs of continuation of the war, the American people would approve the use of gas. After all, he argued, that weapon was not as terrible as others such as the flamethrower or the "petroleum bomb" that had set so many fires in Japan.[48]

There is no evidence that the JCS decided to pursue the use of poison gas against Japan, perhaps because of strong resistance from Leahy. They did consider in some detail the application of biological or chemical agents to destroy the Japanese rice crop, however. In January 1945 Stimson's staff had requested a legal opinion on the use of "LN Agents" to destroy crops. The judge advocate general concluded that the use of such chemicals was legal as long as they were not toxic to humans. He added, "The proposed target of destruction, enemy crop cultivations, is a legitimate one, inasmuch as a belligerent is entitled to deprive the enemy of food and water, and to destroy his sources of supply." The National Academy of Sciences and the US Biological Warfare Committee urged Stimson to approve the use of LN chemicals,[49] and the JCS seriously considered the option. King pushed for a decision by 1 August so that shipping could be arranged in time to ensure the destruction of Japanese crops in June 1946.[50] Considering what we now know about the famine conditions in Japan in the winter of 1945, the impact of such an assault on rice would have been truly catastrophic.

In May 1945 Arnold received the suggestion for a similar plan to attack Japanese food supplies and to use medium bombers to destroy schools of fish. Norstad claimed that the AAF had been working on such a project already, but Eaker asked for further study. By August experiments in Terre Haute, Indiana, had demonstrated that an agent known as VKA was effective in destroying cereal crops such as rice when raw crystals were dropped into paddies from the air.[51]

Arnold's staff continued to search for better ways to achieve victory through airpower over Japan. One of the obvious sources for new ideas was the experience of the USSTAF in the European theater, and many officers were transferred to the Pacific. Anderson warned, "These officers should be selected both for their experience and their flexibility of thought, for those tactics which are sound in the European theater may not be the best for the Japanese theater."[52] Nonetheless, AAF headquarters expected to gain valuable lessons from the air campaign against Germany, especially from the work of the US Strategic Bombing Survey (USSBS).

During June and July Norstad chaired meetings in Washington between the Joint Target Group and the USSBS staff, which had studied bombing results in Europe. Roosevelt's directive, the inspiration for the creation of the survey, recommended that the focus include the "indirect" results of attacks on industries, especially the impact of refugees on transportation, food, medical attention, and morale. Norstad was interested in these aspects in relation to RAF area bombing. He was astonished, however, by reports that workers' morale was affected very little by the attacks. In fact, impressed workers actually worked harder after air raids, "joined in as a common herd against a common enemy." Absenteeism was a problem after major raids as people relocated their families, but otherwise the efficiency of German workers did not decrease materially. The USSBS gave Norstad a detailed study of Hamburg, tracing its recuperation from the firestorm, and Norstad predicted the information would be helpful in plotting the war against Japan.[53]

In final reports to the secretary of war, both the USSBS and the Joint Target Group agreed that a large gap existed between the most important target system, Japanese transportation, and any other objective. Second in priority for the USSBS was ammunition reserves, followed by precision industrial targets and chemical attacks on rice production. Attacks on urban industrial targets were last, and they were to be hit only if there was less than a one-third chance of hitting more precise objectives. The Joint Target Group was in general agreement except that they placed no emphasis on most precision targets or on the rice crop and more on incendiary attacks on cities. Both groups briefed Spaatz, the newly designated commander of the recently created US Army Strategic Air Forces (USASTAF), which included the Eighth and Twentieth Air Forces. He was being sent to the Pacific to take over the direction of most strategic air operations there. Eighth Air Force personnel were due to follow, where they would also be equipped with Superfortresses. Typical of the convoluted command structure in the theater, MacArthur and Kenney retained control over their own heavy bombers, mostly B-24s. In accordance with his record of adherence to precision bombing, Spaatz agreed with the USSBS's recommendations for his forces. He went to Guam with a directive from Eaker to concentrate on Japanese railway targets, aircraft production, ammunition supplies, and industrial concentrations and stores, in that order of priority.[54]

Spaatz could do little to change the course of the air war in the Pacific, however; there was too much momentum behind the fire raids. Ammunition dumps were stocked with incendiary clusters, and operations and training for the strategic-bomber crews were geared for low-level, night area attacks. Statistics covering the number of bombs dropped and the number of factories destroyed were being used to demonstrate the power of the AAF, and data on civilian bombing casualties were ignored. Predictions of potential losses of American lives received much attention, however, and the devastating raids were linked to preparations for the impending invasion. The Twentieth Air Force was fully committed to the firebombing of Japanese cities.

So was General Arnold. While Spaatz was trying to reshuffle priorities, the AAF chief was telling his staff at the Potsdam Conference, "The war with Japan is over as far as creative work is concerned. The die is cast. There is very little we can do other than see the planes and personnel with supplies get over there." Arnold passed out books of photographs showing the destruction of Japanese cities, and when Stalin proposed a toast to a meeting in Tokyo, Arnold boasted, "If our B-29s continue their present tempo there [will] be nothing left of Tokyo in which to have a meeting." His attitude was well received by those assembled. Hatred for the Japanese was evident, typified by Lord Mountbatten's remarks that the Japanese royal family were "morons" and should be liquidated. Arnold was optimistic about his air forces' ability to end the war, betting Portal that it would be over "nearer Christmas 1945 than Valentine's Day 1946."[55]

Arnold would win his bet handily. When Spaatz arrived in the Pacific, an examination of the situation convinced him "that unless Japan desires to commit national suicide, they should quit immediately." The dropping of the atomic bombs helped bring some Japanese leaders to the same conclusion. Appalled by the destruction being wrought on Japan, Spaatz wrote in his diary about the new weapon and the fire raids: "When the atomic bomb was first discussed with me in Washington I was not in favor of it just as I have never favored the destruction of cities as such with all inhabitants being killed." According to the recollections of Spaatz's family, he had been reluctant to take the USASTAF command because of his revulsion over the destruction dealt German cities and his expectations of a worse fate for the Japanese. Directed to continue bombing until arrangements for surrender were completed, Spaatz canceled one raid because of bad weather and tried to limit other attacks to military targets. When the press interpreted Spaatz's cancellation as a cease-fire, Truman ordered him to halt the bombing to avoid a misperception that its resumption indicated a breakdown in negotiations. When the Japanese delayed, Truman ordered more strategic attacks, and Arnold demanded a peak effort to show the importance and power of the AAF. Despite Spaatz's anxious queries, no cancellation was ordered, and more than 1,000 planes hit Japan on 14 August, some even after Japanese radio announced acceptance of the terms of surrender.[56]

Although AAF officers quibbled over the number of American lives saved by bombing, they agreed with Prince Konoye's claim: "Fundamentally, the thing that brought about the determination to make peace was the prolonged fire bombing by the B-29s." The AAF was worried, however, that the Japanese "were conducting an intensive propaganda campaign concerning the bombing of their cities with the view to getting sympathy out of Americans."[57] However, little sympathy was available, even though the B-29s had burned out 180 square miles of sixty-seven cities, killed over 300,000 people, and wounded another 400,000. The Twentieth Air Force reported remarkably light operational losses of only 437 of the very heavy bombers, mostly from technical failures—a tribute to the effectiveness of American tactics as well as to the weakness of Japanese defenses. In contrast, over 3,000 B-17s and 1,000 B-24s had been lost by the Eighth Air Force in European combat.[58]

Hansell, who remains notably objective in his memoirs, makes a strong case that precision attacks on the Japanese electrical industry, using low-altitude attacks at night with new radars and tactics finally perfected by the 315th Wing, would have destroyed Japan's ability to make war and brought it to the peace table "at less cost with fewer undesirable side effects." This alternative strategy would have taken fewer sorties and saved many civilian lives, though it would have taken more time (and perhaps cost more American lives) because of the wait for the arrival of new equipment. Another possibility might have been to expand the B-29 aerial-mining program, but that also probably would have required more time to produce decisive results. In four and a half months, LeMay's 313th Wing sowed over 12,000 mines in ports and waterways, sinking almost a million tons of Japanese shipping. Along with submarines and tactical air attacks, the strategic-mining campaign had almost completely halted Japanese seaborne traffic of raw materials and foodstuffs by mid-August 1945. One can only wonder what would have happened if another leader, such as Spaatz, had commanded the B-29s, someone more committed to precision doctrine and perhaps more experienced and secure in his position. Would he have been more inclined to take the time and effort to explore alternatives before resorting to the extreme of the fire raids? Such a course would have been difficult, especially after Hansell's experience. And if Prince Konoye is to be believed, different tactics or a delay in resorting to the incendiary attacks might have had serious consequences in forcing a Japanese capitulation.

The massive destruction, social dislocation, and psychological impact of the B-29 campaign against Japanese cities perhaps made it key in the series of shocks that produced a surrender. Each separate blow, including the Soviet entry into the war, affected a different group of decision makers and added to the Emperor's burden. Remove any one, and perhaps the end of the war is delayed. Even Hansell concedes that the chosen strategy of the fire raids was "decisively effective" and a "sound military decision," especially with the time pressures that existed in the Pacific. The final result might also have been better for the Japanese, as terrible as it was. At the conclusion of a presentation I gave in Tokyo about the firebombing in 1995, a Japanese historian closed the session by postulating that without the blows of the fire raids and the atomic bomb, his country would have resisted at least into the fall, long enough for the Soviet Union to execute plans to invade Hokkaido. Stalin planned to initiate the operation in late August. The nation then would have been occupied like Germany, with a communist zone in North Japan. In addition to that Soviet threat, Japan also faced a complete breakdown of its transportation system and mass starvation by the winter of 1945 that was mostly alleviated by MacArthur and American occupation forces.[59]

American leaders could not wait for XXI Bomber Command to experiment and train; the invasion was too close and looked too costly, and the will of the home front appeared to be on the wane. With the air resources available, the fire raids seemed to be the easiest and the quickest method for destroying the ability of Japan to wage war. Military and industrial targets were the primary objectives, but just as in Europe, as the war dragged on, civilian casualties from strategic attacks clearly were less of a consideration. Perhaps the culmination of this trend is best exemplified by the message Norstad sent to Spaatz on 8 August: "It is understood that the Secretary of

War in his press conference tomorrow will release a map or photostat of Hiroshima showing the aiming point and the general area of greatest damage. . . . It is believed here that the accuracy with which this bomb was placed may counter a thought that the CENTERBOARD [A-bomb] project involves wanton, indiscriminate bombing."[60] If an atomic bomb dropped on a city could be construed as a method of precision bombing, then that doctrine had evolved to the point where civilian casualties were no longer taken into consideration at all.

11. STRATEGIC AIRPOWER IN LIMITED WARS

I regret the necessities of war have compelled us to bomb North Vietnam. We have carefully limited those raids. They have been directed at concrete and steel and not at human life.

—President Lyndon Johnson[1]

For the men who dropped bombs on Japan, there was little difference between destroying cities with incendiary bombs and with atomic ones. Spaatz abhorred both means, and LeMay wrote of the new weapons, "Nothing new about death, nothing new about deaths caused militarily. We scorched and boiled and baked to death more people in Tokyo on that night of 9–10 March than went up in vapor at Hiroshima and Nagasaki combined." The attack on Hiroshima was followed by the same psychological campaign that had been used for the fire raids. Leaflets emphasized that the new bomb was to be used "to destroy every resource of the military by which they are prolonging this useless war" and ended with the demand, "Evacuate Your Cities!"[2] The atomic bomb would be used as its predecessors had been, to destroy urban industrial and military centers and to terrorize city dwellers into fleeing to the countryside. From the perspective of those airmen dropping bombs on the Japanese, the decision to use an atomic weapon was much easier than the choice to resort to the fire raids, but for Secretary of War Henry L. Stimson, it was a difficult course of action to adopt. Devoted to morality and to keeping the war "within the bounds of humanity," he viewed using such a terrible weapon to destroy a city as contrary to everything he stood for. Yet after confronting weary troops headed for the Pacific, and upon contemplating the costs of more war, he approved "the least abhorrent choice" for the destruction of Hiroshima and Nagasaki, to some extent because "it stopped the fire raids."[3]

The violent precedent established by LeMay's incendiary campaign helps explain the civilian authorities' acceptance of the use of atomic warfare against Japanese cities. Although this new policy troubled Stimson, most of the other leaders in Washington strongly endorsed it, an attitude transmitted through Arnold to the rest of the AAF leadership. Even Spaatz made plans to use a third atomic bomb, proposing that it be dropped on Tokyo to exert "psychological effect on the government officials," using that obliteration of capacity as a way to influence leaders' will.[4] Knowing that more nuclear weapons would be used if they were available, and never one to disobey direct orders, Spaatz probably hoped that this final raid on the enemy capital would end the war and conclude the deadly air campaign against Japanese cities.

Despite the extravagant claims by airmen during the war, the true destructive capacity of airpower was not clear to leaders until they visited conquered enemy cities. When LeMay landed in Yokohama to help arrange the final surrender, he was amazed at the "unpopulated wilderness" his bombers had created. He was proud of his accomplishments; in contrast, Stimson, after seeing the destruction of Berlin, had written, "I felt as though I had done a distasteful duty." Other observers with similar misgivings about the bombing of German cities had their doubts dispelled by the revelations of the barbarism in the concentration camps. USSTAF historian Bruce Hopper noted after visiting Buchenwald in April, "Stench everywhere: piles of human bone remnants at the furnace. Here is the antidote for qualms about strategic bombing."[5]

ANALYZING RESULTS OF STRATEGIC BOMBING

Hopper was on a jeep trip with Anderson when he saw Buchenwald, collecting data for a book on USSTAF operations against Germany. He never published the manuscript. Disillusioned and frustrated by the lack of cooperation from airmen, he found he was considered a "nuisance," and he himself felt he had no role or function. His experience seems indicative of a general mistrust of historians by the image-conscious Air Force. Unlike the ground forces, the AAF had no real combat historians. Teams directed by Colonel S. L. A. Marshall conducted interviews and examined documents for the Army as its units came out of action; officers and especially the enlisted mil-

Aerial view of Mannheim, Germany, taken 19 April 1945, showing the devastation caused by Allied planes and artillery. Scenes such as this prompted Henry Stimson to feel that he had carried out "a distasteful duty." (Special Collections Division, US Military Academy Library, West Point, NY)

itary personnel who were historians had an advantage over civilians in dealing with troops. However, the Army also accepted the historians' role more readily than did the AAF, apparent if one compares the massive "Green Book" series on World War II supported by the Department of the Army's Office of Military History with the seven-volume AAF history, designed more to assist the AAF in justifying independence. Moreover, the historians involved in AAF work admitted that they did not have access to all necessary documents, especially those papers involving controversial issues.[6]

Instead of relying on historians for lessons, the AAF looked to technical experts. The Committee of Operations Analysts appraised target systems for Arnold, Operational Research Sections examined tactical problems with air support in Europe, and the Operations Analysis Section of XXI Bomber Command advised LeMay about dealing with the weather problems affecting strategic attacks on Japan. These experts focused on technical problems without giving much, if any, consideration to ethical or human factors.[7] Air operations are more conducive to statistical analysis than are comparatively subjective land operations, but the AAF approach soon influenced other services. In the postwar period, American military doctrine as a whole began to shift its focus to quantifiable firepower at the expense of more subjective maneuver considerations and to Douhetian formulas on the amount of fire support needed to defeat an enemy. The characteristics of atomic warfare also influenced this trend.[8]

With the postwar focus on firepower formulas and the use of nuclear weapons, neither historians nor analysts systematically examined the ethical aspects of conventional bombing, or were really willing to examine its efficiency or effectiveness objectively. The Air Force concentrated primarily on precise data that could be applied to future target selection. To AAF leaders, the main lessons of the US Strategic Bombing Survey, prepared mostly by economists and scientists, apparently were that better analysis of target systems and an earlier focus on key industrial objectives such as oil would have collapsed enemy economies much sooner. In his detailed analysis of the conduct of the USSBS, Gian Gentile concludes that the process was carefully crafted to come up with results that would support AAF doctrine and its possible decisiveness as an independent service, both with the framing of questions for analysis and the selection of personnel to do it. He asserts, "The civilian analysts of the USSBS accepted the American conceptual approach to strategic bombing . . . made it the analytical framework for their evaluation, and wrote conclusions about air power in World War II that vindicated their conception." Applying these lessons to the future, Anderson and Maxwell believed that the best way to prevent Germany from ever waging war again was to ensure that the country was rebuilt with an economic system and predesignated strategic targets "in a permanently vulnerable position" to air attack.[9]

The use of the atomic bombs on Japan and the relatively short strategic air campaign there tended to obscure any lessons about conventional bombing in the Pacific theater. As a result, those seeking justification for precision-bombing doctrine focused on the European theater. This orientation was reinforced because Arnold's next three successors as chief of staff of the Air Force—Spaatz, Vandenberg, and Twining—had gained their primary wartime experiences commanding major units in Europe. A good indication of their attitudes was revealed by the findings of a board Arnold convened in late 1945 to determine the implications of the atomic bomb for the future air force. The group, headed by Spaatz and including Vandenberg, concluded that because atomic bombs would be few and expensive, conventional pin-point bombing would still be necessary to strike most strategic targets. Spaatz biographer David Metz adds, "Notwithstanding the fire bombing of Tokyo and other Japanese cities, there was little indication in the report that area bombing had gained favor among its writers."[10]

Spaatz maintained his devotion to precision-bombing doctrine and worked for a large air force to carry out both conventional and atomic missions, but a few dissenters led by LeMay were pushing for a "small striking force capable of exploiting the atomic bomb." As the new deputy chief of staff to the commander of the AAF, LeMay continued to demonstrate his penchant for innovative tactics and his commitment to obliteration bombing; he was joined in his campaign by Eaker. With public acceptance of atomic bombs and the growing realization that an independent air force would be needed to employ nuclear weapons properly, Eaker apparently decided that "throwing the strategic bomber at the man in the street" was a good idea.[11]

Most American air leaders came out of the war believing that their doctrine had been vindicated. Conventional bombing could be effective in defeating enemy nations, and adequate accuracy could be achieved. The USSBS also looked to some extent at the psychological effects of aerial bombardment on enemy civilians. In Germany, "the power of a police state over its people" kept them working efficiently even when their will to fight declined. The effects of bombing on civilian morale in Japan were more important, although "the interrelation of military, economic, and morale factors" that produced the surrender was "complex." The ethical implications of conventional air attack could not be measured and were not systematically studied; nor was there any motivation to do so. The AAF encountered none of the postwar criticism over city bombing that RAF Bomber Command experienced.[12] The victorious American public and its warriors were just glad to have the war in the Pacific concluded. Their relief was heightened as postwar reports revealed the extent of strong Japanese defenses against invasion that would have caused many casualties.[13] American decision makers, who had been deluged with glowing reports and carefully selected photographs of AAF bombing results (similar to the optimistic bomb-damage assessments and impressive bombsight videotapes offered at press briefings during DESERT STORM and future US Air Force [USAF] aerial campaigns), believed that the AAF could now exert decisive airpower in any conflict, even without atomic weapons, and with pinpoint accuracy.[14] A more effective analysis of nonquantifiable factors probably would not have changed formal doctrine, but it would have made leaders more aware of the actual effectiveness and the political implications of conventional bombing in urban areas. Such an analysis also might have suggested that different enemy economies and national characters or changing international relations could limit the effectiveness of future strategic air campaigns.

DISAPPOINTING RESULTS IN KOREA

A series of conflicts very different from World War II would soon present severe challenges for a new USAF that still pursued the ideals of a focused strategic bombing campaign aimed at eliminating enemy means. The new Strategic Air Command even considered its atomic missions as "precision attacks with an area weapon," reflecting the same sentiments as Norstad's message to Spaatz after Hiroshima.[15] The dilemma of using strategic airpower in a limited war is that by definition in such confrontations a belligerent is not willing or able to pursue the complete destruction of enemy capacity to resist and therefore must somehow reduce or break will, at least of the decision makers who must be coerced into some sort of agreement to terminate the conflict on terms favorable to those bombing. Civilian morale can be targeted, but as always, affecting that is not enough by itself to create decisive results. In Germany most popular discontent just generated apathy, not Kuter's "call to action" to truly influence leadership decisions. However, Spaatz might have been onto something with his expectations for the third atomic bomb. Although the USSBS was never going to concede the targeting of morale any significant role in producing surrender, an astute observer might have concluded differently. A basis of the British belief in the efficacy of Bomber Command's city raids was a sense among policy makers arising from World War I that urban industrial workers were already under great stress in their normal lives and were therefore especially vulnerable to be incited to rebellion by bombing.[16] This same mistrust of urban populations had led the French to surrender to the Prussians in 1871 when Paris was subjected to prolonged artillery fire while under siege.[17] Richard Frank concludes that a key factor in the Japanese decision to surrender, especially for civilian leaders, was the fear that the hardships inflicted on the population by the sea blockade and aerial bombardment would eventually produce internal upheaval that could lead to the end of Imperial institutions.[18] It appears that the utility of civilian morale as a target system lies not so much in actually inciting populations to overthrow their governments but instead in creating that expectation in the minds of their leaders. In limited wars, where coercion of enemy decision makers is the main strategic goal, the effects of attacks on capacity and will can be closely linked, and in fact can be hard to separate.

The war in Korea presented the USAF with a different set of challenges from those of World War II and should have provided astute observers with some disturbing lessons about the future efficacy of strategic bombing in limited wars. Political constraints restricted the area and nature of operations, and the simple nature of the North Korean economy along with the inviolable sanctuary of Chinese bases made strategic bombing unproductive. American air units entered combat shortly after the June 1950 invasion, and air superiority over the North Koreans was achieved quickly. World War II–vintage B-26s and B-29s destroyed the eighteen major enemy strategic targets by 25 September 1950. By 24 October the FEAF's Bomber Command B-29s had to stand down because of a lack of suitable targets south of the Yalu River. Even this relatively small strategic campaign brought accusations of indiscriminate and barbarous attacks against peaceful civilians, not only from the Russian delegation at the United Nations but also from American, British, and Indian newspapers. This response was a sign of things to come; such international reactions to USAF air strikes in or near urban areas have become commonplace since World War II. When the size of Chinese forces across the Yalu River in Manchuria became apparent in the fall of 1950, the commander of the UN forces, Douglas MacArthur, approved a plan from Lieutenant General George Stratemeyer of the FEAF to firebomb North Korean cities in order to create a zone of destruction to prevent possible intervention. Only a few such raids were conducted before the Chinese entered the war in late November. Strategic bombers then concentrated on interdiction of enemy lines of communication. This campaign had only a limited impact on a stalemated front and did not influence the ongoing peace talks. By October 1951, FEAF B-29s had been driven out of daytime skies by enemy jet fighters.[19]

As frustration with stalemate and enemy intransigence mounted, the FEAF mounted a couple campaigns to pressure communist negotiators into an armistice. The tactics and goals had much in common with the HURRICANE-style operations proposed late in World War II in the European theater. As for Operation THUNDERCLAP, the North Korean capital was an attractive target. Incendiary attacks in January 1951 burned out 35 percent of the city. MacArthur's successor, General Matthew Ridgway, hoped to gain leverage at ongoing peace talks with attacks on the city on July and August 1951, but bad weather caused poor bombing with "regrettable" civilian casualties. In turn, his successor, General Mark Clark, also tried to attack the capital for negotiating leverage. Operation PRESSURE PUMP on 11 July 1952 involved a concentrated assault on thirty military objectives in Pyongyang, though Brigadier General Jacob Smart, FEAF deputy for operations, also intended to exploit the psychological effects of airpower. In a statement reminiscent of the early concept for Operation CLARION, he directed, "Whenever possible, attacks will be scheduled against targets of military significance so situated that their destruction will have a deleterious effect upon the morale of the civil population actively engaged in the support of enemy forces." Warning leaflets were also used to demonstrate the omnipotence of UN airpower and disrupt industry with fleeing workers. As with the emphasis on bombing Berlin in World War II, mass raids on the North Korean capital had the highest priority and included attacks in August 1952 designed "to cause a noise in Moscow" by destroying all public offices. By 1 September no worthwhile precision targets were left in Pyongyang. The campaign caused much damage and dislocated many civilians, but the resolve of enemy leaders was unshaken. Chinese diplomats dismissed the air attacks as "19th century gun boat tactics." FEAF leaders were not even certain which decision makers they were trying to influence—in Pyongyang, Beijing, or Moscow—and how their minds worked.[20]

FEAF planners did not rely only on European precedents from World War II. In a move that resembled LeMay's psychological operations, in July 1952 Fifth Air Force Commander Lieutenant General Glenn Barcus announced to press and radio the names of seventy-eight North Korean towns containing targets to be bombed. Although the USAF considered these warnings "humanitarian and utilitarian" and Radio Seoul warned residents to evacuate, the State Department complained that the American campaign would be exploited intensely by communist propaganda as well as harm the UN position in world opinion, and got the warnings stopped. Operation STRIKE was intended to exploit the impact of a new "Air Pressure" campaign designed to cause enough destruction to finally force the enemy to concede on key issues deadlocking the peace talks, most notably over POW repatriation. First North Korean hydroelectric facilities were attacked, a "dual use" system that had been off-limits before because electricity also went to China and many civilian users. The main impact of those attacks seemed to be in Britain, where there was outcry about escalating the war. To ratchet up pressure further, target systems expanded to include pretty much any industrial target left in North Korea, and eventually any structure that could store

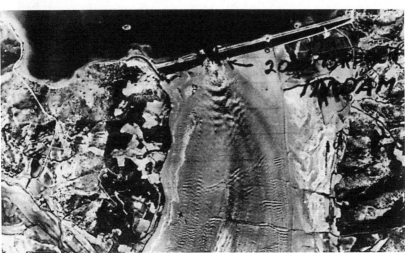

Some examples of USAF targets in North Korea, the central marshaling yard in Pyongyang (top) and the Chasan Dam near Sunchon (bottom). Following many precedents from World War II, considerations for American airpower strategy included pummeling the enemy capital and causing a rice shortage by destroying irrigation dams.

supplies or shelter troops. Yet the pressure of the new air campaign through 1952 and into 1953 failed to bring about evident progress in negotiations.[21]

The official USAF history claims that a combination of aerial pounding of Chinese ground offensives and new strategic attacks against irrigation dams in May 1953 was instrumental in finally persuading the communists to accept armistice terms. One of the planners' reasons for bombing the dams was to destroy North Korean food crops and cause a "rice famine," a tactic that had never been used even in LeMay's total air war against Japan. FEAF commander Otto P. Weyland resisted such attacks, however, until he was persuaded that destroying the dikes was really a way to wash out key rail lines. Soon enemy countermeasures negated the impact of even those raids. Fears of American war weariness and the frustrations of dealing with a stubborn Asian enemy again contributed to an escalation of bombing operations and expansion of acceptable targets with increased risk to civilians. By the end of the war, most North Koreans were living in hidden villages or caves, and eighteen of their twenty-two major cities had been more than 50 percent obliterated. One of the primary motivations for the contemporary North Korean nuclear and missile programs is to deter the United States from ever doing that to their homeland again. According to the USAF official history, "Whether the Reds yielded because they feared an expanding air war, or whether they quit because of the pounding pressure of air attacks against their forces in North Korea, one thing was certain: airpower was triumphant in the Korean War."[22]

While appreciating the contributions of American air forces in the war, few objective observers could make such a positive conclusion after three years of such a bloody and disappointing conflict. Communist concessions at the peace table had more to do with the death of Stalin, riots in Eastern Europe, and war weariness in China than the aerial pummeling of North Korea. USAF doctrine and practice had really not been effective in Korea, including the policies involving nuclear weapons. Perceptions of public opinion and diplomatic reality again worked to limit bombing operations. Although President Truman and his advisers had discussed plans to destroy Russian Far East bases with A-bombs, and despite MacArthur's suggestions, Truman's misstatements, and Eisenhower's hints, American leaders never seriously considered the use of nuclear weapons.[23] Yet USAF doctrine after the Korean War still emphasized the use of strategic bombing with nuclear weapons in a total war against the war-making capacity of a modern industrialized nation; the 1964 doctrinal manuals had no provision for strategic bombardment using conventional munitions.[24] The USAF did not appreci-

ate that fears of the possibility of Russian retaliation or international con-
demnation as well as more restricted political goals might require them to
work with nonnuclear ordnance and to avoid total war. The next conflict, in
Vietnam, would again highlight the inability of the USAF to act decisively in
a limited war and would center attention on the increasing military, public,
and diplomatic demands for accuracy in bombing operations in urban areas.

MORE FRUSTRATION IN SOUTHEAST ASIA

By the time the United States was deeply embroiled in the war in Southeast
Asia, the use of operations research and systems analysis (ORSA) that the
AAF had pioneered during World War II had become almost a religion in
the Department of Defense headed by Secretary Robert S. McNamara. Instead of supplementing strategic and tactical objectives, as in World War II,
the process was now to define these objectives. This rationalistic approach
was characterized by "the pretension to universality of solutions, . . . quan-
tification, simplification, and lack of flexibility." The process proved useful
to structure forces for a war but not to fight it. Human and political factors,
along with the chance and friction of actual war, were incompatible with
operations research and systems analysis, and plans and strategies developed
through the process were too inflexible to deal with alternatives.[25] Yet this
process had influenced the development of USAF doctrine in the 1960s
as well as the plans developed for "Victory through Airpower" over North
Vietnam.

Even before major United States forces were committed to South Vietnam, the USAF had already developed a scheme to shock Hanoi quickly and
decisively with American firepower and resolve. Chairman of the JCS General Earle Wheeler presented McNamara with a plan to strike ninety-four key
targets in sixteen days, an operation designed to convince North Vietnam to
abandon its support of the insurgency in the South. Primarily for political
reasons, President Johnson decided to apply pressure gradually, in the campaign called ROLLING THUNDER. Target lists grew to 240 and then 427 fixed
objectives, and priorities ranking interdiction, oil, industry, and electrical
power fluctuated. Johnson prohibited attacks on many targets near cities,
and Wheeler was sensitive about the prospect of civilian casualties. Military
advisers repeatedly tried to expand and accelerate air attacks on North Vietnam throughout Johnson's presidency, including asking for permission to
destroy rice crops, but with little success.[26]

American fighter-bombers roamed the skies over Vietnam, but any bombing near urban areas was strictly controlled. Enemy tactics and propaganda
forced extraordinary measures. Rules of engagement required air strikes to
be preceded by warnings with leaflets or loudspeakers; pilots could not fly
over friendly populated areas when armed. Despite precautions, friendly
troops or villages were hit, mostly through technical failures or poor communication. Eventually pilots were ordered not to deliver ordnance unless
they were completely sure of their target and equipment. By 1967 only 1
in 6,000 sorties involved accidental bombing of friendly units or towns, a
circumstance reflecting sound training, "smart bombs," and strict control.[27]
Much of this precision can be attributed to technical advances pioneered
during World War II.

However, improved accuracy alone was not enough to ensure a successful
air war. As in Korea, a resolute enemy with a simple economy thwarted superior technology in weapons. Operations such as ROLLING THUNDER (referred to
by some Air Force officers in hindsight as "Rolling Blunder") drew directly
on precision-bombing doctrine to target North Vietnam's vital economic
and military centers and to destroy its capacity to wage war. A combination
of political restrictions, gradualist tactics in the application of force, and
the nature of the enemy's will and infrastructure frustrated these grandiose
plans. Perhaps because of an exaggerated opinion of American success with
air interdiction in World War II and Korea, the USAF concentrated heavy
bombing on enemy supply lines and sources in North and South Vietnam.
In 1967 General Matthew Ridgway wrote, "There were those who felt, at the
time of the Korean War, that air power might accomplish miracles of interdiction. . . . The fact that it could not accomplish these miracles has not yet
been accepted as widely as it should have been." He believed that "some in
high position" still failed to appreciate the "limitations" of airpower. These
deficiencies were evident in ineffective campaigns against precision target
systems such as oil and electric power. As McNamara came to realize that the
agrarian economy and guerrilla forces of the North Vietnamese would never
collapse from bombing, USAF leaders chafed to be free of political restrictions to strike harder at key targets in Hanoi and Haiphong.[28]

A new president, Richard Nixon, gave the Air Force its chance with Operation LINEBACKER I and Operation LINEBACKER II, which included sending
strategic bombers against objectives in North Vietnamese cities. Earlier attempts to destroy small factories with B-52 bombers had just highlighted
their "inability . . . to hit a small target without damage to the surrounding
civilian population," a result that brought a halt to such missions. Nixon al-

*William Westmoreland, the new Army chief of staff (right), confers on strategy with
President Lyndon Johnson (center) and Walt W. Rostow (left) in 1968. Rostow, perhaps
Johnson's most hawkish adviser on the Vietnam War, had analyzed bombing targets during
World War II with the Enemy Objectives Unit of the Economic Warfare Division of the
US embassy in London. The economy of North Vietnam presented different problems
for strategic bombing from those encountered in Germany, however. (Westmoreland
Collection, Special Collections Division, US Military Academy Library, West Point, NY)*

lowed even more extensive targeting of urban storage and transportation facilities. Once again, American aircraft pounded an enemy capital. Accuracy
was relatively good, and evacuations helped keep casualties low. Though 730
B-52 sorties attacking urban targets during LINEBACKER II in December 1972
caused only 1,318 civilian deaths, considerable public outcry arose against
the operation, and world opinion quickly compared the attacks with area
bombing raids such as those against Dresden. The operations did appear to
fulfill the commander in chief's goal to bring the North Vietnamese back to
the peace talks, however, and helped persuade them to accept a cease-fire in
January 1973. Nixon also intended LINEBACKER II to impress the South Vietnamese and to gain their support for the results of the negotiations as well.[29]

Five months of LINEBACKER I had crippled North Vietnam's military capability, and the eleven days of LINEBACKER II had unsettled its urban populace.
Despite harsh criticisms in the American press, Nixon had continued attacks
on Hanoi and Haiphong until the North Vietnamese agreed to return to the
peace table. The aerial operations against cities that had to be defended had

depleted North Vietnam's supply of surface-to-air missiles as well as military and civilian food stocks; thus leaders decided to negotiate to stop further bombing. Air Force proponents used the results of LINEBACKER II to claim that political constraints had prevented them from winning the war, and retired generals Curtis LeMay and William M. Momyer echoed that sentiment by asserting that unrestrained airpower could win any war. Yet as Mark Clodfelter has pointed out, "Most air commanders fail to understand that the 'Eleven-Day War' was a unique campaign for very limited ends." It did not cause the North Vietnamese army or nation to surrender; it simply furthered Nixon's political goal for a negotiated settlement and delayed final victory for his enemies. Linebacker did not vindicate precision tactics or the selection of urban targets. In fact, there is an installation in Hanoi called "The Museum of Victory over the B-52" that asserts that the December 1972 downing of fifteen B-52s in a "Dienbienphu of the air" led to American withdrawal.[30] However, another limited conflict involving an air campaign against a state, this time in Southwest Asia, would produce more USAF arguments for the decisiveness of airpower.

SUCCESS IN SOUTHWEST ASIA

For most of us, the arrival of DESERT STORM was heralded by televised American air raids on another enemy capital. We remember the vivid images of Tomahawk cruise missiles and Stealth fighters over Baghdad and broken Iraqi troops in Kuwait. The systematic development of war-weary bombers, radar bombing, and Azon bombs had evolved into an impressive array of high-technology weapons, constantly displayed in briefings that emphasized the precision and the destructive might of American airpower. Conventional bombing of pinpoint objectives was the rule, with a repeatedly announced goal of avoiding harm to civilians. Theory, practice, and ethics seemed to merge in a clean and decisive air campaign to eject a tyrant at a minimum cost in friendly casualties. One of the designers of the air campaign was Colonel John Warden, who had further evolved precision doctrine with his conception of the enemy state as a system, with five "strategic rings" of targets—leadership, organic essentials, infrastructure, population, and fielded forces. Even more than the creators of original precision-bombing doctrine, Warden emphasized that bombing did not need to destroy the whole structure, just paralyze it, to eliminate the enemy capacity to resist and influence their leaders to change their policies.[31]

From the beginning, limited war aims and concerns about maintaining the fragile Allied coalition influenced the execution of the air offensive. This does not mean that extensive bombing of targets in Iraqi cities did not occur. American air strikes destroyed water, power, and transportation facilities in Baghdad in attacks suggesting Seversky's idea of an aerial blockade. Strategic targets pinpointing electricity, oil, communications, supply depots, and transportation nodes were hit throughout Iraq. From the beginning of the war, administration officials and military leaders emphasized that commanders in the field would be allowed to fight the war free of interference from Washington, and there were few limitations on targeting of military and economic objectives. In one notable exception, Secretary of Defense Richard Cheney ordered the JCS to review all missions over Baghdad after the bombing of the Amiriya bunker that killed many civilians.[32] Otherwise, the USAF exercised proper restraint regarding sacred sites and residential areas, though some collateral damage resulted from near misses or downed cruise missiles. Learning their lesson from Vietnam, leaders in Southwest Asia and Washington responded quickly to counter any claims of indiscriminate bombing with explanations and photographs.

Though the bombing of Iraqi cities disrupted civilian life, it did not break the Iraqi will to resist. However, the air campaign had a different goal: to cripple the Iraqi army in Kuwait through interdiction of its lines of communication and by tactical strikes on its troops and positions so that a ground war might prove unnecessary. The results were impressive. Total air supremacy ensured the success of the efforts to hide the massing of forces on the western flank. Frontline enemy conscripts were demoralized by the bombing and were starving from lack of supplies. Farther to the rear, Republican Guard units were better protected and provisioned, but the degraded Iraqi command-and-control system hampered reactions to the coalition's enveloping attacks. Contrary to initial reports, some strong enemy ground resistance occurred as coalition forces drove deeper into Iraq, but superior troops, equipment, and training were decisive in those engagements. Although weakened by air attacks, the Republican Guard did maneuver units to try to stop VII Corps. Although newscasts implied that the USAF had been the main destroyer of enemy armored vehicles, figures from General Norman Schwarzkopf's Central Command showed that ground forces destroyed 2,162 tanks out of total Iraqi losses of 3,847, and those figures may actually be too low. Lieutenant General Frederick Franks claims that his VII Corps troops, carrying out Schwarzkopf's main attack, destroyed over 1,300 tanks on their four-day sweep into Iraq and 600 more in mopping-up operations.

US Marine forces alone claimed about 1,000 tanks.[33] One of the most widely circulated stories among army officers returning from the war concerned an Iraqi regimental commander in the Republican Guard who admitted to his captors from the Second Armored Cavalry Regiment that after losing only seven of his thirty-nine tanks during a month of bombing, he decided it was time to quit when he lost the other thirty-two tanks after only thirty minutes of combat against VII Corps forces.

Despite this quibbling, no one could deny that American airpower had wreaked impressive havoc on the Iraqis. Apparently the most significant effects of the air campaign were to break the morale of the second-rate troops in frontline defenses and to seriously damage Iraqi command, control, communications, and intelligence systems. The ground war was still necessary but was miraculously easy, helped in part because the land offensive possessed combat power designed to defeat a much larger enemy force, which had been projected by faulty intelligence.[34] However, military budget talks were in full swing, and the Air Force was quick to claim sole credit for victory over Iraq. The USAF spokesman, General Merrill McPeak, in words echoing statements made after the surrender of Pantelleria, announced, "My private conviction is that this is the first time in history that a field army has been defeated by air power." USAF historians quickly began to garner evidence to support McPeak's assertion. For example, in *Storm over Iraq*, Richard Hallion provided a detailed analysis of the air campaign that is noteworthy for its discussions of the impact of technology in the Persian Gulf War and how the versatility of modern airpower has blurred the traditional distinction between tactical and strategic roles. Among the lessons that Hallion draws from the conflict is that airpower demonstrated that it can now seize and hold ground without ground forces, and in future wars it will not only be "decisive" but also "the determinant of victory."[35]

Such claims hardly vindicate theories of strategic bombing designed to defeat an enemy nation by destroying its total war-making capacity or by breaking its national will. Precision doctrine and technology did receive deserved praise for their contribution to DESERT STORM, though some of McPeak's disclosures at the press conference also tarnished the image of the pinpoint accuracy of USAF weaponry displayed in so many videotapes at war briefings. Iraq absorbed half again as many so-called smart bombs in forty-three days as Vietnam did in eight years, but precision munitions made up only 6,250 of 88,500 tons of bombs dropped on Iraq and occupied Kuwait. And although 90 percent of the smart weapons hit their targets, the accuracy rate for unguided bombs was only 25 percent. McPeak admitted that over 62,000 tons of bombs had missed their targets, reflecting a rather disappointing level of precision.[36]

The Air Force did conduct a thorough evaluation of the air campaign in the Gulf War Air Power Survey, headed by Eliot Cohen. Realizing the shortcomings of the USSBS, the survey team strove for objectivity—so much so that the USAF leadership was greatly disappointed that the findings were not more triumphal and restricted their distribution. The report highlighted limits on strategic bombing "encountered as far back as World War II" and admitted that too little of the air campaign, about 15 percent, was directed at the eight "strategic" target categories to achieve significant effects. Great success was achieved against electric power, for instance, but very little against the nuclear program. Problems hunting Scud missile launchers resembled those the Eighth Air Force had against Operation CROSSBOW targets. The report did trumpet the operational successes at weakening Iraqi ground forces, but it also cautioned that airpower, like the military instrument itself, could not by itself achieve political "finality" in such a conflict, presciently noting that the defeated side "may regard the military outcome as a transitory evil to be redressed at a later time by political or other means."[37]

Such figures and analyses should not detract from the impressive successes of the air campaign. Careful targeting ensured that few misses caused collateral damage in urban areas, and one must realize that the psychological effects of a miss can be as devastating as a hit. Many vital targets were destroyed by the 26,000 tons of accurate bombs, but the most important result of the air campaign was to destroy the morale of the Iraqi troops manning the defenses of the "Saddam line" in southern Kuwait. Iraqi prisoners reported that B-52 saturation raids on their positions had especially devastating psychological effects, and intelligence sources estimate that from 20 percent to 40 percent of frontline troops had deserted before the ground campaign.[38] Contrary to McPeak's claim, some precedent does exist for such a result, and it comes from an earlier conflict in the same region.

Interestingly, some commentators have looked at the relative casualties between the coalition forces and Iraq and compared DESERT STORM with examples of colonial warfare, such as Omdurman, where technologically superior armies devastated ill-equipped local contingents. These pundits are more correct than they probably realize. During the 1920s, as part of its search for missions to justify its independence, the RAF developed a doctrine of air control for British colonial mandates in the Middle East. Principles and tactics were perfected in countering an Iraqi insurgency that involved at least 131,000 armed rebels. As in DESERT STORM, bombing and psychological war-

fare were used to generate a sense of helplessness and to induce many deser-
tions and surrenders. In actions foreshadowing occurrences in DESERT STORM,
rebels often gave up at the mere sound of aircraft approaching. In 1920
Britain needed 135,000 troops to maintain order in Iraq; by 1930 it had only
four RAF squadrons and one armored-car company there.[39]

The British ground operations in Iraq in the 1920s were of course much
different from the armored onslaught of Desert Storm, but the results of
the associated air campaigns were similar.[40] A poorly led third world force
in open country was broken by a technologically superior air force. DESERT
STORM gave the USAF a unique opportunity to fight a fast-paced conventional
war against a vulnerable enemy on a battlefield with few political restrictions,
though it was a limited conflict aimed at dislodging an army rather than at
subduing a whole nation. This optimum situation allowed American airmen to demonstrate the full range of their capabilities and the evolution
of modern airpower. Traditional strategic bombing of objectives in cities by
mass raids of B-52s was not a factor in the coalition victory (though they did
pound Iraqi troop concentrations effectively); instead, attacks by individual
aircraft using precision tactics and technology were highly effective against
key targets in enemy urban areas. Pictures of broken bridges and destroyed
factories in Baghdad and a widespread recognition of the sincere and generally successful attempt to avoid civilian casualties in Iraqi cities demonstrated
that American airmen had continued their adherence to precision-bombing
doctrine and had made significant progress toward achieving the ideal capabilities first envisioned at the Air Corps Tactical School almost sixty years
earlier.

AIRPOWER IN THE BALKANS, AND BACK TO IRAQ

The apparent rapid and decisive success of Operation DESERT STORM in 1991
launched a deluge of claims that warfare had changed. Debates raged about
whether the new technologies displayed portended a full-blown revolution
in military affairs. Airpower advocates trumpeted the results of the air campaign against Iraq and later operations in the Balkans to advocate expanding
USAF missions.[41] The bombing campaign to get the Serbs out of Kosovo
inspired historian John Keegan to declare that conflict the first ever successfully won by the air arm alone, and that perceived success helped reinforce
the concept of "Shock and Awe" that gained many adherents before war was
again launched on Iraq in 2003.[42]

The 1990s saw a number of new attachments to contemporary American airpower theory. The Battle of Khafji, where aircraft stopped an Iraqi foray from Kuwait into Saudi Arabia, became the model for a "halt phase" construct where air units alone could hold off a major enemy theater offensive long enough to allow American ground forces to build up. The Shock and Awe concept that appeared in 1996, mostly Warden with a bit of Douhet mixed in, foresaw a swift and powerful air campaign to achieve decisive finality quickly by paralyzing and demoralizing enemies. It advocated a sort of Operation CLARION on steroids, with carefully chosen target sets that did not target civilians directly but would significantly reduce both their capacity and will to resist.[43]

Air operations in the disintegrating Yugoslavia seemed to support these new expectations for airpower. Seventeen days of NATO air strikes during Operation DELIBERATE FORCE in September 1995 helped persuade the Serbs to accept a cease-fire in Bosnia and eventually to sign the General Framework Agreement for Peace in Dayton, Ohio, in November. Though ground threats from Bosnian Muslims and Croats and a rampaging Croatian army were more significant in achieving that result, airpower advocates were again quick to claim decisive independent effects.[44] So when another Balkan crisis erupted and diplomacy failed to resolve it, this time over Kosovo in 1999, American and NATO political leaders were prepared to pin their hopes on an air campaign alone to resolve the situation without a ground invasion.

When the bombing campaign commenced, Pentagon planners admitted they did not expect it to force President Slobodan Milosevic to sign a peace agreement. Instead, President Bill Clinton announced that military operations had three primary goals: stop the ethnic cleansing as the Serbs expelled Kosovar Albanians, prevent even worse Serb depredations against civilians there, and "seriously damage" Serb military capacity to conduct such atrocities. In fact, the ensuing air campaign accomplished none of those objectives and even initially worsened the situation as Serb forces responded to the high-technology aerial assault with a low-technology ravaging of the region. The military forces in Kosovo proved adept at decoys and camouflage as well as hiding in towns and using human shields; postwar surveys revealed that very little damage had been done to them. What significant results the air campaign achieved had to be accomplished through a shift to punishing attacks on Serbia to coerce Milosevic to change his policies.[45]

Having to work with a nineteen member NATO coalition ensured that Shock and Awe would not be applied. The NATO commander, General Wesley Clark, and his joint force air component commander, Lieutenant

General Michael Short, wanted to hit power supplies, communications facilities, and command bunkers in Belgrade on the first night of Operation
ALLIED FORCE, but NATO political leaders would not even approve strikes
on occupied barracks, fearing too many dead conscripts. Targeting was mi-
cromanaged even more than in Vietnam. Eventually Clark got approval for
a wider target array, but he still had to get clearance to attack each objective from any nation participating on the mission. New information systems
facilitated an amazingly complex target review and development process,
linking operational planners in Germany, Belgium, and the United States
with data analysts in England and weapons experts in Italy. Lawyers in Germany assessed each target in terms of the Geneva Convention, confirming
its military nature and evaluating whether its value outweighed any risks of
collateral damage. Clark held daily teleconferences with NATO leaders and
finished the process by passing target lists to the JCS and the White House
for a final blessing.[46]

With high expectations for accuracy and much political squeamishness
among European allies, inevitable but unanticipated errors such as the
bombing of the Chinese embassy and a Yugoslav train eroded support for
the air war and put considerable pressure on NATO political and military
leaders to achieve results. Even meticulous planning and precision munitions could not overcome erroneous maps or prevent that train from running late and right onto the targeted bridge as the bomb arrived. Clark was
close to running out of militarily useful and politically acceptable targets
when he secured approval for the most important raid of the campaign on
24 May. The destruction of the transformer yards of the Yugoslav power grid
disabled everything from the air defense command-and-control network to
the country's banking system. It demonstrated NATO's strength and dominance to the political leaders and the civilian population. Knocking out
the electric system also took away power from hospitals and water-pumping
stations. Military lawyers made the moral implications clear to Clark. One
recalled, "We'd have preferred not to have to take on these targets. But this
was the Commander's call." All major Serb cities experienced extended
power disruptions until a settlement was reached on 10 June after a seventy-
eight-day (and night) campaign.[47]

Despite European attempts to restrain attacks, a less than final settlement
was achieved by the same sort of "imposed cost" strategy applied in Korea
and Vietnam, resulting in massive destruction of the civilian infrastructure
of Yugoslavia. Pentagon spokesman Ken Bacon sounded like Giulio Douhet
by speculating that the main factor in Milosevic's acceptance of terms "was

the increasing inconveniences that the bombing campaign was causing in Belgrade and other cities." As in all strategic air campaigns against states, the list of acceptable bombing objectives expanded as the conflict continued. A broad definition of the term "dual use" opened up a wide array of targets for NATO airmen, including bridges, heating plants, and television stations. Black humor in Belgrade determined that even bakeries were valid targets because "soldiers also eat bread." Serb propaganda videos of the damage and casualties wreaked by NATO airpower in attacks on cities, factories, and power plants gained some international sympathy, but the same images that fanned anti-NATO and anti-American sentiments may have also reinforced a sense of futility in the besieged civilian population because their own air defenses seemed powerless to do anything to stop the mounting devastation. When the conflict ended, 45 percent of Yugoslavia's TV broadcast capability was degraded and a third of military and civilian radio relay networks were damaged. Petroleum refining facilities were completely eliminated. Seventy percent of road and 50 percent of rail bridges across the Danube were down. The whole regional economy was degraded for many years afterward.[48]

It is still unclear exactly why Milosevic gave in to NATO demands. He did get a better deal than the Rambouillet accords offered in March. We will probably never know exactly what the Russians advised him. Despite their vocal opposition to the bombing campaign, they did assist NATO by not upgrading outdated Yugoslav air defense systems. Open discussions about the possibility of a NATO ground invasion and an apparent growing willingness to gather peacekeeping forces in the region probably had some influence on Yugoslav leaders. However, in the end, the air campaign did achieve the adjusted political goals. Postwar analysts highlighted growing fears among Serb leaders that the aerial assault would eventually escalate to the level of World War II city bombing; they also noted that the air attacks increasingly threatened the holdings of Milosevic's most important political supporters. However, there was no systematic official evaluation conducted like USSBS or GWAPS. In October 1999, Secretary of Defense William Cohen did present the findings of a Kosovo after-action review conducted by his office, but the review does not represent a conclusive analysis of the impact of airpower. In fact, the written report submitted to Congress in January 2000 was so devoid of hard facts that Pentagon officials jokingly labeled it "fiber-free."[49]

As the new millennium opened, American airpower advocates were in ascendance. Secretary of Defense Donald Rumsfeld intended to create a reformed Department of Defense relying more on technology than manpower, with a significantly reduced Army. The initial campaign in Afghanistan in

2001 seemed to confirm the correctness of his vision, as US Special Forces calling in air strikes were key in enabling the indigenous Northern Alliance to defeat and displace the Taliban. Airpower was again essential in the fast and relatively easy assault to take Baghdad and bring down Saddam Hussein in 2003. The initial Shock and Awe plan was modified by desires to limit noncombatant casualties and preserve infrastructure, as well as by General Tommy Franks's decision to attack early. That meant that the major air offensive started twenty-eight hours after ground forces had begun their advance and had overrun many areas. As a result, only 39 percent of leadership or command-and-control targets initially scheduled for attack would be struck during the three-week air campaign. However, airpower had already done much with both kinetic and nonkinetic operations to prepare the battle space. Airmen enforcing prewar no-fly zones had already suppressed Iraqi air defenses and gathered a great deal of valuable intelligence. After the full air campaign began on the night of 21 March, the nonstop precision bombardment by ground- and carrier-based aircraft paved the way for allied ground forces so well that their entrance into Baghdad was a virtual fait accompli. Republican Guard units around the city lost over 1,000 of their 2,500 tanks before they were engaged by any ground elements. Losses for other defending divisions were even more severe, greatly reducing possible resistance on every front. Improvements in force connectivity, air–ground communication, time-sensitive targeting capability, command and control, unmanned aerial vehicles, and precision munitions were important in facilitating the success of the military operations, as were Iraqi blunders and ineptitude.[50]

The decisiveness of the campaign led journalist Stephen Budiansky to conclude: "The great historical joke on airmen was that after having struggled for a century to escape the battlefield in their quest for equal status and independence—having fought so many bitter battles to free themselves from the indignity of providing 'mere support' to ground forces—it was on the battlefield where air power finally achieved not merely equality, but its claim to ascendancy."[51] However, those hopes for decisive airpower, even on the battlefield, soon faded as messy insurgencies developed in both Iraq and Afghanistan. Nonstate actors have few vulnerabilities to strategic airpower. Drone strikes against leadership targets have had some impact, but often the negative backlash against collateral damage from such attacks, real or imagined, outweighs positive effects. With the "counterinsurgency fatigue" so evident in the United States after the long conflicts in Afghanistan and Iraq and a national security strategy that proclaims the nation will not engage in such stability operations requiring large-scale or prolonged employment of ground troops, airpower will remain the primary military tool for American decision makers despite the fact it might not be the most appropriate one. Mark Clodfelter argues that the ideal vision of American airpower, surgically applied targeting to achieve political goals with a minimum of casualties and collateral damage, does not suit the basic violent nature of war, especially the nature of contemporary "wars amongst the people" involving so many nonstate actors and adaptive adversaries who are willing to use sophisticated information campaigns, "lawfare" with restrictive international norms, and hiding among populations to thwart dominant American air forces. For him, that vision is "an enticing idea waiting to be victimized by conflicting goals, uncooperative enemies, and the imposing momentum that every war generates."[52]

12. LEGACIES

It was an illusion of the historian to assume that the participants would help prepare history current with operations. It is likewise an illusion of warriors to assume they will do it after hostilities.

—*Bruce Hopper, USSTAF historian*[1]

Strategic bombing in World War II left two conflicting and interacting legacies for American airpower. While for some that conflict set the USAF on the path to achieve true precision bombing, others see it as establishing a precedent for mass aerial destruction. Some observers of the First Persian Gulf War against Iraq disagreed with the prevailing view that coalition air forces were consciously and effectively avoiding indiscriminate bombing of civilians. Yasuo Kurata, a political commentator for *Tokyo Shimbun*, was highly critical of Americans and the USAF after the bombing of the air raid shelter in Amiriya that "slaughtered more than 400 people, including about 100 infants and young children." Discounting official insistence that the underground bunker was a communications center, Kurata claimed that Americans are insensitive to civilian casualties because they have never been bombed themselves, a charge that brings to mind Vera Brittain's writings during World War II. He invoked images of Dresden and Tokyo, describing his own memories of the latter raid in graphic detail, and accused the US military of a tendency to dismiss the loss of life as "collateral damage," an "inevitable byproduct of aerial warfare. . . . Carpet bombing by B-52s is the US Air Force's stock in trade. The huge aircraft can destroy entire cities from 30,000 feet; the collateral damage can well be imagined." He also condemned the use of fuel-air explosives against Iraqi troops as well as the entire American strategy of air superiority and bombing. He implied that Asians and Europeans, sensitized by their own experiences of being bombed, were opposed to the air war against Iraqi cities but that Americans remained ignorant of the costs of such aerial bombardment and did not seem to care.[2] It is easy to criticize Kurata's position. Americans did not ignore the tragedy in Amiriya. It received extensive media coverage, and command authorities from the president on down took action to ensure that such incidents did not recur. The experience of being bombed did not stop British or German raids during World War II, nor did it affect European support for the effort to dislodge Iraq from Kuwait. B-52s have never carpet-bombed cities, though Kurata seems to imply that Americans are uniquely preoccupied with urban area attacks. Obviously this is a distortion of history; he could be reminded that Japanese aircraft conducted the first air war against population centers when they bombed China in the 1930s. Yet one should not completely discount Kurata's perceptions. Fears of massive retaliatory American air raids on Baghdad may have deterred Saddam Hussein from using chemical or biological weapons in the Gulf War. Treatises that argue the American way of war tends toward an overall technological onslaught against an enemy society often use American strategic bombing in World War II as a prime example.

Similar criticisms appeared after Operation ALLIED FORCE, which actually dropped leaflets over Serbia trumpeting how many 500-pound bombs could be delivered by each B-52 as part of the psychological warfare campaign synchronized with the bombing.[3] In Yugoslavia it appears that the growing intensity of attacks on dual-use targets in Belgrade and other cities was significant in achieving NATO's political goals. Accordingly, there is a good probability that Yugoslav civilian casualties exceeded their military ones. For instance, Michael Dobbs estimates that the Serbs suffered 1,600 civilian casualties and only 1,000 military ones. Human Rights Watch completed a study that lowered estimates of Yugoslav civilian dead to 500 from ninety separate attacks but was still critical of NATO targeting practices. It concluded that half the casualties could have been avoided. This is particularly ironic considering the expectations for a bloodless war caricatured so well in *Doonesbury* cartoons and reinforced by NATO briefings on targeting accuracy.[4] These high NATO expectations for extremely low casualties on both sides helped convince the more reluctant coalition members to support the air campaign and increased the negative impact on alliance cohesion of each scene of civilian dead and wounded.

Yet those same images might have also increased Serb fears and weakened their resolve. Ironically, such incidents might have reduced the will to continue on both sides. Media images and accusations motivated UN war crimes prosecutors of the International Criminal Tribunal for the former Yugoslavia to begin assessing evidence in December that NATO commanders had violated the laws of war with their air attacks. (They decided not to pursue formal charges.) Other war crimes charges came from Amnesty International, and the British parliament's top foreign affairs panel criticized the bombing as being of "dubious legality." Michael Ignatieff has aptly pointed out that journalists' accounts of the maneuvering of cruise missiles in Iraq and fascination with precision munitions have reinforced a myth in Western publics that war can now be thought of as laser surgery. In the dogged pursuit of the ideal of precision bombing the USAF has improved its capabilities tremendously, but the term "surgical airstrike" remains an oxymoron. Some targeting errors and technical failures will always occur, and blast effects are often unpredictable. The errant raid on the Chinese embassy looks even more sinister when we claim perfection.[5]

Despite the controversy over that attack or the one on Amiriya, the USAF has demonstrated during numerous conflicts since 1990 that it has vastly improved its ability to apply precision tactics and technology to target capacity effectively without extensive collateral damage. The achievement of this goal was delayed partly because of the AAF's hasty and insufficient historical assessment of its operations during World War II. Ethical and practical implications of strategic air attacks were not adequately examined, and the lessons of victory through airpower gleaned from World War II did not apply to the conflicts in Korea and Vietnam. The industry and infrastructures in those Asian countries were unlike the systems in Germany, Japan, or Italy, and the international climate during those limited wars was far different from that of the 1940s. Yet a thorough AAF analysis of the total effects of strategic bombing in World War II would have prepared the USAF for a better use of airpower in Korea or Vietnam.

Another result of this incomplete assessment by the AAF, as well as contemporary expectations for accuracy, has been the recent criticism questioning the reality of World War II precision bombing. Beginning after the war, and sometimes based on distorted facts, isolated criticisms of individual missions such as the attacks on Dresden and Tokyo have now grown into general doubts about the ethics and practices of the entire strategic air campaign. Hopper's prophecy has come true; the initiative in discussions of AAF performance has passed from participants to critical historians, who are not always as knowledgeable or as sympathetic. Although the ideal of pinpoint air attacks that could send bombs down industrial smokestacks was never

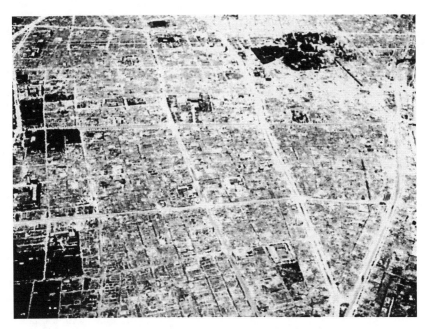

The devastation caused by Major General Curtis LeMay's fire raids on Tokyo. Images such as this have inspired critics to question American sensitivity to civilian casualties.

achieved in World War II, the claim that adherence to precision-bombing doctrine was a myth ignores the operational record.

In Europe, despite many pressures to do otherwise, American airmen consistently followed their doctrine. Precision advocates like Spaatz and Hughes at USSTAF headquarters, Cabell at Mediterranean Allied Air Forces, and Doolittle at Eighth Air Force seemed motivated at least partly by concerns for morality; other leaders in the European theater, such as Anderson and Eaker, were more concerned with bombing effectiveness or public relations. The result, however, was the same. Although theory did exceed technology, American airmen in Europe did the best they could with what they had. Air operations during DESERT STORM again demonstrated the difficulty of achieving accuracy with "dumb bombs" of the kind used by the Eighth and Fifteenth Air Forces against Germany, and their practices generally must be seen as an attempt to halt or at least to slow the rush to unlimited warfare. Although it is difficult to separate efficiency from ethics in AAF doctrine and practice, a limitation on the "uncurbed bestial instincts" of war did emerge. Objective observers can still perceive a definite difference between AAF strategic bombing focused on capacity in Europe and the British area raids on cities or the German Blitz on London, focused instead on breaking morale.

The moral tenets of World War II AAF doctrine are still present in current American military manuals on the law of war. Military necessity for aerial bombardment is defined in terms of precision bombing. One case study explains that the destruction of a city is not justified because of warehouses or transportation routes; only recognized military targets can be attacked. Another emphasizes that the rules of war prohibit attacks that cause "unnecessary suffering and destruction" or attacks against "the civilian population or against cultural, historical, religious, or other protected objects." A third study, inspired by Cassino, asserts that cultural protection can be forfeited if the structure is used for military purposes. The emphasis throughout focuses on the military or economic justification for targets and the protection of civilians as much as possible. The issue of workers as belligerents is not directly addressed, however.[6]

The devotion of men such as Spaatz and Doolittle to the precision doctrine during World War II established an important precedent for later American air operations. Arnold's drive to develop new technology also had important implications. American prototypes for cruise missiles, precision munitions, and radar bombing aids that were so impressive for their pinpoint accuracy during DESERT STORM and after were first tested in combat during World War II. Precision doctrine has influenced the development of technology to the extent that the motivation for recent cuts in American nuclear weapons has come in part from the realization that conventional smart bombs can remove many targets more effectively, especially at the tactical and operational levels of war.

On the other hand, the legacy of the fire raids can be seen in the acceptance of urban targeting policies involving strategic nuclear weapons.[7] Sanctions restricting the bombing of civilians eroded as World War II entered its complex final phases, and pressure increased for the Allies to achieve their stated aim of winning the war "as decisively and speedily as possible."[8] Once Hansell had left the Pacific, no real advocate of precision bombing remained there, and LeMay and his superiors saw the area incendiary attacks as the best method for ending the war quickly, saving American lives, demonstrating a true victory through airpower, and securing a strong position to bargain for postwar status as an independent service. The fire raids and the exploitation of the accompanying terror marked the culmination of the American escalation to total war. Once that course of destroying cities was adopted, with its complete disregard for any restraint against killing civilians, the use of the atomic bomb was logical. Most Americans and their leaders considered the new weapon simply to be a more powerful version of conventional ordnance; recognized restrictions limiting chemical and biological warfare did not appear to apply to nuclear weapons in 1945. The *Chicago Sun* echoed popular sentiment: "There is no scale of values which makes a TNT explosion right and an uranium explosion wrong." Once the fire raids became accepted policy, any form of warfare against Japan seemed permissible. If the invasion of Kyushu in November had been a bloodbath, poison gas and crop destroyers probably would also have been used to support the invasion of Japan's main island in March 1946. As Marshall had noted, those weapons were not as terrible as the incendiary bombs being used to incinerate Japanese urban areas.[9]

Yet we should not make hasty moral judgments about the men who firebombed Tokyo or dropped the atomic bombs. Michael Howard reminds us that "the overwhelming majority of the people concerned, not simply the decision makers but the public that supported them, did not see this as a moral problem at all." He has also observed that when statesmen and their generals deal with the ethical issues of a war threatening their people and nation, "the options open to them are likely to be far more limited than is generally realized."[10] Further, the problems of leaders are much more complex in an era of total war and nuclear weapons. The issues of law, technology, and airpower ethics that every AAF commander faced are part of the problem that Bill Moyers has called "the great unresolved dilemma of our age: Will we go on doing what our weapons make possible?"[11]

However, that is not the only dilemma from such capability. Another remains, reflective of Ignatieff's concerns. If warfare is considered less bloody, it is easier to consider it to be a viable policy option, and its threat is less of a deterrent to aberrant behavior. Fear of massed American airpower is evident in displays in military museums in Beijing and Hanoi. Chinese, North Vietnamese, and Iraqi veterans all remember the catastrophic blast and shock from the deadly loads of heavy bombers.[12] One of the reasons for the relatively easy American advance on Baghdad in 2003 was that so many Iraqi soldiers had surrendered or deserted, many persuaded by one of more than forty million air-dropped psychological warfare leaflets noting that if the soldiers went home then they would avoid the destruction of mass airstrikes remembered from a decade before and being experienced again.[13] Those remain the most fearsome conventional weapon in the American arsenal and must be retained.

At the same time, in contemporary wars amongst the people, both state and nonstate enemies have become more adept at exploiting expectations of accuracy to turn every civilian bombing casualty into a political liability for those with dominant airpower. Few realize the painstaking care involved in contemporary targeting decisions, but war still remains a bloody and unpredictable business. One of the most important missions for today's military leaders is to educate politicians and the public about that fact. We should continue to target carefully, but we must make the world realize that going to war will always have significant costs on both sides. If enemies prolong conflicts, those costs will only rise, especially for states. As one journalist wrote after concluding that the attacks on Yugoslav civilians in 1999 were the key to ending the Kosovo conflict, in a restatement of the airpower ethic that would have been recognized by Giulio Douhet, "That may produce an uncomfortable lesson for the politicians who call the shots during the next war: the most merciful way to conduct a war may be to end it swiftly and violently."[14]

Hap Arnold's dynamic vision to develop and publicize AAF capabilities has molded an unmatched air service that inspires unrealistic expectations for what American airpower can do. The hardest task for future military leaders working with their civilian political bosses will not be to explain all the great things their aircraft can accomplish but instead to honestly admit what they cannot.

APPENDIX: SUGGESTED REPLY TO LETTERS QUESTIONING HUMANITARIAN ASPECTS OF AIR FORCE

The most fundamental difference between beast and man is in the fact that the beast is a realist, taking life at its face value, while man attempts by his emotions to camouflage, and thereby to make more bearable, unpleasant prospects which he faces.

War, no matter how glorious the cause, is horrible by every civilized standard. Clothing it in shining armor does not hide the blood and suffering except from him who would be blind; neither does changing the vehicle of destruction alter the fact that death and destruction form the inevitable body and face of war.

By drawing aside the curtain, we see air warfare as being different only in the range of its potential destruction. The air gives uncurbed bestial instincts a wider field of expression, leaving only humanity and common sense to dictate limitations. Law cannot limit what physics makes possible. We can depend for moderation only upon reason and humane instincts when we exercise such a power.

We believe that we are using those curbs to the proper extent in our application of Air Power, but I can well understand your confusion in the light of propaganda and misguided reports of air operations. The fact that no adequate explanation has ever been offered has likewise confused others in a much better position to understand.

All of us have seen the result of air power as used by the beast. To one such as he, any horror is justified so long as his end is accomplished, but he fails to realize that even his purpose could be better accomplished if he used methods which are more efficient and which happen, at the same time, to be most humane.

This can best be illustrated by our own concept of the proper role of air power in war. It works on the principle of the old adage to the effect that for the lack of a nail the house fell down. We take away the nail.

It has always been recognized that armies can be defeated through the killing of men; but are not modern armies as futile without weapons and equipment? The armored force is nothing without a tank, and we can take the tank by killing its occupants and, at the same time, suffering casualties on our part. But we can also take the tank away, in effect, "before it is born," thereby saving the casualties on both sides. We can hit the factory where it is built, the steel plant where the armor is made, or the refinery from which it gets its fuel. We do not mean the cities containing the factories, but by exercising the precision which is the keynote of America, we mean that we carefully select and, to the best of our ability, hit the precise spot which is most vital to the enemy. We hold no brief for terror bombing. True, that will cause casualties on both sides, and there will still be ground fighting, but the final score in blood will be much less.

Those are the factors of reason and humanity which we allow to curb the awful weapon at our disposal. Those are the factors which the brute mind of the beast cannot conceive. With the understanding cooperation of you and thousands of others like you, we will prove to the beast that humanity pays and that Air Power is the most powerful urge for peace.

—From "Humanitarian Aspects of Airpower" binder,
Papers of Frederick L. Anderson,
Hoover Institution on War, Revolution, and Peace,
Stanford University, Stanford, California

NOTES

CHAPTER ONE. INTRODUCTION

1. Carl A. Spaatz to H. H. Arnold, 27 August 1944, diary (personal), August 1944, Box 15, Papers of Carl A. Spaatz, Library of Congress (LC).

2. Clausewitz, *On War*, 77.

3. Bidinian, *Combined Allied Bombing Offensive*, 160.

4. Weigley, *American Way of War*, 354–358.

5. Craven and Cate, *Army Air Forces*, 1:78, 95.

6. Ibid., 3:638, 733. These include Greenfield, *American Strategy*.

7. Sallagar, *Road to Total War*, 127. John Keegan has also emphasized the superior "moral scruple" of AAF policies in "We Wanted Beady-Eyed Guys Just Absolutely Holding the Course," *Smithsonian*, August 1983, 34–43.

8. Hastings, *Bomber Command*, 124.

9. Schaffer, "American Military Ethics," 319; Schaffer, *Wings of Judgment*, xii.

10. Sherry, *Rise of American Air Power*, 362–363; see also Michael S. Sherry, "The Slide to Total Air War," *New Republic*, 16 December 1981, 24–25.

11. Sherry, *Rise of American Air Power*, 52.

12. For a summary of some of the problems with the York, see "After a Big Gun Comes up a Dud," *US News and World Report*, 9 September 1985, 11.

13. Dougherty, "R&D Strategy in WWII," 44.

14. Doughty, *Evolution of US Army Tactical Doctrine*, 2.

15. Futrell, *Ideas, Concepts, Doctrine*, 1:168.

16. On results and technology of the Libya raid, see William R. Doerner, "In the Dead of Night," *Time*, 28 April 1986, 28–31; see also later coverage in this book in chapter 11 on air operations in the Balkans and Desert Storm.

17. Doughty, *Evolution of US Army Tactical Doctrine*, 1.

18. Fred Reed, "NATO Is in the Business of Projecting Uncertainty," *El Paso Times*, 1 October 1989, 8B.

19. Craven and Cate, *Army Air Forces*, 3:721.

20. Sherry, *Rise of American Air Power*, 222.

21. Sallagar, *Road to Total War*, 156–157.

22. Rostow, *Pre-invasion Bombing Strategy*, 40–42.

23. Operational-level commanders are those who manage campaigns in a theater of war; tactical commanders fight battles and engagements.

24. This goal is from a US Chiefs of Staff memorandum, adopted at a meeting of Combined Chiefs of Staff (CCS) at Quebec on 13 May 1943, US Department of State, *Foreign Relations of the United States: The Conferences at Washington and Quebec*, 222.

25. Fussell, *Wartime*, 14. He has admitted that his impressions are those of a "pissed-off infantryman," and he has no adequate documentation for his view of American airmen.

26. Schaffer, *Wings of Judgment*, does analyze isolated individual operations in some detail, but I believe his focus, especially on European operations, is too narrow. He does not completely examine operational and tactical aspects of operations or the rest of the air war around them.

27. Middlebrook, *Battle of Hamburg*, 340.

28. Sherry, "The Slide to Total Air War"; Hayes, *History of the Joint Chiefs of Staff*, 728.

29. Coffey, *Iron Eagle*, 139, 243.

CHAPTER TWO. DEVELOPING DOCTRINE

1. From a draft text for an Air Corps Tactical School (ACTS) course, *Air Force*, 1 December 1935, para. 28, File 248.101-1, Air Force Historical Research Agency (AFHRA), Maxwell Air Force Base (AFB), Alabama.

2. Holley, *Ideas and Weapons*, 140.

3. Ibid., 140–146, 157–172.

4. Maurer, *US Air Service*, 2:141, 161–163; Biddle, *Rhetoric and Reality*, 38–39, 54.

5. Greer, *Development of Air Doctrine*, 11. Edgar Gorrell first used the metaphor that a nation's army is the point of a drill and the nation the shank that must support it.

6. Maurer, *US Air Service*, 2:141–151.

7. Ibid., 253.

8. Ibid., 4: 363–499.

9. Ibid., 497.

10. Fredette, *Sky on Fire*, 30, 262. The Germans also planned devastating incendiary raids on Paris and London in late summer 1918, but the attacks were canceled out of fear they would harm peace negotiations.

11. Maurer, *US Air Service*, 4:500–503.

12. Biddle, *Rhetoric and Reality*, 69–80; Hurley, *Billy Mitchell*, 25–26.

13. Hurley, *Billy Mitchell.*, 142–145.

14. Hansell, *Strategic Air War against Japan*, 1. Smuts may have been influenced by his South African perspective on the ravages of the Boer War.

15. Warner, "Douhet, Mitchell, Seversky," 489–491.

16. Hurley, *Billy Mitchell*, 75–76.

17. Warner, "Douhet, Mitchell, Seversky," 487–491; Douhet, *Command of the Air*, 10.

18. Kennett, *History of Strategic Bombing*, 50–53.

19. Douhet, *Command of the Air*, 57–61, 69, 188; Howard, *Studies in War and Peace*, 143; Kennett, *History of Strategic Bombing*, 56.

20. Warner, "Douhet, Mitchell, Seversky," 498–500; Smith, "Douhet and Mitchell," 98–99.

21. Hurley, *Billy Mitchell*, 6, 146–147; Shiner, *Foulois*, 48.

22. Futrell, *Ideas, Concepts, Doctrine*, 1:38–39; Douhet, *Command of the Air*, 1; Hurley, *Billy Mitchell*, 146–147.

23. Collins, *Grand Strategy*, 17–18.

24. On the development of British bombing policy, see Hastings, *Bomber Command*, and Terraine, *Time for Courage*. The former is rather critical of British policy and the latter more sympathetic. Biddle, *Rhetoric and Reality*, provides a sort of middle view. Hastings explains the origins of "dehousing" (140–148).

25. Shiner, *Foulois*, 44–45. For a concise history of ACTS, including a list of faculty and students, see Finney, *History of the Air Corps Tactical School*.

26. Snow and Drew, *Introduction to Strategy*, 64–69.

27. Hansell, *Strategic Air War against Japan*, 3.

28. Shiner, *Foulois*, 47–48; Greer, *Development of Air Doctrine*, 57; Hansell, "Harold L. George," 77.

29. Weigley, *American Way of War*, 516.

30. Futrell, *Ideas, Concepts, Doctrine*, 1:33; Greer, *Development of Air Doctrine*, 57–58; Byrd, *Kenneth N. Walker*, 24–36; Clodfelter, *Beneficial Bombing*.

31. Greer, *Development of Air Doctrine*, 57.

32. Ibid., 58; Hansell, "Harold L. George," 78.

33. Greer, *Development of Air Doctrine*, 58; Hansell, "Harold L. George," 78.

34. Schaffer, *Wings of Judgment*, 27; Sherry, *Rise of American Air Power*, 55.

35. From a 1931 ACTS text, *The Air Force*, 54–55, File 248.101-1, AFHRA.

36. Shiner, *Foulois*, 47–48; a copy of the article is in Box 245 of the Papers of Henry H. Arnold, LC; instructor text for 1934–1935 US Air Force course, 3, File 248.101-1, AFHRA.

37. From draft text for US Air Force course, 1 December 1935, para. 28, File 248.101-1, and from lesson plan for "Conference on Air Operations against National Structures," 11 April 1939, 14, File 248.2020A-25, AFHRA.

38. Faber, "Interwar US Army Aviation," 220–221.

39. For an example of the influence on Command and General Staff School, see Sherman, *Air Warfare*. Sherman was an instructor in air tactics at Fort Leavenworth; his writings follow ACTS doctrine of the time and deviate from official policy. He had been one of the real founders of ACTS a few years earlier, along with Tommy Milling. See Faber, "Interwar US Army Aviation," 212–216.

40. Cannon, *Flying Training*, 30–32.

41. Ibid., 27; memorandum from the Department of Tactics to the superintendent, "Analysis of Cadet Military Training and Recommended Changes," 19 January 1939, United States Military Academy (USMA) Archives, West Point, NY.

42. See Tactical Course File 351.051 and Department of Civil and Military Engineering Organizational History/Program of Instruction Files, USMA Archives.

43. Student handouts, "The Sino-Japanese War" and "The Civil War in Spain," Department of Civil and Military Engineering Organizational History/Program of Instruction Files, Academic Year 1938–1939, Box 2, USMA Archives.

44. Goss, *Civilian Morale*, 253; "Franco Exhibits Himself," *New Republic*, 30 March 1938, 205.

45. Irvine, "Misuse of Air Power."

46. P. W. Wilson, "Are Laws of War Scraps of Paper?" *New York Times*, 3 October 1937, sec. 4E, 1.

47. Col. Byron Q. Jones, "Air Forces in War" File, Command Course No. 6, 1939, and Capt. Carter W. Clarke, memorandum for the assistant commandant, 28 February 1940, File 7-1940-87, Army War College Curricular Archives, US Army Military History Institute (USAMHI), Carlisle Barracks, PA.

48. Futrell, "Commentary," 313; Seversky, *Victory through Airpower*, 145–147.

49. Seversky to Maj. Gen. Frederick L. Anderson, 7 September 1943, Box 9A, Anderson Papers, Hoover Institution on War, Revolution, and Peace, Stanford University, Stanford, CA. The film was "designed to educate people on new concepts of air power."

50. Hansell, "Harold L. George," 79.

51. Craven and Cate, *Army Air Forces*, 1:114–116, 146.

52. Memorandum for the chief of Air Staff, "Notes on Preparation of AWPD/1," 19 November 1941, Box 7, Spaatz Papers; Hansell, *Strategic Air War against Japan*, 5; Mets, *Master of Airpower*, 112–113.

53. "Notes on AWPD/1," Spaatz Papers; Hansell, *Strategic Air War against Japan*, 5; Mets, *Master of Airpower*, 112–113; Hansell, "Harold L. George," 86–87; Byrd, *Kenneth N. Walker*, 65–67; quote from Gaston, *Planning the American Air War*, 103.

54. "Army and Navy Estimate of United States Overall Production Requirements," 11 September 1941, AWPD/1, tab 2, sec. 2, pt. 3, app. 2, Joint Army–Navy Board File 355, Serial 707, Record Group (RG) 225, National Archives (NA), Washington, DC; Sallagar, *Road to Total War*, 187, 233.

55. "Notes on Preparation of AWPD/1," Spaatz Papers; Craven and Cate, *Army Air Forces*, 1:146–147; for AWPD/1's long-range impact, see Hansell, *Air Plan That Defeated Hitler*.

CHAPTER THREE. FROM DOCTRINE TO PRACTICE

1. AWPD-42, Part 4, "Report," and Tab B-1-b, "Combined Offensive," File 145.82-42, AFHRA.

2. Craven and Cate, *Army Air Forces*, 1:133–134, 236, 246, 644–645, 662–663.

3. Griffith, *Quest*, 94–97; Cody, *AWPD-42*, 13–18; Hansell, *Strategic Air War against Germany and Japan*, 58–60; AWPD-42, Part IV, Para. 4g.

4. Cody, *AWPD-42*, 13–18, 22; AWPD-42, Part IV, Para. 5d.

5. Griffith, *Quest*, 98–99.

6. Craven and Cate, *Army Air Forces*, 1:607–610, 2:301–303.

7. Ibid., 2:305–307.

8. Ehlers, *Targeting the Third Reich*, chap. 8; Wheeler, *Jacob L. Devers*, chap. 9; Caidin, *Black Thursday*, 30; Craven and Cate, *Army Air Forces*, 2:631–635.

9. Ehlers, *Targeting the Third Reich*, 167.

10. Clausewitz used the term *friction* to describe the inevitable role of chance and unpredictability in war.

11. Craven and Cate, *Army Air Forces*, 2:353–364; Caidin, *Black Thursday*, 17–22.

12. Craven and Cate, *Army Air Forces*, 2:681–686; Miller, *Masters of the Air*, 192–200.

13. Coffey, *Iron Eagle*, 89–92.

14. Caidin, *Black Thursday*, 39, 218; Craven and Cate, *Army Air Forces*, 2:696-704; Speer, *Inside the Third Reich*, 372-373.

15. Caidin, *Black Thursday*, 215-218; Craven and Cate, *Army Air Forces*, 2:705-706, 711; Middlebrook, *Berlin Raids*, 306-325.

16. Davis, *Carl A. Spaatz*, 270-272, 283.

17. Ibid., 272-278; Wheeler, *Jacob L. Devers*, chap. 9.

18. Davis, *Bombing the European Axis Powers*, 269-271; McFarland and Newton, *To Command the Sky*, 155.

19. McFarland and Newton, *To Command the Sky*, 158-164; Doolittle with Glines, *I Could Never Be So Lucky Again*, 352-354.

20. McFarland and Newton, *To Command the Sky*, 168-173.

21. Ibid., 175-191; Davis, *Bombing the European Axis Powers*, 280-288.

22. McFarland and Newton, *To Command the Sky*, 190-192; Davis, *Bombing the European Axis Powers*, 287-289.

23. McFarland and Newton, *To Command the Sky*, 211-212; Murray, *Strategy for Defeat*, 237-255, 303.

24. Craven and Cate, *Army Air Forces*, 3:79-81.

25. Rostow, *Pre-invasion Bombing Strategy*, 3-35. For a fine discussion of the problems with aerial interdiction, see Mark, *Aerial Interdiction*. Robert Ehlers has pointed out that while aerial interdiction operations in Italy did have some success, like for Operation DIADEM in May 1944, they were hampered by exorbitant expectations and a lack of consistent ground pressure to work with the air campaign to strain enemy capabilities. Ehlers, *Mediterranean Air War*, 331-343.

26. Rostow, *Pre-invasion Bombing Strategy*, 36-65; Mierzejewski, *Collapse*, 180-187.

27. Overy, *Why the Allies Won*, 124-125; Ehlers, *Targeting the Third Reich*, 248, 311-315.

28. Davis, *Bombing the European Axis Powers*, 462-463.

29. Davis, *Carl A. Spaatz*, 570-571; Mierzejewski, *Collapse*, 184.

30. Davis, *Bombing the European Axis Powers*, 483-485. The directive was actually issued on the 16th but began to influence operations before that.

31. Ehlers, *Targeting the Third Reich*, 271-326; Miller, *Masters of the Air*, 315.

32. Ehlers, *Mediterranean Air War*, 356-385.

33. Description for 44th Bomb Group missions comes from the monthly reports in Boxes 14 and 15 of the 44th Bomb Group Collection, USAMHI, US Army Heritage and Education Center, Carlisle, PA. An overall listing of all Eighth and Fifteenth air force missions is available on a CD with Davis, *Bombing the European Axis Powers*. The term "10/10ths" means 100 percent cloud cover.

34. Information on the operations of the 455th Bomb Group comes from Asch, Graff, and Ramey, *The Story of the Four Hundred and Fifty-fifth Bombardment Group (H) WWII*, and Mahoney, *Fifteenth Air Force*.

35. The remarkable amount of tonnage dropped on targets around Vienna is evident from graphical depictions of the THOR database at the Air Force Research Institute at the Air University, Maxwell AFB, AL.

36. Miller, *Masters of the Air*, 419-446.

CHAPTER FOUR. ATTITUDES OF LEADERS AND THE PUBLIC

1. Mrs. Katharine A. Hooper to H. H. Arnold, 3 May 1943, "Humanitarian Aspects of Airpower" Binder, Box 9A, Anderson Papers. Many materials originally in that box may have been spread back out through the collection by archivists.

2. Craven and Cate, *Army Air Forces*, 2:238–241.

3. For American dreams about the airplane, see Corn, *Winged Gospel*. On the promotion of "air-mindedness," see Faber, "Interwar US Army Aviation."

4. Parton, *"Air Force Spoken Here,"* 140.

5. Cantril and Strunk, *Public Opinion*, 1067.

6. Sallagar, *Road to Total War*, 187, 233.

7. Cantril and Strunk, *Public Opinion*, 1067–1069.

8. Brittain, *Seeds of Chaos*. "Massacre by Bombing" was actually a reworking of *Seeds of Chaos* without her knowledge after she had sent a copy to a friend in the United States. She found out about it from English papers and noted it "produced much abuse of me—from which I deduced much bad conscience in USA." Brittain, *Wartime Chronicle*, 245-246.

9. Wittner, *Rebels against War*, 59; "Obliteration Raids on German Cities Protested in US," *New York Times*, 6 March 1944, 1.

10. "Letters to the Times," *New York Times*, 9 March 1944, 16.

11. Hopkins, "Bombing," 467–471.

12. Ford, "Morality," 271; for an example of support for Britain, see "Massacre by Bombing," *Politics* 1 (April 1944): 67–68.

13. "City Bombing Backed by Cousins and Elliot," *New York Times*, 31 March 1944, 3.

14. Lyle Evans Mahan to Arnold, 2 July 1945, File 091.412, Box 61, Arnold Papers; Hopkins, "Bombing," 464–466; R. Alfred Hassler, "Slaughter of the Innocent," *Fellowship*, February 1944, 58–62.

15. Ford, "Morality," 286, 304.

16. Batchelder, *Irreversible Decision*, 180–181.

17. See Hopkins, "Bombing," 467–471. He argues that the average American would have denied acquiescence in any attacks on women and children.

18. Howard, *Causes of War*, 104.

19. US Department of State, *Foreign Relations of the United States: Diplomatic Papers*, 1:541–542.

20. Hull, *Memoirs*, 1:671–672.

21. US Department of State, *Foreign Relations of the United States: Diplomatic Papers*, 1: 542–553.

22. Morgenthau, *Presidential Diaries*, 4:952.

23. Sherry, *Rise of American Air Power*, 78–79.

24. Batchelder, *Irreversible Decision*, 176–177; Ford, "Morality," 271.

25. Memo, Franklin D. Roosevelt to Henry Stimson, 26 August 1944, President's Secretary File, File 1944–1945, Box 104, FDR Library, Hyde Park, NY.

26. Lawrence Kuter to F. L. Anderson, 8 August 1944, File 145.161-7, April 1944–May 1945, miscellaneous correspondence of Anderson and Kuter, AFHRA, Maxwell AFB, AL.

27. Arnold and Eaker, *Winged Warfare*, 133–134.

28. Arnold, *Global Mission*, 227; diary of trip to England, April 1941, Box 271, Arnold Papers.

29. H. H. Arnold, "Precision Blows for Victory: A Report to the Nation," text of planned speech scheduled for Soldiers Field, Chicago, on 16 May 1943, Box 9A, Anderson Papers. This wording was typical of Arnold's rhetoric.

30. T. J. Hanley Jr. to assistant chiefs of Air Staff, personnel et al., 30 April 1943, File 385, Box 114, Arnold Papers; War Department transcript of extemporaneous remarks by Arnold at a Pentagon news conference, 18 October 1943, Box 14, Spaatz Papers.

31. Coffey, *Hap*, 358-375.

32. Arnold to Spaatz, 15 September 1942, Box 8, Spaatz Papers; Arnold to Eaker, 29 June 1943, Box 16, Papers of Ira C. Eaker, LC (Arnold's emphasis).

33. Eaker to Lt. Gen. Barney Giles, 29 September 1943, Eaker Papers, LC; Arnold to Spaatz, 26 September 1944, and Giles to Spaatz, 11 November 1944, Box 16, Spaatz Papers; Giles to Curtis LeMay, 11 November 1944, Box Bl 1, Papers of Curtis LeMay, LC.

34. Arnold to Eaker, 26 November 1944, File 000.7, Box 57, Arnold Papers.

35. Memo from Arnold to all Air Force commanders in combat zones, "Evaluation of Bombing Methods and Purposes," Box 121, Papers of Nathan F. Twining, LC; Sherry, *Preparing*, 19.

36. Memo, Arnold to each Air Force commander throughout the world, "Employment of Air Forces," 29 October 1942, Directive File, Box 42, Arnold Papers.

37. Schaffer, *Wings of Judgment*, 16; "Report on Suggestion for Bombing Japanese Volcanoes," 21 May 1942, President Folder, Box 45; and Maj. Gen. V. E. Bertrandias to Arnold, with documents, 4 June 1945, File 385, Japan, Box 115, Arnold Papers.

38. Record sheets reference "Booby Traps," File 400.112, Box 117; Col. E. W. Hill to Vannever Bush, with documents, 28 May 1942, File 452.3, Box 132, Arnold Papers.

39. "Evaluation of Bombing Methods," Twining Papers.

40. Macdonald, *Memoirs*, 76-77.

41. Diary of Henry L. Stimson, 5 September 1944, Yale University Library (microfilm).

42. Ibid., 3 January 1945, 2 July 1945, 6 May 1945.

43. Ibid., 6 June 1945; Chomsky, *American Power*, 167; Giovannitti and Freed, *Decision*, 36.

44. Schaffer, *Wings of Judgment*, 180.

45. Stimson to Arnold, with reply by Eaker, 11 June 1945, Sec. of War File, Box 46, Arnold Papers; on Kyoto, see Schaffer, *Wings of Judgment*, 143-146; Stimson to secretary of state, 11 January 1944, Box 114, Arnold Papers; Stimson diary, 11 October 1944.

46. Weigley, *Eisenhower's Lieutenants*, 104; Spaatz to Arnold, 19 November 1944, Box 16, Spaatz Papers.

47. Statement by Spaatz to public relations officers, 8 April 1944, Box 14, Spaatz Papers.

48. Weigley, *Eisenhower's Lieutenants*, 59.

49. Personal diary, 11 August 1945, Box 21, Spaatz Papers; Spaatz, interview with Noel Parrish and Alfred Goldberg, 21 February 1962, USAF Oral History Program K239.0512-754, Office of Air Force History, Boiling AFB, Washington, DC.

50. Spaatz to Maj. Gen. George Stratemeyer, 14 September 1942, Box 8, Spaatz Papers.

51. Davis, *Carl A. Spaatz*, 592-596.

52. Mann, *Lightning*, 244-245, 252-255; Thomas and Jablonski, *Doolittle*, 173-174, 245-246, 294; Craven and Cate, *Army Air Forces*, 3:638-639, 725.

53. Doolittle with Glines, *I Could Never Be So Lucky Again*, 376.

54. Letter, John P. Doolittle to Jamie Mitchell, 22 April 1993, in author's possession.

55. Material on Anderson's early career is in Boxes 3 and 4 of his papers; "Memorandum to Mr. Murphy," Box 13, Anderson Papers; Anderson to Fulton Lewis Jr., 18 April 1945, File 519.1611, 1945, AFHRA.

56. Schaffer, "American Military Ethics," 324; *Journal of American History* 67 (September 1980): Eaker to Arnold, 5 January 1945, Box 22, Eaker Papers, LC.

57. Parton, *"Air Force Spoken Here,"* 24-25, 41-42, 46-47, 216-228; minutes of meeting of Joint Chiefs of Staff (JCS), 29 March 1943, RG 218, NA, Washington, DC; "General Eaker Explains Strategy of 24-Hour Bombing of Germany," 18 February 1943 release, War Department, Bureau of Public Relations, Box 9A, Anderson Papers.

58. Memo, Eaker to Arnold, 25 August 1939, Box 3, Arnold Papers; Eaker, interview with Joe Green, 1972, Ira C. Eaker Papers, USAMHI, Carlisle Barracks, PA. In 1972 he did believe, however, that without daylight bombing the Luftwaffe would not have been defeated and the invasion would have failed.

59. Minutes of US Strategic Air Forces (USSTAF) Air Commander's Conference, 15 October 1944, Box 16, and Eaker to Spaatz, 1 January 1945, Box 20, Spaatz Papers.

60. See attache reports in G-2 Regional File, Great Britain, 1933-1944, 9600-9670, Box 1620, War Department General and Special Staffs, RG 165, Modern Military Field Branch, NA II, College Park, MD.

61. Report by Anderson, 5 January 1942, Box 2, Anderson Papers; memo, Eaker to Spaatz, "Night Bombing," 8 October 1942, Box 10, Spaatz Papers.

62. Memo, George Stratemeyer to Robert Lovett, 6 February 1943, File 385, Box 114, Arnold Papers.

63. Leahy, *I Was There*, 82-83; "Radio Message from American GHQ to Occupied France," 6 October 1942, Box 10, and personal diary, 20 October 1942, Box 9, Spaatz Papers.

64. Craven and Cate, *Army Air Forces*, 2:240; memo on bombardment policy from Air Vice Marshal J. C. Slessor, 29 October 1942, File 519.318-1, 1942-1945, Combined Bomber Offensive Policy Directives, AFHRA.

65. Bruce Hopper, memo on USSTAF history preparation, 22 September 1944, Box 287, Spaatz Papers.

66. Memo, Lovett to Judge Robert Patterson, 18 March 1943, with supporting documents, File 385, Box 114, Arnold Papers.

67. Craven and Cate, *Army Air Forces*, 2:320; Eaker to Air Vice Marshal Norman Bottomley, 9 April 1943, Box 19, Eaker Papers, LC; Sir Charles Portal to Eaker, 21 April 1943, Box 41, Arnold Papers; draft of letter, Arnold to Portal, "Humanitarian Aspects of Airpower" Binder, Box 9A, Anderson Papers.

68. Weigley, *Eisenhower's Lieutenants*, 58-64; "Review of Oil and Transportation Target Systems," 6 June 1944, File 168.7026-6, January-June 1944, Papers of Gen. Charles P. Cabell, AFHRA.

69. Weigley, *Eisenhower's Lieutenants*, 58-64; "Review of Target Systems," AFHRA.

70. Cabell interview with Hopper, 9 July 1944, Box 135; memo to Eisenhower with cable to JCS, "Loss of Civilian Lives during Overlord Preparatory Phase," from Overlord

Air Support Advisory Committee, 11 April 1944, Box 17; minutes of meeting in Gen. Sir H. M. Wilson's HQ, 30 April 1944, Box 14, Spaatz Papers.

71. Overy, *Bombers*, 425–426; comment from the audience at Conference on the 50th Anniversary of World War II, Siena College, Loudonville, NY, June 1993.

72. "Humanitarian Aspects of Airpower," Binder, Box 9A, Anderson Papers. See Appendix.

73. Howard, *Studies in War and Peace*, 238–241.

CHAPTER FIVE. ATTITUDES AND PERCEPTIONS
OF AMERICAN AIRMEN

1. Melville, "A Utilitarian View of the Monitor's Fight," 40.

2. Fuller, *Generalship*, 13.

3. Marshall, *Men against Fire*, 204. Despite controversy about his methods of gathering data, Marshall still offers many valuable insights.

4. Sherry, *Rise of American Air Power*, 204–218; Schaffer, *Wings of Judgment*, 17–18.

5. Craven and Cate, *Army Air Forces*, 6:538–556; Marshall, *Men against Fire*, 15–17; Grinker and Spiegel, *Men under Stress*, 8; Stouffer et al., *American Soldier*, 2:326–327.

6. See, for instance, MacDonald, *Company Commander*, preface, 293; Charles P. Roland, military historian and former World War II, infantryman, interview with author, West Point, NY, 30 January 1986; Morrison, *Point of No Return*, 241.

7. Kaplan and Smith, *One Last Look*, 20–21; Caidin, *Black Thursday*, 77–79.

8. "Flak versus Heavy Bombers," 24; Elmer T. Lian, *POW*, 1–10, manuscript, Lian Papers, USAMHI, Carlisle Barracks, PA. Flak suits were fifteen-pound aprons with small steel discs sewn in to provide some protection from low-velocity shrapnel.

9. Nalty and Berger, *Men Who Bombed the Reich*, 25–26; letter 197, Letters of Robert E. O'Donnell, USAMHI; Grinker and Spiegel, *Men under Stress*, 33–34.

10. Memo, Eaker to Spaatz, "Lessons Learned from Operations to Date," 25 August 1942, Box 38, Arnold Papers, LC; minutes of USSTAF staff meeting, 28 October 1944, Box 19, Spaatz Papers; survey is in Box 14, Spaatz Papers; Stouffer et al., *American Soldier*, 2:407; Lian, *POW*, 1–25; Fili, *Passage to Valhalla*, 26; Martin E. Kestenbaum, World War II veteran and president of the New Jersey chapter of the Eighth Air Force Historical Society, interview with author, West Point, NY, 23 May 1992.

11. Research Division, Special Service Division, HQ, European Theater of Operations, June 1944, "Survey of Combat Crews in Heavy Bombardment Groups in ETO," 11, Box 18, Spaatz Papers.

12. Thomas and Jablonski, *Doolittle*, 301.

13. Freeman, *US Strategic Bomber*, 87–100; Anderton, *B-29 Superfortress at War*, 19, 23, 35, 123.

14. For a good example, see Ardery, *Bomber Pilot*, 214–219.

15. Kerr, *Flames over Tokyo*, 35, 128; Morrison, *Point of No Return*, 257.

16. See, for instance, foreword to XXI Bomber Command Tactical Mission Report, Mission No. 40, Urban Area of Tokyo, 10 March 1945, dated 15 April 1945, Box 26, LeMay Papers.

17. Craven and Cate, *Army Air Forces*, 6:566–589; see Anderson's September 1941 curriculum, Box 3, Anderson Papers.

18. O'Donnell letters, USAMHI; Newby, *Target Phesti*, 93–98; Ardery, *Bomber Pilot*, 171–174. The O'Donnell letters present a vivid picture of the intense pressure for accurate bombing placed on bombardiers. Copies of the briefing form were examined in the mission reports of the Forty Fourth Bomb Group in that collection at USAMHI.

19. Moran, *Anatomy of Courage*, 102.

20. Muirhead, *Those Who Fall*, 174; Grinker and Spiegel, *Men under Stress*, 34–35; Cleveland Amory, "The Man Even Hollywood Likes," *Parade Magazine*, 21 October 1984, 9; Warren E. Thompson, "Mr. Stewart Goes to Vietnam," *History Net*, http://www.histo rynet.com; Ardery, *Bomber Pilot*, 2–3, 180–181.

21. Grinker and Spiegel, *Men under Stress*, 29; Lian, *POW*, 1–15; Wells, *Courage*, 121.

22. Stiles, *Serenade*, 21, 77–78, 84, 122. This unique book, a combination of philosophical musings and brutal depictions of aerial combat, like the war Stiles describes, "never stays the same for any length of time" (5).

23. Lian, *POW*, 1–9; Bendiner, *Fall of Fortresses*, 148–149, 154–155, 211, 238–239.

24. Collected Letters of Earle C. Cheek, USMA Manuscript Collection, Special Collections, West Point, NY; his death is described in a letter from Sergeant Keenan to Cheek's mother, 25 June 1945, in the collection.

25. Quotes are from Cheek's letters of 29 March 1944, 6 August 1944, 22 October 1944, 8 February 1945, and 28 February 1945.

26. Grinker and Spiegel, *Men under Stress*, 24–25, 35–36; Hastings et al., *Psychiatric Experiences*, 21–22; Roger Spiller, interview with author, Combat Studies Institute, Fort Leavenworth, KS, 28 February 1991; Davis, *Carl A. Spaatz*, 448.

27. Davis, *Carl A. Spaatz*, 417, 448–451. For a fine description of Swiss internment, see Miller, *Masters of the Air*, 331–347.

28. "The Aims and Accomplishments of Strategic Bombing," lecture, Maj. Russell Post to the 2nd Bombardment Division, File 526.716E, 3–29 August 1944, AFHRA, Maxwell AFB, AL; 25,000 men heard this particular lecture.

29. Dubois to Smith, "Flying Stress and Lack of Moral Fibre," War Department File for 1943, Box 104, President's Secretary Files, FDR Library; "Survey of Combat Crews," 22, and Col. Leroy A. Rainey, "Strategical Pattern Bombing," Box 81, Spaatz Papers; Stiles, *Serenade*, 122.

30. Hastings et al., *Psychiatric Experiences*, 137–138.

31. Diary of Henry L. Stimson, 31 December 1944, Yale University Library (microfilm); Polenberg, *War and Society*, 41–43, 135; Stouffer et al., *American Soldier*, 2:157–159; Kaplan and Smith, *One Last Look*, 156–184.

32. *Impact*, 1:vi–viii; April 1943, inside cover.

33. Ibid., April 1943, 2; September 1943, 42–43; June 1943, 18–19; July 1945, 4, 51.

34. Ibid., May 1945, 34; March 1945, 19–21; May 1944, 41; April 1944, 42; "Leaflet Bombing—The Appeal to Reason," lecture, Maj. Russell Post to 2nd Bombardment Division, File 526.716E, 3–29 August 1944, AFHRA.

35. *Impact*, April 1945, 2–23; June 1945, 24–37; August 1945, 19, 34–37.

36. Minutes of USSTAF Commanders Meeting, 20 July 1944, Box 18, Spaatz Papers.

37. Reynolds, *Amazing Mr. Doolittle*, 263. Doolittle also received unexpected support

from his Catholic chaplains, who appreciated the importance of Rome as a communications and supply center.

38. Lt. Sawyer, 5th Bomb Wing asst. A-2 (Intelligence Staff), to Lt. Col. Arthur Clark, 5th Wing A-2, 18 February 1944, Box 17, Twining Papers.

CHAPTER SIX. THE LURE OF TECHNOLOGICAL
INNOVATION: BOMBING AIDS

1. Carl Spaatz to Lt. Gen. Barney Giles, chief of Air Staff, 15 December 1944, Box 16, Spaatz Papers.

2. Spaatz to H. H. Arnold, 19 November 1944, Box 16, Spaatz Papers; Arnold to all Air Force commanders in combat zones, 10 June 1943, Box 121, Twining Papers.

3. Secret report by Major Anderson, 5 January 1942, Box 3, Anderson Papers; notes on accuracy of bombing, A-2 (Intelligence Staff) Report, 6 October 1942, Box 10, Spaatz Papers. The Norden was supposedly accurate within five mils at any altitude, versus thirty to forty mils for the Mark XIV. That would mean a total expected error for the Norden bombsight of only 100 feet for bombs dropped from 20,000 feet, compared with 600 to 800 for the Mark XIV.

4. Kaplan and Smith, *One Last Look*, 193-197; Craven and Cate, *Army Air Forces*, 2:343-346.

5. Smith, *Screaming Eagle*, 144; letter from Milt Groban, *Commentary* 66 (July 1978): 10; letter from Charles M. Bachman, *Commentary* 66 (November 1978): 20; Davis, *Bombing the European Axis Powers*, 177.

6. Arnold to all US Air Force commanders in combat zones, 10 June 1943, Box 121, Twining Papers; Spaatz to Arnold, 20 October 1942, Box 9, Spaatz Papers.

7. Terraine, *Time for Courage*, 473-474, 514-515.

8. Craven and Cate, *Army Air Forces*, 2:690-693; 3: 13-18; minutes, JCS Special Meeting, 29 April 1943, CCS 334, meetings 71-86, RG 218, NA, Washington, DC: Military Attache Reports, Files 9600-9670, Boxes 1621 and 1622, RG 165, NA II; Schaffer, "American Military Ethics," 322; Davis, *Bombing the European Axis Powers*, 176-178.

9. Headquarters, European Theater of Operations, US Army Release No. 8231, 28 December 1943, Box 9A, Anderson Papers.

10. Memo, H. M. McClelland to chief of Air Staff, 24 November 1943, Box 114, Papers of Henry H. Arnold, LC; Arnold to Spaatz, 5 January 1944, Box 14, Spaatz Papers; Office of Chief Press Censor, US Army, London, Edition 7, 13 December 1943, Box 1593, RG 165, NA II; memo, Brooks to Curtis Lemay, 3 December 1943, Box B9, LeMay Papers.

11. Ira Eaker to Barney Giles, 13 December 1943, and Eaker to Col. George Brownell, Robert Lovett's executive officer, 22 December 1943, Box 17, Eaker Papers, LC.

12. Craven and Cate, *Army Air Forces*, 3:17.

13. Mets, *Master of Airpower*, 180-181; Spaatz to Arnold, 14 January 1944, Box 17, and January 1944 Files and Minutes of Press Conference, 13 March 1944, Box 14, Spaatz Papers.

14. Spaatz to Arnold, 4 April 1944, and James Doolittle to Spaatz, 22 March 1944, Box 17, Spaatz Papers; Infield, *Big Week*, 89-90.

15. Intelligence summaries in Box 6 and daily diary, Anderson Papers; on Schaffhausen, see File 519.5991-2, 1944, Indiscriminate Bombing, AFHRA, Maxwell AFB, AL; Collected Letters of Earle C. Cheek, 16 March 1944, USMA Manuscript Collection, Special Collections, West Point, NY.

16. *Impact*, January 1944, 12–14; *Official World War II Guide*, 264.

17. Subject File: Bombing Overcast (H2X), Box 82, Spaatz Papers; Craven and Cate, *Army Air Forces*, 3:190–193. Figures are from Doolittle's remarks in the file; they differ slightly from those of Craven and Cate.

18. Harrison, *Cross-Channel Attack*, 300–302.

19. *Impact*, March 1945, 28–31, and May 1945, 34–38; Reed, *Condensed Analysis*, 34.

20. Minutes of 20 July 1944 USSTAF Commanders Meeting, Box 18, Spaatz Papers.

21. Spaatz to Advisory Specialist Group, 30 September 1944, Box 18; Dr. E. L. Bowles to Spaatz, 9 November 1944, Box 19; Spaatz to Doolittle, 18 November 1944, Box 16, Spaatz Papers.

22. Craven and Cate, *Army Air Forces*, 3:649; Eighth Air Force memo no. 55-24, "Attack of Secondary and Last Resort Targets," 29 October 1944, File 519.318-1, 1942–1945, Combined Bomber Offensive Policy Directives, AFHRA.

23. Craven and Cate, *Army Air Forces*, 3:667; US Strategic Bombing Survey Military Analysis Division, "Daylight Bombing Accuracy of the 8th, 9th, and 15th Air Forces," 27–28, File 137.306.6, 24 August 1945, AFHRA.

24. Minutes, USSTAF Staff meeting, 14 November 1944, Anderson diary, Anderson Papers; Doolittle to Spaatz, 19 December 1944, and Spaatz to Giles, 15 December 1944, Box 16, Spaatz Papers.

25. Craven and Cate, *Army Air Forces*, 3:666–667; Fifteenth Air Force monograph, "Operational Employment of Lone Wolf Tactics," 18 January 1945, Box 82, Spaatz Papers; message, 15th Air Force to USSTAF, 14 November 1944, Anderson diary, Anderson Papers.

26. Msg. CS-533-11E, Eaker to Spaatz, 2 January 1945, Box 17, Twining Papers; Eaker to Giles, 4 January 1945, Box 106, Arnold Papers; Craven and Cate, *Army Air Forces*, 3:667.

27. Mets, *Master of Airpower*, 258–259; entry for 26 January 1945, David Schlatter daily diary, File 168-7052-5, AFHRA; memo, McClelland to Giles, 22 January 1945, File 370.2, England, Box 105, Arnold Papers.

28. Memo, McClelland to Giles, 22 January 1945, Arnold Papers; Giles to Spaatz, 6 January 1945, Box 20, Spaatz Papers.

29. Spaatz to Giles, 23 February 1945, Box 9A, Anderson Papers; "Daylight Bombing Accuracy of the 8th, 9th, and 15th Air Forces," AFHRA, 24; Lauris Norstad to Spaatz, 3 March 1945, File 519.9701-15, 44–45, General Correspondence, AFHRA; on Korean War radar bombing techniques, see Crane, *American Airpower Strategy*.

30. Hastings et al., *Psychiatric Experiences*, 117, 327; memo, McClelland to Giles, Arnold Papers; Craven and Cate, *Army Air Forces*, 3:738–743.

31. Odishaw, *Radar Bombing*, 124–126; Galland, *The First and the Last*, 190; Davis, "Bombing Strategy Shifts," 44; Morrison, *Point of No Return*, 267–268.

32. Craven and Cate, *Army Air Forces*, 5:567.

CHAPTER SEVEN. THE LURE OF TECHNOLOGICAL
INNOVATION: BETTER BOMBS

1. Olsen, *Aphrodite*, 196.

2. Schaffer, *Wings of Judgment*, 85–86.

3. Craven and Cate, *Army Air Forces*, 3:727.

4. Werrell, *Evolution of the Cruise Missile*, 15–16.

5. Arnold, *Global Mission*, 74–76, 227, 260–261. For a more detailed discussion on these "Bugs," officially termed the GMA-1, see Craven and Cate, *Army Air Forces*, 6:253–254; Werrell, *Evolution of the Cruise Missile*, 26–30.

6. Cable, Spaatz to War Department (WAR), 20 June 1944, official diary, Box 18, Spaatz Papers.

7. Weigley, *Eisenhower's Lieutenants*, 258–259.

8. Olsen, *Aphrodite*, 175–176.

9. Telephone conversation, Lawrence Kuter and F. L. Anderson, 22 June 1944, personal diary, Box 15, and cable, Mediterranean Allied AF to WAR, 7 July 1944, official diary, Box 18, Spaatz Papers.

10. Cable WX58750, Washington to commander in chief, Southwest Pacific Area (CINC SWPA), 2 July 1944, Box 11079/22, and cable, George Kenney to Arnold, 3 July 1944, Box 11061/42, 373 files, US Army Forces, Pacific Adjutant General (AF-PAC AG) Correspondence Files, Records of US Army Commands, RG 338, NA II.

11. "Report of Aphrodite Mission, 4 August 1944," 6 August 1944, official diary, Box 18, Spaatz Papers; "Report on Aphrodite Project," 20 January 1945, File 527.431A-1, January 1945, AFHRA, Maxwell AFB, AL; Olsen, *Aphrodite*, 123–126, 165–167, 173, 189–196.

12. "Report on Aphrodite Project," AFHRA; cable UG6379, Spaatz to Arnold, 13 August 1944, and cables UG7658 and UX67648, Spaatz to Arnold, 6 September 1944, Anderson's diary, Anderson Papers; Olsen, *Aphrodite*, 232, 280–288, 298, 302–321.

13. "Report on Aphrodite Project," AFHRA; cable 1E1000CS, Spaatz to Ira Eaker, 13 August 1944, and cable, Spaatz to James Doolittle, 7 September 1944, Anderson's diary, Anderson Papers; Olsen, *Aphrodite*, 327, 360–361.

14. Alfred Maxwell to Anderson, "Plan, Willie Orphan—Phase B," 14 November 1944; cable W61260, Arnold to Spaatz, 11 November 1944; cable, Spaatz to Arnold, 21 November 1944, Anderson's diary, Anderson Papers; "Report on Aphrodite Project," AFHRA.

15. Cable UX70102, Hoyt Vandenberg to Spaatz, 22 November 1944, and cable S71437, Dwight Eisenhower to Arnold, 18 December 1944, Anderson's diary, Anderson Papers.

16. JCS 1150, CCS 729, CCS 729/ 1, CCS 729/2, CCS 729/4, File 373.11 Germany (4 November 1944), Records of the United States Joint Chiefs of Staff, RG 218, NA, Washington, DC.

17. "Newest Attempts of the Luftwaffe," *Impact*, October 1944, 42–43; Kuter to Arnold, 5 February 1945, Box 38, Arnold Papers.

18. Arnold to Spaatz, 23 November 1944, and Spaatz to Arnold, 10 December 1944, personal diary, Box 16, Spaatz Papers.

19. Grandison Gardner to Spaatz, 6 February 1945, official diary, Box 20, Spaatz Papers.

20. Minutes, JCS 190th meeting; memo from Adm. William Leahy to the president, 26 March 1945, CCS 373.11 Germany (4 November 1944), RG 218, NA, Washington, DC.

21. Minutes, JCS 190th meeting; Loewenheim et al., *Roosevelt and Churchill*, 688–689; Giles to Spaatz, 27 April 1945, File 519.9701-15, AFHRA.

22. Donald Hutchinson, chief of Far Eastern Air Forces (FEAF) Air Staff, to S. J. Chamberlin, G-3 SWPA 16 June 1945, Box 11061/42, and cable WX-44043, Washington to Guam, 5 August 1945, Box 11079/22, 373 Files AFPAC, RG 338, NA II.

23. See September to November 1942 correspondence on glide bombs between Arnold, Eaker, and Spaatz in Box 9, and Kuter to Anderson, 10 September 1943, Box 80, Spaatz Papers; Smith, *Screaming Eagle*, 156–157.

24. Muirhead, *Those Who Fall*, 172–175; *Impact*, March 1945, 33–35; Werrell, "Who Fears?" 90–92.

25. Entry for 16 June 1944, journal, trip to England, 8 June 1944-21 June 1944, Box 272, Arnold Papers.

26. Werrell, *Evolution of the Cruise Missile*, 62–63, 68–70.

27. See correspondence in File 452.11, Rockets, Box 131, Arnold Papers; *Impact*, January 1945, 5–7.

28. Msg. WARX 44137, Arnold to Spaatz and Eaker, 10 October 1944, File 519.8671-8, 1943–1944, AFHRA; memo, "Stoppage of Flying Bomb Production," Col. W. F. McKee to Col. Dean, 29 November 1944, File 471.6, Box 137, Arnold Papers; minutes, USSTAF Staff meeting, 23 December 1944, Box 16, Spaatz Papers.

29. Cable W78828, George C. Marshall to Eisenhower, 18 December 1944, Anderson's diary, Anderson Papers; memo, McKee to Barney Giles, "Subject: Buzz Bomb (JB-2)," 19 January 1945, Box 131, and memo, "Buzz Bomb Program," deputy chief of Air Staff to Staff, 12 June 1945, File 471.6, Buzz Bombs, Box 138, Arnold Papers.

30. Giles to Vannever Bush, 13 February 1945, File 471.6, Buzz Bombs, Box 138, Arnold Papers.

31. Stranger ideas on missile guidance were being tested; one, Project Orcon (for "organic control") with psychologist B. F. Skinner, involved using pigeons pecking at a target image. Irving Wallace, "Significa," *Parade Magazine*, 31 July 1983, 19.

32. Memo, D. T. Griggs to Spaatz, "The Role of Controlled Buzz Bombs in the German War," 5 February 1945, Box 23, Spaatz Papers; Griggs to Robert Lovett, 17 February 1945, and memo, Lt. Gen. W. B. Smith to Spaatz, 27 February 1945, Box 41, Arnold Papers.

33. Memo, "Buzz Bomb Program," Brig. Gen. P. W. Timberlake, deputy chief of Air Staff, to Staff, 12 June 1945, and Eaker to Kenney, 5 June 1945, File 471.6, Buzz Bombs, Box 138, Arnold Papers.

34. See Bernstein, "America's Biological Warfare Program."

35. Bernstein, "Why We Didn't Use Poison Gas"; War Cabinet, Inter Service Committee on Chemical Warfare, CCW (44) 2, 23 January 1944, File 519.8085-3, 1943–1945, Chemical Warfare, AFHRA.

36. Arnold to Spaatz, 2 February 1944, Box 14, Spaatz Papers; memo, "Retaliatory Use of Chemical Warfare against the Japanese," Haywood Hansell to Arnold, 20 March 1944, File 385, Japan, Box 115, Arnold Papers. Arnold ordered plans prepared on 7 December 1943.

37. Spaatz to undersecretary of state, Air Ministry, undated, Box 16, and memo, "Gas Attack by Air Forces," Spaatz to Eisenhower, 20 May 1944, Box 17, Spaatz Papers; Bernstein, "Why We Didn't Use Poison Gas," 43.

38. Mountcastle, "Trial by Fire," 136–138.

39. Ibid., 138–140; memo, "BDRC Report on Incendiary Bomb Requirements," Maj. Gen. George Stratemeyer, chief of Air Staff, to deputy chief of staff, War Department, 24 October 1942, File 385, Box 114, Arnold Papers.

40. Memo, "Incendiary Bombs," Arnold to assistant chief of Air Staff, Material, Maintenance and Distribution, 26 April 1943, Box 38, Arnold Papers; Mountcastle, "Trial by Fire," 141, 146–150; translation of article on Braddocks, 19 February 1945, File 520.464, 16 March 1943–18 July 1945, AFHRA.

41. The best account of Project X-ray is Couffer, *Bat Bomb*, a truly amazing book. Truth is stranger than fiction. Further information is in Coffey, *American Arsenal*, 99–103.

42. Mountcastle, "Trial by Fire," 146, 151–154, 163; Supreme Headquarters, Allied Expeditionary Forces (SHAEF), Bedell-Smith to Spaatz, 16 October 1944, Anderson's diary, Anderson Papers; Freeman, *US Strategic Bomber*, 154–155, 160; Coffey, *American Arsenal*, 103.

CHAPTER EIGHT. THE LURE OF THE
DEATHBLOW IN EUROPE

1. "Army and Navy Estimate of United States Overall Production Requirements," 11 September 1941, AWPD/1, tab 2, sec. 2, pt. 3, app. 2, 6, Joint Army-Navy Board File 355, Serial 707, RG 225, National Archives, Washington, DC.

2. Craven and Cate, *Army Air Forces*, 2:415–433; *Impact*, August 1943, 40–41; George Patton to Carl Spaatz, 19 November 1944, Box 16, Papers of Carl A. Spaatz.

3. Craven and Cate, *Army Air Forces*, 2:463; Reynolds, *Amazing Mr. Doolittle*, 262–263; File MR 303, Bombing of Rome, Box 33, Map Room Files, FDR Library; memo, Winston Churchill to JCS, 10 June 1943, and H. H. Arnold's written comments on JCS memo for George Marshall, Ernest King, and Arnold, 3 July 1943, Box 39, Arnold Papers; Overy, *Bombers*, 333.

4. Overy, *Bombers*, 330–333.

5. Memo, Churchill to JCS, and CCS memo, "Bombing of Rome," 22 June 1943, Box 39, Arnold Papers; Craven and Cate, *Army Air Forces*, 2:464; Col. Leroy A. Rainey, "Strategical Pattern Bombing," Box 81, Spaatz Papers.

6. Craven and Cate, *Army Air Forces*, 2:464–465; File MR 303, FDR Library; Rainey, "Strategical Pattern Bombing"; May, *Lessons*, 128; Overy, *Bombers*, 336–339.

7. Memo, Maj. D. Dalziel to Brig. Gen. E. P. Curtis, "Surrender of Bulgaria," 24 October 1943, Box 13, Spaatz Papers.

8. J.P.(43)346, 15 October 1943, "Air Attack on the Balkans," File 512.3171-1, AFHRA, Maxwell AFB, AL.

9. Schaffer, *Wings of Judgment*, 54–59.

10. Memo, F. L. Anderson to director of intelligence, 18 January 1944, and memo, Spaatz to Ira Eaker, 3 February 1944, File 519.318-1, AFHRA; Schaffer, *Wings of Judgment*, 57.

11. Air Ministry messages to Joint Intelligence Committee, 16 February 1944, and to Britman Washington, 10 March 1944, File 621.609-4, AFHRA.

12. Msg. AX779, Air Ministry to USSTAF, 25 March 1944, Box 14, and msg. W13745, Arnold to Spaatz, 24 March 1944, Box 17, Spaatz Papers; Schaffer, *Wings of Judgment*, 57.

13. Msg., Spaatz to Arnold, 6 March 1944, Box 14, and statement, Col. Richard Hughes to Bruce Hopper, 13 June 1944, Box 135, Spaatz Papers.

14. CCS 626, 20 July 1944, US Chiefs of Staff, "Integration of Political Considerations with Military Decisions in Bombing Europe"; enclosures include paraphrase of 23 April 1944 note from John Winant to FDR, ABC 384.5 (25 May 1944), RG 165, NA, Washington, DC; Schaffer, *Wings of Judgment*, 58; Craven and Cate, *Army Air Forces*, 3:411, 652, 748–749.

15. Eaker to Arnold, 17 September 1944, President Folder, Box 45, and secretary of war to secretary of state, 11 November 1944, Box 106, Arnold Papers.

16. Memorandum for personal file, 12 October 1944, Box 38. Papers of General of the Army Omar N. Bradley, USMA Special Collections, West Point, NY.

17. Morgenthau, *Presidential Diaries*, 4:952; Dallek, *Franklin Roosevelt*, 290; coordinator of information, Monograph No. 3, "The German Military and Economic Position," 21, Box 101, Arnold Papers.

18. Office of the Assistant Chief of Air Staff, Intelligence, "The Strategic Aerial Bombardment of Europe: Accomplishments and Potentialities," 10 December 1943, 3:39–41, Box 248, Arnold Papers.

19. Craven and Cate, *Army Air Forces*, 3:76; "Plan for the Completion of the Combined Bomber Offensive," 5 March 1944, pt. 1, suppl., File 519.318-1, AFHRA.

20. E. Frey to Spaatz, 21 August 1942, Box 8, and memo, Spaatz to CGs 15th and 8th Air Forces, "Exploitation of Air Supremacy," 4 March 1944, Box 14, Spaatz Papers.

21. Memo, Capt. John Harris to Brig. Gen. George McDonald, "Operation Shatter," 27 June 1944, File 519.322-1, AFHRA; memo, Charles Cabell to Anderson, "Attacks for Demoralization of the German People," 26 June 1944, Thunderclap File, Box 153, Spaatz Papers.

22. Rostow, *Pre-invasion Bombing Strategy*, 17; Richard Hughes, memo, 5 July 1944, Pointblank Folder, File 519.4511-14, AFHRA.

23. Memo, Lowell Weicker to McDonald, 6 July 1944; memo, McDonald to Charles Williamson, 5 July 1944; undated memo, Charles Taylor to Williamson; Taylor comments on proposed memo, Anderson to Sir Arthur Tedder, 8 July 1944; draft, Psychological Warfare Plan with handwritten note from Taylor to Williamson, 16 July 1944, Pointblank Folder, AFHRA.

24. Laurence Kuter to Anderson, 20 July 1944, and Anderson to Kuter, 27 July 1944, Anderson's diary, Anderson Papers.

25. Memo, Kuter to Arnold, "Attack on German Civilian Morale," 9 August 1944, Thunderclap File, Box 153, Spaatz Papers; Middlebrook, *Battle of Hamburg*, 270–272, 327–328.

26. Craven and Cate, *Army Air Forces*, 2:677, 707–719; Eaker to Robert Lovett, 9 August 1943, Box 17, Eaker Papers, LC; Anderson to Eaker, 13 August 1943, Box 143, Spaatz Papers; Schaffer, *Wings of Judgment*, 66. Hamburg may have influenced Curtis LeMay; see chapter 10 of this book.

27. Kuter to Anderson, 15 August 1944, Thunderclap File, Box 153, Spaatz Papers.

28. Memo, Williamson to Kuter, 4 September 1944, with 6 September Kuter endorsement; memo, Williamson to Anderson, 12 September 1944, Thunderclap File, Box 153, Spaatz Papers.

CHAPTER NINE. DELIVERING THE
DEATHBLOW TO GERMANY

1. Ira Eaker to Carl Spaatz, 1 January 1945, Box 20, Spaatz Papers.

2. Msg. CS93JD, James Doolittle to Spaatz, 30 January 1945, File 520.422, Thunderclap, AFHRA, Maxwell AFB, AL.

3. Spaatz to H. H. Arnold, 5 February 1945, Box 20, Spaatz Papers.

4. Combined Operational Planning Committee 2111, "Tactical Plan for the Air Attack of Targets in and in the Neighborhood of the Ruhr," and memo, F. L. Anderson to Combined Operational Planning Committee, 6 October 1944, Hurricane File, Box 150, Spaatz Papers.

5. Operation Thunderclap, 20 August 1944, File 519.321, and Charles Cabell to Richard Hughes, 8 September 1944, File 168.7026-9, AFHRA; Spaatz to Arnold, 27 August 1944, Box 15, Spaatz Papers.

6. Memo, Spaatz to D. D. Eisenhower, 24 August 1944, with 28 August endorsement from Eisenhower, Box 18, and diary entry, 9 September 1944, Box 16, Spaatz Papers; Weigley, *Eisenhower's Lieutenants*, 268–273; MacDonald, *Mighty Endeavor*, 361–362.

7. Eaker to Robert Lovett, 9 August 1943, Box 17, Eaker Papers, LC; memo, Brig. Gen. Thomas White to Arnold, "Morale and Human Effects of Berlin Bombings," 2 February 1944, Germany File, Box 50, Papers of Henry H. Arnold, LC.

8. Craven and Cate, *Army Air Forces*, 3:284–285; interview, Lt. Col. Cecil Hahn with Brig. Gen. Orville Anderson, 10 November 1944, Box 135, Spaatz Papers.

9. Minutes, JCS 176th meeting, 14 September 1944, CCS Decimal File, Box 179, RG 218, NA, Washington, DC.

10. Arnold to Spaatz, 30 December 1944, Box 20, and msg., Anderson to Spaatz, 1 February 1945, Clarion File, Box 170, Spaatz Papers; diary entry, 29 January 1945, Box 1, Papers of Hoyt Vandenberg, LC.

11. Craven and Cate, *Army Air Forces*, 3:725–726; minutes, USSTAF Staff meeting, 2 February 1945, Box 20, Spaatz Papers.

12. Msg. CS93JD, Doolittle to Spaatz, 30 January 1945; msg. JD104CS, Spaatz to Doolittle, 30 January 1945; msg. UA53649, Spaatz to Doolittle, 2 February 1945, File 520.422, AFHRA.

13. Msg. CS96JD with Spaatz note, Doolittle to Spaatz, 2 February 1945, Box 23, Spaatz Papers; Craven and Cate, *Army Air Forces*, 3:725–726; USSTAF Air Intelligence summaries 66, 67, and 68, AF spec, safe, Box 126, records of interservice agencies, RG 334, NA II; Friedrich, *Fire*, 310.

14. Spaatz to Lovett, and msg. U68773, Spaatz to Arnold, 1 October 1944, Anderson diary, Anderson Papers.

15. Msg. CS139EC, Anderson to Spaatz, 30 September 1944; msg. CS150EC, Anderson to Spaatz, 1 October 1944; memo, Anderson to Combined Operational Planning Committee, "Operation Hurricane," 6 October 1944; msg. W40454, Arnold to Spaatz, 3

October 1944, Hurricane File, Box 150, Spaatz Papers; Craven and Cate, *Army Air Forces*, 3:319–322.

16. Memo, Alfred Maxwell to Spaatz, "Comments on RAF Version of Plan Hurricane," 3 October 1944, Hurricane File, Spaatz Papers.

17. Target Section, USSTAF working papers, on "Plan for Operation Hurricane," 2 October 1944, and untitled, undated work on Transportation Attack Plan, File 519.321, AFHRA.

18. Notes from Allied Air Commanders Conference, 15 December 1944, Anderson diary; Bowles to H. L. Stimson with extracts from Griggs letter, 21 November 1944, Box 2, E. L. Bowles's File, Office of the Secretary of War, RG 107, NA, Washington, DC; Arnold to Spaatz, 14 January 1945, Box 20, Spaatz Papers.

19. "General Plan for Maximum Effort Attack against Transportation Objectives," 17 December 1944, File 168.7026-9, AFHRA.

20. Ibid., includes Cabell's handwritten comments, and memo, "The German Transport System as a Strategic Bombing Target," by Capt. W. A. Salant, 12 October 1944, and N. F. Twining to Eaker, 4 January 1945; Eaker to Spaatz, 1 January 1945, Box 20, Spaatz Papers.

21. Doolittle to Spaatz, 27 December 1944; Maxwell to Anderson, 5 January 1945; msg. AX991, Sir Norman Bottomley to Spaatz, 26 December 1944, File 519.430A, AFHRA.

22. Spaatz to Arnold, 7 January 1945, Box 49, Arnold Papers; Spaatz to Arnold, 5 February 1945, Box 20, Spaatz Papers; msg. UAX 53778, Spaatz to all units, 5 February 1945, File 519.430A, and msg. UAX 64613, Spaatz to all units, 21 February 1945, File 520.3233-40, AFHRA.

23. Schaffer, *Wings of Judgment*, 86–95; memo, F. L. Anderson to O. Anderson, "Press Conference in US," 2 March 1945, Anderson diary, Anderson Papers.

24. Forty-second Bomb Wing Plan for Clarion, File 549.322H, and msg. F6055Al, 28 February 1945, File 519.318-1, AFHRA; msgs. UAX 64905, D1933, D61872, and M47480, 1 March 1945, Anderson diary, Anderson Papers; situation maps, 22–23 February 1945, MR 300, sec. 18, Box 148, Map Room Files, FDR Library.

25. Mierzejewski, *Collapse*, 170.

26. Msg. MSW 305, 6 March 1945, and msg. FWD 17651, 8 March 1945, Anderson diary, Anderson Papers; Clarion summary, Box 20, Spaatz Papers; Doolittle to Barney Giles, 20 March 1945, Box 61, Arnold Papers; Craven and Cate, *Army Air Forces*, 3:732–735; entry for 3 March 1945, Vandenberg diary, Papers of Hoyt Vandenberg, LC.

27. Mierzejewski, *Collapse*, 184.

28. See maps in Bergander, *Dresden im Luftkrieg.*

29. Irving, *Destruction of Dresden*, 151, 177, 186–191. Irving, who gave wide publicity to the higher figure, at times even going as high as 250,000, accepted the lower in 1966. See letter from Max Rosenberg, *Air Force Magazine*, April 1973, 4.

30. Smith, "Bombing of Dresden Reconsidered," 208–209, 237–247; Joseph W. Angell, "Historical Analysis of the 14-15 February 1945 Bombing of Dresden," 11–15, File K239.046-38, AFHRA; Biddle, "Dresden 1945" and "Sifting Dresden's Ashes." Although Biddle misses the pre-raid concerns among American air leaders, she is especially good describing the development of postwar myths and images of Dresden.

31. USSTAF Air Intelligence summary 68, RG 334, NA II; see articles, *New York*

Times, 15 February 1945, 1; notes from Allied Air Commanders Conference, 15 February 1945, File K239.046-38, AFHRA.

32. Craven and Cate, *Army Air Forces*, 3:640, 653, 724–725.

33. Memo, Bottomley to Sir Charles Portal, 31 January 1945, and msg. W37181, Giles to Eaker, 14 February 1944, File 519.318-1, AFHRA; msg. Cricket 38, Lawrence Kuter to Giles, 1 February 1945, Box 316; msg., Giles to Spaatz, 17 February 1945, and msg. UA64462, Spaatz to Arnold, 18 February 1945, Box 20, Spaatz Papers.

34. Memo, George McDonald to Anderson, 19 February 1945, File 519.523-6, AFHRA; memo, 21 February 1945, Anderson's diary, Anderson Papers.

35. M. Smith, "Bombing of Dresden," 70–78; memo, Anderson to Spaatz, 19 February 1945, with msgs. UA64462, W39222, UA64470, W39730, UA64471, W39722, File K239.046-38; Anderson to Kuter, 27 February 1945, File 519.1611, AFHRA.

36. Msg. UA 64555, Spaatz to Eaker, 20 February 1945, Box 23, Spaatz Papers; Diary of H. L. Stimson, 5 March 1945, Yale University Library (microfilm); Schaffer, *Wings of Judgment*, 99–103; "Report of Air Attacks on Targets in Dresden," File 519.523-6, AFHRA.

37. 1 March 1945 Bombardment Policy with Anderson memo, Box 118, Twining Papers; Anderson to Kuter, 26 March 1945, File 519.1611, AFHRA; msg. WAR 65558, 9 April 1945, with Anderson response, 10 April 1945, Box 21, Spaatz Papers; David Schlatter, diary, 15 March 1945, File 168.7052-5, AFHRA.

38. Biddle, "Dresden 1945," 430.

39. Lovett to Spaatz, 27 November 1944, Box 16, Spaatz Papers.

CHAPTER TEN. TORCHING JAPAN

1. LeMay with Kantor, *Mission*, 382.

2. Cortesi, *Target: Tokyo*, 276.

3. Feist, "Bats Away"; Couffer, *Bat Bomb*.

4. Dower, *War without Mercy*, 53–54, 77–93.

5. Thorne, *Allies of a Kind*, 158–159, 168; Diary of Henry L. Stimson, 31 December 1944, Yale University Library (microfilm); memos, Stimson to FDR, 17 September 1943, and JCS to FDR, 22 September 1943, Box 104, Personal Secretary File, FDR Library.

6. Dower, *War without Mercy*, 49–50.

7. Manchester, *Glory*, 268–269; George Kenney to H. H. Arnold, 1 January 1943, Box 121, Twining Papers.

8. Air Raids File, Box 313, Papers of Harry Hopkins, FDR Library.

9. *Retaliation*, 69–77, 142–143; memo, Arnold to George Marshall, 26 May 1945, Box 117, Arnold Papers.

10. Brower, "Joint Chiefs of Staff," 209–210. This excellent dissertation has recently been revised into a book for Palgrave Macmillan, entitled *Defeating Japan*.

11. Spector, *Eagle against the Sun*, xiii.

12. Prime Minister John Curtin to Douglas MacArthur, 7 April 1943, with 10 April reply, 11061/43; memo, Brig. Gen. B. M. Fitch to Allied Commanders, "Air Attack of Objectives within the Philippine Archipelago," 1 November 1944; and msg. to same from MacArthur, 2 September 1944, 11061/41, RG 338, NA II.

13. Correspondence on Intramuros incident, 16-17 February 1945 in File 373.21, 11061/44, and on Rabaul Hospital, 23-24 May 1944 in File 373.11,11061/41, Records of US Army Commands, RG 338, NA II.

14. Dower, *War without Mercy*, 41; MacArthur, *Reminiscences*, 276; Allied Translator and Interpreter Section, South West Pacific Area, Research Report No. 94, "Psychological Effect of Allied Bombing on the Japanese," 21 September 1944, RG 3, Reel 511, microfilm copy of Douglas MacArthur Archives at the USMA Library, West Point, NY; W. F. Craven and Cate, *Army Air Forces*, 5:698-699; Crane, *American Airpower Strategy*, 46-48.

15. Craven and Cate, *Army Air Forces*, 5:628-635; Morison, *Two-Ocean War*, 477-478.

16. LeMay with Kantor, *Mission*, 340-341, 370-372.

17. Coffey, *Iron Eagle*, 4, 34-38, 50, 56, 69, 139, 243; Werrell, *Blankets of Fire*, 140.

18. Craven and Cate, *Army Air Forces*, 2:698-699; Schaffer, *Wings of Judgment*, 66-67; USSTAF Air intelligence summary No. 50, RG 334, NA, Suitland, MD; minutes of 3rd Bombardment Group Commanders Meeting, 15 October 1943, Box B8, LeMay Papers; Coffey, *Iron Eagle*, 99; copy of "Additional Intelligence Briefing Material for 3rd Field Order No. 77" from 9 October 1943, furnished by Trevor Albertson, Air Command and Staff College, Maxwell AFB, AL.

19. Lesson plan for Conference on Air Operations against National Structures, 11 April 1939, File 248.202A-25, AFHRA, Maxwell AFB, AL; plan, "Aircraft Requirements for the Chinese Government," Serial 691, and memo, Arnold to Robert Lovett, 11 June 1941, Joint Army-Navy Board No. 355, RG 225, NA, Washington, DC.

20. For both sides of this issue, see Pogue, *George C. Marshall*, 201-203; Sherry, *Rise of American Air Power*, 109-110; and Werrell, *Blankets of Fire*, 46-47.

21. Memo, Brig. Gen. Martin Scanlon to Barney Giles, "Priorities: Japanese Objective Folder Material," 19 February 1942, File 360.02, Box 101, and Voucher No. 40971, "One Way to Cripple Japan," File 452.3, Box 132, Arnold Papers.

22. Memo, Lawrence Kuter to Arnold, "Radical Air Plans to Defeat Japan," 3 August 1943, Box 113, Arnold Papers.

23. Craven and Cate, *Army Air Forces*, 2:354-355; 5: 27; Schaffer, *Wings of Judgment*, 110-111; Herman S. Wolk, "The B-29, the A-Bomb, and the Japanese Surrender," *Air Force*, February 1975, 55; "Air Plan for the Defeat of Japan," ABC 381 Japan (27 August 1943), File ABC 384.5, Boxes 477-478, Army Staff, RG 319, NA, Washington, DC.

24. Memo, Brig. Gen. Mervin Gross to Giles, "Test of Incendiaries," 5 May 1944, File 400.112, Box 117, Arnold Papers; "Outline of Presentation of Views of Commanding General, AAF, on the Role of the Air Forces in the Defeat of Japan," 22 February 1944, Naval Aide's Files, Map Room, Box 167, FDR Library.

25. Coffey, *Iron Eagle*, 127-128.

26. Craven and Cate, *Army Air Forces*, 5:15-175.

27. Coffey, *Iron Eagle*, 121; Hansell, *Strategic Air War against Germany and Japan*, 167; Pasco to Arnold, 18 December 1944, Box 41, Arnold Papers; Schaffer, *Wings of Judgment*, 124; Werrell, *Blankets of Fire*, 68-74.

28. Schaffer, *Wings of Judgment*, 124; msg., Hansell to Arnold, 16 January 1945; memo, H. E. Lanasberg to Robert Stearns, "Estimate of Possibilities of Visual Bombardment of Primary Targets," 28 February 1945; memo, J. T. Seaver to Donald Loughridge, "Ballistic Winds over Japan," 1 March 1945, File 762.912-1, AFHRA.

29. Craven and Cate, *Army Air Forces*, 5:551-567; Coffey, *Iron Eagle*, 129-132, 144-

145; Kerr, *Flames over Tokyo*, 119; Hansell, *Strategic Air War against Germany and Japan*, 208–215; Arnold, *Global Mission*, 541.

30. LeMay to Lauris Norstad, 31 January 1945, Box B11, LeMay Papers; LeMay with Kantor, *Mission*, 344–345, 368; Norstad to Carl Spaatz, 3 March 1945, File 519.9701-15, AFHRA; Coffey, *Iron Eagle*, 125–126.

31. Craven and Cate, *Army Air Forces*, 5:568–576, 611; Hansell, *Strategic Air War against Japan*, 51; Coffey, *Iron Eagle*, 147–157; Kerr, *Flames over Tokyo*, 156.

32. Foreword to XXI Bomber Command Tactical Mission Report, Mission No. 40, Urban Area of Tokyo, 10 March 1945, prepared 15 April 1945, Box 26, LeMay Papers; Werrell, *Blankets of Fire*, 152–154, 157; Marshall with Thompson, *Final Assault*, 129; Cifelli, *Saipan*, 100–103. It appears that LeMay's intent was to remove all guns, gunners, and ammunition from the B-29s, but that directive was not enforced. The crews did not seem ready to go in completely defenseless.

33. "Pacific Report #90," in United States Strategic Bombing Survey, *Pacific Reports*, 10:70–73; Target Section A-2, XXI Bomber Command, "Target Information Sheet: Tokyo Industrial Area," March 1945, File 760.01. Binder VII, AFHRA.

34. Morrison, *Point of No Return*, 224; Cortesi, *Target: Tokyo*, 233–274; Havens, *Valley of Darkness*, 178–181; transcript of interview of General Thomas Power by Kenneth Leish, July 1960, Box 9, Thomas R. Power Manuscript Collection, Syracuse University Library, Syracuse, NY; Letter, LeMay to Arnold, 11 March 1945, with attached handwritten report from Power, File 312.1-2/59, 1945 AAG, Records of the Army Air Forces, RG 18, NA II; Marshall with Thompson, *Final Assault*, 131; Harold R. Martin, "Black Snow and Leaping Tigers," *Harper's Magazine*, February 1946, 151–153.

35. *New York Times*, 11 March 1945, 1, 13.

36. LeMay with Kantor, *Mission*, 351–352; Morrison, *Point of No Return*, 225; XXI Bomber Command, "Analysis of Incendiary Phase of Operations against Japanese Urban Areas," 39–40, Box 37, LeMay Papers.

37. LeMay with Kantor, *Mission*, 384. This description matches the AAF conception of Japanese home industry described in *Impact*, April 1945, 10–11.

38. Morrison, *Hellbirds*, 156–157.

39. Gleason, "Psychological Operations," 36–37; C. C. Chauncey to Giles, 16 July 1945, File 091.412, Box 61, Arnold Papers; Twentieth AF Mission Reports 297–302, 28–29 June 1945, File 760.331, AFHRA; Havens, *Valley of Darkness*, 167.

40. Psychological Warfare Branch, US Army Forces, Pacific Area, "Report on Psychological Warfare in the Southwest Pacific Area, 1944–1945," RG 4, Reel 617 of microfilm copy of Douglas MacArthur Archives at the USMA Library, West Point, NY; Craven and Cate, *Army Air Forces*, 5:698; Kuter to Anderson, 15 August 1944, Anderson diary, Anderson Papers.

41. Werrell, *Blankets of Fire*, 157; Craven and Cate, *Army Air Forces*, 5:624–625; Arnold to LeMay, 21 March 1945, and Norstad to LeMay, 3 April 1945, Box B11, LeMay Papers; Giles to LeMay, 20 April 1945, Box 106, Arnold Papers; Warren Moscow, "51 Square Miles Burned Out in Six B-29 Attacks on Tokyo," *New York Times*, 30 May 1945, 1 and 4; Stimson diary, 1 and 6 June 1945.

42. Brower, "Joint Chiefs of Staff," 273–281; Craven and Cate, *Army Air Forces*, 5:696–697; Marshall, Arnold, and King, *War Reports*, 275.

43. Amendment No. 1 to G-2 Estimate of the Enemy Situation with Respect to Ky-

ushu," 29 July 1945, and "G-2 Estimate of the Enemy Situation with Respect to an Operation against the Tokyo (Kwanto) Plain of Honshu," 31 May 1945, Quintin S. Lander Papers, USAMHI, Carlisle Barracks, PA.

44. LeMay with Kantor, *Mission*, 373; journal, "Trip to Pacific June 6, 1945, to June 24, 1945," 13 June entry, Box 272, and msg., Arnold to Ira C. Eaker, Anderson, and Norstad, undated, Truman File, Box 45, Arnold Papers; Coffey, *Iron Eagle*, 174-175.

45. Msg., Arnold to Eaker, Anderson, and Norstad; memo, Hansell to Arnold, "Retaliatory Use of Chemical Warfare against the Japanese," 20 March 1944, File 385 Japan, Box 115, Arnold Papers.

46. Memo, Arnold to Marshall, "Comments on Air Aspects of General Stilwell's Memorandum Relative to the Invasion of Japan," 30 May 1945, Box 115, and journal, "Trip to Pacific," 17 June entry, Arnold Papers.

47. Lilienthal, *Journals*, 199-200; J. J. McCloy, memorandum of conversation with General Marshall, 29 May 1945, 11:45 a.m., RG 107, NA, Washington, DC.

48. Memo, Marshall to Ernest King, "US Chemical Warfare Policy," 15 June 1945, Box 75, Folder 35, George C. Marshall Papers, George C. Marshall Research Library, Lexington, VA.

49. Bernstein, "Why We Didn't Use Poison Gas," 45; memo, Myron Cramer to George Merck, "Destruction of Crops by Chemicals," 5 March 1945, and memo, Merck to Stimson, "Destruction of Crops by LN Chemicals," 25 April 1945, Box 84, Folder 27, Marshall Papers.

50. JCS 1371, "Destruction of 1946 Crops in Japan," 30 May 1945, ABC 475.92 (25 February 1944), RG 165, NA, Washington, DC.

51. V. E. Bertrandias to Arnold, 29 May 1945, with attached memo to Arnold from R. P. Proctor; memo, Eaker to Hoyt S. Vandenberg, "Experiment in Destruction of Crops by Air," 3 August 1945, with 10 August reply from Vandenberg, File 385, Japan, Box 115, Arnold Papers.

52. Anderson to Brig. Gen. Joe Loutzenheiser, chief, AAF Operational Plans Division, 20 March 1945, File 519.1611, AFHRA.

53. FDR to Stimson, 9 September 1944, Box 277, Arnold Papers; transcript of meeting of Joint Target Group (JTG) and US Strategic Bombing Survey (USSBS), entry 1, File .001, US Strategic Bombing Survey, RG 243, NA, Washington, DC.

54. Memo, Lovett to Stimson, 31 July 1945, with accompanying "Report on USSBS and JTG Conferences," File Aircraft, Air Corps General, RG 107, NA, Washington, DC; Mets, *Master of Airpower*, 298-299; directive, Eaker to Commanding General, US Army Strategic Air Forces, 26 July 1945, Box 13, LeMay Papers.

55. Diary of Terminal Conference, 10 July 1945-30 July 1945, entries for 13, 15, 17, 23, and 24 July, Box 249, Arnold Papers.

56. Msg., Spaatz to Eaker, 2 August 1945, and diary entry, 11 August 1945, Box 21, Spaatz Papers; Mets, *Master of Airpower*, 302-303; Bernstein, "Perils and Politics of Surrender," 16-17.

57. Craven and Cate, *Army Air Forces*, 5:756; memo, J. E. Hull to Eaker, 13 September 1945, File 091.412, Box 61, Arnold Papers.

58. Wartime History, 20th Air Force (Public Information Office *PIO* version), File 760.01, AFHRA; US Army Strategic Air Forces Communique No. 12, 17 August 1945, Box 121, Twining Papers; Kaplan and Smith, *One Last Look*, 213. Kenneth Werrell has

somewhat different numbers in his book *Blankets of Fire*. He claims 414 B-29s were lost in combat operations, 148 to enemy action, 151 to operational causes, and 115 unknown. Far more, 870, were lost in training and testing accidents.

59. Craven and Cate, *Army Air Forces*, 5:662–674; Hansell, *Strategic Air War against Japan*, 74–93; the best discussion of the process that produced Japanese surrender, and the alternatives, including Soviet invasion plans, is Frank, *Downfall*, 331–360. Other important shocks besides the fire raids included Russian entry into the war, the American submarine and B-29 mining campaigns against Japanese shipping, the inexorable advance by Nimitz and MacArthur toward Japan, and the atomic bombs.

60. Msg. 082328Z, Norstad to Spaatz, 8 August 1945, Box 21, Spaatz Papers.

CHAPTER ELEVEN. STRATEGIC AIRPOWER
IN LIMITED WARS

1. Maclear, *Ten Thousand Day War*, 124.

2. LeMay with Kantor, *Mission with LeMay*, 387; Tactical Mission Report, 509th Composite Group, 20th AF, 60, File 760.331, AFHRA, Maxwell AFB, AL. LeMay's calculations seem inaccurate; the two atomic bombs together were more deadly. See Sherry, *Rise of American Air Power*, 406n.

3. Stimson and Bundy, *On Active Service*, 632–633.

4. Bernstein, "Perils and Politics of Surrender," 13–14.

5. LeMay with Kantor, *Mission*, 387; Diary of Henry L. Stimson, 17 July 1945, Yale University Library, microfilm; Folder, Bruce C Hopper, "Jeeping the Targets in the Country That Was," 17 April 1945 entry, Box 5, Anderson Papers.

6. Hopper documents, Box 5, Anderson Papers, and Boxes 286 and 287, Spaatz Papers; James McGregor Burns interview with author, 11 April 1986, West Point, NY; Schaffer, *Wings of Judgment*, 252–253.

7. *Operational Research in North West Europe*, text for course OA 3655, Naval Postgraduate School, Monterey, CA; see Operations Analysis Section reports in File 762.912-1, AFHRA; Schaffer, *Wings of Judgment*, 162–163.

8. Doughty, *Evolution of US Army Tactical Doctrine*, 12–13.

9. United States Strategic Bombing Survey, *Summary Reports*, 37–39,110–113; Gentile, *How Effective Is Strategic Bombing*, 193; memo, Alfred Maxwell to Anderson, "Creation of Strategic Targets during Reconstruction of Germany," 20 April 1945, File 519.318-1, AFHRA.

10. Mets, *Master of Airpower*, 314–315.

11. Herken, *Winning Weapon*, 212; Eaker, quote, to Spaatz, 1 January 1945 on Operation Clarion, Box 20, Spaatz Papers.

12. *Bombing Surveys: Summary Reports*, 34–39, 92–96; Hastings, *Bomber Command*, 403–404.

13. See, for example, "Defenses of Southern Kyushu," a 3 June 1946 speech by Edmund J. Winslett, Winslett Papers, USAMHI, Carlisle Barracks, PA. Some British citizens had similar sentiments: see Harper, *Miracle of Deliverance*.

14. Good examples of the bombing assessments furnished key leaders are in Box 6 of

the Anderson Papers. These highly selective reports concentrating on target destruction may have led to an exaggerated belief in capabilities for precision.

15. Air University lecture by Dan Dyer, "Horizontal Approach to Target Analysis," 12 December 1951, 7, File K239.716251-55, AFHRA, Maxwell AFB, AL.

16. Biddle, *Rhetoric and Reality*, 76–80.

17. Wawro, *Franco-Prussian War*, 233–235, 295–296.

18. Frank, *Downfall*, 354.

19. Stewart, *Airpower*, 76–82; Futrell, *United States Air Force in Korea*, 186, 285–313; Crane, *American Airpower Strategy*, 23–88.

20. Futrell, *United States Air Force in Korea*, 480–490. Crane, *American Airpower Strategy*, 63–64, 76–78, 122–123. In fairness to the USAF, it must be noted that Pyongyang had also been damaged by severe ground fighting during 1950.

21. Futrell, *United States Air Force in Korea*, 483–493; Acheson, *Korean War*, 135–136; Crane, *American Airpower Strategy*, 110–131.

22. Futrell, *United States Air Force in Korea*, 605–643; Stewart, *Airpower*, 166–188; Crane, *American Airpower Strategy*, 159–169; Harrison, "Missiles of North Korea." Japanese rice probably would have been a target for American bombers if the Pacific War had gone into 1946 (see chapter 10 of this book).

23. US Department of State, *Foreign Relations of the United States, 1950*, 7:159; Blair, *Forgotten War*, 124, 522–523, 971; Crane, *American Airpower Strategy*, 164–165; Crane, "To Avert Impending Disaster."

24. Drew, *Rolling Thunder 1965*, 24–27.

25. Summers, *On Strategy*, 28–30.

26. Clodfelter, *Limits of Airpower*, 39–146.

27. Schlight, *War in South Vietnam*, 258–261.

28. Clodfelter, *Limits of Airpower*, 39–146; Ridgway, *Korean War*, 238.

29. Kreis, *Air Warfare*, 293–296; editorial, *Air Force Magazine*, April 1973, 3; Eschmann, *Linebacker*, 202–203.

30. Clodfelter, *Limits of Airpower*, 194–210; for a USAF view on the effects of political restrictions, see Momyer, *Air Power in Three Wars*. The "Dienbienphu of the air" description comes from a display board at the museum, which I visited in 2004.

31. The best explanation of Warden's ideas, as well as a good analysis of their strengths and weaknesses, is Fadok, "John Boyd."

32. US Department of the Air Force, *White Paper*, 1–2; Tom Mathews, "The Secret History of the War," *Newsweek*, 18 March 1991, 36.

33. Charts accompanying transcript of Schwarzkopf's "Central Command Briefing," 27 February 1991, *Military Review* 71 (September 1991): 100; Lt. Gen. Frederick Franks, CG, VII Corps, interview with author, 30 May 1991, Fort Leavenworth, KS.

34. Mathews, "Secret History," 38. Planners expected 540,000 Iraqi troops in the Kuwait theater, with more than half in Kuwait itself; instead, the actual total was about 250,000, with about 150,000 in Kuwait.

35. Barton Gellman, "70% of US Bombs Missed Their Targets, Figures Show," *Kansas City Star*, 16 March 1991, A15; Hallion, *Storm over Iraq*.

36. Barton Gellman, "70% of US Bombs Missed Their Targets, Figures Show," *Kansas City Star*, 16 March 1991, A15; Hallion, *Storm over Iraq*.

37. Gentile, *How Effective Is Strategic Bombing*, 170–190; Keaney and Cohen, *Gulf War*

Air Power, 64–65, 90, 118–119, 236; Keaney and Cohen, *Gulf War Air Power Survey* 2:377–381. Gentile provides a fine comparison between the conduct of USSBS and GWAPS.

38. US Department of the Air Force, *White Paper: Air Force Performance in Desert Storm*, 5.

39. Dean, *Airpower in Small Wars*; Foster, *Making of Modern Iraq*, 236–237; Horner, "Air Campaign," 25–27.

40. Most British actions were against relatively small parties, often raiding from northern Saudi Arabia. See Glubb, *War in the Desert*.

41. For example, see IRIS Independent Research, *Airpower and the Iraqi Offensive*.

42. John Keegan, "West Claimed Moral High Ground with Air Power," *London Daily Telegraph*, 16 January 2001; Ullman et al., *Shock and Awe*.

43. *Airpower and the Iraqi Offensive at Khafji* was widely circulated to support halt phase proposals; Ullman et al., *Shock and Awe*.

44. Central Intelligence Agency Office of Russian and European Analysis, *Balkan Battlegrounds*, 119–396; Owen, *Deliberate Force*.

45. For the stated objectives of the bombing campaign see R. W. Apple, "A Fresh Set of US Goals," A1, and the text of President Clinton's speech, A15, in the 25 March 1999 *New York Times*. On the Serb use of decoys and estimates of damage, see Steven Lee Myers, "Damage to Serb Military Less Than Expected," *New York Times*, 28 June 1999, 1. On how NATO damage estimates matched their findings after occupying Kosovo, see Richard J. Newman, "The Bombs that Failed in Kosovo," *US News and World Report*, 20 September 1999, 28–30.

46. Ignatieff, *Virtual War*, 96–103.

47. Ibid., 101–108; Grant, *Kosovo Campaign*, 22.

48. Michael Dobbs, "Post-mortem on NATO's Bombing Campaign," *Washington Post National Weekly Edition*, 19–26 July 1999, 23; Grant, *Kosovo Campaign*, 22.

49. Barry and Thomas, "The Kosovo Cover-up," *Newsweek*, 15 May 2000, 22–26; the best analyses of the air campaign are Hosmer, *Conflict over Kosovo*, and Lambeth, *NATO's Air War*. Although both authors wrote studies for RAND at the same time, they come up with very different conclusions.

50. For the best description of the early success in Afghanistan, see Biddle, *Afghanistan*; for the most thorough coverage of the air component of the 2003 invasion of Iraq, see Lambeth, *Unseen War*.

51. Budiansky, *Air Power*, 441.

52. Obama and Panetta, *Sustaining Global Leadership*; Clodfelter, *Beneficial Bombing*, 251–256.

CHAPTER TWELVE. LEGACIES

1. Bruce Hopper, USSTAF historian, memo on USSTAF history preparation, 22 September 1944, Box 286, Spaatz Papers.

2. Yasuo Kurata, "Americans Are Insensitive to Casualties Because Their Country Hasn't Been Bombed," *Kansas City Star*, 5 May 1991, K2.

3. For an example of the leaflets, see Crane, "Peace Dividends."

4. Dobbs, "Post-mortem on NATO's Bombing Campaign," 23; Elizabeth Becker, "Rights Group Says NATO Killed 500 Civilians in Kosovo War," *New York Times*, 7 Feb-

ruary 2000, A10; Garry Trudeau's *Doonesbury* cartoons on the Kosovo bombing ran in early May 1999.

5. Charles Trueheart, "War Crimes Court Is Looking at NATO," *Washington Post*, 29 December 1999, A20; Jamie Dettmer and Jennifer G. Hickey, "British MPs Question Legality of Kosovo Intervention," *Insight on the News*, 3–10 July 2000, 6; Ignatieff, *Virtual War*, 91–92, 210–215.

6. US Department of the Army, *Training Circular 27-10-1*, 44, 52–54. Similar examples are presented in US Department of the Army, *Field Manual 27-2*.

7. Ronald Schaffer notes, however, that counterforce nuclear strategies are often presented as a relatively humane form of warfare, like conventional precision bombing, and rely on pinpoint techniques; see *Wings of Judgment*, 213.

8. JCS memorandum, read at a meeting of the CCS on 13 May 1945, US Department of State, *Foreign Relations of the United States: The Conferences at Washington and Quebec*, 222.

9. Yavenditti, "American People," 231; memo, George Marshall to Ernest King, "US Chemical Warfare Policy," 15 June 1945, Box 73, Folder 35, Papers of George C. Marshall, Marshall Research Library, Lexington, VA.

10. Kohn, "Scholarship on World War II," 376; Howard, *Studies in War and Peace*, 239.

11. Bill Moyers, at the conclusion of "The Arming of the Earth," an episode in his 1984 Public Broadcasting System series, *A Walk through the 20th Century with Bill Moyers*.

12. I have visited the museums in Beijing and Hanoi, and I have talked with Chinese and North Vietnamese veterans at conferences at Texas Tech University. I was also privy to Iraqi POW interviews from 2003 surveys at the Strategic Studies Institute of the US Army War College.

13. Lambeth, *Unseen War*, 122–123, 228–231.

14. Newman, "The Bombs that Failed," 30.

BIBLIOGRAPHY

MANUSCRIPT SOURCES

Air Force Historical Research Agency of the United States Air Force, Air University, Maxwell Air Force Base, AL
  Air Corps Tactical School Files
  Army Air Forces Planning and Operational Records
Franklin D. Roosevelt Library, Hyde Park, NY
  Map Room Files
  President's Secretary Files
  Papers of Harry Hopkins
George Arents Research Library for Special Collections, Syracuse University, Syracuse, NY
  Thomas S. Power Manuscript Collection
George C. Marshall Research Library, Lexington, VA
  Papers of George C. Marshall
Hoover Institution on War, Revolution, and Peace, Stanford University, Stanford, CA
  Papers of Frederick L. Anderson
Library of Congress, Manuscript Division, Washington, DC
  Papers of Henry H. Arnold
  Papers of Ira C. Eaker
  Papers of Curtis E. LeMay
  Papers of Carl A. Spaatz
  Papers of Nathan F. Twining
  Papers of Hoyt S. Vandenberg
National Archives, College Park, MD, and Washington, DC
  Record Group 107, Office of the Secretary of War
  Record Group 165, War Department General and Special Staffs
  Record Group 218, United States Joint Chiefs of Staff
  Record Group 225, Joint Army and Navy Boards and Committees
  Record Group 243, United States Strategic Bombing Survey
  Record Group 319, Army Staff
  Record Group 332, United States Theaters of War, World War II

Record Group 334, Interservice Agencies
Record Group 338, United States Army Commands
Office of Air Force History, Boiling Air Force Base, Washington, DC
United States Air Force Oral History Interviews: Ira C. Eaker, Curtis E. LeMay, and
Carl A. Spaatz
United States Army Military History Institute, at the United States Army Heritage and
Education Center, Carlisle Barracks, PA
Army War College Curricular Archives
Forty Fourth Bomb Group Collection
Letters of Robert E. O'Donnell
Papers of Ira C. Eaker
Papers of Quintin S. Lander
Papers of Elmer T. Lian
Papers of Crawford F. Sams
Papers of Edmund J. Winslett
Senior Officer Oral History Program
United States Military Academy Archives and Special Collections, West Point, NY
Collected Letters of Earle C. Cheek
Department of Civil and Military Engineering Files
Papers of General of the Army Omar N. Bradley
Papers of George A. Lincoln
United States Military Academy Library, West Point, NY
Douglas MacArthur Archives (microfilm)
Sterling Memorial Library, Yale University, New Haven, CT
Diary of Henry L. Stimson (microfilm copies used)

INTERVIEWS BY AUTHOR

Burns, James McGregor. Former enlisted Army historian in World War II. West Point,
NY, 11 April 1986.
Franks, Lt. Gen. Frederick. Commander of US Army VII Corps in Operation Desert
Storm, Fort Leavenworth, KS, 30 May 1991.
Kestenbaum, Martin. World War II veteran and president of the New Jersey chapter of
the Eighth Air Force Historical Society. West Point, NY, 23 May 1992.
Roland, Charles P. Military historian and World War II infantry officer. West Point, NY,
30 January 1986.
Spiller, Roger. Military historian. Fort Leavenworth, KS, 28 February 1991.

WORKS CITED AND CONSULTED

Acheson, Dean. *The Korean War.* New York: W. W. Norton, 1971.
Anderton, David A. *B-29 Superfortress at War.* New York: Charles Scribner's Sons, 1978.
Ardery, Philip. *Bomber Pilot.* Lexington: University Press of Kentucky, 1978.
Arnold, H. H. *Global Mission.* New York: Harper, 1949.

Arnold, H. H., and Ira C. Eaker. *Winged Warfare*. New York: Harper, 1941.

Asch, Alfred, Hugh Graff, and Thomas Ramey. *The Story of the Four Hundred and Fifty-fifth Bombardment Group (H) WWII: Flight of the Vulgar Vultures*. Appleton, WI: Graphic Communications Center, 1991.

Batchelder, Robert C. *The Irreversible Decision, 1939–1950*. Boston: Houghton Mifflin, 1962.

Beck, Earl R. *Under the Bombs: The German Home Front, 1942–1945*. Lexington: University Press of Kentucky, 1986.

Bekker, Cajus. *The Luftwaffe War Diaries*. Translated by Frank Ziegler. New York: Ballantine, 1969.

Bendiner, Elmer. *The Fall of Fortresses*. New York: G. P. Putnam's Sons, 1980.

Bergander, Gotz. *Dresden im Luftkrieg*. Cologne: Bohlan Verlag, 1977.

Bernstein, Barton J. "America's Biological Warfare Program in the Second World War." *Journal of Strategic Studies* 11 (1988): 292–317.

——. "The Perils and Politics of Surrender: Ending the War with Japan and Avoiding the Third Atomic Bomb." *Pacific Historical Review* 46 (1977): 1–27.

——. "Why We Didn't Use Poison Gas in World War II." *American Heritage* 36 (1985): 40–45.

Best, Geoffrey. *Humanity in Warfare*. New York: Columbia University Press, 1980.

Biddle, Stephen. *Afghanistan and the Future of Warfare: Implications for Army and Defense Policy*. Carlisle, PA: Strategic Studies Institute, 2002.

Biddle, Tami Davis. "Dresden 1945: Reality, History, and Memory." *Journal of Military History* 72 (2008): 413–449.

——. *Rhetoric and Reality in Air Warfare: The Evolution of British and American Ideas about Strategic Bombing, 1914–1945*. Princeton, NJ: Princeton University Press, 2002.

——. "Sifting Dresden's Ashes." *Wilson Quarterly* 29 (2005): 60–80.

Bidinian, Larry J. *The Combined Allied Bombing Offensive against the German Civilian, 1942–1945*. Lawrence, KS: Coronado Press, 1976.

Blair, Clay. *The Forgotten War: America in Korea, 1950–1953*. New York: Doubleday, 1989.

Bowman, Martin W. *Castles in the Air*. Wellingborough, UK: Patrick Stephens, 1984.

Brittain, Vera. *Seeds of Chaos*. London: New Vision Publishing, 1944.

——. *Wartime Chronicle: Diary, 1939–1945*. Edited by Alan Bishop and Y. Aleksandra Bennett. London: Victor Gollancz, 1989.

Brodie, Bernard. *Strategy in the Missile Age*. Princeton, NJ: Princeton University Press, 1965.

Brodie, Bernard, and Fawn M. Brodie. *From Crossbow to H-Bomb*. Bloomington: Indiana University Press, 1973.

Brower, Charles F., IV. "The Joint Chiefs of Staff and National Policy: American Strategy and the War with Japan, 1943–1945." PhD diss., University of Pennsylvania, 1987.

Budiansky, Stephen. *Air Power: The Men, Machines, and Ideas That Revolutionized War, from Kitty Hawk to Gulf War II*. New York: Viking, 2004.

Byrd, Martha. *Kenneth N. Walker: America's Untempered Crusader*. Maxwell AFB, AL: Air University Press, 1997.

Caidin, Martin. *Black Thursday*. New York: Bantam, 1981.

Cannon, M. Hamlin. *Flying Training at West Point*. Colorado Springs: US Air Force Academy, 1970.

Cantril, Hadley, and Mildred Strunk, eds. *Public Opinion, 1935–1946.* Princeton, NJ: Princeton University Press, 1951.

Central Intelligence Agency Office of Russian and European Analysis. *Balkan Battlegrounds: A Military History of the Yugoslav Conflict, 1990–1995.* Washington, DC: CIA, 2002.

Chomsky, Noam. *American Power and the New Mandarins.* New York: Pantheon, 1969.

Cifelli, Edward M., ed. *Saipan: The War Diary of John Ciardi.* Fayetteville: University of Arkansas Press, 1988.

Clark, Ronald W. *Tizard.* Cambridge, MA: MIT Press, 1965.

Clausewitz, Carl von. *On War.* Edited and translated by Michael Howard and Peter Paret. Indexed edition. Princeton, NJ: Princeton University Press, 1984.

Clodfelter, Mark. *Beneficial Bombing: The Progressive Foundations of American Airpower, 1917–1945.* Lincoln: University of Nebraska Press, 2010.

Clodfelter, Mark. *The Limits of Airpower: The American Bombing of North Vietnam.* New York: Free Press, 1989.

Cody, James R. *AWPD-42 to Instant Thunder: Consistent, Evolutionary Thought or Revolutionary Change?* Maxwell AFB, AL: Air University Press, 1996.

Coffey, Patrick. *American Arsenal: A Century of Waging War.* New York: Oxford, 2014.

Coffey, Thomas M. *Hap: The Story of the US Air Force and the Man Who Built It.* New York: Viking, 1982.

———. *Iron Eagle.* New York: Crown, 1986.

Collins, John M. *Grand Strategy: Principles and Practices.* Annapolis, MD: Naval Institute Press, 1973.

Copp, DeWitt S. A. *Few Great Captains.* Garden City, NY: Doubleday, 1980.

———. *Forged in Fire.* Garden City, NY: Doubleday, 1982.

Corn, Joseph J. *The Winged Gospel: America's Romance with Aviation, 1900–1950.* New York: Oxford, 1983.

Cortesi, Lawrence. *Target: Tokyo.* New York: Kensington, 1983.

Couffer, Jack. *Bat Bomb: World War II's Other Secret Weapon.* Austin: University of Texas Press, 1992.

Crane, Conrad C. *American Airpower Strategy in Korea, 1950–1953.* Lawrence: University Press of Kansas, 2000.

———. "Peace Dividends, Benevolent Interventions, and the US Army, 1989–2013." In *The West Point History of Warfare.* New York: Rowan Technology, 2014. http://www.westpointhistoryofwarfare.com/.

———. "To Avert Impending Disaster: American Military Plans to Use Atomic Weapons during the Korean War." *Journal of Strategic Studies* 23 (2000): 72–88.

Craven, Wesley Frank, and James Lea Cate, eds. *The Army Air Forces in World War II.* 7 vols. Chicago: University of Chicago Press, 1948–1953.

Current, Richard N. *Secretary Stimson: A Study in Statecraft.* Hamden, CT: Archon Books, 1970.

Dallek, Robert. *Franklin Roosevelt and American Foreign Policy, 1932–1945.* New York: Oxford, 1979.

Davis, Richard G. "Bombing Strategy Shifts, 1944–45." *Air Power History* 36 (1989): 33–45.

——. *Bombing the European Axis Powers: A Historical Digest of the Combined Bomber Offensive, 1939–1945*. Maxwell AFB, AL: Air University Press, 2006.

——. *Carl A. Spaatz and the Air War in Europe*. Washington, DC: Center for Air Force History, 1993.

Dean, Lt. Col. David J. *Airpower in Small Wars: The British Air Control Experience*. Maxwell AFB, AL: Air University Press, 1985.

Doolittle, Gen. James H., with Carol Glines. *I Could Never Be So Lucky Again*. New York: Bantam, 1991.

Dougherty, Kevin A. "R&D Strategy in WWII." *Army Research, Development, and Acquisition Bulletin*, March–April 1990, 44.

Doughty, Maj. Robert A. *The Evolution of US Army Tactical Doctrine, 1946–1976*. Fort Leavenworth, KS: Combat Studies Institute, 1979.

Douhet, Giulio. *The Command of the Air*. Translated by Dino Ferrari. 1942. Reprint, New York: Arno Press, 1972.

Dower, John. *War without Mercy*. New York: Pantheon, 1986.

Drew, Col. Dennis M. *Rolling Thunder 1965: Anatomy of a Failure*. Maxwell AFB, AL: Air University Press, 1986.

Dugan, Gen. Michael. "First Lessons of Victory." *US News and World Report*, 18 March 1991, 32–36.

Dugan, James, and Carroll Stewart. *Ploesti*. New York: Ballantine, 1962.

Dyson, Freeman. *Weapons and Hope*. New York: Harper & Row, 1984.

Ehlers, Robert S., Jr. *The Mediterranean Air War: Airpower and Allied Victory in World War II*. Lawrence: University Press of Kansas, 2015.

——. *Targeting the Third Reich: Air Intelligence and the Allied Bombing Campaigns*. Lawrence: University Press of Kansas, 2009.

Eschmann, Karl J. *Linebacker: The Untold Story of the Air Raids over North Vietnam*. New York: Ivy Books, 1989.

Faber, Lt. Col. Peter R. "Interwar US Army Aviation and the Air Corps Tactical School: Incubators of American Airpower." In *The Paths of Heaven: The Evolution of Airpower Theory*, edited by Phillip S. Meilinger, 183–238. Maxwell AFB, AL: Air University Press, 1997.

Fadok, Lt. Col. David S. "John Boyd and John Warden: Airpower's Quest for Strategic Paralysis." In *The Paths of Heaven: The Evolution of Airpower Theory*, edited by Phillip S. Meilinger, 357–398. Maxwell AFB, AL: Air University Press, 1997.

Feist, Joe Michael. "Bats Away." *American Heritage* 33 (1982): 93–94.

Fili, William J. *Passage to Valhalla*. Media, PA: Filcon Publishers, 1991.

Finney, Robert T. *History of the Air Corps Tactical School, 1920–1940*. Washington, DC: Air Force History and Museums Program, 1998.

"Flak versus Heavy Bombers." *Coast Artillery Journal* 89 (1946): 24–25.

Ford, John C. "The Morality of Obliteration Bombing." *Theological Studies* 5 (1944): 261–309.

Foster, Henry A. *The Making of Modern Iraq: A Product of World Forces*. Norman: University of Oklahoma Press, 1935.

Frank, Richard B. *Downfall: The End of the Imperial Japanese Empire*. New York: Penguin, 1999.

Fredette, Raymond H. *The Sky on Fire: The First Battle of Britain, 1917–1918.* New York: Harcourt Brace Jovanovich, 1976.

Freeman, Roger. *The Mighty Eighth: Units, Men, and Machines–A History of the US 8th Army Air Force.* New York: Orion Books, 1989.

———. *The US Strategic Bomber.* London: McDonald and Jane's, 1975.

Friedrich, Jorg. *The Fire: The Bombing of Germany, 1940–1945.* Translated by Allison Brown. New York: Columbia University Press, 2006.

Fuller, Maj. Gen. J. F. C. *Generalship: Its Diseases and Their Cure.* 1963. Reprint, Fort Leavenworth, KS: Combat Studies Institute, 1987.

Fussell, Paul. *Wartime: Understanding and Behavior in the Second World War.* New York: Oxford, 1989.

Futrell, Robert Frank. "Commentary." In *Command and Commanders in Modern Warfare,* edited by Lt. Col. William Geffen, 277–287. Colorado Springs: US Air Force Academy, 1969.

———. *Ideas, Concepts, Doctrine: A History of Basic Thinking in the United States Air Force, 1907–1964.* 2 vols. Maxwell AFB, AL: Air University Aerospace Studies Institute, 1971.

———. *The United States Air Force in Korea, 1950–1953.* New York: Duell, Sloan and Pearce, 1961.

Galland, Adolf. *The First and the Last.* Translated by Mervyn Savill. 1957. Reprint, New York: Ballantine, 1973.

Gaston, James C. *Planning the American Air War: Four Men and Nine Days in 1941.* Washington, DC: National Defense University Press, 1982.

Geffen, Lt. Col. William, ed. *Command and Commanders in Modern Warfare.* Colorado Springs: US Air Force Academy, 1969.

Gentile, Gian P. *How Effective Is Strategic Bombing? Lessons Learned from World War II to Kosovo.* New York: NYU Press, 2001.

Giovannitti, Len, and Fred Freed. *The Decision to Drop the Bomb.* New York: Coward-McCann, 1965.

Glantz, David M., ed. *Historical Precedents.* Fort Leavenworth, KS: US Army Command and General Staff College, 1981.

Gleason, Robert L. "Psychological Operations and Air Power." *Air University Review* 22 (1971): 35–41.

Glubb, Sir John Bagot. *War in the Desert.* New York: W. W. Norton, 1961.

Goss, Hilton P. *Civilian Morale under Aerial Bombardment, 1914–1939.* Maxwell AFB, AL: Air University Press, 1948.

Gow, Ian. *Okinawa, 1945.* Garden City, NY: Doubleday, 1985.

Grant, Rebecca. *The Kosovo Campaign: Aerospace Power Made It Work.* Arlington, VA: Air Force Association, 1999.

Greenfield, Kent Roberts. *American Strategy in World War II: A Reconsideration.* 1963. Reprint, Westport, CT: Greenwood Press, 1979.

Greer, Thomas H. *The Development of Air Doctrine in the Army Air Arm, 1917–1941.* Maxwell AFB, AL: Air University Research Studies Institute, 1955.

Gregory, Lt. Col. Jesse O. "Headaches of Strategic Bombing." *Coast Artillery Journal* 89 (1946): 26–28.

Griffith, Charles. *The Quest: Haywood Hansell and American Strategic Bombing in World War II.* Maxwell AFB, AL: Air University Press, 1999.

Griffith, Thomas E., Jr. *MacArthur's Airman: General George C. Kenney and the War in the Southwest Pacific.* Lawrence: University Press of Kansas, 1998.

Grinker, Roy R., and John P. Spiegel. *Men Under Stress.* Philadelphia: Blakiston, 1945.

Haines, William Wister. *Command Decisions.* New York: Dodd, Mead, 1974.

Hallion, Richard P. *Storm over Iraq.* Washington, DC: Smithsonian, 1992.

Hansell, Haywood S., Jr. *The Air Plan That Defeated Hitler.* Atlanta: Higgins-MacArthur, 1972.

——. "Harold L. George: Apostle of Air Power." In *Makers of the United States Air Force,* edited by John L. Frisbee, 73-97. Washington, DC: Office of Air Force History, 1987.

——. *The Strategic Air War against Germany and Japan.* Washington, DC: Government Printing Office, 1986.

——. *Strategic Air War against Japan.* Maxwell AFB, AL: Airpower Research Institute, 1980.

Harper, Stephen. *Miracle of Deliverance: The Case for the Bombing of Hiroshima and Nagasaki.* London: Sidgwick and Jackson, 1985.

Harrison, Gordon A. *Cross-Channel Attack.* Washington, DC: Office of the Chief of Military History, 1951.

Harrison, Selig. "The Missiles of North Korea: How Real a Threat?" *World Policy Journal* 17 (2000): 13-24.

Hastings, Donald W., et al. *Psychiatric Experiences in the Eighth Air Force.* New York: Josiah Macy Jr. Foundation, 1944.

Hastings, Max. *Bomber Command.* New York: Dial, 1979.

Havens, Thomas R. *Valley of Darkness.* New York: W. W. Norton, 1978.

Hayes, Grace Person. *The History of the Joint Chiefs of Staff in World War II: The War against Japan.* Annapolis, MD: Naval Institute Press, 1982.

Henshall, Philip. *Hitler's Rocket Sites.* New York: St. Martin's, 1985.

Herken, Gregg. *The Winning Weapon.* New York: Knopf, 1980.

Higham, Robin. *Air Power: A Concise History.* New York: St. Martin's, 1972.

Holley, I. B., Jr. *Ideas and Weapons.* Hamden, CT: Archon Books, 1971.

Hopkins, George E. "Bombing and the American Conscience during World War II." *Historian* 28 (1966): 451-473.

Horner, Lt. Gen. Charles A. "The Air Campaign." *Military Review* 71 (1991): 16-27.

Hosmer, Stephen T. *The Conflict over Kosovo: Why Milosevic Decided to Settle When He Did.* Santa Monica, CA: RAND, 2001.

Howard, Michael. *The Causes of War and Other Essays.* 2nd ed. Cambridge, MA: Harvard University Press, 1984.

——. *Studies in War and Peace.* New York: Viking, 1971.

Hull, Cordell. *The Memoirs of Cordell Hull.* 2 vols. New York: Macmillan, 1948.

Hurley, Alfred F. *Billy Mitchell, Crusader for Air Power.* Bloomington: Indiana University Press, 1975.

Ignatieff, Michael. *Virtual War: Kosovo and Beyond.* New York: Henry Holt, 2000.

Impact: The Army Air Forces' Confidential Picture History of World War II. 8 vols. 1943-1945 periodicals. Reprint, Harrisburg, PA: Historical Times, 1982.

Infield, Glenn. *Big Week.* Los Angeles: Pinnacle, 1974.

IRIS Independent Research. *Airpower and the Iraqi Offensive at Khafji*. Arlington, VA: IRIS Independent Research, 1997. CD-ROM.

Irvine, Dallas D. "The Misuse of Air Power." *Infantry Journal* 44 (1937): 255–256.

Irving, David. *The Destruction of Dresden*. New York: Ballantine, 1965.

Kaplan, Fred. *The Wizards of Armageddon*. New York: Simon & Schuster, 1983.

Kaplan, Philip, and Rex Alan Smith. *One Last Look*. New York: Abbeville Press, 1983.

Keaney, Thomas A., and Eliot Cohen, eds. *Gulf War Air Power Survey*. Volume 2, *Operations and Effects and Effectiveness*. Washington, DC: Government Printing Office, 1993.

——. *Gulf War Air Power Survey Summary Report*. Washington, DC: Government Printing Office, 1993.

Kennett, Lee. *A History of Strategic Bombing*. New York: Charles Scribner's Sons, 1982.

Kerr, E. Bartlett. *Flames over Tokyo: The US Army Air Forces' Incendiary Campaign against Japan, 1944–1945*. New York: Donald I. Fine, 1991.

Kohn, Richard H. "The Scholarship on World War II: Its Present Condition and Future Possibilities." *Journal of Military History* 55 (1991): 365–393.

Kreis, John F. *Air Warfare and Air Base Air Defense*. Washington, DC: Office of Air Force History, 1988.

Lambeth, Benjamin S. *NATO's Air War for Kosovo: A Strategic and Operational Assessment*. Santa Monica, CA: RAND, 2001.

——. *The Unseen War: Allied Air Power and the Takedown of Saddam Hussein*. Annapolis, MD: Naval Institute Press, 2013.

Leahy, William D. *I Was There*. New York: McGraw-Hill, 1950.

LeMay, Curtis, with MacKinley Kantor. *Mission with LeMay*. Garden City, NY: Doubleday, 1965.

Lilienthal, David E. *The Journals of David E. Lilienthal*. Vol. 2, *The Atomic Energy Years, 1945–1950*. New York: Harper & Row, 1964.

Loewenheim, Francis L., et al., eds. *Roosevelt and Churchill: Their Secret Wartime Correspondence*. New York: E. P. Dutton, 1975.

MacArthur, Douglas. *Reminiscences*. New York: McGraw-Hill, 1964.

MacDonald, Charles B. *Company Commander*. New York: Bantam, 1978.

——. *The Mighty Endeavor*. New York: William Morrow, 1986.

Macdonald, Dwight. *Memoirs of a Revolutionist*. New York: Farrar, Straus, and Cudahy, 1957.

Maclear, Michael. *The. Ten Thousand Day War: Vietnam, 1945–1975*. New York: Avon Books, 1981.

Mahoney, Kevin A. *Fifteenth Air Force against the Axis: Combat Missions over Europe during World War II*. Lanham, MD: Scarecrow Press, 2013.

Manchester, William. *The Glory and the Dream*. New York: Bantam, 1975.

Mann, Carl. *Lightning in the Sky*. New York: Robert H. McBride, 1943.

Mark, Eduard. *Aerial Interdiction: Air Power and the Land Battle in Three American Wars–A Historical Analysis*. Washington, DC: Office of Air Force History, 1994.

Marshall, Chester, et al., eds. *The Global Twentieth: An Anthology of the 20th AF in WWII*. 3 vols. Winona, MN: Apollo Books, 1985.

Marshall, Chester, with Warren Thompson. *Final Assault on the Rising Sun*. North Branch, MN: Specialty Branch Publishers, 1995.

Marshall, George C., H. H. Arnold, and Ernest J. King. *The War Reports*. New York: J. B. Lippincott, 1947.

Marshall, S. L. A. *Men against Fire: The Problem of Battle Command in Future War*. 1947. Reprint. Gloucester, MA: Peter Smith, 1978.

"Massacre by Bombing." *Politics* 1 (1944): 67–68.

Maurer, Maurer, ed. *The US Air Service in World War I*. 4 vols. Washington, DC: Office of Air Force History, 1978.

May, Ernest R. *Lessons of the Past*. New York: Oxford, 1973.

McFarland, Stephen L., and Wesley Phillips Newton. *To Command the Sky: The Battle for Air Superiority over Germany, 1942–1944*. Washington, DC: Smithsonian Institution Press, 1991.

McKee, Alexander. *Dresden, 1945: The Devil's Tinderbox*. New York: Dutton, 1984.

Melville, Herman. "A Utilitarian View of the Monitor's Fight." In *Collected Poems of Herman Melville*, edited by H. P. Vincent, 40. Chicago: Packard, 1947.

Mets, David R. *Master of Airpower*. Novato, CA: Presidio Press, 1988.

Middlebrook, Martin. *The Battle of Hamburg*. New York: Charles Scribner's Sons, 1980.

———. *The Berlin Raids: RAF Bomber Command, Winter 1943–44*. New York: Penguin, 1988.

Mierzejewski, Alfred C. *The Collapse of the German War Economy, 1944–1945: Allied Air Power and the German National Railway*. Chapel Hill: University of North Carolina Press, 1988.

Miller, Donald L. *Masters of the Air: America's Bomber Boys Who Fought the Air War Against Nazi Germany*. New York: Simon & Schuster, 2006.

Momyer, Gen. William M. *Air Power in Three Wars*. Washington, DC: Government Printing Office, 1978.

Moran, Lord. *The Anatomy of Courage*. 1945. Reprint. Garden City Park, NY: Avery Publishing, 1987.

Morgenthau, Henry. *The Presidential Diaries of Henry Morgenthau, 1938–1945*. 7 vols. Microfilm edition. Frederick, MD: University Publications of America, 1981.

Morison, Samuel Eliot. *The Two-Ocean War*. New York: Ballantine Books, 1972.

Morrison, Wilbur H. *Fortress without a Roof*. New York: St. Martin's, 1982.

———. *Hellbirds: The Story of the B-29s in Combat*. New York: Duell, Sloan and Pearce, 1960.

———. *Point of No Return*. New York: Times Books, 1979.

Mountcastle, John W. "Trial by Fire: US Incendiary Weapons, 1918–1945." PhD diss., Duke University, 1979.

Muirhead, John. *Those Who Fall*. New York: Random House, 1986.

Murray, Williamson. *Strategy for Defeat: The Luftwaffe, 1933–1945*. Maxwell AFB, AL: Air University Press, 1983.

Nalty, Bernard, and Carl Berger. *The Men Who Bombed the Reich*. New York: E. P. Dutton, 1978.

Newby, Leroy W. *Target Ploesti: View from a Bombsight*. Novato, CA: Presidio Press, 1983.

Obama, Barack, and Leon Panetta. *Sustaining Global Leadership: Priorities for 21st Century Defense*. Washington, DC: Department of Defense, 2012.

Odishaw, Hugh. *Radar Bombing in the Eighth Air Force*. Cambridge, MA: Overseas Office, Radiation Laboratory, Massachusetts Institute of Technology, 1946.

Olsen, Jack. *Aphrodite: Desperate Mission*. New York: Pyramid, 1972.

Overy, Richard J. *The Air War, 1939–1945*. New York: Stein and Day, 1981.
——. *The Bombers and the Bombed: Allied Air War over Europe, 1940–1945*. New York: Viking, 2014.
——. *Why the Allies Won*. New York: W. W. Norton, 1996.
Owen, Robert C., ed. *Deliberate Force: A Case Study in Effective Air Campaigning*. Maxwell AFB, AL: Air University Press, 2000.
Paret, Peter, ed. *Makers of Modern Strategy, from Machiavelli to the Nuclear Age*. Princeton, NJ: Princeton University Press, 1986.
Parton, James. *"Air Force Spoken Here": General Ira Eaker and the Command of the Air*. Bethesda, MD: Adler & Adler, 1986.
Pearton, Maurice. *Diplomacy, War and Technology since 1830*. Lawrence: University Press of Kansas, 1984.
Pogue, Forrest. *George C. Marshall: Ordeal and Hope, 1939–1942*. New York: Viking, 1966.
Polenberg, Richard. *War and Society: The United States, 1941–1945*. New York: J. B. Lippincott, 1972.
Reed, Col. William B., ed. *Condensed Analysis of the Ninth Air Force in the European Theater of Operations*. 1946. Reprint. Washington, DC: Office of Air Force History, 1984.
Retaliation: Japanese Attacks and Allied Countermeasures on the Pacific Coast in World War II. Corvallis: Oregon State University Press, 1975.
Reynolds, Quentin. *The Amazing Mr. Doolittle*. New York: Appleton Century Crofts, 1953.
Ridgway, Matthew B. *The Korean War*. New York: Popular Library, 1967.
Rostow, W. W. *Pre-invasion Bombing Strategy*. Austin: University of Texas Press, 1981.
Sallagar, F. M. *The Road to Total War*. New York: Van Nostrand Reinhold, 1975.
Saundby, Air Marshal Sir Robert. *Air Bombardment*. New York: Harper, 1961.
Sawin, Capt. H. C., and Capt. Mac Harlan. "The Rules of Land Warfare." *Coast Artillery Journal* 87 (1944): 30–33.
Schaffer, Ronald. "American Military Ethics in World War II: The Bombing of German Civilians." *Journal of American History* 67 (1980): 318–334.
——. *Wings of Judgment: American Bombing in World War II*. New York: Oxford, 1985.
Schaller, Michael. *The US Crusade in China, 1938–1945*. New York: Columbia University Press, 1979.
Schlight, John. *The War in South Vietnam: The Years of the Offensive, 1965–1968*. Washington, DC: Office of Air Force History, 1988.
Schwarzkopf, Gen. H. Norman. "Central Command Briefing." *Military Review* 71 (1991): 96–108.
Seversky, Maj. Alexander P. de. *Victory through Airpower*. Garden City, NY: Garden City Publishing, 1942.
Sherman, Maj. William C. *Air Warfare*. New York: Ronald Press, 1926.
Sherry, Michael S. *Preparing for the Next War*. New Haven, CT: Yale University Press, 1977.
——. *The Rise of American Airpower: The Creation of Armageddon*. New Haven, CT: Yale University Press, 1987.
Shiner, John F. *Foulois and the US Army Air Corps, 1931–1935*. Washington, DC: Office of Air Force History, 1983.
Shrader, Lt. Col. Charles R. *Amicicide: The Problem of Friendly Fire in Modern War*. Fort Leavenworth, KS: Combat Studies Institute, 1982.

Smith, Maj. Gen. Dale O. *Screaming Eagle: Memoirs of a B-17 Group Commander.* New York: Dell, 1990.

Smith, Melden E., Jr. "The Bombing of Dresden Reconsidered: A Study in Wartime Decision Making." PhD diss., Boston University, 1971.

Smith, Perry M. "Douhet and Mitchell: Some Reappraisals." *Air University Review* 18 (1967): 97–101.

Snow, Donald M., and Dennis M. Drew. *Introduction to Strategy.* Maxwell AFB, AL: Air Command and Staff College, 1982.

Southworth, Herbert R. *Guernica! Guernica! A Study of Journalism, Diplomacy, Propaganda, and History.* Berkeley: University of California Press, 1977.

Spector, Ronald H. *Eagle against the Sun.* New York: Vintage, 1985.

Speer, Albert. *Inside the Third Reich.* New York: Avon, 1971.

Stewart, James T., ed. *Airpower: The Decisive Force in Korea.* New York: D. Van Nostrand, 1957.

Stiles, Bert. *Serenade to the Big Bird.* New York: Bantam, 1984.

Stimson, Henry L., and McGeorge Bundy. *On Active Service in Peace and War.* New York: Harper, 1948.

Stouffer, Samuel A., et al. *The American Soldier.* 2 vols. Princeton, NJ: Princeton University Press, 1949.

Summers, Col. Harry. "Conventional Forces, Not Nuclear Bombs, Are Now 'Strategic.'" *Kansas City Star,* 26 April 1991, C7.

Summers, Harry G., Jr. *On Strategy: The Vietnam War in Context.* Carlisle, PA: US Army War College, 1982.

Taylor, Joe Gray. "They Taught Tactics." *Aerospace Historian* 13 (1966): 67–72.

Terkel, Studs. *"The Good War": An Oral History of World War Two.* New York: Ballantine, 1985.

Terraine, John. *A Time for Courage.* New York: Macmillan, 1985.

The Official World War II Guide to the Army Air Forces. 1944. Reprint. New York: Bonanza Books, 1988.

Thomas, Gordon, and Max Morgan Witts. *Enola Gay.* New York: Pocket Books, 1978.

Thomas, Lowell, and Edward Jablonski. *Doolittle: A Biography.* New York: Da Capo, 1976.

Thorne, Christopher. *Allies of a Kind: The United States, Britain, and the War against Japan.* New York: Oxford, 1978.

Tillman, Barrett. *Forgotten Fifteenth: The Daring Airmen Who Crippled Hitler's War Machine.* Washington, DC: Regnery History, 2014.

———. *Whirlwind: The Air War against Japan 1942–1945.* New York: Simon & Schuster, 2010.

Toland, John. *The Rising Sun.* New York: Bantam, 1971.

Ullman, Harlan, et al. *Shock and Awe: Achieving Rapid Dominance.* Washington, DC: National Defense University, 1996.

United States Strategic Bombing Survey. *Pacific Reports.* 10 vols. New York: Garland, 1976.

———. *Summary Reports.* 1945–1946. Reprint. Maxwell AFB, AL: Air University Press, 1987.

US Department of State. *Foreign Relations of the United States, 1950: Asia and the Pacific.* 7 vols. Washington, DC: Government Printing Office, 1977–1980.

———. *Foreign Relations of the United States: Diplomatic Papers, 1939.* 5 vols. Washington, DC: Government Printing Office, 1955–1957.

——. *Foreign Relations of the United States: The Conferences at Washington and Quebec, 1943.* Washington, DC: Government Printing Office, 1970.

US Department of the Air Force. *White Paper: Air Force Performance in Desert Storm.* Draft. Washington, DC: Government Printing Office, April 1991.

US Department of the Army. *Field Manual 27-2: Your Conduct in Combat under the Law of War.* Washington, DC: Government Printing Office, 1984.

——. *Training Circular 27-10-1: Selected Problems in the Law of War.* Washington, DC: Government Printing Office, 1979.

US Department of War. *Training Regulations No. 440-15: Air Corps: Employment of the Air Forces of the Army.* Washington, DC: Government Printing Office, 1935.

US Department of War, Bureau of Public Relations. *The Background of Our War.* New York: Farrar and Rinehart, 1942.

Villa, Brian L. "The US Army, Unconditional Surrender, and the Potsdam Proclamation." *Journal of American History* 63 (1976): 66–92.

Walzer, Michael. *Just and Unjust Wars.* New York: Basic Books, 1977.

Warner, Edward. "Douhet, Mitchell, Seversky: Theories of Air Warfare." In *Makers of Modern Strategy,* edited by Edward Mead Earle, 485–503. Princeton, NJ: Princeton University Press, 1941.

Watts, Barry D. *The Foundations of US Air Doctrine.* Maxwell AFB, AL: Air University Press, 1984.

Wawro, Geoffrey. *The Franco-Prussian War: The German Conquest of France in 1870–1871.* Cambridge, UK: Cambridge University Press, 2003.

Weigley, Russell F. *The American Way of War.* Bloomington: Indiana University Press, 1977.

——. *Eisenhower's Lieutenants.* Bloomington: Indiana University Press, 1981.

Wells, Mark K. *Courage and Air Warfare: The Allied Aircrew Experience in the Second World War.* London: Frank Cass, 1995.

Werrell, Kenneth P. *Blankets of Fire: US Bombing Over Japan during World War II.* Washington, DC: Smithsonian Institution Press, 1996.

——. *The Evolution of the Cruise Missile.* Maxwell AFB, AL: Air University Press, 1985.

——. "The Strategic Bombing of Germany in World War II: Costs and Accomplishments." *Journal of American History* 73 (1986): 702–713.

——. *"Who Fears?" The 301st in War and Peace, 1942–1979.* Dallas: Taylor Publishing, 1991.

Wheeler, James Scott. *Jacob L. Devers: A General's Life.* Lexington: University Press of Kentucky, 2015.

Wittner, Lawrence S. *Rebels against War: The American Peace Movement, 1941–1960.* New York: Columbia University Press, 1969.

Wolff, Leon. *Low Level Mission.* New York: Berkley, 1958.

Wolk, Herman S. *Planning and Organizing the Postwar Air Force, 1943–1947.* Washington, DC: Office of Air Force History, 1984.

Yavenditti, Michael J. "The American People and the Use of Atomic Bombs on Japan: The 1940s." *Historian* 36 (1974): 224–247.

INDEX

Accidents
  aircraft, 50 (photo), 88–89, 91, 95,
    118, 120, 184, 241n58
  bombing, 108, 112, 198, 206
Accuracy of bombing, 5
  airmen's concerns about, 88, 90–91,
    95–96
  in AWPD-42, 32
  in Balkans, 212
  on Berlin, 149
  on Dresden, 156
  on Hamburg, 142–143
  on Iraq, 202–203, 213
  on Japan, 171, 174
  in last three months of war,
    49–62
  leaders' views on, 70, 74, 101
  public expectations of, 12, 205,
    211–212, 216
  of radar bombing, 46–47, 105,
    108–115, 114 (photo)
  of RAF, 113
  in right conditions, 35, 58
  statistics on, 35, 58, 60–61, 102–104,
    111–115, 202–203
  on transportation targets, 46–47,
    154–156
  on Vietnam, 197–199
Achmer, bombing of, 55
Afghanistan, 5, 207–208
A-Go Project, 163
Air Corps Tactical School, 12, 14–15, 17,
    21–29, 167–168, 204

Aircraft, 31, 35, 46
  accidents, 50 (photo), 88–89, 91, 95,
    118, 120, 184, 241n58
  B-17 Flying Fortress, 22, 31–32, 37–38,
    67, 87 (photo), 87–88, 117–118,
    124 (photo), 124–125, 168, 184
  B-24, 35, 38, 49–62, 50 (photo), 57
    (photo), 78 (photo), 87–88, 95, 103
    (photo), 183–184
  B-26, 193
  B-29, 86, 88–90, 107 (photo), 110,
    114–115, 163–164, 166–177, 172
    (photo), 183–185, 193, 241nn58–
    59
  B-52, 12, 198–200, 210–211, 215
  Junkers 88, 122
  losses of, 37–38, 40, 42–43, 51, 54–56,
    60, 87, 95, 143, 148–149, 167, 175,
    184, 241n58
  ME-262, 47, 55, 61
  P-38, 38, 41
  P-47, 37
  P-51, 39, 41, 55
  PB4Y, 118
  PV-1, 118
  Spitfire, 37
  Stealth, 200
  See also Fighters
Airmen
  attitudes about aircraft, 89, 171, 176
  attitudes about bombing civilians, 86,
    88–90, 93–95, 100, 174
  attitudes about enemy, 96–97

Airmen, *continued*
  compared to infantry, 86, 94
  concerns about survival, 86–88, 148,
    173, 176
  conditions of combat, 86–88
  cracks in bomber crew morale, 41,
    95–96
  devotion to precision doctrine, 10, 88,
    90, 93, 99–100, 109
  as elite, 85–86
  importance of crews, 35, 95–96
  leaders' perceptions of, 95–100
  reactions to fire raids, 89–90, 174–175
  recruiting, 86
  survival rates, 88
  as technicians, 85, 89
  training, 26, 90, 108, 111–112,
    171–172
  as warriors, 12, 85–87
Airpower ethic, 10, 19, 71, 145
Air War Plans Division (AWPD), 28–32
Allied Expeditionary Air Force, 44, 82–83
ALLIED FORCE, 205–207
Altenbecken, bombing of, 51
American Expeditionary Forces Air
  Service, 14–16
Amiens, bombing of, 45 (photo)
Amiriya, bombing of bunker in, 201,
  210–211
Amstaten, Germany, bombing of, 58
Amsteten, Austria, bombing of, 60
Anderson, Frederick L., 11, 37–38, 41
  background of, 77
  in Dresden controversy, 157–158
  emphasis on efficiency of, 77, 213
  in THUNDERCLAP and CLARION, 142–143,
    150
Andrews, Dana, 162
Andrews, Frank, 22
Anklam, bombing of, 38
Antiaircraft fire. *See* Flak
Anzio, 40
APHRODITE, 116–121
APQ-7 Eagle radar, 107 (photo), 112–115
Ardery, Phillip, 91
Area bombing, 47
  American views on, 75–76, 99, 107,
    113, 116–117, 154, 214

  in AWPD/1, 30
  British use of, 9–10, 98, 107, 113, 154,
    167, 178, 182, 214
  Gorrell's critique of, 15–17
  ground commanders' views of, 144
  on Japan, 99, 173–178, 183–185,
    214–215
  LeMay's views about, 167, 176
  Spaatz's views about, 74
ARGUMENT, 41–43
Army Air Corps, 20–23, 26
Army Air Forces
  adherence to doctrine, 1, 4–13, 84,
    143, 213–214
  attitudes in *Impact*, 97–100
  creation of, 28
  criticism of ethics of, 3–4
  differences with British, 1–2, 9, 44,
    78–83, 136–139, 142–144, 158
  and Pacific command situation, 163
  public perceptions of, 67, 86
  recruiting of, 86
  reliance on technical experts of,
    168–169, 189–190
Army Air Forces Proving Ground
  Command, 117, 121
Army Air Service, 26
Army War College, 27
Arnold, Henry H. "Hap," 5, 11, 28–30,
  29 (photo), 33, 36, 38, 72 (photo),
  77, 180
  convenes board on atomic warfare,
    190–191
  desire for accurate bombing, 70, 101,
    143
  desire for independent air force, 7, 10,
    69–71, 112, 170
  drives command changes, 7, 39–40,
    171
  ethics of, 71
  health of, 7, 69, 157, 159, 166, 173
  influence on operations by, 7, 69, 104,
    148, 166, 171, 180
  interest in incendiary bombing, 130,
    168–169, 173, 178–179
  interest in pilotless flying bombs, 71,
    117–126
  involvement in THUNDERCLAP and

CLARION, 142, 144, 147–148, 150, 153
reaction to bombing of Dresden, 157–159
relieves Hansell, 171
views on bombing civilians and morale, 7, 69, 71, 84, 148, 150, 179
views on bombing Rome, 134
views on chemical warfare, 128, 181–182
views on defeating Japan, 180–183
views on interservice cooperation, 112
views on new technology, 5, 70–71
views on public opinion, 70
views on public relations, 70, 74, 97–98
views on radar bombing aids, 105, 110
Aschaffenberg, bombing of, 52–53
Atlantic Conference, 29
Atomic bomb, 4, 12, 30, 66, 74, 91, 128, 131–132, 166, 179, 183–184, 186–188, 190–191, 196
Atrocities, 71, 73, 97, 161–162, 188
Augsburg, bombing of, 59
Australia, 163
Austria, 42, 56–62
Avisio Bridge, 125
AWPD/1, 28–32, 63, 132, 144
AWPD-4, 31
AWPD-42, 31–33, 48, 63
Azon bombs and guidance, 118, 119 (photo), 125, 200

Bacon, Ken, 206–207
Baghdad, bombing of, 201, 204, 211
Balkans, 40, 56–62, 136–139, 141, 158, 160, 204–207
Balloons, 71, 163
Barcus, Glenn, 194
Basilica of San Lorenzo, 134
Batbombs, 130–131
Battle of the Bulge, 8, 46–47, 56, 148
Belgian protests about bombing, 81
Belgrade, bombing of, 5, 206–207
Bendiner, Elmer, 93
Berlin, bombing of, 39, 43, 51–52, 54, 65, 71, 88, 91, 93, 113, 131, 142–144, 146–149, 156–157, 188, 194

Betzdorf, bombing of, 54
Biddle, Tami, 15, 160
Bielefeld, bombing of, 53 (photo), 54
Big Week, 41–44
Biological warfare, 66, 128, 163, 181, 211, 215
Bischofhofen, bombing of, 58–59
Bissell, Clayton, 28
Bitterfeld, bombing of, 52
BOLERO, 31
Bombardiers, 16, 77, 83, 90–91, 95–96, 171
Bomb damage assessment, 16, 37, 108, 114 (photo), 191
Bomber Command. See Royal Air Force
Bombing, through overcast. See Nonvisual bombing
Bombing targets
    aircraft plants, 15, 32, 35, 37, 41, 47
    airfields, 55, 58, 61
    ball bearings, 35–38, 40–41
    capitals, 10, 17, 136, 148 (see also Belgrade, bombing of; Berlin, bombing of; Bucharest; Budapest; Hanoi, bombing of; London, bombing of; Pyongyang, bombing of; Rome, bombing of; Sofia, bombing of; Tokyo)
    dams, 195 (photo), 196
    factories, 9–10, 15, 17, 22, 27, 30, 49–62, 67–68, 82, 99, 107, 140, 171, 174–175, 198
    food and water, 23–24, 28, 67, 181–182, 196, 201
    historical and religious sites, 65, 98–100, 134–135, 201, 214
    occupied countries, 34, 80–84
    oil, 30, 43–62, 75, 111–112, 114 (photo), 115, 137, 149–150, 153, 157, 159, 190, 197–198, 201, 207
    power, 23–25, 28, 30, 32, 184, 194, 197–198, 201, 203, 206
    submarine pens, 32–34, 35 (photo), 47, 55
    transportation, 8, 17, 23, 25, 27, 30, 32, 43–62, 82–83, 115, 150–158, 176, 182–183, 201, 207
    troops, 16–17, 26, 133–134, 201–202, 205–206, 208

Bombing targets, *continued*
   workers, 9, 15, 21, 82, 107, 176, 182,
      192, 214
Bombs
   glide, 124–125
   guided, 5, 125
   high explosive ("dumb"), 102,
      202–203, 213
   precision ("smart"), 5, 59, 125, 198,
      202, 206
   See also Incendiary bombs and
      bombing
Bombsights, 15–16, 22, 77, 102, 171
Bottomley, Sir Norman, 47, 157–158
Bounheim, bombing of, 50
Bourdeaux, bombing of, 37
Braddock incendiary device, 130
Bradley, Omar, 127, 139, 148
Bremen, bombing of, 38
Brenner Pass, 125
Brescia, bombing of, 19
Brissac, bombing of, 112
Brittain, Vera, 65–66, 224n8
Brod, Yugoslavia, bombing of, 60
Broz, bombing of, 56
Bruck-Leitha, bombing of, 60
Brunswick, bombing of, 55, 91
Bucharest, 136–138, 154
Buchenwald, 188
Budapest, 87 (photo), 137
Budiansky, Stephen, 208
Bulgaria, 136–138
Bulitt, William, 68
Burg Reuland, bombing of, 49
Burma, 125
Bush, Vannever, 126

Cabell, Charles P., 83, 128, 140, 147, 153,
      213
Cairo Conference, 39
Candee, Robert, 81 (photo)
Canton, bombing of, 26
Casablanca Conference, 33, 78
Casablanca Directive, 34
CASTOR control system, 117–118, 120
CENTERBOARD, 186
Cheek, Earle C., 94, 108
Chemical warfare, 19–20, 24, 66, 101
   considered against Germany,
      128–129
   considered against Japan, 181, 215
Chemical Warfare Service, 129–131
Chemnitz, 156–157
Cheney, Richard, 201
Chennault, Claire, 169
Chicago Sun, 215
China, 5, 215
   B-29s in, 169–170
   Japanese bombing of, 26–27
   in Korean War, 193–194, 196
   plans to bomb Japan, 168
China–Burma–India theater, 125,
      169–171
Churchill, Winston, 44–46, 77
   approves Combined Bomber
      Offensive, 33, 78
   blamed for Dresden raid, 156
   and bombing of Rome, 134
   resistance to war-weary bombers, 123
   views on chemical warfare, 128
Civilian bombing casualties
   in Amiriya, 201
   in Bucharest, 138
   in Dresden, 156
   in Hamburg, 142
   in Japan, 8, 175–176, 179
   in LINEBACKER II, 199
   in occupied countries, 80–84
   in World War I, 16
Civilian morale, as a target, 9, 15
   American doctrine concerning, 20,
      22–25, 30, 133
   American resistance to, 1, 9, 17,
      22–25, 136, 154
   Douhet's ideas on, 19
   early wartime lessons, 26–27
   in Korean War, 193–194
   in operations against Germany, 30,
      133, 139–160
   in operations against Japan, 161,
      177–178, 183–185
   in operations against the Balkans,
      136–139, 204–207
   perceptions of German vulnerability
      of, 15, 21, 139–144, 146–148,
      152–153, 182

perceptions of Japanese vulnerability of, 162, 176–178, 184–187

postwar conclusions of USSBS about, 191

prewar perceptions of, 21–25

Seversky's views on, 27–28

CKD Lieben tank works, 61

CLARION, 7, 48, 52, 58, 62, 146, 151–155, 160, 194, 205

Clark, Mark, 194

Clark, Wesley, 205–206

Clausewitz, Carl von, 1, 20, 26, 62, 180

Clergy attitudes about bombing, 65–67, 100, 229n37

Clodfelter, Mark, 22, 200, 209

Cohen, Eliot, 203

Cohen, William, 207

Cologne, as bombing target, 15, 37

Combined Bomber Offensive, 33–34, 41, 78, 81, 136

Combined Chiefs of Staff, 34–35, 39–41, 81, 107, 136–138, 148, 150, 157

Combined Operational Planning Committee, 41

Command and control, 6–7, 12, 137, 163, 166, 182–183

Command and General Staff School, 26, 221n39

Committee of Operations Analysts, 36, 38, 168–169, 189

Copilots, 91, 93

Cottbus, as bombing target, 157

Cousins, Norman, 66

Coventry, bombing of, 161

Cowan, Howard, 158

CROSSBOW, 45, 117

Cruise missiles, 200, 214

Curry, John F., 21

Czechoslovakia, 61, 88

Dalziel, D., 136

Danzig, bombing of, 38

Davis, Richard, 47, 75

Daylight versus night bombing, 1, 16, 79–80, 143–144, 170–171, 173–174

Deathblow, search for aerial. See *Todestoss*, search for

DELIBERATE FORCE, 205

DESERT STORM, 5–6, 12, 191, 200–204, 210–211

Devers, Jacob, 40, 112

Disney, Walt, 28

Doctrine, process to develop, 5–6, 21. See *also* Precision bombing doctrine

Donovon, William J., 130, 139

Doolittle, James "Jimmy," 7, 75–77, 76 (photo), 124

and bombing of Rome, 75, 98, 100, 134, 135 (photo)

as commander of Northwest African Strategic Air Force, 82, 134

concerns about bombing civilians, 82, 88, 146, 149

devotion to precision bombing, 146, 213–214

ethics of, 75–76

involvement in CLARION and THUNDERCLAP, 143, 146–147, 149, 153, 160

involvement in war-weary bomber project, 116, 118, 120

mistrust of radar bombing, 108–110, 115

raid on Tokyo, 75, 98, 162

reaction to bombing of Dresden, 156

releases Eighth Air Force fighters to hunt enemy fighters, 40–41, 95

takes command of Eighth Air Force, 39–40, 82, 106

Dortmund, bombing of, 51

Douhet, Giulio, 26–27

background of, 18–19

influence on American doctrine, 19–20, 23–24, 133, 190

views of, 19, 216

Dower, John, 161

Dresden, bombing of, 51, 149, 154–159, 199, 210, 212

Drones, 208

Dugway Proving Ground, 130–131, 169

Dunkirk, bombing of, 79 (photo)

Eaker, Ira, 7, 32

as AAF deputy chief of staff, 77, 180

on bombing French civilians, 81–82

Casablanca presentation, 33, 78

Eaker, Ira, *continued*
  as commander of Eighth Air Force,
    33, 37–39, 77–78, 81, 124
  concern about, for public relations, 7,
    77–78, 146, 153, 213
  enthusiasm of, for radar bombing, 48,
    104–107, 111–112
  ethics of, 78
  involvement in CLARION, 146,
    152–153
  on precision bombing, 78
  postwar views on air force roles, 191
  reaction to Hamburg firestorm, 143
  relations with Arnold, 39–40, 77–78
  takes command of MAAF, 39–40, 106,
    137
  and testing of new bombs, 124–128
  views on targeting civilian morale, 78,
    106, 146, 152–153
Early, Stephan, 68
Economic Objectives Unit, Economic
    Warfare Division, US embassy,
    London, 44
Edgewood Arsenal, 129
Eglin Field, FL, 117, 121, 169
Eighth Air Force, 75, 77, 88, 95, 97, 102,
    127, 130–131, 140, 182–183, 213
  and bombing of France, 80–82
  and bombing of oil and transportation
    targets, 43–48
  compared with Fifteenth Air Force, 8,
    48, 58, 62–63, 95, 111
  conduct of final air campaign, 48–55
  gaining air superiority over Europe,
    39–43
  in Hamburg raid, 142–143
  initial operations, 31–39
  and nonvisual bombing, 48–55,
    104–112
  in THUNDERCLAP, 51, 147–149
  and war-weary bombers, 118, 120
VIII Bomber Command, 32–33, 37, 108,
    143
  First Bombardment Division, 37
  Second Bombardment Division, 38,
    50–55, 95, 108
  Third Bombardment Division, 37,
    112

Eisenhower, Dwight David, 35, 77, 81
    (photo), 129, 134, 158, 196
  and air command changes in Europe,
    39–40, 44
  and bombing of Balkan cities, 136
  choice of transportation plan, 44–45,
    83
  and JB-2, 126
  relations with Spaatz and USSTAF, 8,
    40, 44, 47, 108, 110, 112, 147
  on THUNDERCLAP, 147, 160
  on war-weary bombers, 121
Eliot, George Fielding, 66
Escalation, 13, 115, 129, 214, 216
Essen, bombing of, 55
Ethiopia, 27

Far Eastern Air Forces, 117, 166, 177,
    193–194, 196
Fellowship of Reconciliation, 65
Fersfield, England, 117
Fifteenth Air Force, 40, 91, 94–95, 106,
    131, 137, 140, 213
  bombing oil and transportation
    targets, 43–48
  compared with Eighth Air Force, 8,
    48, 58, 62–63, 95, 111
  conduct of final air campaign, 56–61
  gaining air superiority over Europe,
    39–43
  and nonvisual bombing, 48, 56–62,
    111–112
Fifth Air Force, 194
Fighters
  Allied, 32, 37–42, 55, 79, 93, 113, 148,
    150–152, 198, 200
  German, 35, 37–43, 55, 62, 74, 87, 94,
    108, 115, 167
  Japanese, 89, 171, 173
Firebombing. *See* Incendiary Bombs and
    Bombing
Fiume, bombing of, 58
Flak, 12, 51, 54, 59, 62, 87, 94, 108, 118,
    124, 152, 167, 173–174, 180
Florence, bombing of, 99
Florisdorf, bombing of, 56, 60
Foggia, Italy, 56, 58
Ford, John C., 66

Formation bombing, 102-104, 154-155
Fort Leavenworth, 17, 26
44th Bomb Group, 49-55
Forward director posts, 109
Foulois, Benjamin, 15
455th Bomb Group, 56-61
466th Bomb Group, 50 (photo)
Fourteenth Bomb Wing, 51-55
France
    Allied bombing of civilians in, 44,
        80-84
    reaction to bombing of Poland, 68
    transportation targets in, 44, 45
        (photo), 82-83
Frank, Walter, 81 (photo)
Frankfurt, bombing of, 54
Franks, Frederick, 201
Franks, Tommy, 208
Frey, E., 140
Fuller, J. F. C., 20, 85
Fussell, Paul, 10

Galland, Adolf, 41, 115
Gas. See Chemical warfare
GB-1 glide bombs, 124 (photo), 124-125
Gdynia, bombing of, 38
GEE navigation aid, 49-54, 104,
    108-109, 111
General Framework Agreement for Peace,
    205
George, Harold, 22-24, 27-29, 29 (photo)
Germany
    airpower strategies against, 8, 30,
        32-34, 41-48, 99, 139-160
    American images of, 68-69, 71, 96-
        97, 139-144, 147-149, 152-154,
        158-159, 188, 190, 214
    Blitz on London, 10, 89, 214
    bombing of Romania, 138
    bombing policies, 2, 7, 67-68, 211
    defenses of, 139-140, 152, 167
    effects of bombing on, 2 (photo), 3
        (photo), 46, 142, 151 (photo), 151,
        155 (photo), 155, 182, 189 (photo),
        189-191
    reactions of civilians to bombing in,
        12, 142, 182, 191
    response to FDR's pleas on Poland, 68

    vulnerability of morale in, 68, 139-143
    Zeppelin attacks by, 16, 18-19
Giles, Barney, 112-113, 126, 179
Gmund, bombing of, 59
Göring, Hermann, 41
Gorrell, Edgar S.
    and World War I air studies, 14-17,
        23-24, 30
Gotha bombers, 16, 18
Gottingen, bombing of, 52
Graz marshaling yard, 60
Great Britain, 7
    Air Ministry of, 80, 82, 137, 142
    Air Staff of, 15
    commitment to morale attacks, 9
    concerns about war-weary bombers,
        116, 122-123
    concerns for French civilians, 80-83
    desire to knock out Balkans, 136-138
    German bombing of, 10, 16, 18, 78,
        89, 161, 214
    political considerations of, 80,
        137-138
    protests against US bombing in Korea
        by, 194
    reactions of civilians to bombing in, 65
    response to FDR's pleas on Poland, 68
    See also Royal Air Force
Grierson, C. M., 158
Ground support, 109, 112-113, 121, 159
Guam, 166, 171, 179-180
Gulf War Air Power Survey, 203
Gutersloh, bombing of, 54

Haiphong, bombing of, 198-199
Halberstadt, bombing of, 40
Halle, bombing of, 52
Hallendorf, bombing of, 51
Halsey, William, 70
Hamburg, bombing of, 12, 16, 36 (photo),
    142-143, 148, 156, 167, 182
Hamm, bombing of, 51
Hankow, fire raid on, 169
Hanoi, bombing of, 198-199
Hansell, Haywood S., Jr., 7, 28-29, 29
    (photo), 164 (photo)
    adherence to precision doctrine, 11,
        170-171, 214

Hansell, Haywood S., Jr., *continued*
on best way to defeat Japan,
184–185
contributions to doctrine, 22, 28
difficulties commanding XXI Bomber
Command, 170–171
writing AWPD-42, 32–33
Harburg, bombing of oil refinery at, 3
(photo), 51, 53
Harris, Sir Arthur "Bomber," 21, 39, 44,
48, 64–65, 82
Hassler, R. Alfred, 66
Hastings, Max, 3
Heligoland, attack on submarine pens
at, 120
Hemmingstadt, bombing of, 50, 155
Herford, war-weary attack on, 120
Himalaya Mountains, 170
Hirohito, emperor of Japan, 162, 180,
183, 185
Hiroshima, atomic bombing of, 12,
186–187
Historians
AAF reluctance to use, 188–189
criticisms of bombing by, 1–4, 212
Eaker's concerns about, 77
Hitler, Adolf, 46, 97, 115, 129, 179
Hitzacker, bombing of, 55
Hodges, Courtney, 127
Hohengandern, bombing of, 52
Honshu, invasion of, 180, 215
Hopper, Bruce, 188, 210, 212
Howard, Michael, 84, 215
Hoya ammunition depot, 55
H2S radar, 104
H2X radar, 49–62, 83, 105–115, 155
Hughes, Richard, 141, 147, 150, 213
Hull, Cordell, 68, 138
"Humanitarian Aspects of Airpower," 84,
217–218
Hungary, bombing of, 61, 87 (photo),
137–138
Hunter, Frank, 81 (photo)
HURRICANE I and II, 146, 150, 193
Hussein, Saddam, 203, 208, 211

Ignatieff, Michael, 212, 215
Impact magazine, 97–99, 108, 126

Incendiary bombs and bombing, 19, 102,
163
development of, 129–131, 168,
181
postwar legacies of, 191, 214–215
raid on Hankow, 169
raids on Germany, 131, 142, 156, 159,
178
raids on Japan, 4, 7–8, 10, 162,
172–179, 178 (photo), 180–181,
183–185
results of incendiary bombing, 142,
156, 175, 179, 184–185
Intelligence, 35–36, 38, 44, 48, 138, 154,
176
International Red Cross, 138
Intervalometer, 102, 103 (photo), 154
Invasions
of Europe, 10, 33, 35, 39, 82, 93, 109,
139–140
of Japan, 10, 176, 179–181, 185, 215
Ipswich, 118
Iraq, 12, 117, 213–214
RAF air control of, 203–204
reaction to Amiriya bombing in, 201,
210–211
results of DESERT STORM against, 12,
200–203, 213
results of 2003 bombing against, 208
Isarco-Albes railroad bridge, 59
Italy, bombing of, 35, 44, 56–62, 65,
98–100, 133–135
Iwo Jima, 9

Japan
airpower strategies against, 8, 32, 99,
122–123, 160, 163, 166, 168–180,
182–185, 214–215
American images of, 73, 97–99,
161–163
atomic bombing of, 179, 183–188
atrocities of, 26, 97, 162
attacks on continental United States
by, 163
Chinese cities bombed by, 2, 26, 211
defenses of, 89, 174, 180, 184, 191
fire raids against, 7–8, 10–12, 73, 99,
166, 174–179, 178 (photo)

home industries in, 99, 175–176
inflammability of, 168–169
last air attacks on, 184
mining campaign against, 184–185,
        241n59
precision attacks against, 99, 114
        (photo), 115, 171, 173, 176, 182,
        184–185
results of bombing on, 99, 178
        (photo), 179, 184–185, 187–188,
        192, 213 (photo)
use of chemical warfare considered
        against, 181–182
JAVAMAN, 123
JB-2 buzz bomb, 125–128
"Jeb Stuart" fighter units, 152
Jesenice, bombing of, 59
Johnson, Lyndon, 187, 197, 199 (photo)
Joint Chiefs of Staff, 12, 33, 74, 78, 83,
        134, 137–138, 144, 163, 197, 201
    defeat of Japan, pursued by, 179–181
    and war-weary bombers, 121–123
Joint Intelligence Committee, 138, 154
Joint Planning Staff of the British War
        Cabinet, 136
Joint Staff Mission, Washington, DC, 136
Joint Target Group, 182
Judge Advocate General, 181

Kaiserslautern, bombing of, 49
Kamaishi Iron Works, 166
Kamikazes, 166
Kammon Tunnel, 123
Kantor, MacKinley, 65
Kapfenberg, bombing of, 61
Keegan, John, 204
Kellogg, Crawford, 129
Kennedy, Joseph P., 120
Kenney, George, 22, 118, 123, 125, 128,
        166, 177, 183
Kettering Liberty Eagle, 117
Khafji, battle of, 205
Kiel, bombing of, 54, 106
King, Ernest, 163, 181
Klagenfurt, bombing of, 58
Koblenz–Lutzel, bombing of, 49
Kokotai Bridge, bombing of, 175
Konoye, Prince, 184–185

Korean War, 212
    effectiveness of airpower in, 193–194,
        195 (photo), 196, 198
    PRESSURE PUMP, 194
    public reaction to bombing in, 194,
        196
    strategic bombing in, 193–196
Korneuburg oil refinery, 58
Kosovo, 204–207
Kralupy oil refinery, 61
Krueger, Walter, 165
Kurata, Yasuo, 210–211
Kuter, Laurence, 28–29, 84, 122–123, 168
    contributions to doctrine, 22, 28
    involvement in Dresden controversy,
        157–158
    involvement in THUNDERCLAP and
        CLARION, 142–144
Kuwait, 200–203, 205
Kyoto, 73
Kyushu
    bombing of, 166, 177
    invasion of, 180, 215

Lampedusa, bombing of, 133
Landau, bombing of, 49
Lawfare, 209
Leaflets, 98, 176–177, 187, 194
League of Nations, 27
Leahy, William, 123, 148, 181
Leigh-Mallory, Sir Trafford, 44, 82
Leipzig, bombing of, 41, 42 (photo)
LeMay, Curtis, 10, 165 (photo)
    background of, 167
    bombs center of Munster, 113,
        167–168
    commanding XX Bomber Command,
        169–170
    conducts Hankow fire raid, 169
    improves XXI Bomber Command,
        171–174
    initiates incendiary raids on Japan,
        7–8, 12, 89–90, 115, 131–132,
        173–176, 214
    innovations of, 105, 112, 131,
        167–168, 188
    postwar views of airpower, 188, 191,
        200

LeMay, Curtis, *continued*
  practicality of, 12, 167
  psychological warfare campaign of,
    176–177, 187, 194
  relations with other commanders, 163,
    166
  replaces Hansell, 7, 11, 163, 171
  results of incendiary campaign,
    174–179, 184, 188
  Schweinfurt raid, 37
  service in Europe, 37, 105, 112–113,
    131, 167
  strategy to defeat Japan, 178, 180, 183,
    185, 196, 214
  views on bombing civilians, 131, 133,
    187–188
Leuna, bombing of, 101, 115
Libya, bombing of, 5
Liddell Hart, Basil, 1, 20
Lille, bombing of, 80
Limburg, bombing of, 54
LINEBACKER I and II, 198–200
Linz, bombing of, 56, 59, 61
LN chemicals, 181
London, bombing of, 10, 18–19, 78, 161,
    220n10
Lone-wolf raids, 57, 61, 111
Lovett, Robert, 73, 81, 97, 106, 126, 141,
    146, 150, 152, 160
Luce, Henry, 98
Luftwaffe, 10, 32–33, 37–48, 59, 61,
    106–108, 111, 115

MacArthur, Douglas, 12, 163, 171, 177,
    183, 193, 196
  on chemical warfare against Japan,
    181
  restrictive bombing policies of,
    163–166
Madrid, bombing of, 27
Magdeberg, bombing of, 51, 53
Mahan, Alfred Thayer, 20, 27
Malmedy massacre, 97
Malta conference, 156–157
Manila, retaking of, 165
Mannheim, bombing of, 189 (photo)
Mao Tze-tung, 173
March, Peyton, 14

Marianas Islands, 168, 170–172, 172
    (photo), 183
Maribor, Yugoslavia, bombing of, 58–60
Marienberg, bombing of, 35, 38
Marshaling yards, 8, 32, 45 (photo), 47,
    49–62, 102–103, 113, 120, 134,
    135 (photo), 136–138, 151 (photo),
    152–157, 160, 195 (photo)
Marshall, George C., 30, 32–33, 40, 157
  on chemical warfare against Japan, 181
  desire to force early German
    surrender, 46, 110, 148–149
  on German people, 71, 96
  on incendiary bombs and bombing,
    168, 181, 215
Marshall, S. L. A., 85, 188
Maruzen, Japan, 114 (photo)
Maxwell, Alfred, 150, 190
McDonald, George, 141, 157
McNamara, Robert S., 197–198
McPeak, Merrill, 202–203
Mediterranean Allied Air Forces, 39–40,
    99, 106, 111, 141, 152, 157
MEETINGHOUSE, 174–175
Melville, Herman, 85
Micro-H radar/beacon system, 111
Microwave early warning stations
    (MEWS), 109
Mierzejewski, Alfred O., 44, 47, 155
Miller, Donald, 62
Millis, Walter, 1
Milosevic, Slobodan, 205, 207
Mining campaign against Japan, 184–185,
    241n59
Mining of Danube, 48
Misburg oil refinery, 52
Mitchell, William "Billy," 18 (photo), 26,
    27
  background of, 17–18
  influence on American doctrine,
    19–20
  influences on his thought, 17–18, 20
Momyer, William M., 200
Monte Cassino, bombing of, 99–100, 214
Moosbierbaum oil refinery, 56
Morality of bombing
  airpower ethic as one view of, 10, 19,
    71, 144–145, 214, 216

Arnold on, 69, 71, 159
Buchenwald compared to, 188
controversy over, 1
criticisms of AAF over, 3-4
criticisms of RAF over, 2-3, 9, 191
difficulties considering, in strategy, 9,
    215
Doolittle on, 75-76
Eaker on, 78, 146, 152-153
Hughes and Weicker SHATTER debate
    over, 140-142
Kurata's critique of DESERT STORM,
    210-211
Kuter on, 143-144
LeMay on, 161, 174, 176
MacArthur on, 164-166
questioned in Poland, 68
questioned in Vietnam, 199
questioned in Yugoslavia, 207,
    211-212
in shaping precision doctrine, 8,
    22-25, 84, 217-218
Spaatz on, 74-75, 183-184
Stimson on, 71, 73, 187-188
Vera Brittain on, 65-66, 68
World War II public debates over,
    65-67
Moran, Lord, 91
Morgenthau, Henry, 68
Morrison, Wilbur H., 90
Moscow, 194
Mountbatten, Lord Louis, 171, 183
Moyers, Bill, 215
Muhldorf, bombing of, 61
Muirhead, John, 91
Munich, bombing of, 2 (photo), 61,
    148-149, 151 (photo)
Munster, bombing of, 38, 51, 54, 113,
    167-168
Mussolini, Benito, 97, 134-135

National Academy of Sciences, 181
Navigators, 93-94, 96, 167
Neratovice, Czechoslovakia, bombing of,
    61
Neuburg, bombing of, 54, 61
Neunkirchen, bombing of, 49
New York city, 23

New York Times, 65-66
Night bombing, 1, 16, 33, 79-80, 98, 115,
    170, 173-175
Nimitz, Chester, 12, 163, 166, 171
Ninth Air Force, 109, 112, 121
Ninth Tactical Air Command, 152
Nixon, Richard, 198-199
Nonvisual bombing, 8, 32, 83, 94, 98-99
    in Europe, 8, 48-62, 83, 104-115,
        137, 167
    in ground support, 109, 112-113
    on Japan, 115, 170, 172-174, 184
Norden bombsight, 22, 102
Norstad, Lauris, 113, 171-173, 179, 182,
    185, 192
North Atlantic Treaty Organization,
    205-207
Northwest African Air Forces, 33, 81, 136
Northwest African Strategic Air Force,
    82, 134
Norwegian bombing protests, 73
Novezamke, bombing of, 60
Nuclear weapons strategy, 187-188,
    190-192, 196, 214-215, 244n7
Nuremburg, bombing of, 52

Oberstein, bombing of, 49
Oberstraubling airdrome, 58
OBOE radar navigation aid, 104, 113
Office of Scientific Research and
    Development, 126
Oil targets. See Bombing targets
Okinawa, 9, 166, 180
Oldenburg, war-weary attack on, 120
Omura, Japan, 107
Operations Research and Systems
    Analysis, 189, 197
Oppenheimer, Robert, 73
Oschersleben, bombing of, 40
OVERLORD, 10, 44-46, 82, 93, 107-108,
    137-140
Overy, Richard, 46, 135

Pacifism, 65
Pankow railyard, 52
Pantelleria, bombing of, 44, 133, 202
Paris, bombardment of, 19, 78, 80, 192,
    220n10

Parona railroad bridge, 60
Patrick, Mason M., 14, 16
Patterson, Judge Robert, 81
Patton, George S., 70, 94, 127, 134
Paulding, C. C., 66
Pearl Harbor, 31, 168
Persian Gulf War, 200–203. *See also*
    DESERT STORM
Pforsheim, bombing of, 51
Philippine Islands, 20, 31, 164–165, 168,
    173
Pilots
    Allied, 41, 84, 91–94, 96
    German, 43, 46–47
Ploesti, bombing of, 45, 48–49, 137
POINTBLANK, 35, 41
Pola, bombing of, 58
Poland, 38, 68
Politz, bombing of, 101
Polls, 65, 161
Portal, Sir Charles, 34, 36, 81, 122,
    137–138, 154, 156, 159, 183
Porto Nuevo marshaling yard, 56
Potsdam Conference, 183
Power, Thomas, 175
Prague, bombing of, 61
Precision bombing doctrine, 4–6, 11, 33,
    63, 143
    ACTS development of, 21–25
    airmen's belief in, 10, 88, 93
    British roots of, 15
    contributions of Gorrell's studies to,
        15–17
    Doolittle's support of, 75–76, 146,
        149, 213
    Eaker's mixed support of, 78
    expressed in AWPD/1, 28–30
    failure of, against Japan, 8, 170–171,
        173–174, 184–185
    faulty assumptions, 25
    Hansell's devotion to, 11, 171, 214
    highlighted in *Impact*, 97–99
    in "Humanitarian Aspects of Air
        Force," 84, 217–218
    persistence in field, 6, 10–11, 116, 171,
        212–214
    post–World War II, 5–6, 12, 190–212,
        216

    and Progressive ideas, 22
    Spaatz's adherence to, 74–75, 78, 101,
        147, 159, 183, 214
    World War II advocates for, 214
PRESSURE PUMP, 194
Prisoners of war, 97, 153, 160, 162
Prussia, 19, 159, 192
Psychological effects of bombing, 9–10,
    15, 19, 109, 136, 144, 185, 192,
    194, 203–205, 207, 211, 215
Psychological warfare, 10, 98–99, 136,
    140, 176–177, 181, 187, 194,
    203–204, 211, 215
Psychoneurotic casualties, 91, 94–95
Public opinion about bombing
    American, 64–67, 97, 141, 158, 193,
        199
    international, 24, 140, 193, 207,
        210–212
    leaders' concerns about, 10, 67–68,
        70, 77, 141, 158–159, 196, 199
Purple Heart, The, 162
Pyongyang, bombing of, 193–194, 195
    (photo)

Quadrant Conference, 35
Quebec Conference, 169
Quesada, Elwood, 152

Rabaul, 165
Racism, 4, 161–162, 183
Radar bombing aids, 104–110, 200, 214.
    See also Nonvisual bombing
Rand, Henry James, 118
Regensberg, bombing of, 37, 57–58, 60
Republican Guard, 201–202
Restrictions on bombing, 46–48
    in Balkans, 205–207
    in Iraq, 201, 208
    in occupied countries, 47, 80–83
    in Vietnam, 197–200
Rheine, bombing of, 52, 55
Rheinmetall Borsig Armament Works, 54
Rice crops as a target, 181–182, 196–197
Ridgway, Matthew, 198
Riem airdrome, 61
ROLLING THUNDER, 198
Romania, bombing of, 48, 136–138

Rome, bombing of, 65, 98–99, 134–135, 135 (photo)
Roosevelt, Franklin D., 28, 32–33, 39, 81, 138, 154
   attitudes about bombing civilians, 7, 67–69, 139
   on bombing Rome, 134
   on chemical warfare, 128
   directs creation of USSBS, 182
   perceptions of Japanese, 97, 161
   pleas to halt bombing of cities, 68
Rostow, Walt W., 199 (photo)
Rothensee oil refinery, 51–53
Rotterdam, bombing of, 84, 161
Rouen, bombing of, 32
Royal Air Force, 33, 37, 39
   in Big Week, 41–42
   bombing accuracy, 102, 113
   colonial air control of, 203–204
   doctrine of, 1, 17, 21, 78–79, 192
   in Dresden raid, 156
   and Hamburg firestorm, 12, 142–143, 148
   help with oil targets, 48
   limitations of, 78–79, 102, 151
   night area raids of, 1, 10, 16, 33, 65, 78, 98, 113, 178, 214
   postwar criticism of, 191
   reasons for bombing strategy, 20–21, 79, 192
   search for *Todesstoss* against Germany, 142–143, 146–154
Royal Flying Corps, 17
Ruhland, bombing of, 50
Ruhr, bombing of the, 48
Rumsfeld, Donald, 207–208

Saddam Line, 203
Sallagar, F. M., 7
Salzbergen oil refinery, 52
San Francisco, fears of Japanese attack on, 163
Scanlon, Martin, 29 (photo)
Schaffer, Ronald, 3–4, 6, 105, 116, 136, 153, 244n7
Schaffhausen, bombing of, 108
Schlatter, David, 159
Schwabisch Hall, bombing of, 55

Schwarzkopf, Norman, 201
Schweinfurt, bombing of, 36–38, 40, 93, 167
Scientific Advisory Group, 126–127
SCR-584 radar, 109, 127
Scud missiles, 117, 203
Segar, Gerhart, 66
Seoul, 194
Sergeant York air defense gun, 5
7th Bomb Group, 125
VII Corps, in DESERT STORM, 201
Seversky, Alexander P. de, 27–28, 148, 201
Shanghai, Japanese bombing of, 26–27
SHATTER, 140–141, 150
Sherry, Michael, 3–4, 6–7, 12
Shimonoseki Straits, 123
Shipdham, Norfolk, 49–50, 50 (photo), 52
"Shock and Awe," 204–205
SHORAN directional guidance system, 109, 113
Short, Michael, 206
Sicily, 44, 143
Siegen, bombing of, 52, 54
Sino-Japanese War, 26
Smart, Jacob, 194
"Smart" bombs. *See under* Bombs
Smokescreens, 11, 53, 57, 62, 112
Smuts, Jan, 18
Sofia, bombing of, 40, 136–137
Sorenson, Edgar, 29 (photo)
Spaatz, Carl, 11, 28, 29 (photo), 31, 74–75, 78, 81 (photo)
   on atomic bomb, 183–184, 188, 191
   attempts to alter Japanese campaign, 160, 182–183
   on bombing civilians, 74–75, 129, 137–138, 159, 183–184, 187
   on bombing Rome, 134
   commands NAAF, 33, 81
   commands USASTAF, 182–184
   concern for French civilians, 80, 82–83
   contributions to precision doctrine, 22, 28, 30, 75
   cooperation with RAF, 75
   devotion to precision doctrine, 22, 74–75, 78, 101, 147, 159, 183–184, 191, 213–214

Spaatz, Carl, *continued*
    directs ARGUMENT, 41–43
    ethics of, 7, 74–75, 183–184
    extends combat tours, 95
    fears of morale bombing backlash, 1,
        147
    involvement with CLARION, 140, 142,
        144, 146, 150–154
    involvement with radar, 104–113
    involvement with war-weary bombers,
        117–123
    postwar views on air roles, 190–191
    on public relations, 74, 153, 158
    pushes oil campaign, 44–46, 75,
        82–83, 149, 157
    reaction to Dresden controversy,
        158–159
    relations with Eaker, 40
    relations with Eisenhower, 8, 39–40,
        112, 147, 163
    resistance to Balkan city raids, 40,
        137–138
    resistance to chemical warfare,
        128–129
    resistance to glide bombs, 124
    resistance to JB-2, 126–127
    resistance to THUNDERCLAP, 147–149
    resistance to transportation plan,
        82–83
    takes command of USSTAF, 39–40,
        82
Spain, 27, 166 Spanish Civil War, 27
Special Attack Unit 1, 118, 120
Speer, Albert, 38, 42–43, 46–47, 155
Sperry bombsight, 22
Squier, George O., 17–18
Stalin, Josef, 156, 181, 183, 185, 196
Stewart, James "Jimmy," 91, 92 (photo)
Steyr, bombing of, 61
Stiles, Bert, 93, 97, 228n22
Stilwell, Joseph "Vinegar Joe," 181
Stimson, Henry L., 30, 33, 68, 72 (photo),
        181
    and atomic bomb, 179, 187–188
    background of, 71
    concerns about American war
        weariness, 73, 179, 187
    concerns about Dresden raid, 158–159

    concerns about fire raids, 73, 179
    influence on military operations, 6,
        73–74
    perceptions of enemies, 71, 73, 96
    regrets about bombing results, 73,
        187–188
    views on bombing Rome, 134
    worries about bombing civilians, 71,
        73, 179
Stormede, bombing of, 55
Strategy, schools of, 20
Straubling, bombing of, 58
St. Valentin tank works, 61
Submarine pens, targeting of, 32–34, 35
        (photo), 47, 55, 104, 120
Sunchon, Korea, bombing dam at, 195
        (photo)
Supreme Headquarters Allied
        Expeditionary Forces, 112, 127,
        129, 140, 142, 152, 154, 156–159
Sweden, 96, 120
Switzerland, 59, 96, 108, 159
Szombathely, Hungary, bombing of, 61

Taylor, Charles, 141–142
Technology
    Arnold's fascination with, 5, 70–71
    effects on warfare, 101, 200, 215
    influence on American way of war,
        4–5, 211
    relationship with doctrine, 5, 21–23,
        79, 214
Tedder, Sir Arthur, 44–45, 82, 152
Terror bombing, 1, 20, 26
    American resistance to, 1–2, 10,
        22–25, 27, 84
    Arnold on, 7, 69
    in the Balkans, 136–139, 158
    British escalation to, 7, 21, 79, 178
    Douhet on, 19
    pursued against Germany, 139–160
    Seversky on, 27–28
    used against Japan, 177–178
    See also Area bombing; Civilian
        morale, as a target; *Todestoss*, search
        for
Thomas, Norman, 66
304th Bomb Wing, 56

313th Bomb Wing, 184
314th Bomb Wing, 175
315th Bomb Wing, 114 (photo), 115, 184
THUNDERCLAP, 7, 48, 51, 146-150, 160,
    193
Tiverton, Lord, 15
Todestoss, search for
    against Balkans, 136-139
    against Germany, 133, 139-153,
        159-160
    against Japan, 133, 145, 160, 179-185
    in AWPD/1, 30, 132-133
Tokyo, 213 (photo)
    as atomic bomb target, 188
    Doolittle's raid on, 75-76, 162
    great fire raid of 9-10 March 1945, 8,
        16, 86, 99, 161, 163, 173-176, 187,
        191, 210, 212, 215
    other air attacks on, 99, 166, 177, 178
        (photo), 183-184, 214
Tokyo Shimbun, 210
Tomahawk cruise missiles, 200, 212
TORCH, 33
Transportation plan, 44-46, 82-83, 139
Transportation targets, 8, 17, 25, 27, 30,
    44-62, 82-83, 113, 150-160, 176,
    182-183, 201, 207
Trenchard, Hugh, 17-19
Trident Conference, 35
Trieste, bombing of, 58
Truman, Harry, 91, 123, 179-181, 184,
    196
Twelve O'Clock High, 91
Twentieth Air Force, 8, 90, 113, 131, 160,
    163, 183-184
XX Bomber Command, 107 (photo),
    169-171
XXI Bomber Command, 166, 170-171,
    185
    incendiary campaign, 174-179,
        183-184
    mining campaign, 184-185
Twining, Nathan, 39-40, 112, 152, 190

Union of Soviet Socialist Republics, 6, 60,
    62, 137-138, 173, 185, 193-194,
    196-197
    bombing assistance for, 48, 136,

156-157
United Nations, 193
United States Air Force
    bombing Serbia, 205-207
    faults in doctrine of, 196-198, 209
    in Iraq, 200-203, 208, 213-215
    in Korean War, 193-196
    in Vietnam, 197-200
United States Army, 12, 21-22, 166
United States Army Combat Studies
    Institute, 5
United States Army Strategic Air Forces,
    182-184
United States Biological Warfare
    Committee, 181
United States Congress, 22, 24, 141
United States Department of Defense,
    197, 207
United States Department of State, 138,
    194
United States Department of the Navy, 28
United States Department of War, 28-30
United States Navy, 12, 21-22, 33, 166
United States Strategic Air Forces, 7-8,
    11, 37, 74, 77, 188, 213
    in Big Week, 41-43
    bombing the Balkans, 137-138
    and CLARION, 150-154, 160
    in Dresden controversy, 156-159
    and radar bombing, 104-115
    in THUNDERCLAP, 147-149, 160
United States Strategic Bombing Survey,
    182-183, 190-192
Urban bombing attacks
    in the Balkans, 136-139, 206-207
    in China, 26-27, 169, 211
    incomplete AAF assessment of,
        188-192
    in Iraq, 200-203
    in Italy, 134-135
    in Germany, 48, 142-143, 147-149,
        154-160
    in Japan, 173-179, 214-215
    in Korea, 193-194, 196
    in Spain, 27
    in Vietnam, 198-200
    in World War I, 15-16, 18-19, 220n10
Urban bombing attacks, *continued*

See also Belgrade, bombing of; Berlin, bombing of; Bucharest; Budapest; Dresden, bombing of; Hamburg, bombing of; Hanoi, bombing of; London, bombing of; Pyongyang, bombing of; Rome, bombing of; Sofia, bombing of; Tokyo
Utah Beach, 109

Vanaman, Arthur, 29 (photo)
Vandenberg, Hoyt, 121, 190
Vatican protests against bombing, 134
Vegesack, bombing of, 38
Verona, bombing of, 56, 60
Very Heavy Bomber program, 169–171
    Arnold's concern about, 171
    problems with B-29 aircraft, 89, 170
Vicenza, bombing of, 56
Victor Emmanuel, king of Italy, 135
Vienna, as bombing target, 56–58, 57 (photo), 60
Vietnam, 12, 187, 212
    bombing restrictions in, 197–199
    effectiveness of airpower in, 198–200
    LINEBACKER in, 198–200
    public reaction to bombing in, 12, 199
    technology in, 5, 125, 198, 202
Villard, Oswald Garrison, 66, 161
VKA chemicals, 182
V-1 buzz bombs, 118
    American copies of, 125–128, 127 (photo)
    Arnold's fascination with, 71, 117, 125–126
    British desire to retaliate for, 143
    CROSSBOW campaign against, 40, 45, 117–118
    German changes in launching techniques, 120
Walker, Kenneth, 22, 28–29

Warden, John, 200
Warsaw, bombing of, 161
War weariness of the American people, 73, 144, 148, 163, 179, 187, 196
War-weary bombers, 7, 116–123, 127, 200
"Weary Willies." *See* War-weary bombers
Weather, 37, 87
    over Germany, 8–9, 11, 35, 39, 41, 46–62, 104, 111, 113, 115, 157
    over Japan, 122, 171, 189–190
Webster, Robert, 22–24, 27
Wedemeyer, Albert, 169
Weicker, Lowell, 140–141
Weigley, Russell, 74
Weimar, bombing of, 52
Wels, bombing of, 61
Westmoreland, William C., 199 (photo)
West Point, 26–27, 77
Weyland, Otto P., 196
Wheeler, Earle, 197
Wiener-Neustadt, bombing of, 59–60
Wilhelmshaven, bombing of, 55
Williamson, Charles G., 141–142
WILLIE ORPHAN, 121–122
Wilson, Donald, 22–24
Wilson, Sir Henry Maitland, 137
Winant, John, 138
Wright Field, Ohio, 117

X-RAY, Project, 130–131

Yalta Conference, 156–157
Yalu River, 193
Yenan, China, 173
Yokohama, devastation in, 188
Yugoslavia, 58–60, 136, 205–207

Zeppelins, 16, 18
Zossen, bombing of, 54
Zuckerman, Solly, 44